THE WORLD ENCYCLOPEDIA OF COINS & COIN COLLECTING

THE WORLD ENCYCLOPEDIA OF COINS & COIN COLLECTING

The definitive illustrated reference to the world's greatest coins and a professional guide to building a spectacular collection, featuring more than 3000 images

DR JAMES MACKAY

LORENZ BOOKS

AUTHOR'S DEDICATION
This book is dedicated to my granddaughter, Isabel.

This edition is published by Lorenz Books, an imprint of Anness Publishing Ltd, 108 Great Russell Street, London WC1B 3NA; info@anness.com

www.lorenzbooks.com; www.annesspublishing.com; twitter: @Anness_Books

A CIP catalogue record for this book is available from the British Library.

Publisher: Joanna Lorenz
Editorial Director: Helen Sudell
Project Editor: Catherine Stuart
Designer: Nigel Partridge
Photographer: Mark Wood

NOTE
Every effort has been made to reproduce coins at their actual size. However, readers should treat the images of coins in the book as representative of actual dimensions, rather than literal size. Some coins have been enlarged or reduced slightly to make some of the features more legible, but such modifications have been kept to a minimum.

PUBLISHER'S NOTE
Although the advice and information in this book are believed to be accurate and true at the time of going to press, neither the authors nor the publisher can accept any legal responsibility or liability for any errors or omissions that may have been made.

The illustration on page 2 shows coiners at work in Germany during the 16th century.

CONTENTS

Introducing Coins and Numismatics 6

A GUIDE TO COLLECTING COINS 8

WHAT ARE COINS? 10
The History of Barter 10
Early Currencies 12
Chinese Coinage 14
Greek Coinage 16
Roman Coinage 18
Byzantine Coinage 20
Other Ancient European Coinage 22
Medieval European Coinage 24
Middle Eastern Coinage 26
Indian Coinage 28
Mints 30
Common Currency and Trade Coins 32
Money of Necessity 34

PARTS AND PROCESSES 36
Denominations 36
Metals and Alloys 38
Specifications 40
Hammered and Cast Coinage 42
The First Milled Coinage 44
Industrial Developments 46
Special Production Techniques 48
Combating the Counterfeiter 50
History of Portraiture 52
Non-Figural Motifs 54
History of Pictorialism 56

HOW TO COLLECT 58

Origins of Numismatics 58
Grade and Condition 60
Looking After Coins 62
Housing Coins 64
Using Guides and Catalogues 66
Collecting by Country 68
Collecting by Group 70
Collecting by Mint 72
Collecting by Period 74
Collecting by Denomination 76
Collecting Pictorial Coins 78
Collecting Purpose of Issue Coins 80
Collecting Service Tokens 82
Collecting Coin Lookalikes 84
Collecting Errors and Varieties 86
Collecting Patterns, Proofs and Ephemera 88
Buying and Selling Coins 90
On-line Numismatics 92

WORLD DIRECTORY OF COINS 94

AMERICA 96

Canada 96
United States Definitives 98
American Commemorative and Special Issues 100
The State Quarters of 1999–2008 102
Bahamas, Bermuda and West Indies 104
Cuba, Hispaniola and Jamaica 106
East Caribbean 108
Mexico 110
Central America 112
Colombia, Ecuador and Venezuela 114
Brazil and Guyana 116
Bolivia, Chile and Peru 118
Argentina, Paraguay and Uruguay 120
South Atlantic Islands 122

EUROPE 124

Western Scandinavia 124
Eastern Scandinavia 126
The Olympic Games 128
England, Scotland and Ireland 130
United Kingdom 132
Ireland and Offshore British Islands 134
British European Territories 136
Benelux Countries 138
Switzerland 140
German States 142
German Reich 144
Postwar Germany 146
Austria and Hungary 148
Czechoslovakia 150
Poland 152
Baltic States 154
Russia 156
Commonwealth of Independent States 158
Yugoslavia 160
Albania, Bulgaria and Romania 162
Greece 164
Italy 166
France 168
Iberian Peninsula 170

AFRICA 172

North Africa 172
Egypt and Sudan 174
South Africa 176
Southern Africa 178
Africa's Fauna 180
Central Africa 182
East Africa 184
Horn of Africa 186
West Africa 188
Sahara and Equatorial Africa 190

ASIA 192

Turkey 192
Palestine, Israel and Jordan 194
Lebanon, Iraq and Syria 196
Arabia 198
Gulf States 200
Iran and Afghanistan 202
Burma, Pakistan and Bangladesh 204
Early India 206
Indian Princely States 208
Colonial and Modern India 210
Indian Ocean 212
Indochina 214
China 216
Floral Coins of Asia 218
Chinese Territories 220
Himalayan States 222
Korea 224
Japan 226
Indonesia and the Philippines 228
Malaysia and Singapore 230
Thailand 232

AUSTRALASIA AND OCEANIA 234

Australia 234
Australia's Commerce and Industry 236
New Zealand 238
New Zealand Dependencies 240
PNG, Nauru and Vanuatu 242
Fiji, Solomons, Kiribati and Tuvalu 244
French Pacific Islands 246
Polynesian Kingdoms 248

Glossary 250
Index 253
Picture Acknowledgements 256

INTRODUCING COINS AND NUMISMATICS

In his First Epistle to Timothy, St Paul declared that the love of money was the root of all evil. Clearly, he did not have numismatists (as coin collectors like to style themselves) in mind. Were there coin collectors back in the 1st century? Quite possibly, for the design and production of coins had risen to a very high level by that time and today we regard the Greek coins of the late pre-Christian era as some of the most exquisite works of art ever produced.

In St Paul's day the coins of the early Roman Empire were already showing their character, with accurate likenesses of emperors and their families on one side and generally a female figure representing some abstract concept such as Justice, Concord or Agriculture on the other. From the relatively large numbers of classical coins that have survived in fine condition it must be assumed that wealthy Greeks and Romans were laying aside beautiful specimens to admire rather than spend. Certainly, by the Renaissance in the 15th century, princes and magnates had their coin cabinets, and it was the appreciation of classical coins that inspired the revolution in coin design and production from the 1450s.

Today the role of coins in everyday life is being supplanted by plastic in the form of credit cards and cash cards. There is a popular anecdote about a little boy who went into a grocery store, picked up a packet of ice cream and at the checkout proffered a used telephone card as payment. He had often seen his mother handing over something similar, which was accepted instead of cash. This story indicates

Above: New Zealand 3 pence of 1946 with a portrait of George VI and a reverse motif of Maori war clubs.

how a generation of children are growing up more accustomed to plastic than metal – they may never experience the tactile pleasure of jingling a handful of coins in their pockets.

Despite this gradual narrowing of the actual usage of metal money, coins as collectables have developed dramatically. Not only are the mints and treasuries of the world producing more and more deluxe items for collectors, but the coins in general circulation are more varied than at any time since the fall of the Roman Empire. For centuries coin collecting was the preserve of the upper classes, who had the wealth to indulge their passion, as well as the classical education to appreciate the designs and inscriptions. Today coin collecting is a hobby pursued by people of all ages and incomes.

STARTING A COLLECTION

A good place to begin is at home, with the small change in daily circulation. The collection can very quickly be extended to past issues of your own country, often readily available from local coin dealers, and then to the coins of related territories. These may be similar in denomination and appearance, but the coins of every country are distinctive, such as the 1946 silver 3 pence of New Zealand shown above, with the profile of George VI on one side, just like the British coins, but a pair of Maori war clubs on the other.

The names and nicknames of coins can give clues to their history. The American quarter dollar is still referred

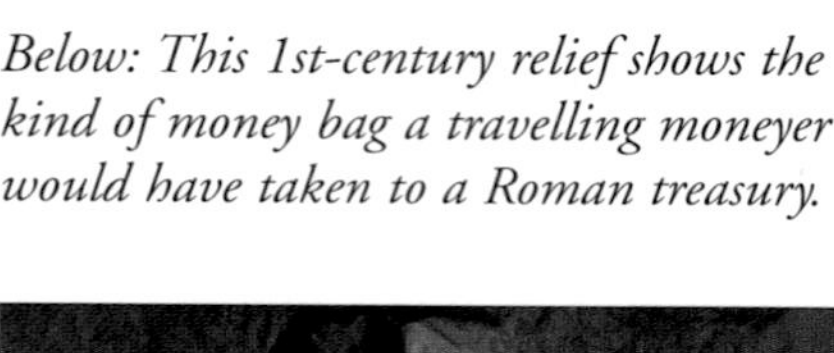

Above: An interesting coin of ancient Rome featuring a serrated edge and a sacrificial bull ritual on the reverse.

Above: An early Roman coin showing Apollo (left) on the obverse side. Later, portraits of emperors replaced deities.

Below: This 1st-century relief shows the kind of money bag a travelling moneyer would have taken to a Roman treasury.

Below: Coining is entwined with metal craft. The Gold Weigher, *by Dutch artist Gerard Dou, appeared in 1664.*

to as a two-bit coin, but few realize that the bit was originally the eighth part of a Spanish dollar, the *peso a ocho reales* (or "piece of eight" in pirate lore). The dollar sign ($) itself is a relic of this – it was originally a figure 8 with two vertical strokes through it.

Coins are usually identified by their inscription, and sometimes the denomination is helpful. Ancient coins are more of a problem; in the absence of any lettering, the effigy or emblem may be the only clue to identity. Where inscriptions exist and are legible, you can look for dates or the mint-marks identifying the place where the coins were struck. For example, American coins found without a mint-mark indicate that they were struck at the US Mint in Philadelphia, while those produced at the branch mints in Denver and San Francisco bear an initial letter D or S alongside the date.

The current range of American coins may seem limited – effectively the only coins in everyday use are the bronze cent (penny), 5 cents (nickel), 10 cents (dime) and 25 cents (quarter) – but in any handful of change you will find different dates and mint-marks. It is not surprising, therefore, that coin collecting at its most basic, known by many as change-checking, should have developed into a national pastime in the United States.

Below: A page from an American coin album designed to house Lincoln cents of each date and mint-mark.

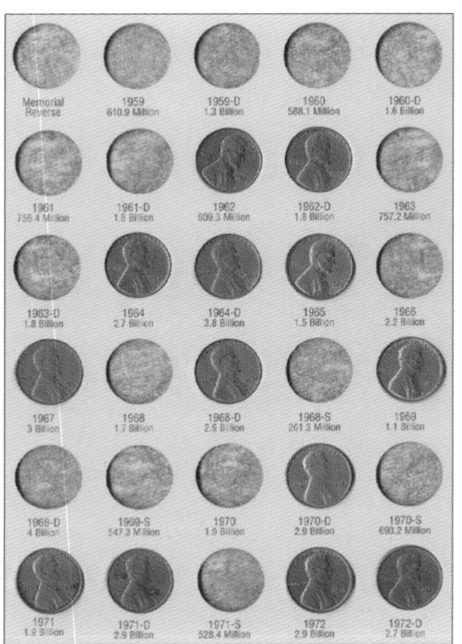

Above: Many mints now sell complete year sets, attractively packaged.

This has led companies to produce a variety of housing options, such as albums of stout card pages with holes punched out to take the entire range of a particular denomination. The holes are annotated with the dates and mint-marks, and this encourages people to look for all the date and mark varieties.

Sooner or later you may want to start trading your coins, to finance new purchases and get rid of those in which you have less interest. Today there are many on-line businesses devoted to the sale of coins, while coin fairs – national and local – are great occasions to meet collectors and learn about your coins.

THE TRUE VALUE OF COINS

There are many opportunities nowadays to expand a coin collection at little cost, and the inclusion of related, non-coin items contributes colour, variety and context. My first trip abroad was to Greece in 1950, where there were no coins at all, just ragged paper printed with lots of noughts, reflecting the horrendous inflation of the immediate post-war years. In early 1950s, Holland I handled my first real foreign coins, but also saw massive silver 2½ gulden coins worn as buttons on the traditional jackets of Dutch men.

Rare vintage coins may sell for enormous sums, but most coins have a value of a different nature. When my father uncovered various copper coins of George III's reign in our garden, I took them to the local museum. The curator opined that someone, perhaps a farm labourer, had probably dropped his purse. Although I was disappointed to learn that the coins were very common and virtually worthless, I got a tremendous thrill imagining that they were the hard-won earnings of some poor ploughboy 150 years earlier. Today, when I handle a chunky Alexandrine tetradrachm of the 4th century BC I still get that tactile thrill, thinking that self-same piece of silver was earned, handled and spent by someone almost 2400 years ago.

Above: The reverse of a Netherlands 2½ gulden of William II, shown at actual size. These coins were often mounted and worn as buttons by Dutch people.

LINDNER

A GUIDE TO COLLECTING COINS

Coins have been in existence for almost 2800 years and, taking into consideration differences in dates, mint- and die-marks, the number of collectable varieties is countless. Even a general collection of world coins, confined to major differences in design, would run to many thousands. This part of the book is divided broadly into three key sections. The first takes a look at how coins originated and evolved in different parts of the world, from the earliest currencies to the astonishing range of articles that have been used as substitutes for metal coins in times of crises. The second section helps the reader to understand the different factors that determine the identity and circulation of a coin: from weight and denomination to the metals used and methods of production, including the transition from hammering by hand to mechanical processes, the designs of coins and the security features employed to defeat counterfeiters. The final section traces the evolution of numismatics, especially from the late 19th century, gives advice on the care and conservation of coins. It also surveys some of the different approaches to collecting – by country, reign or period, or by theme or topic – and examines the byways of the hobby, including bogus coins, errors and oddities.

Left: Different methods of housing coins, plus magnification aids.
Above, left to right: Influential Greek design on an ancient Egyptian coin, a pictorial thaler of medieval Germany, and a gold mohur struck at Calcutta by the East India Company.

WHAT ARE COINS?

Pieces of metal stamped with a device guaranteeing their worth developed more or less simultaneously in China and Asia Minor (modern Turkey) in the 7th century BC. Generally round and flat, modern coins may have different designs and inscriptions but are akin to the coins used centuries ago, like this 12th-century copper 10 cash of the Chinese Song dynasty.

THE HISTORY OF BARTER

Long before coins were invented, goods were traded by other means. The earliest civilizations of the Middle East and the Mediterranean were pastoral and their wealth was represented by flocks of sheep and goats and herds of cattle. Naturally, the earliest forms of money used by these peoples consisted of animals, meat and hides. Many of the words used in connection with money originated in this way. From the Latin word *pecus*, meaning "herd", we get the adjectives "pecuniary" and "peculiar" (that portion of the herd assigned to the cowherd for his own use). The word "talent", which now means an asset or natural gift, denoted a sum of money in Biblical times, but long before that the Greek word *talanton* meant a cowhide. When metal began to be used as money, these tended to mimic the traditional currencies. Large pieces of copper were shaped roughly like cowhides to form money talents.

The modern word "bourse" is used to describe a place where merchants and businessmen meet to buy, sell and exchange goods. This is also derived from cattle, the ancient word *byrsa* meaning "cowhide". Even some of the terms still used to indicate the denominations of coins are derived from animal skins. Thus, the Croatian unit of currency, the kuna, takes its name from the pine marten, whose pelt was the basis of trade, while the rouble is named from the Russian word for a strip of leather.

Salt was an indispensable commodity, highly prized for its use in the preserving of meat, and therefore very desirable in barter. From the Latin word for salt (*sal*) we get the modern term "salary", and we still use the expression "worth his/her salt". Bars of salt were still being used as currency in Ethiopia until the early 20th century.

When we discuss the fineness of gold coins, we use the term "carat" (US "karat"), which is derived from *keration,* the Greek word for a carob bean. These beans, being of a uniform size, were used for weighing things. The Greeks also coined the words *drachma* ("handful") and *obol* (from *belos*, meaning "dart" or "spit"). The Anglo-Saxons had coins called sceats and in the Baltic states a skatiku was a small coin, but both came originally from a Teutonic word *scaz*, simply meaning "treasure" (like the modern German *Schatz*). The German mark got its name from the scratch on a gold ingot, while "shilling" comes from Old Norse *skilja*, "cut".

Forms of Barter Currency

Native Americans, shown here at a trading post in Manitoba, bartered animal skins for guns. From beaver pelts and buckskins came the "made beaver" tokens of the Hudson's Bay Company and the continuing use of the expression "buck" to mean a dollar.

Below: A 15th-century illustration of Russian and Scandinavian traders bartering, from the Historia Gentibus Septentrionalibus *by Olaus Magnus.*

Above: Tea-junks are loaded at Tseen-Tang, depicted in this 1843 engraving of a typical Chinese scene.

Below: Tobacco ships dock on the James River, Virginia in the 18th century, from Bryant's History of America.

PAYMENT IN GOODS

Barter is a system of trade whereby one commodity is exchanged for another, or for a service of some kind, without the use of money. It takes many forms, depending on whether it is carried out within a community or between different communities, and also according to the customs of the people and what goods they have to exchange. It probably arose informally but eventually led to indirect barter, where some objects were invested with a fixed value, whether traded or accumulated as status symbols or signs of wealth. Among the commodities that have acquired a monetary value at different times are almonds (India), rock salt (Rome and Ethiopia), dried fish (Scandinavia), tea bricks (China), cacao beans (Mexico), tobacco (North America, Central Africa, Indonesia and Melanesia) and potatoes (Tristan da Cunha). In Cambodia's recent history, Pol Pot's moneyless society banned all forms of currency except rice, which was traded or bartered in tins from 1975 to 1979.

Generally, barter eventually gives way to some form of money, but commodities have been pressed into service as money in times of emergency, in war or periods of economic upheaval. The best example of this is the cigarette, which was widely used as currency in Germany (1945–8) and the Soviet Union (1990) when money in the traditional sense had ceased to have any value. Candy and chewing gum circulated in Italy in the 1970s during shortages of small change. In 1811, Henri Christophe confiscated the Haitians' accumulated stock of gourds and made them the island's unit of currency, using them to buy coffee, with which he re-established foreign trade. To this day the unit is the *gourde*, alluding to this drastic measure.

Potato Stamp

During World War II the remote island of Tristan da Cunha was occupied by the Royal Navy. Previously the islanders had had no use for coined money, but for the convenience of the sailors the local barter commodity (potatoes) was integrated with sterling at the rate of 4 potatoes to the penny. This dual system was even expressed on the postage stamp, designed for local island mail.

Below: Soviet soldiers rolling cigarettes in World War II. Hard-to-find items such as tobacco and chocolate were often traded between soldiers and civilians.

EARLY CURRENCIES

From actual goods, such as potatoes, salt and tea, which were useful in themselves, it was a logical progression to use objects as currencies which, while lacking a practical use, came to represent an actual value against which the worth of goods and services could be measured. While an assortment of cigarettes or chewing gum may be of little interest to a collector of coins, the same is not true of various forms of early money, some of which are collected as "curious currencies".

SHELL MONEY

From a very early date, people have been fascinated by sea shells. They are often attractive in appearance and not easy to come by, so it is hardly surprising that they should have acquired a monetary value. Strings of *Dentalium* shells were used as money by the native American tribes of the north-western Pacific coast, while armlets composed of *Tridacna* shells were traded in New Guinea. Strings of polished shell discs were used as money all over the Pacific, variously known as *diwara* (New Britain), *pele* (Bismarck Archipelago), *biruan* (Solomon Islands), *mauwai* (Bougainville), *rongo* (Malaita) or *sapisapi* (New Guinea).

Above: An Egyptian tomb painting showing workers recording and banking payments in grain.

By far the most popular forms of shell money were the cowrie species *Cypraea moneta* and *C. annulus,* which were threaded to make necklaces. According to Chinese tradition it was the so-called Yellow Emperor, Huangdi (2698 BC) who established this ancient monetary system, though written records point to the ancient Shang and Zhou dynasties as the chief developers of the cowrie unit. The Chinese ideogram *pei* means both a cowrie shell and money in general. Cowrie shells were found only on the most southerly shores of China, which enabled the emperor to control the supply and thus maintain their value. As the population expanded, the number of genuine cowries was insufficient to meet demand, so the Chinese resorted to various substitutes in stone, bone, ivory or jade, carved to resemble a cowrie, and later bronze cast in the shape of the shell. Cowries were used as money in China until about 200 BC, but their use spread to India and Arabia and thence to Central and East Africa, and the cowrie survived as currency until about 1950. The shells even circulated as small change alongside metallic coins, tariffed at 60–400 to the franc in French West Africa (1900), 200 to the Indian rupee in Uganda (1895) and up to 1200 to the West African shilling in the Gold Coast (now Ghana). They even inspired coins in India and Africa – the kori of Kutch and the cauri of Guinea. The cedi, used in Ghana, is named from a local word meaning "small shell".

Above and right: "Money cowries" featured in J.G. Wood's Natural History, *1854. The cowrie continues to be used as a motif on coins, a rather crude design appearing on this 17th-century lead bazaruk of the Dutch East India Company.*

Below: Two ancient currencies that circulated until quite recently: a Japanese silver chogin of 1865–9 (right) and a gold bar from Vila Rica in Brazil (below), used during the regency of Don João of Portugal, 1799.

It is strange that such a sophisticated society as that of ancient Egypt seldom used coins. However, the Egyptians had a highly complex currency system based on units of weighed metals, called *deben* and *qedet*, which enabled the values of goods to be compared with each other. Taxes could be paid in barley or other grains. The royal granaries acted as banks; people deposited and withdrew the goods, and interest-bearing loans of grain were also made.

ORIGINS OF METAL MONEY

A metallic standard was adopted in Mesopotamia (modern Iraq) as long ago as 2500 BC. By 1500 BC metal rings and copper utensils of standard quality, size and weight were being used as money and were interchangeable with articles of gold and silver. Deals were recorded in terms of copper bowls and pitchers, while gold and silver (originally valued equally) were worth 40 times their weight in copper. By the 10th century BC a ratio of 1:13:3000 was established in the Middle East for gold, silver and copper respectively.

Curious Currency

Bracelets in the shape of horseshoes, known by the Spanish name *manilla* ("manacle"), circulated as money on the Slave Coast of West Africa. Far from trying to stamp out this currency, British traders imported vast quantities made in Birmingham in an alloy of copper, lead and pewter, and the indigenous tribes came to prefer these to their own productions. A manilla was originally worth 30 cents but fell to 20 cents by 1900.

Such systems were by no means confined to the ancient world. Small bars and ingots stamped with the weight, fineness and issuing authority circulated as money in the Portuguese territories of Brazil and Mozambique in the 16th to 19th centuries, rather than the standard coinage of Portugal. Curiously shaped silver bars known as Tiger Tongues and bent rings sometimes called Banana Bars were used in Thailand and Vietnam, while copper bars known as Bonks circulated in the Dutch East Indies. These areas had coinage, introduced from India in the 7th and 8th centuries, but by the 11th century it had disappeared and been replaced by silver ingots, of which these are just a few varieties.

It can be hard to understand why certain kinds of currency should sometimes have been preferred to coins. In some cases, as in colonial Brazil, the local currency was employed of necessity because of poor communications with the mother country. In another example, playing cards marked with values were used in 17th-century Canada instead of French coins. In South-east Asia, however, the curiously shaped pieces of silver were used, rather than flat discs, merely because that was the traditional style. For the same reasons, many of the petty kingdoms and states in India preferred copper and silver bars. It was traditional, and people had confidence in money of that kind, whereas coins in the Western sense were unfamiliar and not trusted.

During the Shogunate of the 17th to 19th centuries, Japan had the most elaborate metallic system of all, involving bars of copper (kwan-ei) and silver (chogin), rectangular gold ingots (ichibu and nibu kin) and large elliptical gold plates known as oban and koban. These had a ribbed surface on which symbols and inscriptions were countermarked. The oban were additionally inscribed with their weight and the mint-master's signature in black ink, using traditional brush techniques.

Above: A beautiful example of a gold koban of pre-Meiji Japan, with large piercing on the reverse.

NON-METALLIC SUBSTITUTES

Pieces of leather have served as money at various times in many parts of the world. As recently as 1923–4, during the German hyperinflation, pieces of shoe leather were stamped with values in millions of marks, and circular pieces of leather embossed with coin images were used in Austria. Pottery and porcelain tokens were used in China and Thailand in the mid-19th century, while in 1945 Japan resorted to terracotta coins of 1, 2 and 5 sen to combat wartime inflation. In the 19th and early 20th centuries the Chinese exchanged bamboo sticks stamped with brands to denote transactions from 100 cash upwards. Apart from a series of commemorative coins in 1977, the only currencies to circulate in the Cocos (Keeling) Islands are tokens of porcelain or plastic, which are used on the coconut plantations.

Below: Tokens exchanged on colonial plantations were often given actual currency values. This brass 1 dollar token is from the Dutch East Indies.

CHINESE COINAGE

The development of the earliest coinage was roughly simultaneous in China and Asia Minor. The first Chinese "coins" were small pieces of bronze, cast and fashioned into representations of the useful agricultural implements used in barter, such as spades and bill-hooks. The small knives, spades, keys and other domestic articles, symbols of the earlier barter system, were invested with a notional value and had no utilitarian purpose. But they represented a real value and could be exchanged for goods or services accordingly.

The knives were about 15cm/6in long and bore the value and the name of the issuing authority. The bu currency, a modified form of the bronze spades, circulated widely in the 5th and 4th centuries BC, and their image has even been reproduced on Chinese coins in modern times.

THE ARRIVAL OF CASH

By the 4th century BC, bronze circular discs with a hole in the centre were in circulation. Over several generations these pieces evolved into the regular banliang (half-ounce) coins minted by the Emperor Shi Huang-di, founder of the Qin dynasty, in 221 BC and known as cash. In 118 BC the banliang were replaced by wuzhu (5 grain) coins by the Han emperor Wudi. These were used all over China, even after the empire was split into a number of smaller states in AD 220. In 621, after the empire was reunified, the Tang emperor Gaozu replaced the wuzhu with a new design with four, rather than two, characters. This style remained in use until 1911. Thus, the Chinese cash, with its distinctive square hole and inscriptions in ideograms, was in circulation for over two millennia. The four Chinese characters that appear on the traditional cash signify "current money of", followed by the

Right: Bronze knife money used during the Warring States period.

Below: A cast imitation cowrie (with a central hole), and an example of the round-hooked "spade" money.

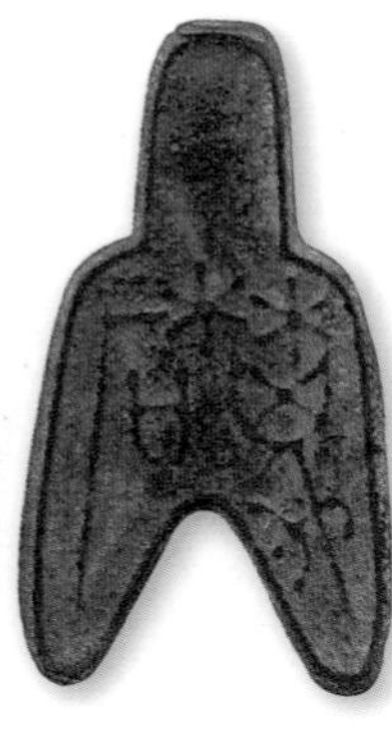

The Silver Yuan

Spanish, Mexican, British and American trade dollars circulated extensively in China and filled the need for coins of higher denominations, so it was not until the late 19th century that China began minting silver coins of its own. The yuan (dollar) was introduced in 1889 at par with the Mexican peso. It circulated alongside the foreign silver, but in order to provide pieces of the same weight and fineness as the other trade dollars already in circulation the Chinese had to produce coins of odd values, based on the traditional Chinese weight and value system of mace and candareens. A handsome piece, nicknamed the Sichuan rupee and issued in Tibet, appeared in the closing years of the century and was the only coin actually to portray the Manchu emperor.

Above: Pattern silver dollar produced by the central Tianjin mint in 1911.

Above: Silver dragon and phoenix dollar of the Chinese Republic, 1923.

Right: An iron cash coin bearing Chinese and Manchu legends, produced by the Qing dynasty.

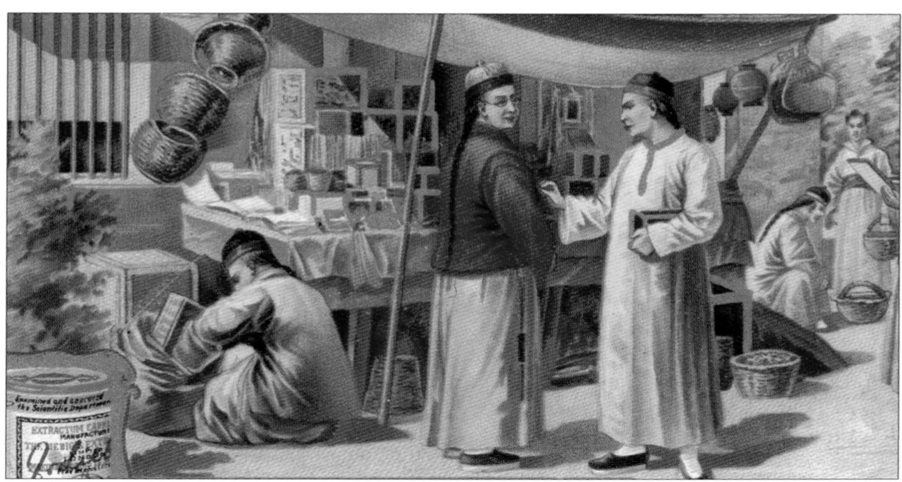

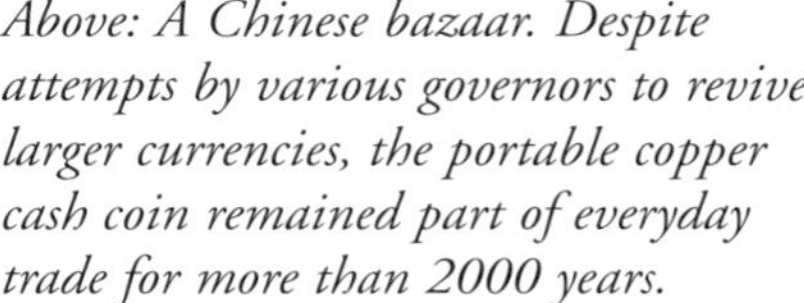

Above: A Chinese bazaar. Despite attempts by various governors to revive larger currencies, the portable copper cash coin remained part of everyday trade for more than 2000 years.

symbol of the appropriate reign. The currency name is not related to the English word for ready money (which comes from the French *caisse* and Italian *cassa,* meaning "money box"). Rather, it appears in slightly different forms in many Oriental languages, from the Sanskrit *karsa* and Persian *karsha* ("weight") via Tamil *kacu* and Portuguese *caixa,* denoting a small copper coin.

Below: Copper cash obverses from the reigns of Emperors Hongxian (1915) and Guangxu (1905).

Above: Reinstated bu (bronze knife and key) money of Wang Mang.

Bu money was briefly revived by the usurper Wang Mang (AD 7–23), but decimalized. Copper cash spread to Korea in the 3rd century BC and Japan (AD 708). Cash continued as the money of China itself and was not superseded until the overthrow of the Qing dynasty and the proclamation of the republic in 1911. Even then, Western-style bronze coins, introduced in 1912 and featuring the crossed flags of the new regime, continued to be denominated in cash, and it is believed that traditional copper cash continued to circulate in rural areas until 1925.

THE ARRIVAL OF CASH

Although various denominations of cash existed, the basic cash unit had a very small value, and the Chinese got into the habit of creating larger values by stringing them together into the shape of a sword. By the time of the Tang dynasty, between AD 650 and 800, merchants found the transportation of huge wagonloads of cash around the country not only cumbersome but insecure, at the mercy of bandits, so they invented *fei-ch'ien* (literally "flying money"), consisting of paper drafts negotiable in bronze currency. These drafts were not authorized paper money in the modern sense but undoubtedly paved the way for the bank notes introduced much later, that serve the world for higher amounts of money.

Above: A Chinese watercolour depicting a moneylender weighing out coins under the Qing dynasty.

Below: The Chinese were pioneers of the use of paper money. This 1000 cash note was issued in 1854, under the Qing dynasty. The rectangular red stamp is the seal of the Fukien Yung Feng Official Bureau.

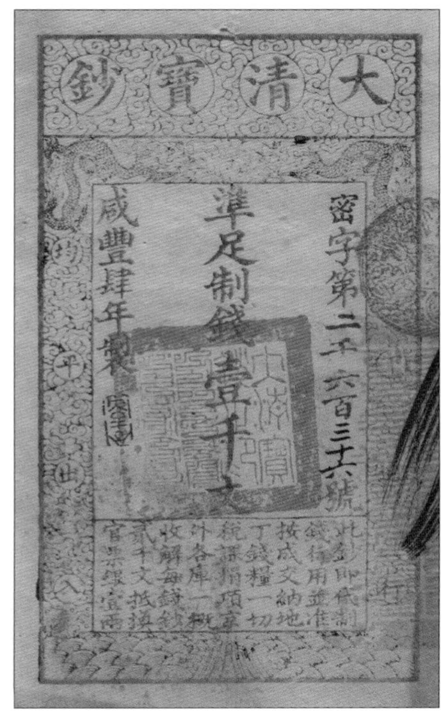

GREEK COINAGE

Copper was worked in Cyprus from at least 3000 BC (indeed, the name of the island is derived from the Greek word for the metal) and by the middle Bronze Age it was being cast into bullion bars, called talents. An ancient Greek talent of bronze (an alloy of copper and tin) weighed about 60lb/127kg. The talent used at the time of Homer, in the 9th century BC, was said to be made of gold, while the talent of Attica, the district surrounding Athens, was of silver, divided into 60 units known as *minae*, worth 100 drachmae each. These units of weight were widely used for high-value transactions in the ancient world.

LEAVING A MARK

Gold was regarded as being worth 13 pieces of silver of equivalent weight, or 3000 pieces of copper. An alloy of gold and silver called electrum, often referred to as pale gold or white gold,

Below: Leaden coin weights used in ancient Greece. The inscriptions on the bottom two suggest that they are equivalent to 8 and 2 drachmae.

Above: Electrum coinage of the Lydian kings with an open-mouthed lion on the obverse (top). The Turtles of Aegina (bottom) circulated widely through the Greek Empire and beyond. The reverse of this stater from 700–500 BC bears an interesting incuse (recessed) punch mark.

was popular in the earliest period. For centuries merchants were accustomed to weigh out lumps of metal at every transaction, but gradually a more convenient system was devised. A rich merchant, or a prince on whose land the metal was mined, would cast it into lumps of uniform size and weight and guarantee the weight of these lumps by applying his personal mark to them. At first this stamp consisted of an irregular mark, made by striking the metal with a broken nail. The jagged edge of the nail left an individual mark that served to identify the person who issued the metal. Sometimes these lumps had several marks struck on them in the form of a pattern. As a rule, the marks appeared on one side only, though the reverse might have a pattern of lines, where the anvil had dug into the metal during striking.

COINS IN A MODERN SENSE

According to the Greek historian Herodotus, the Lydians were the first people to use gold and silver coins. From the evidence of coin hoards and archaeological research it is now believed that the earliest coins of Lydia were produced in the late 7th century BC. By 630 BC the crude nail mark had developed into a proper design, the lion's head emblem of the Mermnad dynasty of Lydia, of which King Croesus – whose wealth was proverbial in the ancient world – was the fifth and last ruler. This emblem was applied to the obverse, or "heads" side, by placing the lump of metal (called a blank or flan) on an anvil whose top had been engraved with the design. The flan had been heated until it was very soft, and striking it with a hammer impressed the image into the surface of the metal. At first the hammer had no mark on its surface, and the earliest coins were uniface (one-sided), but gradually it became customary to include a simple geometric design that bit into the reverse, or "tails" side, of the coin, giving an "incuse" reverse (a simple hammered design). The authority that these simple designs afforded came to be regarded as a guarantee of their value. The value was still linked to the

Below: Ancient Greek coins were highly innovative. This Corinthian stater (top) has a winged Pegasus with a concave reverse showing a helmeted Athena. The coin of Lucania (now Italy) bears a wheat ear with a simple incuse reverse (middle), while the coin of Miletus, a coastal colony in Asia Minor, bears interesting geometric designs (bottom).

The Ornate Shield of Macedon

Philip of Macedon welded the Greeks into a nation and his son Alexander the Great created an empire in the 4th century BC. After his death, the empire was divided and Macedon passed to his general, Antigonus. His descendant, Antigonus Gonatas (277–239 BC), struck this shield-shaped coin bearing the head of Pan. The reverse shows Athena Alkis holding a shield and thunderbolt. These ornate coins survived until Macedon was absorbed by the Roman Empire in the 2nd century BC.

weight and precious metal content, but it was no longer necessary to weigh each piece at every transaction.

THE SPREAD OF COINS

The first electrum coins were found in the river bed of the Pactolus in Asia Minor and may have been struck under the authority of King Ardys of Lydia, ancestor of Croesus. From there they spread to other parts of western Asia Minor, being adopted by the Greek coastal towns of Abydus, Chios, Miletus and Phocaea. These early coins needed no inscriptions, as they circulated only within their own territories, but their motifs were clues to their identity, such as the sphinx of Chios and the man-bull of Miletus. One of the earliest Greek coins showed the civic emblem of a stag and was inscribed "I am the sign of Phanes". It is still the subject of debate as to whether Phanes was a place or a person.

Below: Electrum and silver trihemibols of Phocaea (Ionia), in western Anatolia.

Coin production spread from Asia Minor to mainland Greece in the 6th century. Aegina led the way with its silver "Turtles", whose reverse had a geometric incuse pattern not unlike a Union Jack. Nearby Corinth followed with drachmae showing the winged horse Pegasus. Athens possessed silver mines that enabled it to strike a vast quantity of coins, which were soon accepted all over the Greek world. The earliest featured a range of motifs, but in 546 BC Pisistratus instituted the coins bearing a helmeted profile of Athena on the obverse and an owl, symbol of wisdom, on the reverse. This pattern survived until the early Christian era, though latterly the coins were confined to bronze and permitted by the Romans only for local circulation. The designs were faithfully reproduced in the coinage of modern Greece and survive to this day on the national reverses of the euro coinage.

By the 4th century BC coinage was in general use throughout the Greek world, including colonies as far afield as Syracuse (Sicily) and Marseilles. Silver predominated and coins ranged in size from the tiny hemi-obol to the massive decadrachm (10 drachmae). Portraiture was generally confined to gods and heroes, but after the death of Alexander his profile appeared on coins of the Hellenistic kingdoms created by his generals, and later they used their own portraits.

Above: One of many posthumous coins struck for Alexander the Great, after his death in 323 BC.

Below: The coinage of Alexander the Great, depicted in battle on this ceramic vase, greatly influenced ancient and medieval coins in Europe and Asia.

ROMAN COINAGE

Our connection with the Roman world can be detected in many of our units of currency and weight. The Latin word *pondus*, for example, has given us such words as "ponder" (to weigh up), "ponderous" (heavy) and "pound", used both as a weight (lb) and a unit of currency (£). The abbreviations for the pound in weight and money both came from another Latin word – *libra*, meaning a pound. This is preserved in many European currencies, as *lira* (Italy, Israel and Turkey) or *livre* (France).

Although an imperial mint to supply silver and gold coins was not established in Rome until 269 BC, the Romans had been striking bronze coins locally for several decades prior to this. These bronze currencies began with the aes rude, whose name refers to the crudeness of unmarked lumps of metal, which had to be weighed out at each transaction. Gradually, the lumps were replaced by bars or ingots of a uniform shape and weight. They were known as aes signatum ("signed bronze") because they bore the stamp of the issuing authority on both sides. Significantly, one of these was a bull, alluding to the importance of cattle as a form of barter currency in earlier times.

Below: The Romans were highly skilled in financial dealings. This relief from a Gallo-Roman mausoleum shows a tax collector at work.

Above: Roman aes grave coins, denominated as triens and sextans.

After aes signatum came aes grave ("heavy bronze"). These pieces were roughly circular and fairly flat – like coins, but very much heavier. The basic unit was the as, weighing a pound (*libra*) and bearing the Roman numeral I. Half of this was the semis, indicated by the letter S. A third of an as was the triens, which, being worth four Roman ounces, bore four little pellets to indicate its weight and value. Smaller units were the quadrans ("fourth"), sextans ("sixth") and the uncia ("ounce", indicated by one pellet).

This heavy bronze coinage coincided with the inception of the Roman Mint, which issued a series of silver coins, influenced by the penchant for figures of deities and their familiars in Greek coin design. The series consisted of didrachms (2 drachmae) and their subdivisions of litra, half-litra and silver as. Ten asses of silver or bronze were worth a silver didrachm. The silver coins were inscribed "Roma" or "Romano".

At this point, bronze coins began to fall out of favour. Their weight and consequent value were progressively reduced, until the bronze as eventually weighed no more than the original uncia coin.

GOLD AND SILVER COINS

The Romans preferred silver coins because the metal was abundant, and could be made into a hard-wearing alloy by adding a little copper. Gold was regarded primarily as a medium for jewellery; it was very rarely used for coins. Gold staters were struck in 216 BC during a shortage of silver as a result of the wars against Carthage. (A small silver coin, equivalent to a drachma but known as a victoriate, was struck to celebrate the defeat of Carthage.)

Its victories in the Punic Wars made Rome the most powerful state in the western Mediterranean. Its prosperity led to the adoption of a new currency in 211 BC, based on the silver denarius – the forerunner of the deniers and dinars used by many European and Asiatic countries (and preserved in Britain until 1971 in the symbol "d" to denote the penny). The denarius of 10 asses was divided into the quinarius (5 asses) and the sestertius (2½ asses). A board of moneyers, consisting of three officials elected annually, was created, and their names, initials or family emblems began to appear on the coins.

PORTRAITURE AND ALLEGORY

From the 2nd century BC, Roman coins became more elaborate in their design. The most popular images were Roma and Bellona on the obverse and the heavenly twins, Castor and Pollux, on the reverse. From 146 BC, when the Romans finally destroyed the city of Carthage, Rome expanded rapidly, acquiring territory in North Africa, Gaul (France) and Iberia (Spain), suppressing the Greek colonies in southern Italy and advancing into the Balkans. Coins of this period featured Victory, Mars and Jupiter on the obverse, with elaborate designs illustrating characters and events in classical mythology.

In 141 BC the currency was revalued on the basis of the denarius of 16 asses. Scholars have many theories concerning the motive for this, the general view

Coins in Memoriam

The Emperor Augustus struck coins in memory of his predecessor Julius Caesar, while the coin shown here was struck by Tiberius in memory of Augustus.

now being that silver had become much more plentiful, leading to a decrease in the value of the as. The increase from 10 to 16 asses in the denarius seems to have been a balancing adjustment.

Coins became more varied in design as the moneyers rivalled each other in depicting emblems and events alluding to their illustrious ancestors. By the first century BC, portraits of ancestors were appearing, while Rome was splitting into political factions under such men as Marius, Sulla, Pompey and Julius Caesar. Caesar struck coins in Gaul that included the numerals LII (52, his age) – one of the earliest attempts at putting a date on a coin. After 49 BC, when he became master of Rome, his coins took on a more personal character, with lengthy inscriptions referring to his various public offices. The last coins under Julius Caesar's authority actually bore his portrait.

Below: The expanding Roman empire struck denarii following acquisitions in France (Gallic shield on coin, top) and the Balkans (head of Victory, bottom).

THE ROMAN EMPIRE

From Caesar's assassination in 44 BC until the battle of Actium in 31 BC, a period of civil wars was marked by coins struck on behalf of Brutus, Cassius, the sons of Pompey, the triumvirate of Mark Antony, Lepidus and Octavian, and finally for Octavian himself, having assumed the title of Augustus and set about transforming Rome into an empire. In 27 BC he accepted the title of emperor and instituted a new coinage based on the gold aureus, worth 25 silver denarii. Smaller coins included the brass sestertius and the dupondius (2 asses). Although the weights and sizes of these coins varied, the denominations remained in use for most of the Roman Imperial period.

Imperial coins were prolific and served as propaganda for the emperor, extolling his virtues and achievements and often portraying his wife and family as well as himself. They were generally well produced, with realistic portraits, and elaborate allegorical compositions on the reverse. The seated figure of Britannia shown on British coins since 1672 was actually modelled on the Britannia featured on coins of Antoninus Pius (138–61), in whose reign the Antonine Wall across the isthmus of the Forth and Clyde was built.

Below: Seminal coins issued by the Roman Republic to mark the assassination of Julius Caesar (top) and the suicide of Mark Antony (bottom).

Above: The coins of Antoninus Pius featured a seated Britannia (right).

Above: Some imperial gold coins circulated as far as India, like this holed gold aureus of Caracalla (top). A solidus of Valens appears below.

The double denarius, or antoninianus, was introduced in AD 214 under Caracalla. By that time inflation had caused the demise of the denarius and thereafter the antoninianus was the basic unit of currency. Although nominally silver, it was progressively debased and eventually was no more than a copper coin with a thin silver wash, which soon wore off. New coins were the follis (AD 294) and the gold solidus (309), ancestor of such European coins as the soldo, sol and sou, and the source of the "s" denoting the shilling in pre-decimal British currency.

The nummus, introduced by Diocletian between AD 295 and 310, played a major part in the development of Byzantine coinage. During the 4th century there were two new silver coins, the miliarense and the siliqua, and finally the tremissis, a gold piece worth a third of a solidus.

BYZANTINE COINAGE

In AD 364, Valentinian divided the Roman Empire into eastern and western provinces, assigning the Eastern Empire to his brother Valens. From that time there were two Roman Empires, based in the cities of Rome and Byzantium (Constantinople) respectively. The Western Empire came to an end in 476, when the last emperor, Romulus Augustulus, was defeated by the Ostrogoths. Their ruler, Theodoric, minted coins with his portrait on one side and a figure of Rome on the other, with the caption "Invicta Roma" ("Unconquered Rome"), but these coins were very crude by comparison with the classical issues, and they formed an ironic tailpiece to seven centuries of Roman coinage.

THE IMPERIAL TRADITION

In the east, the Roman Empire survived a further thousand years, until the capture of Constantinople by the Turks in 1453. At the height of its power, the Byzantine Empire extended over the eastern Mediterranean, including even parts of Italy. It retained the ancient Roman provinces in the Balkans and controlled Asia Minor, Syria and Palestine.

Above: Constantine V (left) and a portrait of Christ (middle) on a coin that shows the joint rulers, Basil II and Constantine VIII on the reverse (right).

Below: Allegorical designs on coins of Anastasius and John II portray the emperors flanked by Victory.

Byzantium became the repository of Roman technology, science and the accumulated wisdom of the classical world, and it was the flight of scholars and scientists from Turkish rule after the conquest that triggered off the Renaissance (the rebirth of learning) in the West. Just as the Byzantine Empire kept alight the lamp of learning and civilization in early medieval times, so did it continue the traditions of Greece and Rome in its coins. A new feature, however, was the portrayal of the emperor full-face instead of in profile.

Since the time of the Emperor Constantine (who believed that the victory that gave him the throne had been aided by the one God of the Christians), Christianity had been the official religion of the empire, and from its foundation in 324 his capital at Constantinople, on the site of the ancient Byzantium, had been a Christian city. This religious devotion found expression on the coins of the Byzantine Empire. The figure of Jesus Christ appears on the obverse of Byzantine coins from about 450, followed by the Virgin Mary. From the 9th century onward many saints of the Orthodox Church – Theodore, George, Michael and John among others – were portrayed on the reverses. Christian symbolism replaced the pagan allegory of the Roman Empire.

Above: Crusaders at the walls of Constantinople in 1204, depicted in De la Conquête de Constantinople *by Geoffroi de Villehardouin.*

CHANGING STYLES

As time went by, Greek replaced Latin in the inscriptions on these coins, and it is interesting to note how the Greek letters gradually took over from their Roman counterparts. Inevitably the standards of design and production slipped over the centuries, although

Saucer-shaped Coins

Coins were produced on a flat disc flan until the reign of Constantine IX (1042–55), when a curious concave shape was adopted for all denominations except the smallest bronze pieces. These are known to collectors as *nummi scyphati* (literally "boat-shaped coins"). In succeeding reigns the flan became thinner and slightly cup-shaped, but the strange shape endured until the Latin conquest of 1204.

Byzantine coinage continued to be far superior to that produced anywhere else in the medieval world. Unlike their Roman predecessors, Byzantine coins were relatively neglected by collectors, who regarded their designs as stereotyped and rather monotonous, but recently collectors have developed a keen interest, discovering the subtle developments in design as well as the light they shed on a period of European history that is not well documented in written records. Not surprisingly, coins that not so long ago were comparatively cheap have soared in value.

Although it lasted a millennium, the Byzantine Empire was not a static entity but expanded and contracted, assailed by foreign invasion and torn by civil wars, and these highs and lows of its history are reflected in the coinage. Constantinople was besieged by the Arabs in 674 and the Bulgars in 923. In 1204, during the Fourth Crusade, it fell to these holy warriors and was under Latin (that is, Western European) rule from then until 1261.

The Byzantines minted coins in bronze, silver and gold, although their silver coins are comparatively scarce and usually debased by a high copper content. Justinian I was the first emperor to add a date to his coins, in the form of the year from the beginning of his reign, 526. As well as the increasingly bewildering mixture of Roman and Greek lettering, often reducing inscriptions to little more than an apparent jumble of initials, the collector has to contend with the use of letters to denote numerals in dates and denominations. New titles, such as "Autokrator" (Emperor) and "Basileus Romaion" (King of the Romans) in Greek capitals vie with the cryptic "MP QV" (*Meter Theou* or Mother of God) and "IC" or "XC" (Jesus Christ).

Below: Emperor Justinian I and his wife Theodora, both of whom featured on Byzantine coins.

Above: Lengthy Graeco-Roman inscriptions on post-Justinian coins.

Below: Byzantine coin weights: a 2 solidi square weight (left), a nomisma square weight (right) and a ⅓ nomisma circular weight (bottom).

DENOMINATIONS

The currency was originally based on the gold solidus and its subdivisions, down to the tiny sixth, which was the equivalent of two silver hexagrams. Gradually, the Byzantines adopted a new name for the solidus, calling it a nomisma. In the reign of Nicephorus II a lighter coin than the solidus was adopted, known as a tetarteron, on par with the Arab dinar. In the time of Michael IV (1034–41) the nomisma underwent progressive debasement. Its gold content had dropped to about 26 per cent by the time Alexius I reformed the coinage in 1092 and introduced the hyperper, nominally of pure gold but averaging 21 carat fineness.

The basic silver coin was originally the miliaresion. This word literally means a thousandth part – but of what remains a mystery, as it was tariffed at 12 to the solidus. It was replaced in the reign of Heraclius (610–41) by a crude coin of the same value known as a hexagram. By the 9th century the miliaresion was much thinner and lighter and seems to have been worth half a hexagram. Silver coinage did not recover until the end of the 13th century and was then modelled on contemporary Venetian types, reflecting Venice's control of Byzantine trade.

Copper coins were based on the follis of 40 nummia, the number being represented by a large M. The half (20 nummia) was indicated by the letter K and the quarter by the letter I. Billon (an alloy of copper with a small amount of silver) was used for the trachy, tariffed at 48 to the hyperper.

Above: The basic silver coin of the Byzantine Empire: the miliaresion.

Below: The follis of 40 nummia, a large and cumbersome coin, widely used as small change.

OTHER ANCIENT EUROPEAN COINAGE

Parallel with the main developments of coinage in the great civilizations of the Greek, Roman and Byzantine worlds were the attempts by the peoples beyond the fringes of the civilized world to emulate them. The groups discussed here are the ones of major interest to coin collectors. There were many others that are either obscure, or that produced relatively little coinage, or were content to copy the coins of their more powerful neighbours.

CELTIC COINAGE

The Celtic peoples settled the valley of the Danube and occupied the area now forming the countries of Switzerland, France, Spain, Germany, Belgium and the Netherlands. They migrated to the British Isles around 600 BC and their cultural legacy, especially in Ireland, the Scottish Highlands, Cumbria, Wales and Cornwall, remains strong to this day. Paradoxically, the Celtic fringes of the British Isles did not produce distinctive coinage, but elsewhere, including the southerly and eastern areas of what eventually formed Roman Britain, distinctive Celtic coins developed in the late pre-Christian era.

The Danubian Celts imitated the gold and silver coins with which they were most familiar, the silver tetradrachms and gold staters of the Alexandrine Empire and its Hellenistic successors, but because they were illiterate they blundered the inscriptions or abandoned them altogether. At the same time, the profiles of Philip of Macedon and Alexander the Great were reduced to caricature and then all but vanished, only curls and headbands surviving. Similarly, the horseman on the reverse was reduced to a stylized, abstract shape.

Below: Celtic coins of France and Spain include this Iberian coin of Osca with a horseman (top) and a Gallo-Belgic stater with a large flan depicting Apollo.

Above: Celtic designs: a vine leaf stater of Verica (top), the Phoenician goddess Tanit on a coin of the Danubian Celts (middle) and a stater of the Iceni with a horse and wheel (bottom).

Not so long ago, Celtic coinage was dismissed as barbaric because of this abstraction of classical patterns, but now scholars and collectors are discovering the extraordinary vitality of Celtic art and the religious symbolism of the human heads and even the curvilinear motifs, which are startlingly avant-garde in appearance. British Celts latterly included brief inscriptions that identify the rulers of the Atrebates, Durotriges, Catuvellauni, Iceni, Trinovantes and others in the period immediately before the Roman conquest in AD 43.

THE FALL OF ROME

The minting of coins was one of the technologies lost in the collapse of the Roman Empire. Crude copies of Roman coins were produced by the Ostrogoths, Germanic people who eventually ruled the Romans, from the end of the 5th century. Theodoric the Great not only paid homage to the memory of Imperial Rome but slavishly copied the gold coins of his Byzantine contemporary Anastasius, even going so far as to copy his titles and inscriptions. His successors, Athalaric and Theodahad, substituted

Below: A Celtic punch-marked coin of the Durotriges (top) and an Ostrogoth imitation of a Roman 40 nummia.

Anglo-Saxon Portraiture

The vast majority of early Anglo-Saxon coins had some sort of cross on the reverse. Portraits were seldom attempted and were extremely crude and virtually unrecognizable as such. Unique gold coins of Offa (*c.* 780) and Archbishop Wigmund of York (837–54) have portraits in the Roman or Byzantine style, but these were quite exceptional. It was not until 973 that a royal effigy became standard: the image was composed of tiny punch marks, such as on this penny of Edward the Martyr of 975.

Above: Coins of early medieval France include this tremissis struck by the Visigoths in the name of Severus (top) and 12th-century billon deniers of Burgundy (bottom).

their own portraits. For a time the Byzantine rulers recovered the Balkans and Italy from the Goths and struck coins at Rome and Ravenna in the 8th and 9th centuries.

Elsewhere in the early medieval world, coins based on Roman models were struck by the Vandals in North Africa, denominated in both Roman siliquae and denarii, the Suevians in Spain, the Lombards in Italy, the Burgundians in northern France, the Visigoths in the south of that country, and the Anglo-Saxons in England.

In the majority of cases these coins followed Roman precedents, incorporating crude portraits of local rulers and a wide variety of local inscriptions. Whereas coin production was centralized at the Roman Mint, the rulers of the early medieval European kingdoms dispersed the process and granted the right to strike coins to many towns, and even to monasteries. In the Merovingian kingdom of the 6th and 7th centuries, for example, there existed more than 800 mints. The Merovingians, who ruled over parts of present-day France and Germany, introduced a new coin, the silver saiga, based on the Roman denarius. The legacy of this coin was far-reaching: it led to the denier or penny, introduced by Pepin the Short in 755.

Above and right: The Vikings established extensive trade links. Viking pennies, such as these of Daegmund and Arus, have been found throughout Europe.

VIKING AND ANGLO-SAXON COINAGE

The money that was used in Britain between the withdrawal of the Roman legions, early in the 5th century, and the advent of William the Conqueror, in 1066, is generally described as Anglo-Saxon, although distinctive types were adopted in the seven main kingdoms (Northumbria, Mercia, Kent, East Anglia, Essex, Sussex and Wessex), which emerged as a united England in 959 under Eadgar and adopted the silver penny as the standard unit of currency in 973.

The earliest coins were known as sceats or sceattas (derived from the Old English word meaning "wealth"), and were small pieces of base silver and latterly copper with a uniquely eclectic mixture of symbolism derived from Roman, Byzantine, Teutonic and Celtic coins. Offa of Mercia (757–96) introduced the silver penny, adapted from the Carolingian denier (denarius) with a crude effigy on the obverse and a cross on the reverse. The thrymsa was a small gold coin derived from the tremissis (or third solidus), which was struck between 575 and about 775.

The Vikings traded as widely as they raided and made use of the coinage of other countries, notably England, whose silver penny became the model for the earliest distinctive coins in Denmark, Norway and Sweden. Hedeby in Denmark and Birka in Sweden, the major trading centres of Scandinavia, produced vast quantities of silver pennies with distinctive motifs and runic inscriptions. English sterlings were also extensively copied, not only in the Danelaw (that part of England under Danish rule from the late 9th century), but also in the Norse kingdoms in Ireland and the Isle of Man.

Below: Anglo-Saxon silver pennies issued in Mercia (top) and by the authority of King Eadgar (bottom).

MEDIEVAL EUROPEAN COINAGE

With the collapse of the Roman Empire in Western Europe, social structures became more localized and the coinage system was fragmented. Under the Carolingian rulers, who rose to power as kings of the Franks in the 8th century, a new standardized system was imposed. The gold coins in the realm were demonetized, and in 752 Pepin the Short issued a new silver coin, the silver denier (based on the Roman denarius), which became the basic unit of currency.

BIRTH OF THE SILVER PENNY

The denier was a practical coin for the early Middle Ages, when barter was still prevalent and most people required coins only as a means of converting a small agricultural surplus into cash, and it remained the standard unit for nearly six centuries. In 793, Charlemagne increased the weight of the denier by a third, and as his empire grew, so his coinage was imitated in the denar of the Balkans (hence the dinar of Serbia to this day), the denaro of Italy and the dinero of Spain. It also provided the model for the penny, which travelled from 9th-century England to Scandinavia and northern Germany, giving rise to the pfennig or pfenning in the German states, the fenigow in Poland and the penni in Finland.

By the 11th century the use of the denier was more or less confined to France, where it was struck at many mints – royal, baronial and ecclesiastical. The inconvenience of having no larger coins led to the introduction by Louis IX (1226–70) of the gros (from the French for "large"), which spread across Europe in many different forms – grote, groat, groschen, groszy, grush and even the Turkish kurus.

Below: An enormous salut d'or of Henry VI, with the arms of England and France, to which Henry laid claim, and a depiction of the annunciation.

Below: A 13th-century silver gros tournois of Philip III of France (top), and papal testones of Pius IV (middle), with St Peter enthroned, and Sixtus V (bottom), with St Peter standing.

Above: Workers of the 15th century being paid by the Commune of Siena, in a painting by Pietro di Sano.

Below: A cavallino d'oro of Sicily (top) and a 16th-century zecchino of Venice.

ITALIAN AND GERMAN COINS

After the collapse of the Roman Empire, Italy disintegrated into a multitude of petty principalities and city states. It was the crossroads of civilization and came under the influence of Romans, Byzantines, Goths, Franks and Arabs, reflected in complex coinage of many different types. Pope Adrian I (772–95) minted the first papal coins, which continue to this day.

By the 12th century the city states of Italy were in the forefront of the commercial revolution, and their prosperity was reflected in the size and quality of their coins, as well as the extent to which they were coveted and

Above: A Venetian silver ducato, showing the Doge kneeling before St Mark, and the winged lion.

Bracteates

Coins so thin that they can be struck on only one side are known as bracteates, derived from *bractea*, the medieval Latin word for gold or silver leaf. Coins so described range from the "shadow" coins interred with the dead in ancient Greece to those used in Viking jewellery. The term is also used for the extremely thin silver coins popular in the German states in the 12th to 14th centuries, with emblems struck on one side showing through to the reverse. Popularly known as *Hohlpfennige* (hollow pennies), they circulated alongside more orthodox coins and may have served purely as local small change.

Above (from top): Gold guldens of medieval Hungary and Germany; Crusader coins range from this copper type of Tancred of Antioch to this ornate silver gros of Bohemond VI.

copied elsewhere. Venice, the greatest trading city of this period, introduced the zecchino or sequin, while its rival Florence produced a large silver coin in 1189 depicting a lily (the flower from which it derived its name). The coin, called a fiorino or florin, eventually passed into the currency of many countries, surviving until 2002 in the Netherlands (where the written symbol for a gulden was "fl"). From Genoa in the mid-13th century came the genovino, one of the first great trade gold coins. Worth 20 solidi or 240 denari, it helped to bolster the Roman £sd system, previously confined to money of account rather than actual currency.

In Germany the Franks were at first content to imitate the Romans and Byzantines. In the 14th century, Louis of Bavaria introduced the grossus, modelled on the French gros, and many of the German states adopted thin silver bracteates. It is hard to understand why these were so popular, because they were fragile and easily damaged, but it meant that a small amount of silver went a long way and enabled much larger coins to be struck.

ARABIC INFLUENCES

Gold coins were reintroduced in Western Europe from the 13th century, as the general level of prosperity recovered after the Early Medieval period. This was first evident in southern Italy, where the gold tari and copper follari, originally modelled on the Byzantine system, were inscribed in a mixture of Latin and Arabic. Byzantium was also the inspiration for the silver ducat, so-called because it was first struck in the Duchy (*ducatus*) of Apulia.

From the end of the first millennium the nation-states of Europe gradually emerged, but the process of centralizing coin production and introducing uniformity went on for several centuries. As well as the numerous coins issued by nobles in their own fiefdoms, Crusader coins emanating from the Latin kingdoms briefly flourished in various parts of the Balkans, Asia Minor, Syria and Palestine in the 12th and 13th centuries. Interestingly, it was in the Crusader kingdoms that the pattern of French feudal coinage was most closely followed, although while imitating the deniers of the West they were often influenced by the sizes, weights, specifications and designs of their Islamic contemporaries.

Below: A bilingual tram of Armenia with an inscription citing the Seljuqs of Rum (top) and imitation dirhams of the 13th century (bottom).

MIDDLE EASTERN COINAGE

The inhabitants of Arabia had no coins of their own and were content to use Sassanian drachmae of Persia and the copper folles of Byzantium. Even after they began their dramatic expansion throughout the Middle East, borrowed coinage remained the norm, but in the mid-7th century Caliph Abd al-Malik introduced coinage based on the gold dinar (denarius aureus), the silver dirham (drachma) and the bronze fils (follis). At first the caliph was content to use Byzantine gold solidi, but because they bore the image of Christ he decided to issue his own gold coins with non-figurative motifs, hence the dinar, whose appearance coincided with the rise of iconoclasm in Islam.

DYNASTIC COINS

By the mid-7th century the great empires of Persia and Byzantium had fought each other to a standstill. In the resulting power vacuum the religious zeal of the Arabs gave their aggressive expansion a powerful incentive and explains why they were able to overrun the Middle East so rapidly. Umar, the Commander of the Faithful, established Basra in Mesopotamia and Fustat in Egypt as major centres from which the Arabs spread across the Middle East and North Africa, and thence into Central Asia and the Iberian Peninsula.

Below: An Abd al-Malik dinar of AH 78 (top) and a dirham of AH 81.

Above: More than a thousand years of Arab influence on Spanish coin production can be seen in this 18th-century dirham of Marrakesh struck at Madrid (top) and in this Arab-Byzantine dirham circulated in 8th-century Spain (bottom).

First and foremost of the Arab dynasties were the Umayyads. At the height of their power they ruled over a vast territory from Seville to Bokhara, but they were overthrown in 750. From their chief mint at Wasit they produced the first of the silver dirhams with Koranic inscriptions on both sides, establishing a pattern that lasted for centuries, imitated by their successors, the Abbasids, and later rival dynasties such as the Fatimids of Egypt and the Ghaznavids of Afghanistan.

THE MONGOL INVASION

Early in the 13th century the Mongols under Genghis Khan swept out of the steppes of Central Asia and first overran China (1211–14), then in 1220 advanced westward against the Empire of Khwarizm (modern Iran, Turkestan and north-western India). Before he died in 1227, Genghis had conquered a vast territory from the Black Sea to Korea. In a series of lightning campaigns his immediate successors conquered most of Russia and, by 1241, had advanced into Poland and Hungary. By 1260 the Mongol Empire was divided among the descendants of Genghis and out of this developed separate dynasties in Siberia and the

Above: A Kay-Khusraw II type drachm (top) shows Byzantine influences, and the distinctive concentric design of an 11th-century Fatimid dinar (middle) is reflected in an anonymous silver dirham of the Golden Horde (bottom).

Above: An 18th-century Ottoman coin of Osman III.

Below: An Islamic street scene with a porter and a metalworker.

Crimea, and most notably in China under Kublai Khan. Their impact on coinage was considerable. They generally made use of the coins they seized as booty, or made crude copies of them, but later the khans of the Golden Horde produced small silver coins distinguished by their inscriptions, while the Ilkhans of Persia struck handsome coins in gold, silver and bronze reciting their titles and family tree. They did not contribute to European coinage and their impact on Islamic coins was slight, though coins of the Seljuks of Rum, struck at Qonya, include the adjective *mahrusat* ("well-defended" – against the menace from the east).

SELJUQS OF RUM

In 1055 Tughril Beg the Seljuq seized Baghdad and founded a dynasty that eventually controlled most of Anatolia, otherwise known as Asia Minor or Rum ("land of the Romans"). The Seljuqs of Rum were the most powerful of the Turkmen tribes and eventually prevailed over the others, establishing their capital at Qonya. In turn, they were defeated by the Mongols but remained significant until the early 14th century, producing a vast series of coins mostly distinguished by square frames within a circle. Coins of a similar type were struck by the Mamluks of Egypt.

Islamic Calendar

Most Islamic coins are dated from the Hegira, the flight of Muhammad from Mecca to Medina in AD 622. The Islamic calendar consists of 12 lunar months (as opposed to solar, or luni-solar), so it falls shorter than the Gregorian year. The date 1201, below, equates to 1786 in the Gregorian calendar.

Above: Modern coins of Islamic countries often show the ruler, as in this Iraqi coin of the 1950s portraying King Faisal II (top). Square silver dirhams of Morocco (bottom), a type introduced by Abd al-Mumin c. *AH 550, were popular for 250 years.*

As Seljuq power declined, the Turkic tribes of western Anatolia became more independent, and distinctive coins were struck by the Qaramanids from about 1300, and the Jandarids soon after. Coins were also minted by the Sarukhan, Isfendiyarids and Eretnids, before the emergence of the Ottomans about 1350 under Bayazid bin Murad. His son Suleyman was the first Ottoman ruler to adopt the *toughra* or sign-manual of the sultan as a coin symbol; it survives in some Arab coinage to this day.

OTTOMAN EMPIRE

The Ottoman rulers of Turkey and western Asia began minting coins in the 15th century in gold, silver and bronze, featuring the toughra of the ruler and inscriptions in Arabic script. This type of coinage continued in Turkey until 1933, when the lira of 100 kurus was adopted. The portrait of Kemal Ataturk then began to grace the coins, emphasizing Turkey's transformation into a secular country, and henceforward inscriptions were in the modified Roman alphabet.

ISLAMIC COINS TODAY

Egypt, Morocco and the Yemen all have a long history of distinctive coins, clinging to Islamic tradition with lengthy inscriptions in place of portraiture, and numerous variations of the Bismillah ("There is no God but God and Muhammad is His Prophet"). Morocco's main concession to symbolism was the inclusion of the national emblem, a five-pointed star. All these countries have now adopted portraiture. By contrast, Saudi Arabia retains strong conservative traditions. It used Ottoman coinage until distinctive coins were minted in the early 1900s, apart from a few small copper pieces minted at Mecca from 1804. Foreign coins, notably the Maria Theresia thaler of Austria, were countermarked in Arabic.

Persian coins followed the Arab pattern, but under the reforming Shah Nasr-ed-Din (1829–96) a central mint was established at Tehran and coins on European lines were introduced.

Below: An early 20th-century dinar of Saudi Arabia.

INDIAN COINAGE

The Indian subcontinent developed a distinctive coinage, although at various periods it was influenced by political and artistic developments in other parts of the ancient world. Very little is known about hundreds of dynasties other than what can be gleaned from their coins. Ancient languages, such as Kharoshthi, have been deciphered from bilingual Indo-Greek coins.

EARLY INDIAN CURRENCIES

The earliest coins appeared *c.* 500 BC, when silver from Persia and Afghanistan began to flow into India. They were irregular in shape but of uniform weight. The use of such symbols as hills, trees, animals and human figures suggests issue by royal authority, rather than merchants' marks.

Coins recovered from a hoard at Mathura in central India, bearing up to seven punch marks, are regarded as the earliest known. Around the same time Taxila, which traded with Mesopotamia, produced curved ingots with punch marks at either end. Most punch-marked coins conform to the Karshapana standard weight of 32 rattis (1 ratti being 11mg/0.17 grains, the weight of a gunja seed). From the presence of coins of Alexander the Great in Indian hoards it appears that punch-marked coins continued long after the advent of Indo-Greek coins in the 4th century BC. Many were circular, showing the influence of Greek models. Later types included copper coins, relatively thick and often square, with various symbols punched on both sides.

Below: A conical copper currency item of ancient India bears designs also found on Mauryan coins.

Above: Indo-Greek tetradrachms and staters struck by the kings of Bactria.

HELLENISTIC COINS

Alexander the Great began his conquest of India in 327 BC and subjugated the territory as far as the Indus before his death in 323, when his vast empire was divided among his generals. Seleucus Nicator seized Persia, Bactria (Afghanistan) and Syria, and struck gold staters and silver tetradrachms, combining Greek and Indian inscriptions. He was checked by a powerful Maurya state ruled by Chandragupta, who married a daughter of Seleucus.

The Mauryan Empire covered most of India beyond the limits of Greek penetration and struck distinctive coins until its disintegration in 180 BC. Many other kingdoms and dynasties (such as the Satavahanas, Kshatrapas and Maitrakas) then emerged, each producing its own coins. In southern India the best known coinage was that of the Ardhras, who used lead coins inscribed with native characters.

After the death of Seleucus in 281 BC, his empire broke up into several kingdoms, which continued with Indo-Greek coinage. Arsaces became king of Parthia, while Diodotus seized Bactria in 256 BC. The gold staters and copper tetradrachms of Bactria had inscriptions in both Greek and Prakrit. This Indo-Greek kingdom continued for more than a century before it was absorbed into the Kushan Empire.

The Kushans were a nomadic people of north-western China who moved into the Oxus valley in AD 78 and ruled most of what is now Afghanistan, Pakistan and north-west India. Kushan coins portrayed the ruler on the obverse, with a legend in cursive Greek, while the reverse featured Hindu deities with Sanskrit text. After AD 220 the Kushan Empire disintegrated into

Below: Allegorical subjects on Kushan coins range from Graeco-Roman figures such as Nike to the Hindu god Shiva.

Below: Gold dinars struck by kings of the Kushan.

Princely Coinage

Many Indian princes retained the privilege of striking their own coins until 1947, varying in content and denomination according to the ruler's whim. They range from crude, non-figural pieces to sophisticated coins on Western lines, often produced in London or Birmingham, such as this 1941 silver nazarana rupee of Faridkot, with the bust of Harindar Singh on the obverse and the state arms on the reverse.

numerous petty kingdoms, whose gold dinars and copper coins remained current until the 5th century, latterly with more emphasis on Hindu deities and inscribed in Brahmi script. Were it not for the extraordinary range and beauty of their coins, very little would be known about the Kushans.

THE GUPTAS

A Magadha (Bihar) kingdom, with its capital at Patna, emerged in the late 3rd century AD under Srigupta, founder of a dynasty that lasted for 300 years. His grandson, Chandragupta I (305–25), created the splendid Gupta Empire. The Guptas were noted patrons of the arts and their magnificent coins mirror their taste, with beautifully executed inscriptions in Sanskrit, written in Brahmi characters. The empire, which extended over most of modern India, had collapsed by 650.

Below: Indian Islamic coins include silver horseman tankas of Delhi (bottom) and gold mohurs of the Mughals (right).

CENTRAL ASIAN INVASIONS

Internal dissension and rebellions made the Gupta Empire easy prey to the Hephthalites or White Huns, migrating westward in the 5th century. From time to time, various local dynasties briefly arose, such as the Vardhanas and Pratiharas, but the poor quality of their coins reflect the dark ages of Indian history under successive invasions.

From 717 to 920 several Turko-Hephthalitic kingdoms occupied what are now Afghanistan and Pakistan, and embraced Hinduism, reflected in the symbolism of their coins. Conversely, by the 9th century, many different coins in central India also reflected the influence of Islam, with motifs derived from Turkic and Sasanian coins, often combined with Hindu deities. In the 10th century various Hindu rulers founded petty kingdoms and minted their own coins, often depicting a seated goddess or a bull and horseman, the latter being a type popularized by the Rajput kingdoms.

ISLAMIC COINS

Arab penetration of India began in the 8th century, and by the end of the 9th century they had conquered Afghanistan, Baluchistan and the Punjab. Mahmud of Gazni (998–1030) raided India and struck silver dirhams at Lahore, with Arabic inscriptions on the obverse but Sanskrit text in Devanagri script on the reverse.

Muhammad Ghori (1173–1206) and his successor Qutub-ud-din Aibak created the Sultanate of Delhi. Qutub, originally a slave, founded the so-called Slave Dynasty, which welded together the petty kingdoms and laid the foundations of the mighty Mughal Empire. In the 13th and 14th centuries crude silver and gold tankas were struck, the forerunners of the beautiful gold and silver coins in which the Arabic script is particularly fine. They often bore verses of Persian poetry, and sometimes the signs of the zodiac. From the beginning of the 18th century, the quality of Mughal coins deteriorated. As the empire broke up, petty rulers began producing their own coins, a privilege that continued under British rule.

India holds the record for the world's largest coins, the stupendous gold 1000 mohurs of Shah Jahangir, struck at Agra in 1613, which weighed over 12kg/26lb. India also produced some of the smallest, the pinhead-sized gold coins of Colpata, weighing only 1 grain (65mg).

Below: A Parthian-style coin with a bearded king and a fire temple.

Above: A Gupta dinar with a king drawing his bow at a rearing tiger.

MINTS

The modern mint is a large complex of secure buildings, but early mints were little more than smithies equipped with a furnace for melting gold and silver, moulds for casting blanks, and hammers and anvils for striking the coins.

As soon as coinage came into being, representing the wealth and power of a country as well as providing a means of trade, coins assumed considerable importance. Reflecting the prestige of the ruler as well as creating commercial confidence, they had to be struck to exact specifications with clearly defined images and inscriptions. This could best be achieved in a central workshop, or provincial workshops using equipment supplied by a central authority. A typical mint, until the advent of mechanization in the 16th century, might consist of a small team of men engaged in melting and refining the raw metal, beating it into sheets and cutting it into roughly circular pieces, which were finally struck as coins by the hammermen. The anvils, with their coining irons (dies), were simple in design, and the equipment could be moved from place to place as occasion demanded.

As trade expanded and demand for coins grew, royal powers and privileges were often devolved to mint-masters or moneyers. In medieval Europe there was a proliferation of local mints, as the privilege of striking coins often passed to feudal lords and Church prelates.

Above: A 2nd-century Roman coin shows Moneta holding scales and a cornucopia (top); a Phoenician tetrashekel of the Sidon Mint (middle); and half groats of Henry VII, produced by the ecclesiastical Canterbury Mint.

This trend was reversed in the 16th century as government became more centralized, and the coining privilege was restricted to the Crown.

AN ANCIENT TERM

The word "mint" is derived from the Latin word *moneta*, because the place where Roman coins were originally struck was the temple of the goddess Juno Moneta (literally Juno who monitors or warns) on the northern peak of the Capitoline Hill. The goddess had earned her nickname because she was said to have warned the Romans not to undertake any but just wars, promising in return that they would never run short of money. Moneta was personified in Roman myth and was usually depicted on Roman coins as a woman holding a balance and a cornucopia, or horn of plenty. Many Roman coins, from the reigns of Caracalla to Valens, have a reverse showing three figures of Moneta, holding scales and cornucopiae with lumps of gold, silver and bronze at their feet.

Above: The 15th-century Austrian Emperor Maximilian I is given a tour of a German mint.

The name Moneta was later used to signify the workshop attached to the temple, and the bronze asses coined there were known as *monetae*. This use of the same term to describe pieces of money and the place where they were produced continues today in many European languages. In German, for example, the word *Münze* is used for "coin", "money" and "mint", and

Below: Solidi of Constans, struck at the Siscia Mint (left), and Valentinian III with the mark of the Ravenna Mint.

Siege Pieces

During the English Civil War, the besieged Royalist stronghold of Newark-on-Trent was one of four towns with a temporary mint. It issued pieces of silver plate cut into diamond shapes and stamped on one side with the crown and monogram of Charles I above the value in Roman numerals (30 pence). The reverse bore OBS (for the Latin *obsidium*, "siege") above the name of the town and the date.

Above: The circular symbol above the 'M' on this 18th-century Spanish reverse distinguishes the Mexico City mint from the Casa de Moneda, Madrid.

Dutch *munt* and Swedish *mynt* have the same meanings. In the Romance languages the same word is used for coin and money but not the mint. Thus, French *monnaie*, Italian *moneta*, Spanish *moneda* and Portuguese *moeda* can all mean "coin" or "money", but "mint" is *hotel de monnaie*, *zecca*, *casa de moneda* and *casa da moeda* respectively. In English, "money", "monetary" and "mint" come from the same root. The word "coin" comes from the French word for a corner, which is derived from the Latin *cuneus*, a wedge.

ANCIENT MINTS AND MINT-MARKS

The names, abbreviated or in full, of the places where coins were issued began with Athens ("Athe") inscribed on coins of the 5th century BC, but it was not until the time of Alexander the Great that mint names were explicitly marked. By the end of the 4th century BC, standardization of coin types throughout the empire was the norm, and coins of the same design might be struck in many different mints. The coins of Alexander from Damascus and the Phoenician mints at Sidon and Akko, however, bore inscriptions that identified them. This system was revived by the Romans from the time of Probus (AD 276–82), the abbreviated names or initials of mints usually appearing in the exergue (the separate area below the design) on the reverse.

The Romans operated a highly complex system. Those cities that enjoyed the coining privilege had establishments that consisted of one or more monetary workshops (*officinae monetae*). On the coins of Valentinian II, Valens and Gratian in the 4th century the *officinae* were often designated by the letters P, S, T or Q (*prima*, *secunda*, *tertia* and *quarta*, denoting first, second, third or fourth). These letters may be found on their own in the field (the background of the design), in the exergue or before or after the initials of the mint town.

Mints in the Western Empire generally had a few *officinae*, though Rome had as many as 12. In the Eastern Empire, mints were much larger, and Constantinople had up to 11, while Antioch had 15 and Alexandria 19. Eastern workshops were sometimes denoted by 'OFF' on coins, followed by Roman numerals or Greek letters.

MEDIEVAL TO MODERN

After the fall of the Roman Empire in the west, European coin production was reduced to bare essentials, reflected in crude designs and irregular shapes. Early medieval production was split between numerous small workshops, and every town of any size had at least one. Over a thousand locations have been recorded in inscriptions found on the gold triens of Merovingian France.

In medieval England the names of mints were included on the reverse of coins from the 10th century onwards and at least 109 place names have been identified on Anglo-Saxon, Norman and early Plantagenet coins. Thereafter production became more centralized, and the number of mints decreased.

A similar pattern applied to other European countries in the same period. Medieval Germany consisted of many kingdoms, principalities and duchies, each with its own mint. Today, Germany is the only European country to divide production between several mints, in Berlin, Hamburg, Karlsruhe, Munich and Stuttgart. The United States has operated eight mints at various times since 1793, many of which have now ceased production.

Below (clockwise from top-left): Souvenir medals commemorating the assay office of New York and mints of San Francisco and Denver. (Bottom-left): The Royal Canadian mint has branches at Ottawa and Winnepeg (pictured), the former minting collector coins, the latter circulating coins.

COMMON CURRENCY AND TRADE COINS

There is a scene in Stevenson's *Treasure Island* in which Jim Hawkins and his mother sort through the possessions of the old buccaneer who has died at their inn. Mrs Hawkins wishes to collect what he owed her in board and lodging. "'I'll have my dues, and not a farthing over,'" she says as they count the coins: "It was a long, difficult business, for the coins were of all countries and sizes – doubloons, and louis-d'ors, guineas, and pieces of eight, and I know not what besides, all shaken together at random."

Above: A Mercia penny (top) and a 13th-century Scandinavian imitation of a radiate-type penny.

Below: Hernán Cortés and his Spanish troops discover Aztec treasure.

This sentence vividly conveys the manner in which coins of many countries were widely accepted because of the purity of their gold or silver content. This was not a new phenomenon, for certain gold and silver coins of ancient Greece circulated far beyond the boundaries of the cities that issued them. The Turtles of Aegina, the Foals of Corinth and above all the Owls of Athens were readily accepted all over the Mediterranean and probably even further afield, if the evidence of coin hoards is to be believed. Roman denarii and aurei, the staters and didrachms of Macedon and the darics and sigloi of Persia ranked among the leading trade coins of the ancient world.

From the time of King Offa of Mercia the English silver penny was prized for its high production values and metal content. The adjective "sterling", meaning of the highest character, is derived from the silver penny, which was 92.5 per cent pure. To this day sterling silver is an alloy of 925 parts silver to 75 parts copper, a composition that makes for great durability. The popularity of the penny caused some consternation for the local economy, however. As these good quality coins began increasingly to drain abroad, periodic shortages resulted in England itself, and conversely the country was prone to invasions of poor quality imitations, known as pollards or crockards, from continental Europe. Successive monarchs were perplexed by the mixed blessing of producing a strong currency.

Above: A speciedaler of Christiania (Oslo) of 1663 (top) and a jefimok rouble of Russia, counterstamped on a Salzburg thaler of 1625 (bottom).

THE MIGHTY DOLLAR

The history of the world's most popular coin is an interesting one. Its origins are not in the New World but in an obscure valley in Bohemia (now part of the Czech Republic). Jachymov was known in German as Joachimsthal, and it was near this town, in 1519, that a large strike of silver was made. The Counts of Schlick coined the metal into large coins known as guldengroschen, which came to be nicknamed Joachimsthalers. Shortened to "thaler", the name was adopted for a wide range of large German silver coins, ranging from 60 to 72 kreuzer in value, some beautifully inscribed, which survived until 1872. The name was corrupted in other languages to talar (Saxony), tallero (Italy), tolar (Slovenia), talari (Ethiopia), tala (Samoa), dala (Hawaii), daalder (Netherlands), daler (Denmark and Sweden) and dollar. The term "dollar" was first used in Scotland for the 30 shilling piece of James VI in 1567–71, while coins denominated in dollars and fractions of a half, quarter, eighth and sixteenth were struck at Edinburgh in the reign of Charles II (1676–82), long before the dollar became the standard unit of currency in the American colonies. Just to be different, the Russians adapted the first part of the original name (Joachim) for their large silver coins, jefimki (singular *jefimok*).

The thaler crossed the Atlantic in the form of the crude but vigorous silver coins minted in the Spanish colonies. The silver was cast into circular bars which were sliced to form "cobs" that could be stamped with the Spanish regal device. These were the coins that Jim Hawkins referred to as "pieces of eight" – *pesos a ocho reales* (literally, a weight of 8 reals or bits). The American silver dollar became almost as popular as its Spanish counterpart,

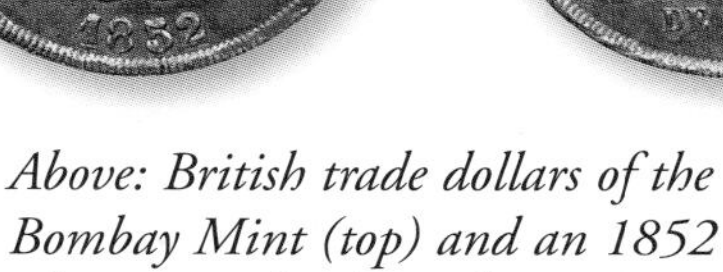

Above: British trade dollars of the Bombay Mint (top) and an 1852 silver peso of Bolivia (bottom).

although it was its paper equivalent that conquered the world and is the only truly international currency of the present time.

Doubloons

The English term "doubloon" was widely, but loosely, applied to many Spanish-Mexican gold coins, which poured into Europe from the 16th century onward. It was derived from the Spanish *doblone*, the augmentative of *dobla* ("double"), which was applied originally to the 2 escudo denomination.

SILVER TRADE DOLLARS

To challenge the supremacy of the Spanish peso, England introduced a trade dollar in 1600, when its "merchant adventurers" were setting out to establish trade in Muscovy (Russia) and the Indies. British trade dollars, mainly circulating in China and the Far East, continued to be struck at the Royal Mint until World War II.

The United States also minted trade dollars for use in the Pacific, rivalling the beautiful pesos of Mexico, which were so pure that the silver was soft and easily knocked. The Chinese, who used these foreign coins for large transactions, eventually produced silver yuan, or dollars, of their own, which were likewise traded readily all around the Pacific area.

GOLD TRADE COINS

Certain gold coins achieved world popularity that endured for many centuries. From the late medieval period, the florins of Florence and the ducats of Venice were traded internationally and they inspired similar coins in the Netherlands, Austria and Hungary down to recent times. From 1816, however, the preferred gold coin was the British sovereign.

BULLION COINS

Coins struck in gold, silver or platinum, whose value is not determined by any inscription as such but by the weight and fineness usually inscribed on them, are known as bullion coins. Their value depends on the prevailing price of precious metals in the leading world markets on any particular day. They came to prominence in the 20th century, when gold and silver disappeared from everyday currency, affording a means of trading in these metals on a small scale. Thus, the Mexican 50 peso coin, known as the Libertad, was re-issued from 1943, with the value omitted and its weight and fineness substituted. This was the forerunner of the Krugerrand (South Africa), followed by the Maple Leaf (Canada), the Panda (China), the Nugget (Australia), the Angel (Isle of Man) and the Britannia series (Britain).

Below: The popular six-ducati of Naples and Sicily, 1768 (top). Under Queen Victoria, the British sovereign (middle) became the world's most widely traded gold coin. Today, common currency in the form of the euro (bottom) encourages trade between member countries.

MONEY OF NECESSITY

From time to time in history, proper coins have been either in short supply or non-existent. Such situations often arose in wartime, because people tended to hoard good gold and silver coins. Wars and civil conflicts also gave rise to situations where towns were besieged and the governor or garrison commander resorted to temporary measures to pay his troops. More often than not, however, it was an economic crisis that drove coins out of circulation, leading merchants and tradesmen to take matters into their own hands and issue tokens.

INTRINSIC VERSUS NOMINAL VALUE

A token is any piece of money whose intrinsic value is less than its face value. In that sense all modern coins are tokens, because their metallic worth is almost invariably less than their nominal, legal tender value. Until the 19th century, however, most countries issued coins that contained metal up to the value at which they circulated.

This applied mainly to gold and silver, but it should be noted that Britain's first copper penny and 2 pence (1797) were very cumbersome because they contained 1 and 2 ounces of metal respectively, copper being then valued at a penny an ounce (28g). The difference between real and nominal value has widened over the years, with the debasement of silver coins and finally the complete replacement of silver by cupro-nickel and other base alloys. Conversely, there have been instances of small copper or bronze coins having a greater intrinsic worth than their face value and actually costing twice as much to produce as they were worth in circulation.

Below: A Roman provincial coin struck at Tyre during the reign of Hadrian (top); an Abbasid coin struck by a local governor, under the caliphate but in his own district (bottom).

Above: British tokens often imitated the designs of real coins: a George and Dragon freehouse token reading, "At the George in Cheapside Markett" (top), a Sussex halfpenny token (middle), and a Suffolk 1s 6d (bottom).

FILLING THE GAP

Token coinage was either sanctioned or permitted in ancient Greece and Rome, and was struck by many towns for local circulation. Tokens were generally made of copper or even lead and used for small change. They are of immense interest, as they often bear symbols and images of purely local significance.

Many of the small civic coins of the Middle Ages really come into the same category, although they have attained the status of coins. In many European countries, notably France, Germany and Italy, these local coins continued until the 19th century, either officially sanctioned or unofficially condoned because they served a useful purpose. This was also true of the numerous local issues in India and China. Similarly the copper cents and sous that

Protest Piece

This imitation of the Cartwheel penny of 1797 bears the inscription: "No landlords you fools/ Spence's Plan for ever". The reference is to Thomas Spence (1750–1814), the pioneer of agrarian socialism, who published a pamphlet in 1801 attacking the great landowners. Spence was convicted of seditious libel, fined £20 and sentenced to a year in prison. He also produced the "Hive of Liberty" trade token in 1793.

Below: A citizen exchanging assignats, *the paper notes that replaced coinage during the French Revolution.*

Above: An Anglesey copper halfpenny of 1788 (left) and an Irish silver 10 pence bank token, 1805 (right).

were circulating in Canada before Confederation in 1867 are regarded as coins, although they were issued by the various provincial banks.

BRITISH TOKENS

As money of necessity, tokens cast or struck in lead, pewter or copper enjoyed a purely local circulation in England from the early 15th century-onward. These farthings and half farthings were tolerated but had no official sanction. Periodically, the government tried to stamp them out, but as the monarch was reluctant to issue any coins other than in silver or gold, there were times when merchants and shopkeepers were forced to produce tokens to use as small change for the benefit of their customers.

There was such an acute shortage of small coins by the end of the English Civil War in 1649 that tokens proliferated, and it has been estimated that there were more than 4000 different types in London alone. After the Restoration, regal halfpence and farthings were adopted in 1672 and tokens were suppressed by 1674. They were revived in 1787, however, when silver pennies disappeared from general circulation, as small copper coins had not been minted since 1775. The Anglesey Copper Mining Company led the way with its Druid penny, which circulated widely. Over the ensuing decade hundreds of different tokens, mostly halfpence and pennies, were produced by businessmen, merchants and shopkeepers and are of immense social interest on account of their commercial advertising. John Palmer, Mayor of Bath and pioneer of the mail coach, issued a halfpenny that showed his invention on the reverse. Some of the pennies bore an inscription stating that 240 of them could be redeemed for a pound note.

Copper tokens were outlawed in 1797 when the Cartwheel copper pennies were introduced, but a shortage of silver coins during the Napoleonic Wars even led to tokens for 1s 6d and 3 shillings being issued by the Bank of England in the early 19th century. Copper tokens were again issued from 1811 until the 1830s.

Below: An American tin token of James II, struck in 1688.

AMERICAN TOKENS

Tokens were struck in the American colonies, or imported from private manufacturers in England and Ireland, to fill gaps in the coinage supplied from the mother country, and this continued until the 1790s pending the supply of coins from the US Mint.

Hard Times tokens, also known as Copperheads, appeared in 1834–44 during a shortage of cents and half cents. Many of them bore political slogans reflecting the power struggle between President Andrew Jackson and the Bank of the United States. There was a rash of tokens during the Civil War, often of a patriotic nature, when coins were in short supply. Even postage stamps were pressed into service, encased in small circular discs that carried commercial advertisements on the back.

WARTIME SHORTAGES

During and immediately after World War I, coins were in short supply in France, Germany, Italy and other countries, and this was remedied by the issue

Above: An aluminium-bronze 2 franc token issued by the French chambers of commerce during the economic crisis of 1922–3.

of tokens by chambers of commerce and local authorities, usually recognizable by the inscription "Bon Pour" ("good for") or its equivalent in other languages. Tokens also appeared during the Spanish Civil War (1936–9), including circular discs with stamps affixed to them. In Russia, stamps were reprinted on stout card and had an inscription on the back signifying their parity with small silver coins. Stamps affixed to cards circulated in lieu of coins in Rhodesia during the Boer War, and this practice was followed by some French colonies in World War I and parts of India in World War II.

OBSIDIONAL CURRENCY

From the Latin word *obsidium* ("siege") comes the term for coins produced by the defenders of besieged towns. The first record of this practice comes from the Siege of Tyre during the First Crusade in 1122, when stamped pieces of leather were used as money. Leather coins were also produced at Faenza (1240) and Leiden (1573–4), when the bindings of hymn books were pressed into service. The first metal pieces were uniface lead coins produced in Saint-Omer in 1477.

The issue of siege coins has been recorded on more than 130 occasions and they include silver and even gold pieces crudely cut from commandeered plate and stamped with a mark of value and usually with the civic arms. This custom appears to have been confined to Europe, although paper notes for the same purpose were produced during the sieges of Khartoum (1885) and Mafeking (1900).

PARTS AND PROCESSES

This section looks at the various factors that distinguish coins by type and value, and the different techniques used to produce them. We also investigate the history of counterfeiting coins and the security features that have evolved to combat the circulation of bogus coins and imitations, like this one shilling and sixpence token of 1811, produced in Suffolk, England.

DENOMINATIONS

Traditionally, the denomination of a coin was determined solely by the weight and fineness, and thus the intrinsic value, of the metal used. We have already touched upon the weight systems based on the ancient Greek talent or Roman libra, but many other value systems were used in antiquity.

One of the earliest was based on the *shoti* of the Middle East, weighing about 120 grains. The grain, still used in weights and measures today, was derived from a grain of barley. The unit of weight in Egypt was the *deben*, made up of 10 *qedets*, and numerous qedet weights have been discovered not only in Egypt but also at Troy and at Knossos in Crete. The system of weights that evolved in Mesopotamia was used across the Persian Empire throughout Asia Minor, Greece, southern Italy and as far west as Ireland in pre-Roman times. In this system 60 um made a sikkur, 6 sikkur a shekel, 60 shekels a maneh and 60 maneh a talent.

Below: In The Banker and his Wife, *by the 15th-century Flemish artist Quentin Metsys, the husband counts and weighs his gold coins while his wife studies a book of devotions.*

MONEY OF ACCOUNT

Broadly speaking, all monetary systems (including money of account) are based on the relationship of one unit to another. In Britain, for example, 12 copper pennies were worth 1 silver shilling and 20 silver shillings were worth one gold sovereign or pound. It is usually convenient to use different metals to express this relationship, but the ratio of one to another has differed over the centuries in many parts of the world. Often, different denominations

Above: During the 11th and 12th centuries, British silver pennies were often simply cut in half to accommodate the need for small change in everyday commercial transactions.

Gold Guineas

The guinea was first issued in 1663 under Charles II (below); its name arose because much of the gold came from Guinea in Africa. It was valued at 20 shillings, but this increased as the price of gold rose. The last guinea was issued in 1813, as the "Great Recoinage" of 1816 replaced it with the pound, though it continued as money of account, valued at 21 shillings, until 1971.

Below: A Roman aes grave, marked with heads of barley and pellets.

Above: A sixpence of Charles II with interlocking Cs.

evolved from the earliest monetary systems. The £sd system used in Britain until 1971 was derived from the Roman system, in which the libra was divided into 20 solidi or 240 denarii. Adopted by the Carolingian Empire, this survived in many European countries. Pre-Revolutionary France had the livre of 20 sols or 240 deniers, while Italy had the lira of 20 soldi or 240 denari.

In Germany, by contrast, the mark was divided into 4 vierding, 16 loth, 32 setin, 64 quentchen, 256 richtpfennig or 512 heller, but only the pfennig and heller existed as coins. However, all these units could be used as "money of account". The latter is, as its name suggests, any unit employed in the keeping of accounts: it is sometimes represented by actual coins but quite often not.

Above: George III shillings of 1787 and 1817 (back left and right), and silver Maundy pennies marked, unusually for the period, with Arabic numerals.

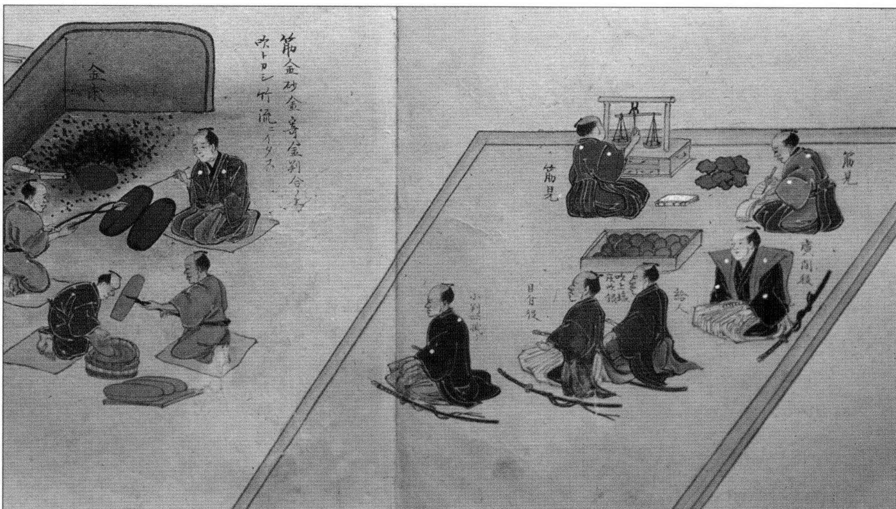

Above: Gold oban and koban coins being marked in 18th-century Japan.

Just as metric and imperial systems are concurrent today, multiple value systems sometimes existed in the same country. In the later medieval period England had gold coins in different finenesses: 22 carat was used for the sovereign (20 shillings), half sovereign (10 shillings) and crown (5 shillings), but 23.5 carat for the noble (6s 8d) and its sub-divisions. The gold guinea (21 shillings) was replaced by the sovereign in 1816 but remained as money of account until the advent of decimal currency in 1971.

The denominations within each system were relative to each other, but different values could be attributed to the same units in different systems. In France the livre was worth 2 marks, but in England the mark was equivalent to two-thirds of a pound, both in weight (8 ounces) and value (13s 4d).

MARKS OF VALUE

The earliest coins bore no mark of value: this was implicit in their size and weight. Most Roman coins were undenominated apart from the aes grave, on which different values were indicated by varying numbers of pellets. Some Byzantine gold coins were inscribed OB, followed by Greek letters forming the number 72. This was an abbreviation for *obruson* ("pure"), and indicated that the coins had been struck at the rate of 72 to the pound of pure metal. Roman numerals XII, XXI or XLII may be found on Vandal coinage to indicate denominations, while some English silver coins of Tudor and Jacobean times were inscribed with Roman numerals behind the monarch's head to denote their values in shillings or pence.

MULTIPLE DENOMINATIONS

Most countries get by with six or eight coins in everyday circulation. Before the general advent of paper money to represent higher values, coins played a much more prominent role, hence the need for high-denomination coins in gold and silver. Today the number of different coins in general use tends to be governed by the lowest paper denomination that is practical (which is dependent on the average life of a banknote). In Britain, for example, this is now £5: eventually the note may be replaced by a coin, as the life of a £5 note is only about three months.

The USA is virtually unique in persevering with a $1 bill (worth about 1 euro), whereas in Europe coins of 1 euro and 2 euros are in everyday use. Lower denominations merely serve the purpose of small change. Such factors as payment of taxes and the facilitation of trade, formerly served by large silver or gold coins, are now entirely supplied by paper or electronic bank transfer.

METALS AND ALLOYS

With very few exceptions, coins are made of metal. Pure, unadulterated metals are seldom used, although even the ancient Greeks managed to achieve a relatively pure gold for some coins. In the main, two or more metals are combined to form an alloy, giving greater durability. We think of copper, silver and gold as traditional coin metals, but a surprising range of other metals has been employed, ranging from platinum and palladium to pewter, tin, and even relatively dense compositions of lead.

Above: A Roman gold aureus with a lump of gold added to it to make up the correct weight.

Above: A platinum noble (1983) and a deluxe silver coin (1993) struck by the Pobjoy Mint in the Isle of Man.

METAL FINENESS

In the ancient world coins were simply pieces of precious metal, which could, of course, be weighed at each transaction. However, it was more convenient to accept the mark stamped on a coin as a guarantee not only of its weight but also its purity. For this reason, units of value were usually tied to specific weights and these, in turn, were derived from particular seeds or grains. Nowadays the fineness of precious coinage metals is measured in thousandths, using a much more precise system than the carat used in ancient times, though this unit has been retained in the assessment of jewellery.

Right: A Russian platinum 3 rouble coin of 1830.

Below: Spanish settlers in Mexico smelting mined gold in imitation of the Aztecs.

ELECTRUM

The earliest coins of the Western world were made of electrum, a natural alloy of about 73 per cent gold and 27 per cent silver, found in riverbeds in the Tmolus Mountains of Lydia (present-day Anatolia in Turkey). Electrum was widely used for the coins of the 6th and 7th centuries BC. Latterly, the Greeks' love of white gold encouraged them to produce an artificial alloy consisting of one part gold and ten parts silver. The Celts copied electrum staters but severely debased them with copper and silver, and the Merovingians produced base electrum coins in which the gold content was minimal.

Theoretically any alloy of gold less than 75 per cent should be described as electrum, but in practice this is confined to classical and medieval coins. Some coins of the Isle of Man were struck in an alloy containing 9 carat gold (.375 fine), when the bullion price of gold was exceptionally high.

GOLD

The most popular of the precious metals was preferred by Croesus, King of Lydia (560–546 BC), who abandoned electrum for a bimetallic system with a gold–silver ratio of 40:3 (or 13.3:1). Coins were struck in relative weights, so that one gold piece was worth 20 of silver. This arrangement, fixed by the Lydians and Persians in the 6th century BC, continued in Rome and the Carolingian Empire and survived in Britain until World War I, the gold sovereign being worth 20 silver shillings.

The fineness of gold was based on the carat which, in addition to being a weight, came to represent a 24th part. Thus, pure gold is described as 24 carat fine. The purest gold for medieval coinage was 23 carat 3½ grains (.997 fine), which was as pure as the primitive metallurgy of the period could get. English gold was debased to 20 carat by 1545, but was eventually standardized at 22 carat (.9167 fine), originally

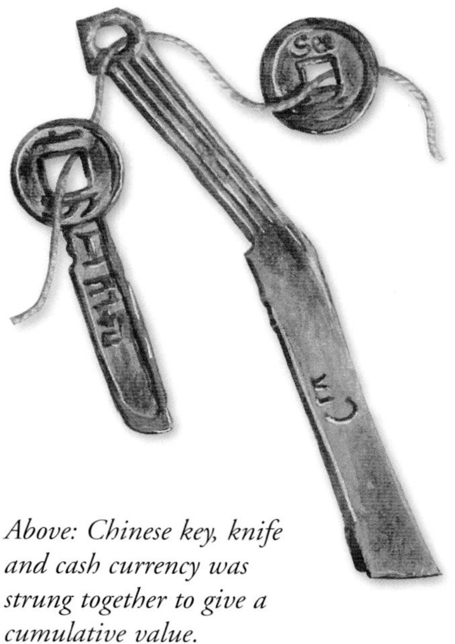

Above: Chinese key, knife and cash currency was strung together to give a cumulative value.

known as "crown gold" due to its first being used for the crown series. It was alloyed with .083 copper to produce a durable alloy with a reddish lustre and continues in the sovereign to this day.

The USA used the same fineness from 1795 to 1834 but later settled on .900. Mexico preferred .875, while France and Germany opted for .900 fine. The world's first major bullion coin of recent times, the Krugerrand, was minted to .9167 standard (the most practical and hard-wearing fineness), but later bullion coins strove for the utmost purity. Canada achieved .999 pure gold for the Maple Leaf (1979), but improved refining techniques led to the famous "four nines" gold first used in 1983. Bullion coins have both the weight and fineness of the metal inscribed on them.

SILVER

Used for coinage by the mid-6th century BC, mainly for the drachma and its sub-divisions, silver remained the preferred medium for the denarius, the denier and the penny, as well as most of the everyday coins of the world until the middle of the 20th century.

Medieval silver was .958 pure but was too soft to be practical, and .925 silver was the widely used sterling standard, usually alloyed with .075 copper. On many occasions, however, governments resorted to debasement of silver. Mexico, for example, struck coins in .903 silver until 1905 but, under pressure from inflation, then progressively debased it to .420 (1935), .300 (1950) and finally .100 (1957–67). Low-grade silver alloys are often described as

Below: The "Rosa Americana" (1722), a British colonial brass 2 pence, was cheaply minted and consequently rejected by the American colonists.

Above: Wartime shortages led to the use of base metals for this Norwegian coin of the German occupation (top) and Belgian zinc 5 cents of 1915 (bottom).

billon. While base alloys are now used for circulating coinage, de luxe and collectors' coins are generally struck in silver of a high quality.

BASE METALS

As copper was tariffed at 3000 to 1 piece of gold, it was very cumbersome, and for that reason it was seldom used for coins at its intrinsic value. The strings of Chinese cash are an example; the enormous copper plates of 17th-century Sweden, known as plåtmynt, are another. More or less pure copper was used for subsidiary coins in Britain from the 17th century until 1860, but then the size was reduced and the copper alloyed with tin to form bronze. A small amount of zinc is often added.

Brass is an alloy of 80 per cent copper and 20 per cent zinc, used by the Romans and revived by Switzerland during World War I. Modern brass coins are alloys of bronze with aluminium or nickel. Aluminium, noted for its lightness, was first used in British West Africa (1/10 penny) and British East Africa (half cent and cent) in 1907–8. Adopted as an emergency measure in Europe during World War I and revived in World War II, it has since become much more widespread, usually for the lowest denominations.

Nickel has been used in coins since the 3rd century BC but was adopted by Belgium in 1860 as a substitute for billon in the smallest coins. Pure nickel coins have been used as a substitute for silver in many European countries. Although Canada is the largest producer of nickel, it did not use it in coins until 1922, when nickel replaced silver in the 5 cent coin. The USA adopted an alloy of 75 per cent copper and 25 per cent nickel ("cupro-nickel") for the 3 cent coin of 1865. Cupro-nickel 5 cents appeared in 1866 and circulated alongside silver half dimes until 1873. The 5 cent coin is still popularly known as a nickel, but since 1964 this metal has also been used for the dime and higher denominations.

BIMETALLIC AND CLAD COINS

Clad coins have a core of one metal and an outer layer in another, such as stainless steel clad with copper (like most pennies and cents today).

Bimetallic coins have a centre in one metal and an outer ring in another. Tin farthings of Charles II (1684–5) had a copper plug in the middle. In the 19th century there were experiments with base metal coins with a silver plug to raise their intrinsic value. Since Italy pioneered bimetallic coins in 1982, alloys of gold and silver colour have been widely used for higher denominations. There are even trimetallic coins, but generally the central "plug" is of the same metal as the outer ring.

Coins on a Coin

This large gold-on-silver bimetallic coin from the Isle of Man reproduces an entire series of Cat crowns issued over the previous ten years.

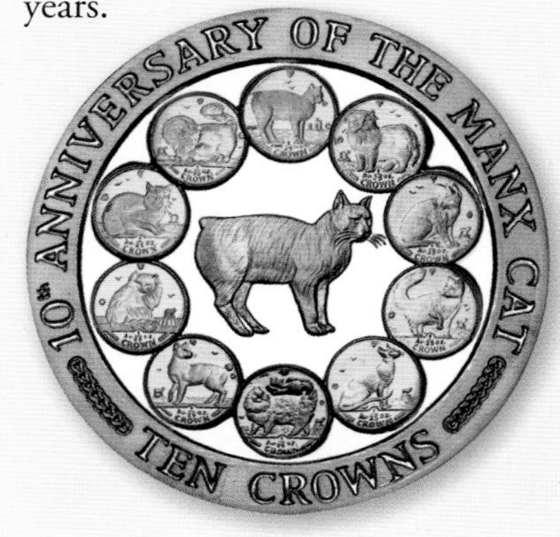

SPECIFICATIONS

All coins are produced within particular parameters. As well as the purity of the metal or alloy, they must conform to particular weights, and certain specifications such as diameter and thickness. As well as the conventional round shape, many coins are polygonal or scalloped, with or without a central hole – all features that help users to distinguish the different denominations.

Above: Silver Tiger Tongue money (top) and Leech money (bottom) from Thailand, and square and diamond-shaped coins of ancient India (middle).

Above: A gold ingot issued by the Central Mint of China in 1945.

THICKNESS

In general, thick coins were common in ancient times because they started life as lumps of precious metal of a particular weight, which were cast in moulds and then struck. Only when the use of sheet metal became more practical were blanks cut with shears, enabling thinner coins to be produced.

Nowadays we are accustomed to coins that are neither too thick nor too thin, that handle easily and stack well. The surface of modern coins is relatively flat and great care is taken in their design to ensure an even balance between the obverse (heads) and reverse (tails). Modern coins have to be stackable in tall piles or, more importantly, operate smoothly in the acceptor–rejector mechanisms of pay-phones, slot machines and automats.

Below: Unusual shapes of modern coins (clockwise from top left) include scalloped (Israel), octagonal (Malta, and Macao) and heptagonal (Jordan).

SHAPE

The earliest coins were small electrum dumps of irregular shape. Some Celtic coins were globular, while the mameita gin of feudal Japan were bean-shaped. Thailand's so-called "bullet money" consisted of silver balls or gold cylinders, which were bent into rough balls.

Chinese sycee currency was given its name (*hsi ssu*, meaning "fine silk") in allusion to the purity of its silver. One form was a thick oblong oval, raised at the ends because it was rocked as the metal was cooled partially, before being stamped with maker's and assayer's marks. Sycee was current from the 8th century AD until 1933, when it was suppressed by the Kuomintang government.

UNUSUAL SHAPES

Oval coins have been produced in Japan and the ancient Persians had elliptical coins. The original kopeks of Russia were made from heavy silver wire, which was cut into short strips, then hammered into ovals. They were extremely light and only about 15mm/⅝in long, providing small change from 1534 until about 1700. Many copper farthings of James I and Charles I (1613–42) had an upright oval shape.

Square or rectangular coins were common in Asia from pre-Christian times to the early 20th century. The style was popular in the Indo-Scythian and Indo-Greek coinage of the 2nd century BC, and continued under the Mughal Empire, down to the Indian feudal states. These coins were true squares with sharp corners, but in India and the Far East, modern square coins have rounded corners, which are much more user-friendly. The Netherlands is the only European country to have adopted this shape: 5 cent coins of 1913–40 had a diamond format, followed by a square format in 1941–3.

Rectangular coins were also popular in Asia and ranged from the long, narrow vertical gia long of Annam to the more elegantly proportioned silver cho gin and gold koban of Japan before the Meiji Revolution of the 1860s.

Klippe

Square or lozenge-shaped coins, known as *klippe*, were produced in many of the German states, and the form later spread as far afield as Poland, Hungary and Denmark. These coins were originally struck in times of emergency, when pieces were cut from silver plate, but later the shape became fashionable and coins were made as presentation pieces, with ornament in the corners. Pictured here is a klippe thaler of Friedrich Augustus I of Saxony, issued in 1697.

POLYGONAL COINS

The only true pentagons (with sharp corners) are the 1/16 and 1/8 ahmadi riyals of the Yemen (1947–60), but five-sided coins with rounded corners have been issued by Belize (1981) and the Solomon Islands (1983). Six-sided coins include the 50 cent coins in aluminium, zinc, brass or bronze from Djibouti (1920–2), the brass 2 francs of the Belgian Congo (1943) and Egypt's silver 2 piastres (1944). In all of these a format with flat sides at top and bottom was adopted. Hexagonal coins with points at top and bottom have been issued by the Yemen (1948), Sudan (1981) and the British Virgin Islands (1982–3).

Below: A Russian denga of the 11th century (top) and a Mongol silver dirham (bottom).

In 1969, the Royal Mint created a 50 pence coin (worth 10 shillings) from the same weight and alloy as the obsolescent half crown, which had a quarter of the value of the new coin. The only variable in design was the shape; the new coin was given seven sides, a shape later extended to the 20 pence. Heptagonal coins later appeared in many Commonwealth countries. Octagonal (eight-sided) coins with flat top and bottom were favoured by some of the German states in the mid-18th century, and have been produced sporadically in more recent times, notably in Senegal (1920) and Egypt (1933).

Octagons with points at the top and bottom have so far been confined to the $50 gold coin commemorating the Pan-Pacific Exposition (1915) and the gold $200 of the Netherlands Antilles (1976). Thailand (1972), Kenya (1973) and Tuvalu (1976–81) have had nine-sided coins, while Colombia (1967), Afghanistan (1979), the Dominican Republic (1983), Jamaica (1976) and Tanzania (since 1971) have had ten-sided coins.

Dodecagons or 12-sided coins are very popular and were pioneered by Britain for the nickel-brass 3 pence of Edward VIII (1936) and subsequent coins of this value until 1967. Just as Britain was abandoning the shape, it was taken up by many other countries, notably Argentina and Australia. When Canada changed the alloy of its 5 cent coin from nickel to tombac brass in 1942, a 12-sided format was adopted and retained until 1962. Its cent switched from circular to dodecagonal in 1982, saving 10.7 per cent in weight – before the change it was costing 2 cents to produce each cent!

Triangular coins with rounded corners have been produced by the Cook Islands and (appropriately) Bermuda, but the only three-sided coin with sharp corners was the 20 centime of Gabon (1883). The 10 centime had an over-all triangular shape but the points were truncated, so that the coin was actually six-sided.

SERRATED OR SCALLOPED EDGES

The Carthaginians and Seleucids had circular coins with serrated edges, but many modern coins have scalloped edges, a useful feature for distinguishing coins of different values but similar sizes. A "nicked" edge is a feature of the brass 20 euro cent, making it distinct from the 50 cent. Burma has even had polygonal scalloped coins.

Many Asian coins (notably Chinese cash) have a central hole, but this feature was not used elsewhere until 1883 (in Bolivia). It is a means of reducing weight and metal while retaining a relatively large diameter and is now widely practised all over the world.

Above: A square Indian rupee of the Indo-Scythian kings.

HAMMERED AND CAST COINAGE

Although a few coins were cast in moulds, most were struck by hand until the late 17th century, relying on the strength of the craftsman to hit the flan with a hammer. This technique sounds extremely crude, but, thanks to the skill of coiners, and the revival of intaglio techniques first developed in the classical world, intricate portraits, emblems and other designs were achieved long before the industrial age.

CAST COINS

In casting, metal is melted and then poured into a mould. The simplest moulds were merely hollows in a bed of fine sand, which produced the small, roughly circular lumps of metal that were then punch marked. Well into the 17th century, flans or blanks for struck coins were cast in this manner, although cutting blanks from thin sheets of metal gradually superseded this. A refinement was to carve a mould from a piece of stone, enabling detailed designs and lettering to be engraved. Double-sided moulds of this kind were used for double-sided coins.

This technique was used exclusively to produce Chinese cash until 1889, and some provinces continued to cast coins as late as 1908. Latterly multiple moulds were employed to cast several coins simultaneously. They resembled a tree with the coins as the fruit at the ends of "branches" created by the channels along which the molten metal flowed. A few of these "trees" have survived intact, but normally the coins were broken off and the rough edges carefully filed.

Cast coins were used in Japan until 1871, Morocco until 1882, Korea until 1888 and Vietnam until the 1930s. They were seldom produced in Europe, but noteworthy exceptions were the first coins of the Isle of Man (1709), where the halfpenny and penny were cast in a foundry at Castletown. These coins can be recognized by the flash marks on the rim and the slight excrescences where the connecting channels of molten metal were broken off. More recent examples are the copies of 8 real coins of Potosi cast by the garrison of Chiloe in South America (1822), coins cast from gunmetal at Terceira in the Azores for Maria II in exile (1829) and Andorran 1, 5 and 10 diners (1984).

The casting technique produced very crude coins compared to struck examples and was latterly used only in extreme cases when more sophisticated coining equipment was not available.

Below: Early Italian cast coin (top); cast Korean bronze cash or mun (bottom).

Multiple Punch Marks

This coin of Asia Minor, dating from around 400–380 BC, shows similar designs on the obverse (crested Athena standing, left) and reverse (Apollo holding a bow). The reverse contains two rectangular countermarks made by the same punch. Early coins often bear various punch marks applied by different authorities to guarantee their value.

HAMMER AND ANVIL

The hammermen formed one of the most prestigious trade guilds of the Middle Ages, a measure of the importance and value of their skill. Generally, they worked in groups in which individuals were responsible for specific aspects of the process (smelting and refining, moulding the blanks or cutting them from sheet metal rolled out to a uniform thickness). The coining irons were generally supplied by the central government, but engravers sometimes used dies produced locally.

The earliest blanks or "flans" for hammered coins were cast in moulds, a natural progression from the original dumps and globules. The round blank was relatively thick. It was heated to make it malleable, then placed on an anvil of bronze whose face had been engraved with a device (the obverse). The upper die, a punch, was hit by a

Above: A Crusader "knight" follis from the 12th century with the design struck off-centre.

Below: In Venice, coins continued to be struck by hand until the 18th century.

Above: These medieval German hammermen are working individually, but this was not typical: the striking of coins was usually a two-man operation – one to hold the blank on the anvil with pincers and the other to hammer.

hammer to raise the design on the coin. Subsequently, a metal block with the reverse device engraved on its lower face was placed over the coin and struck, thus producing a double-sided coin. Later, blanks were cut from sheets of metal and roughly trimmed to shape with large shears. This method of coining continued in Europe until the 17th century and survived in some parts of the world until the 1950s.

The dies were normally lined up so that both obverse and reverse designs were vertical, but in many cases an upset position, or alignment of 180 degrees, was preferred – a custom that prevails in many countries to this day. Nevertheless, because coins were struck by hand, it is not uncommon to find the obverse at right angles to the reverse, or some variation to the left or right of the normal upright position.

PILE AND TRUSSEL

By the 11th century a more advanced technique was beginning to evolve in France and Germany, though it did not completely supplant the traditional method until the 17th century. The "pile and trussel" method avoided progressive wear on the face of the hammer and the need to engrave the die on to the anvil by using dies engraved on pieces of iron or steel.

The pile (bearing the obverse) had a spike on the end, which could be driven into a large tree stump, before which sat the coiner, who then positioned the hot, malleable flan on the pile with a pair of tongs. The trussel, or reverse die, was then positioned over the flan. The hammerman used great force to strike impressions simultaneously into both sides of the coin.

One refinement was the use of tongs or pincers with circular ends, which held the blank and trussel in position on the pile. The force of striking made the metal spread and flow, but the tips of the tongs formed a collar around the blank, which kept the coin reasonably circular in shape. However, the creation of a circular coin with nicely centred images depended entirely on the skill of the hammerman. Many ancient and medieval coins have off-centre images, and these "mis-strikes" are highly prized by some collectors.

DIES AND ENGRAVING

The dies used in coining have evolved through the ages. Those used by the Greeks were engraved on a very hard, durable bronze with a high tin content. The Romans, however, pioneered the use of iron dies, and occasionally used steel, though this did not become the norm until the 15th century.

The intaglio technique of die-cutting, perfected over many centuries, developed in the ancient civilizations of Egypt, Greece and Rome, primarily for the carving of gems and seals. It must have seemed a logical extension to carve into a piece of iron planed smooth to create the indented image necessary for a coin. The technique of direct engraving reached its peak during the Roman Empire and resulted in coins of remarkable beauty. Like most other arts, it vanished during the Early Medieval period and was not revived in western Europe until the 11th century, although there were isolated examples, such as the gold penny of Offa of Mercia (759–96), the gold solidus of Louis the Pious (814–40) and the silver deniers of Charlemagne from the Palatine Mint of about 800. Direct engraving continued in the Byzantine Empire and it was from there that it was re-introduced to Western Europe.

An interesting example of the transition between old and new is provided by the silver pfennigs of the Holy Roman Empire of about 1010, in which the images were engraved on to the die, but the coin inscriptions were produced using wedge-shaped punches. Direct engraving was largely responsible for the production of bracteates, the thin, button-like coins used in Germany, Switzerland, Poland and Hungary from the late 12th to 14th centuries.

Below: Quadripartite (four-part) incuse punches on ancient Greek coins.

THE FIRST MILLED COINAGE

Mechanical processes revolutionized coin production in the 16th and 17th centuries, but they evolved over a long period. There was considerable opposition to their adoption, as the mintworkers, especially the hammermen, saw machinery as a serious threat to their traditional jobs.

EARLIEST MILLED COINS

Around 1500, Leonardo da Vinci produced a detailed diagram for a double press, which would produce a perfectly circular coin blank and then strike it. Like many of his inventions, this remained only a drawing for centuries, but in the 1960s IBM constructed a blanking and coining press to his specifications, which is now part of the collection of the Smithsonian Institution in Washington DC.

Donato Bramante, working on the principle of the fruit press, created a screw press that produced blanks in 1506, and in 1550 Max Schwab of Augsburg improved it, making it capable of both blanking and striking coins. A decade earlier he had created a device like a giant mangle, which squeezed out sheets of metal of an even thickness, harnessed to a machine like an enormous cookie-cutter, which cut out circular blanks. Unable to interest the German or Italian mints, Schwab sold his inventions to the French. They established a special plant at the tip of the Ile du Palais in Paris, where the River Seine produced the power to drive the water mills needed to operate the machinery. It was known as the Moulin des Etuves ("mill of the baths"), as it stood on the original site of the palace spa. It was because of this use of water mills that the new coins came to be described as "milled".

Right: A French milled coin of Charles III, Duke of Lorraine (1593–1607).

Below: An English milled coin of Elizabeth I (1563).

Above: A pattern shilling of Charles I (top) and Nicolas Briot's first issue milled penny (middle) and second issue milled shilling (bottom).

Sample coins, or "patterns", were struck in 1551 and the following year went into general production. But output declined after 1554, due mainly to the entrenched hostility of the hammermen, and in 1563 the mint was ordered to confine its activities to medals. Nevertheless, it was reactivated in 1577 to produce France's first copper coinage, and milled coins were also struck there in 1573 for Henry of Navarre as Lord of Béarn. The early milled coins were distinguished from their hammered counterparts by the evenness of their flans, their perfect impressions and the beauty of the engraving and lettering. That they were not an immediate success was due not only to the strenuous opposition of vested interests but also to the fact that hammered coins were then much cheaper to produce.

ROLLER PRESSES

In other parts of Europe, the rolling and blanking machinery was operated differently. An alternative technique was devised at Augsburg, a city then at the heart of technological progress. This involved pairs of rollers on which the obverse and reverse dies were engraved. Strips of sheet metal were passed between the rollers under high pressure and took up the impressions of the coins, which were then carefully cut out of the strip.

Roller presses and dies of this type were used at the main Habsburg Mint in Kremnica from 1566. The machinery, perfected at Augsburg, was eventually used throughout the Holy Roman Empire until the late 18th century. Several dies (for up to six thalers or 18 smaller coins) could be engraved on the cylinders side by side; entire sheets of metal could then be passed between the cylinders and the resultant

Above: An Oliver Cromwell milled crown of 1658.

Above: A milled papal testone of 1623–44.

coins cut out after striking. The dies were engraved in a slightly elliptical form to compensate for the curvature of the rollers, so that the finished coins emerged perfectly circular.

Roller dies and presses were phased out after the appointment of Daniel Warou as chief engraver at the Kremnica Mint (1699–1703), for he introduced the screw press and made many improvements to it. The screw press remained in use in the Holy Roman Empire until the 1890s, when it was gradually superseded by the hydraulic press.

Ornament and Safeguard

When milled coins became standard in the British Isles in 1662, Pierre Blondeau applied an edge inscription using a secret process of his own invention. The inscription read "Decus et Tutamen Anno Regni ..." ("An ornament and a safeguard in the year of the reign ...") followed by the Latin ordinal number, for example "Vicesimo" (twentieth). The first part of the inscription now appears around the edge of the current English pound coin. Scottish and Welsh pounds bear different inscriptions, the latter reading Pleidiol Wyf I'm Gwlad ("I am true to my country").

THE SPREAD OF MILLED COINS

Etienne Bergeron, master of the Moulin des Etuves, was ejected from France in 1559 because he was a Huguenot (Protestant). He fled to Navarre, then a separate kingdom, and in 1562 became master of the mint set up by the Huguenots at Orleans, where he converted church plate into milled coins. In 1561, Eloi Mestrel of the Moulin des Etuves also fled from religious persecution. He went to England, where he installed coining machinery in the Tower of London. The first English milled coins were produced here and appeared in 1561–2, but Mestrel fell foul of the English hammermen and was dismissed in 1572.

In 1586 the mint at Segovia in Spain acquired some roller presses and began producing good quality coins, in stark contrast to the crude hammered coins that continued to pour our of the other Spanish mints. Rolling machines, blanking machines and screw presses also spread to the German states and to Bohemia in the early 17th century, and the production of milled coins received stimulus both from the greater output of silver and the propaganda requirements of the Thirty Years War (1618–48).

Above: A 1632 thaler of Archduke Leopold V of Tirol, struck at Hall Mint.

Above: Mis-strikes continued to occur with milled coinage, as in these shillings of Queen Anne (1709, top) and George III, struck off-collar (1819, bottom).

A second experiment with milled coins took place in England in this period. Nicolas Briot was chief engraver at the Paris Mint from 1606 to 1625. In 1615 he invented the *balancier*, an improved machine for striking coins, but it was rejected by his superiors. Briot fled from Paris in 1625 to escape his creditors, and brought his machinery to England. He was allowed to install his presses at the Tower Mint in 1628 and produced some milled gold in 1631–2 and silver until 1639. Later, his beautifully engraved dies were utilized for coins produced by the traditional hammered process. He himself was sent to Edinburgh in 1635 and installed mill and screw machinery there, which resulted in some excellent but short-lived Scottish milled coins.

The outbreak of the English Civil War in 1642 was a major setback, but in 1649 the Commonwealth government revived the idea and invited Pierre Blondeau from the Paris Mint to London. The result was the milled coinage of 1656–8, portraying Cromwell. Hammered coinage continued after the Restoration (1660), but two years later machinery operated by horsepower was installed – the animals powering a treadmill – and thereafter all English coins were milled. Elsewhere in Europe, milled coinage was now the norm, except in Holland where hammered coinage survived until 1670.

INDUSTRIAL DEVELOPMENTS

Although the first coining machinery made use of waterpower and horsepower, the advent of steam, and later electricity, totally transformed the production of coins. The maximum output by horsepower was about 40 coins a minute. Steam presses immediately doubled that rate and today's high-speed electric presses can produce over 700 coins a minute.

Above: These coining presses, photographed in 1910, were capable of striking up to 120 coins per minute.

STEAM-POWERED MACHINERY

Matthew Boulton and James Watt invented milling and blank-cutting machinery powered by steam. It was installed in 1786 at their Soho Mint in Birmingham, where it was used to strike coins of the East India Company and many British trade tokens. This mint struck the British Cartwheel pennies of 1797, followed by Manx coins in 1798–1813. In 1809 the firm began supplying the Royal Mint with steam-powered machinery, which was first actually used in the "Great Recoinage" of 1816–17. Boulton also started negotiations with the US Mint in 1799, but it was not until 1816 that steam-powered machinery was installed at the Philadelphia Mint.

Right: The "Cartwheel" copper pennies of 1797 were named for their broad rims.

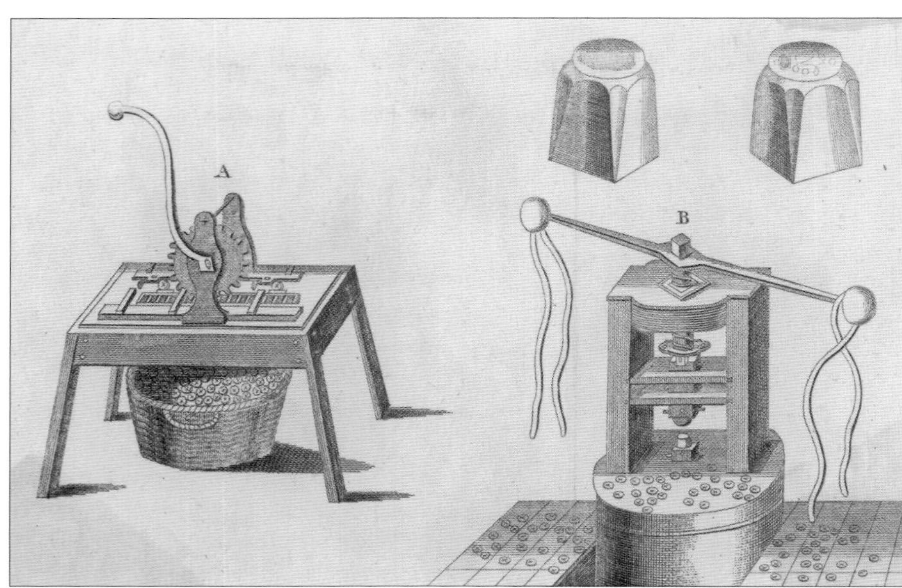

Below: A 1797 illustration of a coining press, dies and a machine designed to engrave coin edges.

HIGH-SPEED PRESSES

In 1817, Dietrich Uhlhorn of Grevenbroich, near Cologne, invented the automatic, high-speed coining press. A year later he demonstrated his knuckle-joint knee-lever press at Dusseldorf. Between 1820 and 1847, Uhlhorn steam-powered lever presses were installed at the mints in Germany and also at the Royal Mint. In 1835 a French engineer named Thonnelier invented an improved steam press, which was in use at the Paris and Philadelphia Mints by 1840.

Thereafter, steam presses spread rapidly to the world's mints. Electric power was substituted in the 1880s and presses capable of striking 200 coins a minute, under a pressure of 180 tonnes, were developed during the 20th century. Today the Cincinnati Milacron presses of the Royal Mint and US Mint can strike up to 700 coins a minute.

DIE PRODUCTION

Dies continued to be engraved by hand in the time-honoured fashion until the mid-19th century. Everything still depended on the skill of the engraver, who cut the design directly into the face of the die. The discovery that steel could be chemically hardened, however, meant that it was possible to produce secondary dies, via an intermediate punch called a hub, from the master die. Alternatively, a positive image could be cut in relief on a metal punch and struck into a piece of softer metal, which was then hardened for use as a die. The technique of hubbing appears to have been known in classical times, although no hubs have survived from antiquity. This technique meant that working dies could be rapidly multiplied, greatly accelerating the mass production of coins.

Around 1715, Konstantin Nartov of the Moscow Mint invented a machine that could reduce a large sculpted model to the size required for a coin die. This revolutionized coin production by eliminating the hand engraving previously carried out on the master die, although it has been argued that the change of practice resulted in more stereotyped, less artistic designs.

Improved models were built in Paris between 1757 and 1824, and were applied with varying success to the production of steel dies from large plaster models. Perfected by M. Collas, these machines were in regular use at the Paris Mint from then onward, but it was not until 1839 that they were adopted by the Royal Mint; they spread to other European and American mints in the mid-19th century. The process is now carried out by the Contamin portrait lathe and the Janvier die-cutting machine.

Hubbing

Using a reducing machine, the enlarged image is transferred to a piece of steel known as the hub, in the precise dimensions of the coin. The next stage, known as hubbing, transfers the positive image from the hub to the working die, which is the negative image used to strike the coins.

Above: The large-scale plaster model is perfected before the design is reduced to create a hub of the correct size.

FROM WAX MODEL TO FINISHED COIN

The progression from original concept to finished coin involves a number of different skills and processes, and since the 1830s, a series of mechanical processes have replaced the direct engraving of dies. A sculptor makes a wax model at least four times the size of the required coin. A plaster cast is created from the wax model, and from this a nickel-faced copper electrotype is produced. This is placed on the reducing machine, which operates on the pantographic principle. A tracer at one end of the proportional arm moves over the entire surface of the model. At the other end a cutting stylus, like the needle of a record player (but moving from the centre outward) cuts an exact but mathematically reduced reproduction to produce a positive punch, or hub. The hub is chemically hardened and driven into a cone of soft steel to produce the working die. In turn, this is also chemically hardened and is then ready for striking.

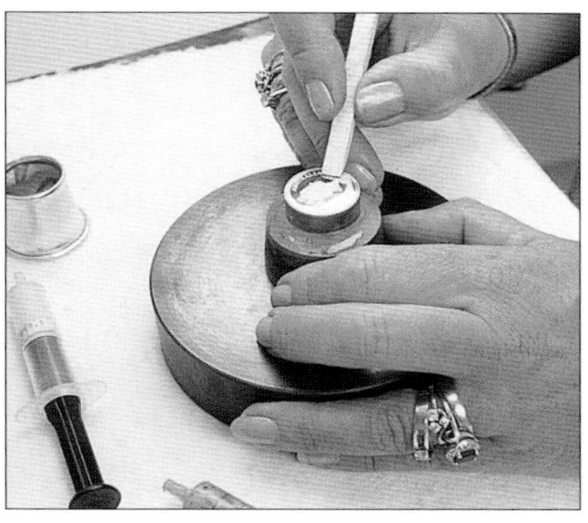

Above: The hub is coated with chemicals to harden it so that it can be used to produce a working die.

CIRCULATING AND PROOF COINS

Today, all coins intended for general circulation are produced on high-speed presses. The blanks are fed into the dial plates and pass through two checking points, which determine that they are of the correct thickness and diameter before they reach the coining station.

Each coin, as it is struck, passes a security counter, which keeps a record of the precise number of coins the machine has struck. The coins are then check-weighed and examined carefully for any flaws. After this examination they are counted again and hermetically sealed in the bags in which they will eventually be distributed to banks.

Proof coins were originally pieces struck to test the dies to ensure perfection before the start of production. They were struck individually by hand, often using specially polished blanks. From this arose the use of proof coins for presentation purposes, but since the mid-19th century they have increasingly been produced expressly for sale to collectors. Today, proof versions of coins are often struck in precious metals, while the circulating versions are in base metals. Although modern proofs are produced by machine like other coins, they are generally struck up to four times, using special dies with frosted relief and polished blanks to provide a sharper contrast between the image and the background.

SPECIAL PRODUCTION TECHNIQUES

Proof coins, intended not for general circulation but for collectors, are not only struck to a much higher standard than circulating coins, but are usually produced in precious metals and consequently sold at a much higher price than ordinary coins. In recent years many special techniques have evolved, which have revolutionized the production of coins intended for the numismatic market. These include the addition of coloured finishes, precious stones and even holographic designs.

Jewel-Studded Coins

A very recent development has been the incorporation of precious stones in the surface of a coin to create a jewelled effect. One of the first coins of this type celebrated the centenary of the Diamond Jubilee of Queen Victoria, appropriately with a diamond inset.

Above: A gilt copper proof 2 reas of the East India Company, produced in 1794.

PROOFS

It is probable that test impressions have been made from coinage dies since the striking of coins began. In the days of direct engraving they were struck for the purpose of checking details of the positive image, such as ensuring that the lettering was the right way round. Proofs were often pulled on blanks made of lead or some very soft alloy, which enabled the details to be more clearly seen. From this arose the custom of striking proofs in metals other than those that were to be used for the issued coins – variations now termed "off-metal strikes". Nowadays, coins issued in base metals, such as cupronickel, are often struck as proofs in silver or even platinum, while gold is sometimes used for proofs of coins normally circulating in brass.

Below: Working mints keep a large stock of coin blanks for striking proofs. These are handled with great care.

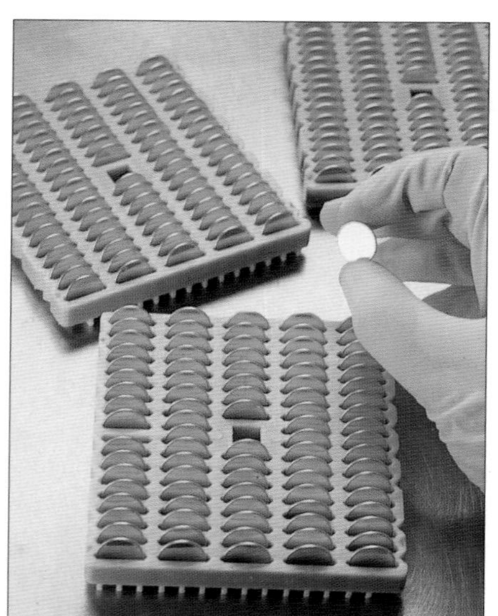

What was a widespread minting tradition has now become an important aspect of the numismatic business, as proofs are prepared specially for the collector. Proofs of this type were first marketed in the middle of the 19th century, the US Mint producing such sets for sale from 1858 onward. Royal Mint proof sets had first been produced in 1826 as presentation issues for a privileged few (such as members of the royal family and senior government officials), but in Britain proof sets sold to the public date from the golden jubilee of Queen Victoria in 1887.

The practice of issuing proofs has now reached the point at which many modern sets exist only in proof form and are not backed by any circulating coins. Modern proofs and deluxe versions of coins are struck on special slow-speed presses, in which each piece is struck up to four times to bring up the fine detail. The blanks are specially polished with mops made of linen, calico and swansdown to produce the "mirror table" effect, and the dies are often specially engraved so that the high points have a frosted relief that contrasts with the mirror-like surface.

Until not so long ago it was the norm for blanks to be prepared to produce an overall polished appearance. This is still employed but is often relegated to a version of the base-metal coins sold to the public under such descriptions as "specimen", "library finish" or "special select". These, with a better finish than the circulating coins, are usually marketed in special folders, whereas proofs may be contained in leatherette cases with a velvet lining.

The Franklin Mint (1975–77) frequently offered coin sets in three distinct versions, classified as "matte", "special uncirculated" and "proof". The Pobjoy Mint devised the terms "Proof 4" (proof coins struck four times), "BU2" (brilliant uncirculated struck twice) and "diamond finish" for base metal coins in a finish superior to the general circulating coins.

PATTERNS

In many cases, when a new coin is being considered, the authorities will commission several trial designs, developed all the way to actual production, so that the coinage committee can examine actual pieces before making their decision. Those pieces that are

Above and below: Special-edition coins produced for the collectors' market may have unusual features such as coloured enamelling.

rejected and not put into production are known as patterns. Patterns may also arise if the design has been altered or modified in some way before going into production. Patterns of this type are often uniface or bear words such as "Specimen", "Trial", "Prova", "Prueba" or "Probe" (which actually signify "test" in other languages). Many mints, when tendering for a contract, would prepare sample coins to demonstrate design. If the contract were eventually awarded to a competing mint, these samples would be regarded as patterns.

The numismatic appeal of patterns is partly psychological; the rejected design often seems superior to the accepted one because the latter is debased by familiarity. On the other hand, though many patterns have been rejected because they were judged to be impractical as actual coins, they are beautiful works of art. Patterns have a special appeal to collectors as examples of what might have been. In many cases they are very similar to the issued coins, but minted in different metals. Most interesting of all are the patterns that went one stage further, being initially accepted but never actually progressing to legal tender for a variety of reasons, usually (though not always) political. For example, a pattern 5 kuna coin for Croatia was produced in 1934, the year that Croat terrorists assassinated King Alexander of Yugoslavia as a prelude to declaring independence, but the plot was suppressed. Patterns for French and German wartime coins exist with portraits of Petain and Hitler respectively: they were never issued as they were overtaken by events.

SPECIAL EFFECTS

Most modern coins have the design and inscription standing out in relief, but from time to time "intaglio" images occur, which appear as if cut into the surface, and an inscription may be "incuse" (cut into a raised surround). Incuse lettering on raised rims was a distinctive feature of the British Cartwheel copper coins of 1797, while the USA issued gold quarter and half eagles (1908–29) in which the Indian head (obverse) and eagle (reverse) were intaglio. Unfortunately such coins tended to accumulate grime in circulation and ended up looking rather dirty. The technique was revived by the Royal Mint for the 20 pence coin in 1982, but in this case only the inscriptions are incuse.

Raised edges with incuse inscriptions have been used to startling effect by the Pobjoy Mint since the 1980s. This private mint has been at the cutting edge of minting technology for many years and has pioneered the use of special surfaces. In 1990, for example, the crown coins celebrating the 150th anniversary of the Penny Black stamp had a black surface: the technique remains a closely guarded secret but the coin won the coveted Coin of the Year Award. Subsequent issues, appropriately coloured, have reproduced other famous stamps, such as the Blue Mauritius and the Black on Magenta 1 cent of British Guiana. The Pobjoy Mint has also, in recent years, led the way in the development of coins with holographic surfaces.

The Royal Canadian Mint pioneered coins in silver with a small motif inset in gold, used effectively in a series tracing the development of aviation, with portraits of aviators in gold. This technique has since been copied by other mints, notably Pobjoy, which took it a step further with insets of diamonds and other precious stones. Several mints, notably the Singapore Mint, have produced coins with latent images that change, like a hologram, as the surface is tilted.

While the enamelling of existing coins, to transform them into jewels for watch chains, earrings or brooches, has been practised for centuries, a number of special issues are now actually produced with multicoloured surfaces. The effect is usually achieved by adapting silk-screen and lithographic processes to this very exacting medium.

Below: The reverse of the silver crown celebrating the 150th anniversary of the Penny Black, the world's first adhesive postage stamp, in 1990. The surface was specially treated to produce an image of the stamp in black.

COMBATING THE COUNTERFEITER

For as long as coins have existed, there have been attempts to forge them, undermining public confidence as well as losing revenue for the issuing authority. The term "counterfeit" is derived from the French word for imitation and applies to copies of coins (and banknotes) that are intended to deceive and defraud people.

Throughout coin-producing history, strenuous efforts have always been made to deter counterfeiters, by threat of severe punishment as well as by making coins very difficult to imitate.

DEBASEMENT

Counterfeiting may not be the world's oldest profession but it has certainly existed as long as coinage itself: coin hoards dating from the 6th century BC have been found to include staters of Aegina with a copper core and a silver wash, passed off as genuine silver coins. There is even a case of official counterfeits, such as the lead pieces covered with gold, which Polykrates of Samos (532–21 BC) is said to have used to buy off the Spartans.

In the classical and medieval periods counterfeiting occurred frequently and was particularly prevalent in the Middle Ages, when genuine coins were often poorly struck. The fact that many governments deliberately debased their coinage from time to time did not help.

Below: A clipped groat of Richard III (top) and clipped shilling of Charles I (bottom). The latter circulated until 1694, when they were finally demonetized and melted down.

The most blatant examples were the "crockards" and "pollards" manufactured by many petty lordships in Europe, which copied highly prized English sterling pennies. They flooded England in the 13th century, and when all attempts by Edward I to suppress them failed he made a virtue of necessity by legitimizing them and allowing them to pass current as halfpence. As the imitations contained more than a halfpennyworth of silver, this was a pretty shrewd decision. As a result, the crockards rapidly vanished, although they were not actually demonetized and declared illegal until 1310. This did not prevent a recurrence in the reign of Edward III (1327–77), when England was flooded with base coins known as "lushbournes" (a corruption of the name Luxembourg, whence they came).

CLIPPING COINS

Another age-old method of counterfeiting involved the slicing off of tiny slivers of gold or silver from the edges of coins. The edges were then filed down to give the appearance of normality. Sometimes forgers produced imitation gold and silver coins from base metals, but more often they bought clippings and melted them down to produce counterfeits with a reasonable proportion of precious metal, alloyed with copper.

COUNTER MEASURES

The major breakthrough against counterfeiting came with the widespread adoption of milled coins in Europe during the 17th century. This made it possible to employ sophisticated techniques to improve the appearance of coins generally, making it harder to produce accurate copies. The minting process also used specific methods to stamp out dishonest coining practices.

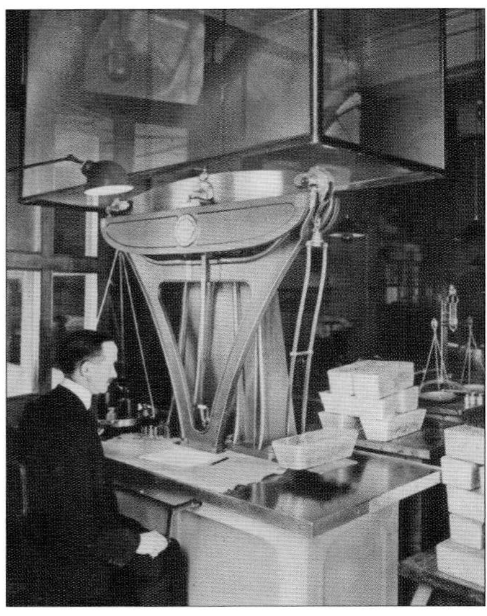

Above: The trials carried out by the Pyx office of the Royal Mint, London, were instrumental in distinguishing legitimate coins from copies.

SECRET MARKINGS

Various marks have been used to defeat the forger. Medieval English coins had tiny symbols, known as mint-marks, which appeared at the beginning of the inscription and denoted the period between Trials of the Pyx (the periodic assaying of coins at Goldsmiths Hall to test the gold and silver, named from the chest the coins were carried in). In more recent times mint-marks have identified the place where coins were struck and either appear as initials or tiny symbols in various parts of the design.

Privy or secret marks are intended for security purposes and include die numbers or letters engraved microscopically. In some cases privy marks have been used to transform definitives into commemorative coins, such as the baby's crib on Manx coins that greeted the birth of Prince William in 1982.

SECURITY EDGES

The milling process allowed the use of a specially engraved collar to impress an inscription on the edges of coins.

Counterfeit Coins Today

It has been estimated that more than 1 per cent of the pound coins circulating in Britain are counterfeits. They are easy to detect as even newly forged coins do not "ring true" when bounced on a table. Most lose their brightness very quickly and quite often the edge inscription does not match the reverse motif. Here, the tarnished English arms (left) are the reverse of a forgery, whereas the Welsh motif is the genuine article.

The milled coins that went into general circulation in Britain in 1662 bore a Latin motto around the edge – "Decus et Tutamen" ("An ornament and a safeguard") followed by "Anno Regni" ("in the year of the reign") and a date in Roman numerals. This effectively stamped out the practice of clipping. Many countries have resorted to edge inscriptions of this kind as a security feature. The lettering may be either raised or incuse, and often includes tiny ornamental flourishes.

Below: Today, subtle security inscriptions are incorporated into the designs of all coins to foil counterfeiters.

GRAINING

The most common form of safeguard against the clipping of coins is a pattern of fine grooves running across the edge, at right angles to the rim. In common parlance this is often referred to as "milling", but this is a misnomer.

The grain on British and American coins usually consists of fine vertical serrations, but some coins have been produced at various times with a coarser or finer grain, and having to count the number of notches threatens the advanced numismatist with a nasty headache and crossed eyes!

An interrupted grain may be found on some coins, with sections of vertical grooves alternating with plain sections. Its purpose is to assist partially sighted and blind people in distinguishing between coins of high and low value. In some countries graining takes the form of short lines set at an angle, and this is known as a cable edge. When Britain adopted pound coins in 1982 both graining and an incuse edge inscription were used.

PENALTIES

The treatment of counterfeiters has varied over the centuries and from country to country. Forgery was frequently a capital offence, and very special gruesome punishments were reserved for this crime. In England forgers were usually hanged, but the forgery of coins by women seems to have been regarded as particularly heinous, for several female counterfeiters were publicly burned at the stake as late as 1789. Boiling in oil was the preferred punishment in Germany, while in France it was breaking on a wheel; beheading was a common punishment elsewhere. In Russia counterfeiters had molten lead poured down their throats. First offenders were sometimes dealt with more leniently, merely losing a hand or an eye.

In Britain, the Coinage Offences Act of 1861 set out a series of penalties ranging from two years' imprisonment to penal servitude for life. The more severe penalties were meted out for

Above: The practice of graining or inscribing the edges of coins, to mark them as genuine, continues today.

counterfeiting gold or silver coins. Lesser offences included the gilding of farthings and sixpences to pass them off as half sovereigns, the possession of moulds, machines and tools clandestinely removed from the Royal Mint, and the impairment or diminution of gold and silver coins by filing or clipping (or even the possession of such filings and clippings). The Coinage Act of 1870 made provision for the counterfeiting of base metal coins of any kind. Today, US law dictates that counterfeiting is a felony, punishable by a large fine and a maximum of ten years' imprisonment.

Below: The arrest of a pair of coin counterfeiters in the early 19th century.

HISTORY OF PORTRAITURE

We talk about "heads" and "tails" to denote the obverse and reverse of coins. The former nickname derives from the fact that it is the side often reserved for the most important aspect of the coin, the effigy of the head of state.

By the time of the Hellenistic kingdoms, portraiture on coins was exceedingly lifelike. It attained its peak during the Roman Empire, but the Romans rarely attempted a facing portrait – something that modern mints attempt occasionally, but seldom with any real success. The full-face portraits on Byzantine coins tended to become stereotyped, and the full-face portraits on European medieval coins were very crude and undoubtedly symbolic rather than true likenesses.

During the Renaissance the large silver coins of Italy revived the art of portraiture. Modern portrait coins are still predominantly generated by the age-old method of sculpting a profile; photo-engraving has also been used in many instances, though the results are invariably much flatter.

EARLY PORTRAITS

There are examples of coins from the 6th century BC that show a human effigy, such as the head of a warrior (Ephesus), the head of a discus thrower (Cyzicus, *c.* 520 BC) and a helmeted profile (Kalymna), but it is not known whether these represented real people.

Below right: The Persian satrap Tissaphernes was the first ruler to appear on a coin, in 411 BC.

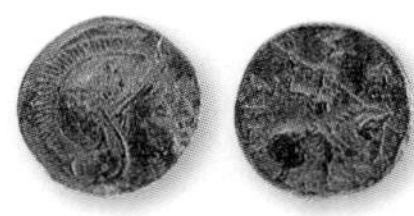

Below: Head of Apollo on a coin of the 4th century BC.

Liberty and Presidents

In 1987 the Isle of Man celebrated the bicentenary of the US constitution with this crown showing the Statue of Liberty and the heads of ten presidents, from Washington to Reagan. The odd man out was Benjamin Franklin (next to the date 1987). This design echoed the multiple thalers of the 17th century (see opposite page).

The earliest coins bearing identifiable portraits came from the Greek cities. Aphrodite and Athena were followed by Herakles, Zeus and a whole host of deities and heroes, but it was left to Persia to depict the first living person, Darius the Great (521–485 BC), on the gold daric and silver siglos. The figure appears as an archer and remained unchanged for 200 years, but is identifiable as Darius because he wears the spiked crown or *orthe* of the Persian ruler. Coins of Abdera (*c.* 425 BC) bear a profile identified by the inscription as Pythagoras, who flourished a century earlier, but the first coin to bear a close-up portrait of a living person was the silver tetradrachm of Miletus (411 BC) with the Persian satrap Tissaphernes.

After the death of Alexander the Great his generals carved up the empire into separate kingdoms and his profile began to appear on their coins. The horn of Ammon sprouting from Alexander's temple signified that he had now become a god. This established a precedent, and subsequent rulers of the Hellenistic kingdoms began portraying

Above: The Roman rulers Philip I (244–9, left) and Galerius (305–11, right) featured their wives on coins.

themselves. The notion spread to Rome in the late-Republican period, and Pompey the Great and Julius Caesar were thus honoured. Portraiture flourished in the Roman Empire, featuring not only the emperor but his wife and children, creating a veritable portrait gallery renowned for its realism.

Medieval coins were very crude by comparison, with stylized portraits of rulers on the verge of parody. Most were full-face portraits but they seldom bore any resemblance to the living ruler. There are rare instances of queens being mentioned, though not actually depicted, including Cynefryth, wife of Offa of Mercia (757–96) and Adelaide, wife of Emperor Otto (931).

REVIVAL IN THE WEST

The Byzantine Empire was indirectly responsible for the revival of realistic portraiture on the coins of Western Europe. Shortly before Constantinople fell to the Turks in 1453, Emperor John Palaeologus paid a state visit to Italy, an occasion commemorated by a handsome bronze medal. This triggered a fashion for large portrait medals in Renaissance Italy, which spread to other countries and also inspired the production of coins by the Italian city states. These relatively large coins came to be known as testone (from Italian *testa*, a head), and from this come the English words "testoon" and "tester", once synonymous with "shilling". In England the first testoon, of 1504, bore the first realistic profile of Henry VII, engraved by Alexander Brugsal, but it

Above: This full-face portrait on a Henry VIII testoon is a good likeness of the king. The testoon provided a good medium for larger portraits.

was not until 1544 that the stereotyped full-face portrait disappeared from the penny. Henry VIII adopted a full-face portrait and when he debased the silver content in his shillings the silver wore off the highest point – his nose – hence the nickname Coppernose given to these coins.

DIFFERENT STYLES

Since the revival of realistic portraiture in the 15th century most images have been profiles. In many monarchies, notably Britain, the custom developed of showing alternate rulers facing left or right. (Both George V and George VI faced left, because Edward VIII – whose coins were never issued – would have faced right.) Two or more facing portraits were fashionable in Byzantine coinage and this treatment is also found on many of the multiple thalers of the German states. The most spectacular examples were the Achtbruderthalers of Brunswick, which had side-by-side facing portraits of eight brothers, hence the name.

Vis-à-vis, or face-to-face, portraits have occasionally appeared. They include some Roman imperial coins, notably those of Septimius Severus.

Below: Successive British monarchs, Edward VII (left) and George V (right), facing alternately left and right.

Above: A multiple thaler of Friedrich I, Duke of Saxe-Gotha-Altenburg, of 1690, with seven busts in roundels.

The style was adopted by English coins showing Mary Tudor and Philip II of Spain, and Scottish coins showing Mary Queen of Scots and her first two husbands, either Francis II of France or Henry, Lord Darnley. A crown from the Turks and Caicos Islands (1976) has confrontational portraits of George III and George Washington, and the style was also used for coins marking the wedding of Prince Charles and Lady Diana Spencer in 1981.

Most coins that have two portraits show them as overlapping profiles, with the more important person (such as a king) at the front and the lesser profile behind. These are described as "jugate", "accolated" or "conjoined" profiles, and they have been in use since the gold staters of the Brutii (282 BC). In Britain the style was used for coins of William III and Mary II (1689–94), those of 1981, 1986, 2000 and 2005 celebrating British royal marriages and the Golden Wedding coins of 1997.

The strangest portrait coin of all time must be the Zurich thaler of 1512, with full-face standing portraits of the three martyred saints, Regulus, Exuperant and Felix, beheaded and holding their heads in their hands.

PORTRAITS OF PERSONALITES

The depiction of royalty other than the reigning monarch was popular during the Roman Empire, when relatives of the emperor were often portrayed. The practice was revived in 16th-century Italy, when the large silver coins that were being produced afforded scope for it, but the portraits were still confined to royalty.

Right: Triple conjoined portraits of Carol I, Ferdinand and Carol II on a Romanian 20 lei of the latter (1944).

Bavaria appears to have produced the first coins commemorating historic personalities other than royalty, beginning with the thaler of 1826 mourning the deaths of the engineer Georg Friedrich von Reichenbach (1772–1826) and the physicist Joseph von Fraunhofer (1787–1826), whose face-to-face profiles appear on the reverse. Several Bavarian coins of 1840–9 depicted the statues of famous men from Albrecht Dürer to Orlando di Lasso. This notion was not copied elsewhere until 1893, when the USA struck a half dollar portraying Christopher Columbus (followed by many other similar coins) and Brazil similarly honoured Pedro Cabral in 1900.

Below: Personalities featured on recent coins include (clockwise from top left) sporting heroes (Roger Bannister, Britain), poets (Robert Burns, Isle of Man), explorers (Captain Cook, New Zealand) and royalty (Charles and Diana's engagement, New Zealand).

NON-FIGURAL MOTIFS

After their adoption of Islam as the prominent faith in the 7th century, Arab countries did not place any effigy of a living creature, either man or beast, on their coins. Although the portrayal of animate objects was considered to be closely linked to idolatry, and was thus declared taboo by the teachings of the Koran, there was no such ban on the depiction of inanimate objects. Nevertheless, until the middle of the 20th century, Islamic coins continued to be devoid of either portraits or pictures, and the space on both sides of the coins was entirely given over to inscriptions in Arabic. This restraint created a need to be innovative with the use of text, leading to some of the lengthiest – and most poetic – inscriptions ever to appear on coins anywhere in the world.

Above: The fusion of Persian and Arab styles has resulted in a few ancient examples of portraiture. This coin depicts Mus'ab bin al-Zubayr.

Below: Abbasid coins usually have the name of the current ruler's heir on the reverse. The bottom example is unusual for bearing the name of an unborn heir.

PIOUS INVOCATIONS

Not only did the countries that produced these coins develop increasingly ornate styles of script, but the inscriptions themselves became more flowery as time passed. The standard formula that appears on Islamic coins is known as the Bismillah, and is the first word of the affirmation, "There is no God but God, and Muhammad is His Prophet." By tradition Allah had 99 excellent names, but opinions differ as to what those 99 names were. In fact, no fewer than 132 epithets for Allah are recorded on Islamic coins. They range from the simple "The One" to "The Ever Self-existing One". Other versions found in inscriptions include "He Who Hath Not Been Begotten", "The Very Next Adjoining One" or the more prosaic "The Numberer" and "The Road Guide".

Muslims had no monopoly on the name of God by any means, but what made their coins so special was their purity of design: they were not sullied by portraits or images of animals or anything else that might distract the thoughts of the faithful.

WIDESPREAD USE OF ARABIC

Arabic was widely used, not only in Arabia and the lands conquered by the Arabs, from Spain to Mesopotamia, but also for the Farsi inscriptions on the coins of Persia and Afghanistan, and for the Malay texts on coins of Java, Sumatra and Malaya. Arabic was the script used by the Mughal emperors, the princely states and even the Honourable East India Company. On some coins of the Indian states Queen Victoria was named (though she was not portrayed) and styled in Arabic as Empress of India.

The earliest Islamic coins combined Arabic with Graeco-Roman or Sasanian (Pehlevi) inscriptions. Siculo-Norman coins were copied from Ayyubid coins but with a Christian formula in Arabic, "Victorious by the Grace of God" on gold taris of Tancred. Alfonso VIII of Castile struck coins inscribed in Arabic, "Amir of the Catholics and the Pope the Imam of the Church of the Messiah".

For the purposes of trade with Muslim merchants in Morocco, Portuguese copper ceitils were struck with a three-line Arabic inscription bearing the name and title of King Manuel I (1495–1521).

Above: Ornate punches replaced effigies on some post-Gupta Indian coins. The lotus motif is a good example of the use of recognized emblems.

Above: Zubayda, the wife of the Abbasid governor Al-Rashid, was perhaps the first woman to strike a coin in the history of Islam. The inscription reads: "By the command of the lady, mother of the heir apparent, may God preserve her, so be it."

TITLES

Islamic coins bore the names and titles of rulers, and Abbasid coins often mentioned the heir to the throne as well – even if the heir was as yet unborn and unnamed. Titles, although extavagant and self-aggrandizing, were also carefully worded to underline religious commitment and the earthly confines of the territories over which a ruler presided. They included "Excellent King of the Surface of the Earth" (used by the Mongol rulers of Persia),

Sun Motif

While some coins of Hyderabad depicted the Char Minar gateway, its feudatory dependency of Indore struck coins with a smiling sun motif, the nearest thing to a portrait without actually being one.

"Emperor of the World" (for the Jahandar of Delhi) and "Lord of the World" (for the Atabeg of Mosul). By contrast, the most self-abasing title of all time was inscribed on Islamic coins, Shah Tahmasp I of Persia (1514–76) being content to refer to himself as "Slave of Ali". Not to be outdone, Shah Rukh was styled "Hound of the Threshold of the Pleasing One" and his successor, Shah Husain, went a step further with "Hound of the Threshold of Ali, of the Amir of the Faithful".

The most charming title found in an Islamic inscription was that favoured by some of the Indian princely states in the 19th century, after the proclamation of the Empire of India in 1877: "Queen Victoria, Adorning the Throne of Inglistan [England] and Hind". The saddest title was "Deceased", inscribed in Arabic on the coins of Aziz Sheikh of the Golden Horde and Tipu Sultan, ruler of Mysore, which were issued shortly after their deaths.

SIGN OF THE TOUGHRA

The *toughra* found on Turkish and Arab coins is the Islamic counterpart of the royal monogram on European coins. It consists of an elaborate Arabic inscription giving the names of a ruler and his father and incorporating three vertical lines. These date from the reign of Sultan Murad I (1359–89), who, when signing important documents, dipped three fingers into the inkwell and drew them down the page.

CHRONOGRAMS

A chronogram is an inscription in which some letters can be read as Roman numerals, which make a date when added together. (The term is derived from the Greek and means "time writing".)

This unusual practice was popular in Europe in the Renaissance and the 17th century, when it was often used to signify dates in inscriptions on tombstones and foundation stones, but it was derived from the Arab custom of giving the letters of the *abjad* (the Arabic alphabet) a numerical value. From this came the fashion for concealing the date in inscriptions on Islamic coins, which could be deduced by adding up the value of the letters composing the word or words.

Thus, coins inscribed in the name of the ruler Fakhr al-Din Qara Arslan, Artuqid of Hisn Kayfa, contained a final word whose letters signified 500, 50 and 6, making the date 556 AH. On the reverse of coins of Nadir Shah appeared the inscription, "By the Tarikh, Whatever Happens is Best." The letters of this phrase as written in Arabic had the values 70 + 100 + 6 + 1 + 40 + 10 + 80 + 200 + 10 + 600 + 30 + 1, which together made 1148 AH.

A mohur of Jahangir bears the inscription: "The letters of Jahangir and Allahu Akbar's are Equal in Value from the Beginning of Time", and, indeed, when added up the letters of their names each total 289.

Below: The toughra is a feature of Ottoman coins (top) and Islamic coins of the Indian princely states (bottom); Egypt included an actual portrait of King Fu'ad I in 1921, and Morocco worked the national star emblem into an ornate reverse of 1900.

Below: Ancient Islamic coiners sought innovative ways of displaying their lengthy inscriptions, from hexagonal, circular and star-shaped arrangements to densely packed central legends.

HISTORY OF PICTORIALISM

The obverse of a coin was traditionally reserved for the portrait of a deity or ruler, while the reverse (the "tails") was used for an image of lesser importance. The distinction has been blurred in more recent times by the adoption of arms instead of a portrait (especially in republics) or, conversely, the use of portraiture on both sides.

Because of the symbolic importance of coins, pictorial elements often arise out of armorial emblems and they, in turn, may be traced back to mythology. The use of animals (particularly cattle and horses) may symbolize power and wealth. From the 1900s onward, as coins in general have become more pictorial, they have often illustrated national aspirations. By the 1930s a didactic or propaganda element was creeping in, particularly on coins of the USSR and fascist countries.

CLASSICAL IMAGES

The simple motifs on the obverse of the earliest electrum dumps probably represented the personal badges of the merchants and magistrates who authorized them. In the heyday of classical Greek coinage the civic emblem was the dominant feature of many issues. Among the earliest examples were the winged boar (Klazomenai), boar (Methymna), calves' heads (Lesbos), lion's head (Lindos), amphora (Andros), frog (Seriphos), dolphins (Thera) and bull's head (Athens). Some of the emblems were a pun on the name of the city or district. Thus the *bous* or cowhide shield graced the coins of Boeotia, while a crab and a turtle were featured on the coins of Akragas and Aegina respectively. Others featured mythical figures associated with the area, such as the boy Taras riding a dolphin (Tarentum) and Athena with her owl (Athens).

Below: Motifs on ancient Greek and Persian coins include ordinary animals as well as mythical creatures such as a winged Pegasus or Gorgon.

Heraldic reverses related to portrait obverses developed in the 5th century BC, and from matching deities with their familiars, such as Zeus and the eagle, it was but a short step to the coins of imperial Rome, with the emperor on one side and an allegorical subject on the other. The Romans, however, eventually produced coins that had a wide range of subjects on the reverse, including the famous buildings and landmarks of the Roman Empire. It is on some of these that we find the earliest representation of the original Tower of London.

MEDIEVAL DEPICTIONS

Most medieval coins tended to show the stylized portrait of a ruler on the obverse and a cross on the reverse, partly out of Christian sentiment but also partly for the practical purpose of showing where the coin could be cut into halves or quarters. The revival of symbolism came in the early 10th century when Pope Benedict I sanctioned denarii whose reverse showed an open hand flanked by the letters R and O. The hand (*manus* in Latin) was a pictogram substituting for part of the word "Romanus". The hand of God raised in benediction was a popular theme on coins, especially as the dreaded millennium approached and people feared the end of the world. Extremely rare pennies of Aethelred the Unready had an obverse of the Lamb of God and reverse of a dove, and are believed to allude to the millennium.

Below: Favoured motifs for Roman coins included a standing bull (left) or landmarks such as the Temple of Jupiter (right).

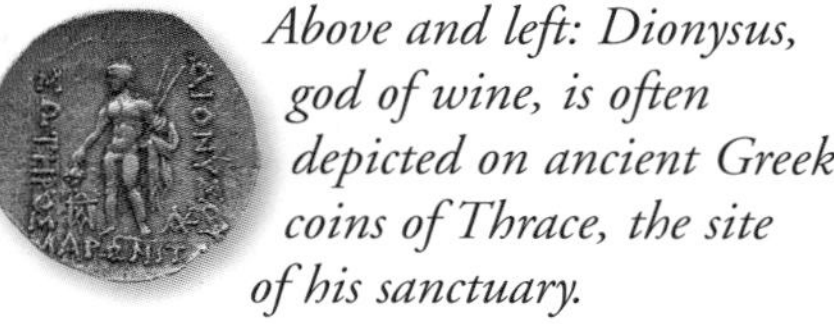

Above and left: Dionysus, god of wine, is often depicted on ancient Greek coins of Thrace, the site of his sanctuary.

Heraldic reverses were adopted by the Frankish rulers. Early coins had a stylized temple, but with the growth of chivalry in the 12th and 13th centuries it became fashionable to place the emblem from the ruler's escutcheon on the reverse. Thus began the convention, prevalent on many coins to this day, of having the ruler's portrait on the obverse and the national arms on the reverse. English gold coins may be found with the Archangel Michael slaying the serpent or the monarch armed and standing in a galleon, but it was not until the neo-classical Britannia (1797) and St George and the Dragon (1816) that pictorialism truly emerged.

MODERN PICTORIALS

In classical times, coins could be startlingly graphic in the subjects they featured. Drunkenness, rape and debauchery appeared on Greek

Above: A "death thaler" of the ruler August II of Saxony, showing a skull lying at the base of a tree.

staters from Thasos (Thrace) and Lete and tetradrachms of Mende and Naxos, reflecting a very earthy approach to subjects considered taboo in later times. Pictorialism as such, however, really began with the large thalers and guldengroschen from the 16th century. Their modern counterparts, dollars and crowns, offer considerable scope for elaborate pictorial motifs.

The large silver coins of the German states tended to be allegorical or propagandistic, particularly during the Thirty Years War (1618–48). Republican France's first pictorial coin, the 5 décime piece of 1793, was in the same genre. Popularly known as the Robespierre décime, its elaborate obverse depicts Nature as an Egyptian goddess expressing the water of life from her breasts. Robespierre (the President of the Convention) is offering a cup of the fluid to a delegate of the Assembly.

Austria and the German states took the lead in developing pictorial coins in the 19th century; the earliest issues to depict ships and locomotives come from that area. But it was in the course of the 20th century that pictorial coins really came into their own. Pictorialism was no longer confined to large commemorative pieces but extended right down to the lowliest definitive circulating coins. The Irish Free State (later the Republic of Ireland) adopted distinctive coins in 1928 and these bore reverse motifs showing such subjects as a sow and piglets (halfpenny), a hen and chickens, a hare (3 pence), a hound (6 pence) and a bull (shilling). The Barnyard series, as it was nicknamed, continued for many years, surviving until 1968. Canada, Australia and New Zealand adopted pictorial motifs in the 1930s, while Britain introduced a series in 1937 depicting a wren (farthing), Sir Francis Drake's ship (halfpenny) and a clump of sea thrift (3 pence); other denominations retained the seated figure of Britannia (penny) or clung to heraldic themes.

Beginning with Lincoln in 1909 (the centenary of his birth), American coins have favoured portraits of dead presidents (obverse) and buildings associated with them, such as the Lincoln Memorial (1 cent) and Monticello, the home of Thomas Jefferson (5 cents), but otherwise heraldic and symbolic motifs predominate. The only truly pictorial United States coin was the nickel of 1913–38, which had the head of a Native American on the obverse and a buffalo on the reverse. In 2005 these much-loved motifs were revived after a gap of 67 years.

Pictorialism today is prominent in the coins of the emerging nations, but examples are also found in Scandinavia and Britain's crown dependencies. For Greece, Italy and Israel the wheel has come full circle, with heavy reliance on classical or biblical pictorial motifs.

Sunrise and Hope

The world's newest country, the Democratic Republic of Timor-Leste, consists of the eastern part of the island of Timor. Formerly a Portuguese colony, it was occupied by Indonesia but fought a long campaign for liberation (1975–99) and, with the backing of a UN peacekeeping force, achieved full independence in 2002. It has the lowest GDP in the world, about $400 a year. The cockerel on the coin symbolizes the sunrise (Timor in Tetum means "sunrise") and hope for the new country.

Below: Coins of the Weimar Republic depicting Cologne Cathedral (top) and a scenic river reverse to mark the liberation of the Rhineland.

Below: A naval obverse of Virginia (top) and a mountain lion reverse of Vermont are just two of the pictorial subjects used on American commemorative issues.

HOW TO COLLECT

Numismatics boasts distinguished enthusiasts, many of whom used the hobby to develop a keen interest in history. Once you have decided on a focus for your collection, you can begin to make new acquisitions. Although it's tempting to seek out rarities, many issues of recent years – such as this enamelled coin of the Isle of Man – are truly resplendent.

ORIGINS OF NUMISMATICS

Numismatics is the name given to the study and collecting of coins and medals, and is derived from *nomisma*, the Greek word for coin. It is probable that coins were prized for their aesthetic qualities from the earliest times, while their importance in socio-economic development was appreciated by Herodotus and other early historians.

There were certainly coin collections during the earliest times – but not, perhaps, in the modern sense. In the era before banking existed, people stored their surplus wealth in leather bags or in earthenware jars, which could be buried in troubled times. Most hoards were presumably retrieved by their owners when the crisis passed, but many others were never recovered until turned up by the plough or (more likely nowadays) discovered by the metal detector. Coins from such hoards, large and small, have long held a fascination for the archaeologist and antiquary, and they are undoubtedly the source of much of the material now in the hands of museums and some collectors. Unfortunately, until relatively recently, such hoards were not carefully preserved and studied scientifically, although laws now exist in some countries to safeguard archaeological finds, including those of numismatic interest, until they can be properly catalogued by the appropriate authority.

Above: Great royal coin collectors include (clockwise from top left) Carol I of Romania, Christina of Sweden, Habsburg Emperor Charles VI and Prince Rainier of Monaco.

Right: Chocolate replica of the 1 euro coin, produced in 2000 to publicize the new currency.

Below: Chinese gold panda coin, distributed as a Lunar New Year gift in a red silk purse.

EARLIEST COIN CATALOGUES

Although St Thomas Aquinas (1225–74) touched on coinage in his philosophical writings, the earliest works dealing with numismatics, or the antiquarian aspects of coins, as opposed to the monetary and financial aspects of current coins, appeared early in the 16th century. The French antiquary Guillaume Budé (1467–1540) published *De Asse et Partibus Eius* ("Concerning the Roman As and its Parts") and *Libellus de Moneta Graeca* ("A Pamphlet of Greek coins").

Many other books appeared in the 17th and 18th centuries, in France, Germany and Italy, dealing with various aspects of ancient and medieval coins. By the early 19th century, the practice of coin-collecting was well enough established to support periodical literature. The earliest magazine devoted to numismatics was *Blätter für Münzkunde*, published in Hanover from 1834 until 1844 by Dr Hermann Grote. *The Numismatic Chronicle*, founded by John Young Ackerman, made its debut as a quarterly in 1836 and is still going strong as the journal of the Royal Numismatic Society.

The second half of the 19th century witnessed the publication of a profusion of catalogues and handbooks, consisting of either systematic listings of coins in the world's major public collections or studies of particular regions and periods, predominantly Greek and Roman but with a developing interest in medieval European and Islamic coins. From the tone and contents of these early works it is clear that the emphasis was on ancient coins, which collectors who had had the benefit of a classical education could appreciate.

Numismatics continued to be predominantly classical in character until the late 19th century. By that time, some wealthy collectors in North America were taking a keen interest in

Royal Collector

Victor Emanuel III of Italy (1900–46) succeeded to the throne on the assassination of his father, and by his own abdication hastened the end of the Italian monarchy. Today he is best remembered for his magnificent coin collection, now in the Palazzo Massimo alle Terme, Rome.

the coins of the United States, yet the earliest book on the subject was not published until 1899.

Catalogues of the coins of the various European countries began to appear in the 1880s, but a similar coverage of the coins of India, China, Japan, Korea and other Asiatic countries did not develop until the turn of the century. These catalogues varied considerably in detail and illustration. No attempt was made to produce priced catalogues until the 1920s, when such books covering specific countries or periods began to appear regularly. The only catalogues that cover world coinage as a whole are the Krause catalogues, published in the USA (and confined to the modern period).

GREAT COIN COLLECTIONS

From the Renaissance onward, it was fashionable for gentlemen to possess a coin cabinet (which in some cases was an entire room, shelved from floor to ceiling to house their treasures). Outstanding among early collectors were the Italian poet Petrarch, the Medici rulers of Florence, Pope Paul II, Queen Christina of Sweden and the Habsburg Emperor Charles VI. In Britain, King George III set a fine example, and his interest in coins was shared by his personal surgeon, Dr William Hunter (1718–83), whose wide-ranging collections, including coins and medals, were the nucleus of the Hunterian Museum in Glasgow, opened in 1807. The collections formed by his brother, Dr John Hunter (1728–93), and their contemporary, Sir Hans Soane, formed the basis of the numismatic collections in the British Museum. Britain is unusual in having several great institutional collections, including those in the Ashmolean Museum (Oxford), and the Fitzwilliam Museum (Cambridge), as well as the Royal Scottish Museum (Edinburgh). Elsewhere, large and all-embracing collections are housed in the Bibliothèque Nationale (Paris) and the Smithsonian Institution (Washington).

Among more recent monarchs who had an abiding passion for coins were King Carol of Romania and Prince Rainier of Monaco, but King Victor Emmanuel III of Italy was a lifelong numismatist, whose studies and scholarly writings on the subject are still widely respected. Conversely, King Farouk of Egypt, another royal collector, was really the pack rat par excellence, whose collections ranged from stamps and coins to glass paperweights and ladies' underwear. Some of the greatest collectors of more recent times were Americans, such as the pharmaceuticals magnate Eli K. Lilly and the Texan tycoon Nelson Bunker Hunt, who famously tried to corner the world silver market back in the 1970s. The late Mary Norweb was arguably the world's leading female numismatist, and the sale of her incomparable collections in the 1980s was spread over many auctions.

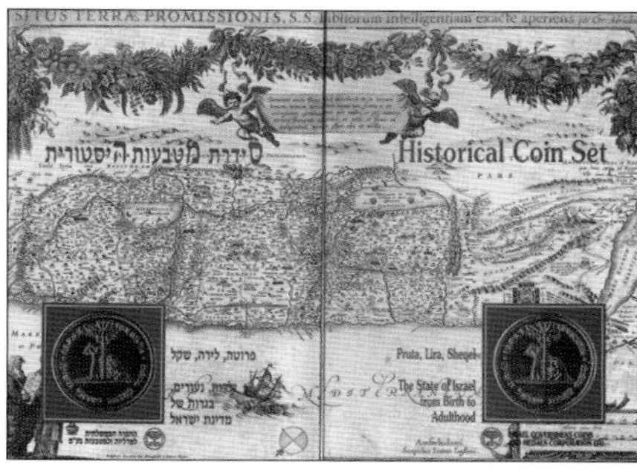

Above: Promotional sets and souvenir folders are contemporary methods of encouraging budding coin collectors.

Below: The coin collection of William Hunter (bottom-left), anatomist and surgeon of fellow collector George III (pictured on this 1796 guinea, right), formed the nucleus of Scotland's oldest museum, the Hunterian in Glasgow. The museum, as it was in 1807, is shown in the engraving (bottom right).

GRADE AND CONDITION

Coins are the most durable of all the antiquities and have survived in remarkable condition considering their age. Gold coins have been dug out of the earth gleaming as brightly as the day they were minted. Conversely, modern coins may show rapid signs of wear due to frequent circulation and the rough treatment meted out in slot machines. It follows that the condition of a coin plays a major part in determining its value to a collector.

COIN GRADES

Newcomers to the hobby are often amazed at the enormous disparity in value or price between a coin in impeccable mint condition, with neither scratches on its surface nor irregularities in its edges, and its twin in worn condition. The effigy on the obverse of the latter may have lost its fine detail but surely it is still recognizable? And the coat of arms on the reverse may be reduced to a mere outline, but the date is still readable, so why should it be regarded as worthless?

Everything is relative. Collectors may be quite happy to acquire a medieval coin in generally poor condition because (a) it is a major rarity, or (b) that is the condition of all the known examples of the coin and it would be virtually impossible to find a specimen in a better state. It seems to be the case that, when it comes to medieval coinage, you will often have to be content with a piece that would otherwise never be considered worthy of a place in your collection. Supply falls far short of demand in this particular area of numismatics. On the other hand, Greek and Roman imperial coins generally exist in such large quantities that their relative condition is a major factor in determining their value.

As for modern coins, anything less than the highest grades of condition should be unacceptable to a collector – a fact that is reflected in the coin catalogues, which usually confine their prices to the two top grades. At the apex of the pyramid, proof coins are collectable only in pristine condition, exactly as they left the mint; anything less makes them unacceptable to the discerning collector.

Below: These 18th-century British spade guineas are judged by one auctioneer to be "fair to very fine", though it often takes an expert to discern variations in condition, and reach an overall grading.

Viewing and Assessing Coins

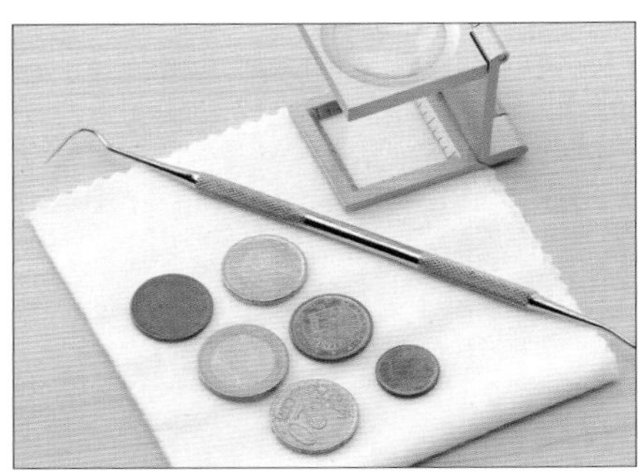

Above: A soft, lint-free cloth offers good protection against surface scratching when setting coins down to view.

Above: If you must handle coins – not recommended for rarities or those in mint state – hold them at the very edges.

Above: A range of magnification tools exist; generally x10 is the maximum strength required to view coins.

Above: Common, circulating coins will arrive in various states, and may be in need of cleaning before viewing closely.

HOW TO ASSESS GRADE AND CONDITION

The ability to appraise a coin accurately comes only with years of experience. A good magnifier is an absolute necessity, but nowadays you can also scan coins at a high resolution and then view them on screen, focusing on the particular details you wish to examine more closely.

In the highest grade of condition a coin should still possess the original lustre characteristic of a freshly minted coin. Next comes a coin that may have lost some or most of its lustre but on which the finest detail of the design is absolutely sharp. Lower down the scale are coins that show slight evidence of wear on the higher points of the design, such as the hair on the portrait, the fine folds of clothing or the intricate detail

Classification of Condition

Because the conventional terms have tended to become subjective, the American Numismatic Association (ANS) has devised a more scientific and objective system, combining terms or abbreviations with numbers to give a more precise classification. This is now used worldwide by dealers when encapsulating or "slabbing" coins in sealed folders (pictured), to bolster confidence in buying and selling. These grades are as follows:

Proof-70	Perfect proof
Proof-67	Gem proof
Proof-65	Choice proof
Proof-63	Select proof
Proof-60	Proof

Uncirculated coins are graded by Mint State (MS):

MS-70	Perfect
MS-67	Gem
MS-65	Choice
MS-63	Select
MS-60	Uncirculated

The lower grades combine the traditional abbreviations with numbers:

AU-50	About uncirculated
EF-45	Choice extremely fine
EF-40	Extremely fine
VF-30	Choice very fine
VF-20	Very fine
F-12	Fine
VG-8	Very good
G-4	Good
AG-4	About good
BS-1	Basal state

in a coat of arms. Below that, you will notice wear in the inscriptions, with the lettering looking thick or blurred.

Beyond that state, coins showing extensive signs of wear are not worth collecting unless they are very rare. The same is true for coins that bear signs of rough handling – scuff marks, scratches or edge knocks. Coins that have suffered actual damage, such as piercing for use as jewellery or clipping to remove slivers of gold or silver from the edges, should be avoided altogether, except as historical curiosities.

Below: Special peel-back holders are available to preserve the condition of individual coins.

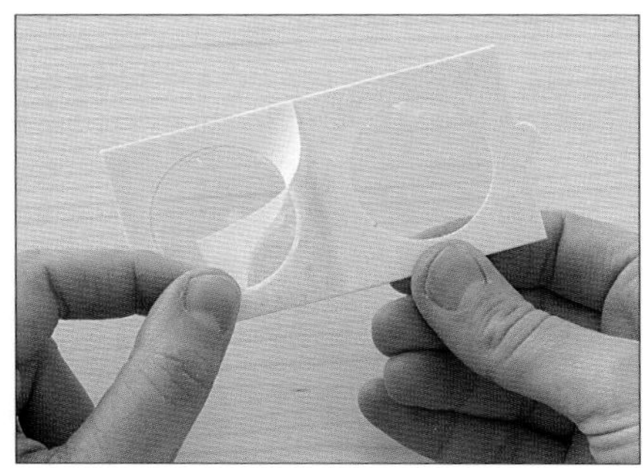

NOMENCLATURE

Over the years dealers and collectors have attempted to classify the condition of coins, adopting various terms to define the various states, from "brilliant uncirculated" to the lower grades of "fair", "medium" and "poor". The trouble is that the terms, like the coins themselves, have tended to become worn or debased with the passage of time and as a result new terms have been devised to upgrade the system. At one time, for example, the term "good" meant just that, but nowadays a coin given that epithet would, in fact, be pretty poor and not worth considering unless it was a very elusive item.

Auctioneers and cataloguers should include the quality of the strike with their description. Countermarked coins will not necessarily lose value if the mark itself is sufficiently clear and complete. Both sides of the coin are assessed during grading: the final evaluation will be based on the slightly weaker of the two sides, if they are not particularly different, or the coin will be given a "split grade" in the catalogue entry. If the two sides are found to be more than one grade apart, this suggests that the design of either the obverse or reverse has been subject to greater wear and tear, and the coin will be graded on the weaker side alone. Coins bearing a small motif, such as a crown symbol, may be graded solely on the condition of this easily worn element of the design. A guide to nomenclature is given with the glossary to this book.

Below: This gold half-anna restrike of an 1892 copper denomination (top left), struck for use in British India, is judged to be in "brilliant" state as it has almost no surface markings. "Peripheral" weakness on the obverse (top right) of a 13th-century issue from Bukhara earns it a split grade of "good/very fine". The "unique" status of these Anglo-Saxon "bonnet-type" pennies (middle) increases value despite their time-worn condition, while this 2 shilling coin of George VI (bottom), sold with its original 1937 proof-set packaging, was graded "about as struck".

LOOKING AFTER COINS

Coins are tough – they have to be in order to carry out their function. For this reason, they have been produced using hard-wearing materials designed to be handled frequently, and to withstand the grime and sweat of hands in every climate and working condition. They have to be robust enough to withstand harsh treatment, such as being shoved into slot machines or dropped on the ground or, worst of all, jostled constantly with other coins in purses and pockets.

Right: Manage your expectations when caring for your coins. If, for example, they display signs of "copper sickness" such as the coins on the left of this picture, you will never be able to restore them to their original state, like those on the right.

PRESERVING CONDITION

Coins are often expected to circulate for decades and, unless there is a change in the currency or a denomination is withdrawn, only when they are too old and worn to be recognizable are they taken out of service. However, even coins bearing the marks of time should be preserved in the condition in which they are found.

Unless you are confining your acquisitions to coins neatly packaged in their pristine state by the mint or numismatic bureau, or slabbed by a dealer of high repute, you will acquire coins in their naked and unadorned state. At best they will have been passed from hand to hand to some extent, even if they are still bright and shiny and bear the current date. At worst they will have been in circulation for some time, perhaps for many years. They may latterly have reposed in a dealer's oddment tray, the convenient repository for so many unconsidered trifles, waifs and strays, which are too poor or of insufficient value to make it worth the dealer's time and trouble to sort and grade properly. Collectors love sifting through these bargain trays as the cheaper material generally ends up there, where quick turnover is the name of the game.

CLEANING WITH CARE

Once you have borne away your treasures and taken them home for closer examination and identification, before putting them into the appropriate place in your collection the first thing is to attend to their appearance. The plain fact is that most coins that will come into your possession in the ordinary way will be dirty, dull and grimy, even if they still possess some of their original lustre. The oils secreted by human hands, atmospheric pollution and everyday dust and dirt all combine to give circulated coins a fairly unattractive appearance.

Generally speaking, a good degreasing solvent will work wonders in removing surface grime. A drop or two of a good quality lighter fuel on the surface of a coin, gently wiped off with a very soft cloth, will remove all or most of the dirt. For more persistent cases, especially when dirt accumulates in and around the lettering or the more intricate parts of the design, brushing with a soft brush with animal bristles – never use nylon or other artificial fibres – is efficacious.

The watchwords here are gentleness and persistence. It is preferable, when handling coins, to wear latex or fine plastic surgical gloves. If you are not wearing gloves, always hold coins at the very edge, as shown, left, so that any contact between your fingertips and the coin surface is minimal. You would be surprised how indelible fingerprints can be; once a fingerprint marks the surface of a coin, it can never be removed and is etched there for all time.

Cleaning Coins

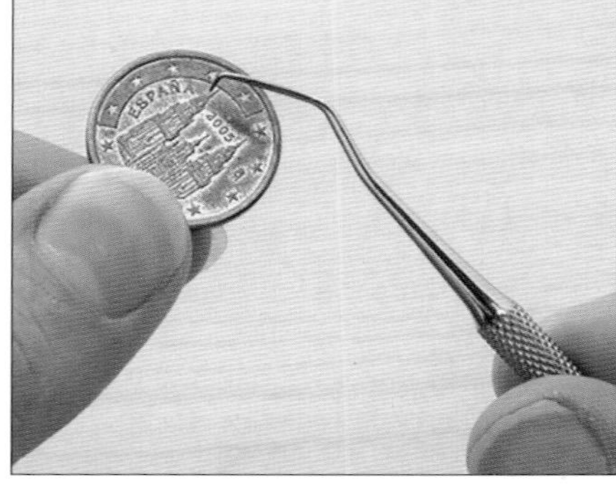

Above: A specially designed coin 'pick' will help to remove encrusted grime.

Above: This coin cleaning brush causes minimal damage to the metal.

SOLUTIONS FOR DIFFERENT METALS

If all coins were made of gold or silver the problems of caring for them would be simple. Gold does not rust, it is impervious to oxidation or atmospheric pollution and it resists most of the chemicals found in the soil. Of course gold coins do get grimy from constant handling, but surface dirt can be easily removed with a solution of lemon juice in an equal amount of warm water. Silver responds well to a bath in warm water to which you have added a few drops of ammonia.

Copper or bronze coins are more of a problem because these metals are prone to oxidation and form the green patina called verdigris. Where this is evenly distributed over the coin, it actually protects the surface from further deterioration, and it is not unattractive in, for example, Roman coins. But where verdigris appears as bright green patches, it is regarded as "copper sickness" and needs special attention. Fortunately, there are now various products on the market that are designed specifically for the cleaning of coins made of different metals. Read the instructions on the label and follow them carefully, and you should be able to cope with this problem.

Below: Basic household items such as an empty jam jar and caustic soda are useful for coin care.

The Perils of Polish

If cleaning should be approached with the utmost caution, polishing is definitely a bad thing! Beginners sometimes fall into the trap of assuming that a vigorous rub with metal cleaner will improve the appearance of a coin, but short of actually hitting it with a hammer and chisel, this is the worst thing you can do. Polishing a coin may briefly improve its superficial appearance, but such abrasive action will destroy the patina and reduce the fineness of the high points of the surface. Even if a coin is polished only once, it will never be the same, and an expert can recognize this immediately.

Above: You should never remove coins from any form of sealed packaging unless it is really necessary.

The lower down the electromotive series the metals are, the greater the problem, as these materials have a greater tendency to rust and corrode. This applies particularly to coins minted in times of shortage, such as wartime, which may be made of tin, zinc, iron or steel. In this case, immersion in a 5 per cent solution of caustic soda containing some aluminium foil or zinc filings works well, but care must be taken to rinse the coins thoroughly afterwards in clean water. Cotton buds can be extremely useful accessories for dealing with troublesome patches of dirt or grease. Dry coins carefully with a soft cloth – never use paper towels as these can scratch the metal surface – and always blot coins dry rather than rubbing them.

SALVAGED COINS

Coins recovered from being buried in the ground, or found on the sea bed, may present special problems due to chemical reactions between the metals and the salts present in earth or sea water. Buried silver coins, for example, will acquire a dark patina of silver sulphide. In such cases, the best advice is to take them to your local museum or friendly coin dealer and let the conservation experts decide what can or should be done to improve their condition and appearance.

Left and below: The packaging in which special edition mint sets are issued is designed to preserve the coins into perpetuity.

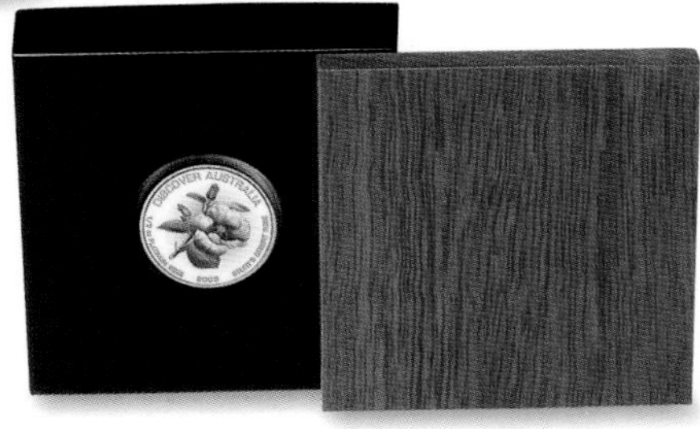

HOUSING COINS

Like any other collectables of value, coins need to be properly housed. Although they are far less bulky than even small antiques, they are much more cumbersome than stamps or postcards, and have their special requirements in order that they should be kept in a safe and orderly manner. Storage options range from special items of furniture to boxes, cases and albums. Each has its good and bad points, but, in the end, what you use is a matter of personal choice.

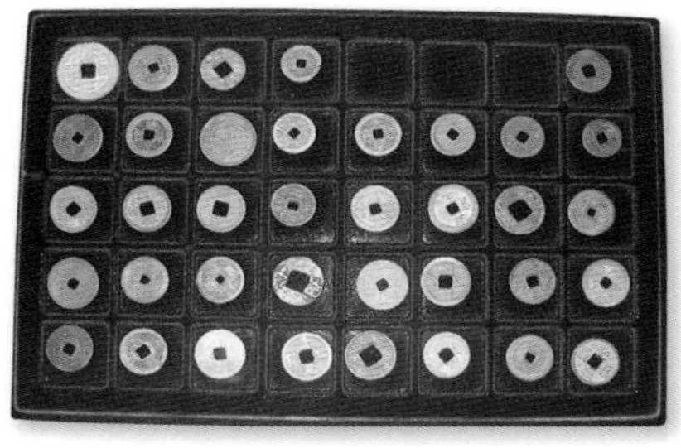

Above: Modern plastic coin trays have a felt lining and compartments, often with a transparent lid and slipcase.

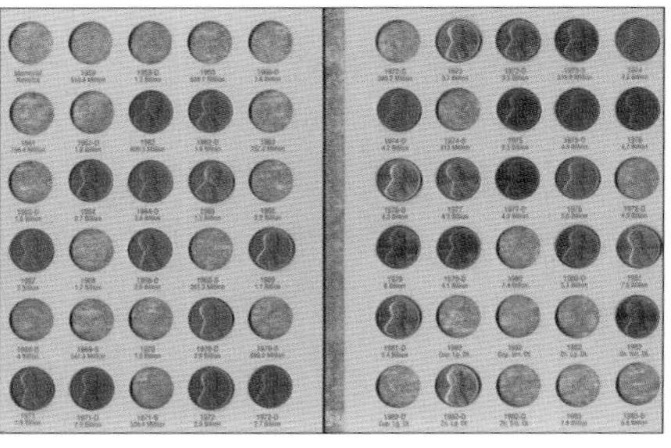

Above and top: A Harris & Co. Memorial Cent coin folder which, when opened, reveals holes to contain all the variants of a particular denomination, arranged by date and mint-mark.

Above and left: A set of Australian transport tokens in a presentation folder.

BOXES AND CASES

For those seeking to establish a fairly extensive collection, with room to grow, boxes and cases not only give the "classic" feel of a small library, but are also a useful aid to cataloguing. Companies such as Abafil of Italy and Lindner of Germany produce a large range of cases suitable for coins. They are constructed of steel or stout plastic, and open to reveal several shallow trays, often stacked in such a way that each can be slid in or out of place without disturbing the other trays. The trays themselves have compartments of various dimensions tailored to fit coins of different sizes and are felt lined. Most of these boxes have a good locking system and a carrying handle, so they are particularly popular with dealers travelling to and from coin shows. When the case is locked the trays are held securely in place and there is no danger of the coins slithering around or falling out in transit. These cases often have separate compartments for such handy accessories as a good magnifier and callipers for accurately measuring diameters and thicknesses. Another useful feature consists of side pockets inside the box for hygroscopic crystals, which ensure that the coins are kept in a dry atmosphere.

The same companies also produce individual cases on the same principle, usually constructed in stout plastic lined with felt, with a sliding plastic lid and a handle. In turn, the case fits inside a slipcase on which you can write the details of the contents. Unlike the boxes, however, these cases seldom have a lock, so they are much less secure. While coin boxes are best simply

Left: There are a number of different ways to house coins, from felt-lined trays to ring-bound albums with clear plastic sleeves, with compartments into which individual coins can be slotted, enabling both sides to be viewed in the sleeve.

stacked on the floor, the cases can be stored on bookshelves – always making sure that you do not overload them. There are also stacking systems that enable you to build up boxes and cases in a single all-purpose storing unit. The German company Mobel-Element, for example, produces a cabinet with a steel frame that can be adapted or added to as your collection grows.

COIN ALBUMS

Stout card coin folders produced by such firms as Harris and Whitman, with holes drilled for different denominations and the date, mint-mark and brief description printed below each hole, have long been immensely popular with American collectors. Similar albums have been produced for coins of other countries. While they are ideal for change-checkers intent on completing all the dates and mint-marks of a particular coin, they lack the flexibility required for a general collection.

In the 1960s, when coin collecting grew dramatically in popularity, a number of stationers began producing coin albums. These had a leatherette binder and a stout steel post with two or four rings on to which transparent pages with pockets of various sizes could be threaded. These albums have the advantage of allowing you to see both sides of the coin merely by turning the page – a big improvement over traditional cabinet trays. If they are stored upright on bookshelves the weight of the coins tends to distort the pages and may even pull the steel post away from the spine, so for this reason they are best laid flat, like coin cases.

Below: A souvenir presentation case with a slipcase, housing a set of coins celebrating the Chinese Year of the Dog.

WALLETS

Plastic wallets are designed to hold individual coins, and are used in conjunction with larger containers such as albums. They often have a small sleeve into which a card giving details of the coin can be inserted. These wallets have largely superseded traditional manilla envelopes, but both can be stacked upright in narrow cases. You can buy cases for this purpose that build into storage systems, but many collectors are content to use any long, narrow box. Today many mints issue coin sets in special folders or wallets, and these can be stored in the compartments of coin cases, or slotted into albums.

CABINETS

Wealthy collectors of former times generally stored their treasures in a coin cabinet, a substantial piece of furniture in its own right. Splendid examples with marquetry doors and elegant cabriole legs come up at auction from time to time, and cost the earth, but plainer examples turn up occasionally in second-hand furniture stores, and as there is little general demand for them you might be lucky and get a bargain.

There are still specialist cabinet makers who produce modern coin cabinets in air-dried mahogany, walnut or rosewood (never oak, cedar or any highly resinous timber, which would react chemically with the contents). These cabinets have tiers of shallow drawers containing felt-based trays made of the same wood but with half-drilled holes of various diameters, suitable for every size of coin from the smallest copper to

Above: A souvenir wallet produced by the Royal Mint in 1968 to publicize the introduction of decimal coinage in 1971.

the largest crowns and dollars. As these cabinets are largely constructed by hand, they are more expensive than machine-made furniture, but prices vary widely, depending on size, number of drawers and such refinements as lockable double doors and brass fittings. Certainly, budget options exist.

The smaller cabinets will sit comfortably on a stout table (bear in mind the weight of the contents), but the more expensive versions are free-standing. When the doors are shut, these cabinets look no different from a drinks or television cabinet and can stand discreetly in your living room without attracting undue attention.

Hidden Dangers of PVC

PVC, once the preferred medium for sleeves, is not chemically inert. After a year or two, coins inserted in these sleeves begin to change their colour and appearance. Bronze coins turn green while "silver" turns to "gold", or, rather, acquires a sickly yellow slime. Thankfully, the rigid pages of albums are now plasticizer-free.

USING GUIDES AND CATALOGUES

Books dealing with aspects of coins and money have been in existence for many centuries, but in the past hundred years the spate of literature devoted to the subject has been enormous. There are thousands of books now available, ranging from beginners' guides to the subject to detailed studies of a single coin or series.

The old maxim "Knowledge pays off" is seldom truer than in the case of coin collecting and trading. A study of the literature appropriate to your chosen field will repay you handsomely. Coin dealers are very knowledgeable people, but numismatics is such a vast subject that no one could ever know everything. The money laid out on buying up-to-date catalogues alone will soon show an excellent return on the investment.

Right: Popular contemporary coin literature ranges from the massive, and indispensable, compendia on coins of the world, published by the American company Krause (top of picture), to smaller guides detailing the coins of single countries, and specialist periodials and catalogues.

CATALOGUES

The essential tools that no collector should be without are the coin catalogues. Not so many years ago numismatics lagged behind philately in the provision of good catalogues covering the whole world, but this deficiency has been remedied by the splendid range now published by Krause Publications of Iola, Wisconsin.

It may seem strange that a small town in the American Midwest should be the centre of a publishing concern of global stature, but the *vade mecum* for most collectors is Krause's *Standard Catalog of World Coins*, published annually. It started out in 1972 as a single volume encompassing all the coins of the modern world, from about 1800 onward. Today it has expanded back in time to 1600 as well as right up to the present day and has been divided into four volumes, covering the 17th, 18th, 19th and 20th centuries respectively. Each of the current volumes is thicker than a London or New York telephone directory. Along the way the "phone book" (as it is affectionately known the world over) has spawned a range of more detailed catalogues, dealing with specific countries or periods

The Krause catalogues are in a class of their own, but at the next level there is an enormous range of rivals that concentrate on single countries or periods. In the USA, for example, the collector has the choice of several excellent works such as *The Handbook of United States Coins* (known as the "Blue Book"), and *The Guide Book of United States Coins,* (known as the "Red Book"), both issued by Whitman Publishing of Atlanta.

In Britain the pre-eminent catalogues are those formerly published by B.A. Seaby but now kept up to date under the imprint of Spink & Son. These catalogues group coins by reign, but a different approach has been adopted by the Coincraft *Standard Catalogues,* in which coins are classified according to denomination. These two radically different approaches reflect the contrasting ways in which coins are collected and studied.

Below: Comprehensive catalogues even include entries on contemporary imitations of coins, such as this poor copy of a George II halfpenny dated 1758 (top) and unofficial patterns, such as this issue portraying Edward VIII (bottom), released specifically for collectors years after his abdication.

Below: Specialist catalogues may not tell the full story about mintage and availability of coins.

There are authoritative specialized coin catalogues for virtually every country now, most of them compiled and published in the countries concerned. Although many are not in English, they are generally well illustrated and include a glossary of terms in different languages, so using them is not difficult. Besides, the collector who wishes to concentrate on the coins of France or Germany, for example, will very soon acquire a working knowledge of the relevant language anyway.

A number of catalogue producers also publish yearbooks, which generally incorporate price guides as well as containing a wealth of other reference material. Auction catalogues for sales of important collections are invariably well illustrated, with scholarly descriptions of each lot, and these are much prized as permanent reference works.

CATALOGUE PRICES

A salient feature of catalogues is that they contain prices, which gives the collector a pretty good guide to current market values. Some catalogues are published by dealers, and so the prices are essentially those at which coins in the different grades are offered for sale. Most catalogues, however, are produced by a team of dealers and experts and the prices quoted tend to reflect the prevailing state of the market more accurately and objectively.

Catalogues often include mintage figures, which can give a pointer to the relative scarcity of a coin, although these statistics have to be used with caution for they seldom take account of the vast quantities of coins melted down by the mints and therefore do not truly reflect the availability of material on the market.

WHERE TO FIND OUT MORE

Whereas catalogues tend to set out the bare details of coins with prices alongside, handbooks have a more discursive approach. Most of them do not provide prices (which would soon be rendered obsolete) but are designed as monographs that will stand the test of time. In this category come the sumptuous series published by the British Museum

Above: Try an on-line numismatic book store for helpful guides.

over more than a century, and now running to many volumes, dealing in considerable depth with the coins of Greece and Rome.

An impressive runner-up is the series compiled by members of the British and Royal Numismatic Societies and published under the generic title of *Sylloge of Coins of the British Isles,* which has been in progress since 1958. It started out as volumes that catalogued in detail the coins in the great national collections, beginning with the Fitzwilliam Museum in Cambridge and the Hunterian Museum in Glasgow. Ignoring the British Museum collections (which were already well-documented) apart from the Hiberno-Norse series, it covered the collections of other provincial museums in the British Isles, but also recorded British coins in the leading European and American museums and has latterly concentrated on the great private collections such as those formed by Emery Norweb, R.P. Mack and John Brooker. These handsome volumes were originally published by the British Academy but have recently been issued by Spink.

Browsing through these scholarly works makes you realize the complexities of British coins alone – and these are a drop in the ocean compared with the coinage output of the whole world. There is now a definitive handbook for just about anything, no matter how esoteric, from the *Pobjoy Encyclopedia of Isle of Man Coins and Tokens* (1977) to *Jewish Ghettos' and Concentration Camps' Money* by Zvi Stahl (1990).

International Coin Literature

The main English-language periodicals for coin collectors are published in the USA: *COINage* (Miller, Ventura, California), *Coin World* (Amos Press, Sidney, Ohio) and *World Coin News*, (Krause, Iola, Wisconsin). Krause also publish a range of more specialized titles such as *Coin Prices* and *Coins and Numismatic News*. America also takes the lead with *Celator* (Lancaster, Pennsylvania), the only magazine aimed specifically at collectors of ancient coins. *Canadian Coin News* (Trajan, St Catharine's, Ontario) and *Coin News* (Token Publishing, Honiton, England) also have a worldwide readership. *Cronica Numismatica* (Domfil, Barcelona), *El Eco* (Vilanova) and *Cronaca Numismatica* (Bolaffi, Rome) are the leading magazines in Spanish and Italian, while *Revue Numismatique* and *Numismatique et Change* (Paris), *Münzen und Medaillen* (Berlin), *Münzen Revue* (Switzerland) and *Money Trend* (Vienna) serve French and German collectors respectively. *Munt Kourier* is published for collectors in the Netherlands.

COLLECTING BY COUNTRY

Traditionally, collectors have naturally tended to concentrate on the coins of their own country as the most readily available. They would begin with the coins they encountered in their small change in everyday life, gradually exchanging worn specimens for examples in better condition. Then they would work backwards in time, seeking examples of obsolete coins in second-hand or junk shops. Finally, they would begin buying from coin dealers and auctions to fill the gaps in the older issues; coins of a previous regime or those pre-dating economic upheavals and monetary reforms.

This is probably still the usual approach to coin collecting, but the rise of mail-order and on-line trading has made the choice infinitely wider. It is now feasible for even the novice collector to acquire coins from any country that appeals on account of the diversity of its coinage, the type of coins or the subjects pictured on them.

Above: The more research you do into the coinage of your chosen country, the better idea you will have of what is available to collect.

Below: If the coins of a country run into thousands, you can opt to focus on the output of a specific region, such as these coins of Bengal: post-Gupta coins (top) struck under the authority of Sasanka, King of Gauda, 600–630; silver tankas of the Sultans of Bengal (middle); and gold mohurs of the East India Company, Bengal Presidency, struck at the Calcutta Mint (bottom).

CHOOSING A COUNTRY

Many collectors are attracted to a particular area for religious reasons. Thus the coins of Israel have an immense appeal to Jewish collectors all over the world. Similarly, Catholics are drawn to the beautiful and prolific issues of the Vatican City State. In both cases, there is infinite scope in the earlier coinage, on the one hand that of Judaea and the Nabatean kingdom as well as the coins of the Jewish revolts against Roman rule, and on the other the fascinating coins of the Papacy stretching back to early medieval times.

As the collection becomes more advanced, the collector may wish to narrow the scope to a single period or reign and concentrate on different coin types, die variants and mint-marks. Hand in hand with the amassing of specimens goes the study of the history, geography, economic structure and monetary policies of the area, all factors that have an impact on the size, choice of metal or denomination of the coins at different times, not to mention the portraits of rulers and changes to inscriptions and armorial devices.

Other factors that may have some bearing on the choice of country may include the frequency of issue and the

Right: Ireland's history has been chronicled in coins: (clockwise from top left) the Hiberno-Norse penny, a Henry VIII "Harp" groot, a "Gun-money" half crown of James II, a halfpenny of William and Mary, a halfpenny struck during the Siege of Limerick, and the "St Patrick" farthing of Charles II.

balance between the definitive series and the number of commemorative or special issues. In general, the latter are phenomena belonging to the past half century, but even the most conservative coin-issuing countries seem to be producing more and more of these coins, which are essentially intended for the collectors' market rather than for general circulation.

THE IRISH EXAMPLE

When considering the variety of definitive issues you will find countries such as San Marino, which changes its designs each year, at one extreme and at the other countries such as the USA, whose basic series has remained unchanged for many years. In the middle are countries whose modern coinage does not go back very far, has not changed much since its inception, and which does not include too many special issues. These can be useful building blocks for putting together a comprehensive but not complex single-country collection.

A good example of this is provided by Ireland, whose modern coinage began in 1928 with a harp obverse and various animals on the reverses. Apart from the change of Gaelic title in 1939, when "Saorstat Eireann" (Irish Free State) was replaced by "Eire" (Ireland), the Barnyard series continued until the advent of decimal currency in 1971. On the decimal coins, the harp obverse remained the same, and the animal motifs were retained on the cupro-nickel coins; only the bronze low values were given new reverse designs, based on ancient Celtic art, in a series that continued until Ireland adopted the euro in 2002.

Only a handful of Irish special issues have appeared since 1966. On the other hand, Ireland has a numismatic history that stretches back more than a thousand years to the Norse kingdom of Dublin. Interesting coins for collectors include the Anglo-Irish pennies, the "gun money" of the Williamite Wars and the tokens and coppers of the 18th and early 19th centuries.

Above and left: The inscribed names on the 20th-century coins of Congo, Central Africa, chronicle its transition from French colony to People's Republic.

Island Coinage

Another fairly manageable group that has considerable appeal is the Pacific islands. Apart from Hawaii (which had its own coins only in the 19th century) and former German New Guinea (pictured), none of these territories has a history of distinctive coinage going back before World War II, and in most cases their coins have only appeared within recent years.

THE INDIAN EXAMPLE

Apart from the usual country approach, many collectors in earlier generations gravitated towards the coins of ancient Greece and Rome. In the 1950s an interest in the Byzantine series began to develop, and recently an increasing number of collectors worldwide have been focusing on Islamic coinage, which had, naturally, always been popular with Muslim collectors. Now the numerous issues of the dynasties of the Indian subcontinent are attracting a growing following outside India. It is interesting that, while Greek and Roman coins appealed to early collectors everywhere because they had all received a classical education, the attraction of Islamic or Indian coins is also transcending the barriers of race, religion or language, the lure of the relatively unfamiliar being a large part of their appeal.

CHANGING BORDERS

Sometimes it is difficult to define the scope of a country from the collector's standpoint. In Europe there have been sweeping changes in the latter part of the last century, as a result of the reunification of Germany on the one hand and on the other the fragmentation of the USSR, Yugoslavia and even Czechoslovakia, resulting in many new names appearing in the coin catalogues.

The political changes in Africa have seen many former colonial territories adopting new names. The Congo is a particularly confusing example: the former Belgian Congo became the Democratic Republic of the Congo (1960), then Zaire (1977) and is now the Democratic Republic once more (since 1999). The neighbouring French Congo became the Popular Republic of the Congo and issued coins thus designated until 1993, when the name was changed to the Republic of the Congo.

It is important to note that most general catalogues list coins only from the 18th century onward. The collector delving into the coins of earlier periods therefore has to seek out more specialized handbooks and monographs to get the full story.

Above: Mints now produce country-themed sets of coins to tempt collectors and promote tourism.

COLLECTING BY GROUP

Rather than concentrating on the coins of a single country, many collectors prefer to study the coins of a group of territories that are related to each other, either geographically or politically. This might mean countries that have a shared colonial or Commonwealth history, or neighbouring countries with a shared language or culture. This approach provides more variety and interest in the collection generally, as well as allowing the collector to develop the theme of common interest, even exploring links in the design and production of the coins themselves.

SHARED IDENTITIES

A prime example of the geopolitical approach is to take a group of modern countries that, on account of their contiguity, have much in common, which is reflected in the development of their coinage. The Scandinavian countries – Denmark, Norway, Sweden and Finland – provide considerable scope for this kind of treatment. They have a shared cultural heritage, similar languages and a history that has frequently been intertwined.

Below: The "C5" monogram of Christian V of Denmark and Norway (1670–99) appears on the coins of both of these territories (top and middle). Christian V and his son Frederick IV appeared on the same coin of 1699 (bottom), Frederick on the obverse.

Above: Examples of religious imagery include a small cross on both sides of a coin of Canute (top), the hand of God on a penny of Aethelred (middle) and highly pictorial Christian imagery on a Habsburg thaler of Joseph II (bottom).

Although they developed as separate kingdoms they were actually united under Margrethe I of Denmark (1387–1412) in a federation known as the Union of Kalmar. This lasted until 1523 when Gustav Vasa expelled the Danes from Sweden and founded a separate dynasty. Finland remained under Swedish rule until 1809, when it was ceded to Russia and became a separate grand duchy under the tsar.

When Finland gained its independence in 1917 it was the lion rampant emblem of the Vasa kings that became the motif on the coinage. Linguistically, Finland belongs to the Finno-Ugric group (which includes Estonia and Hungary) but there is still a large minority of inhabitants who are linguistically and ethnically Swedish, and ties across the Baltic remain strong.

American Colonial Coins

John Hull and Robert Saunderson operated a mint in Boston, which struck the first American coinage long before the United States gained independence from Britain. It was simply inscribed "NE" (New England) with denominations in Roman numerals, and was followed by coins featuring willow, pine (pictured) or oak trees. The Willow Tree shilling first appeared in 1652, but the other tree designs were not issued until the following decade. However, they all bore that original date to get around the fact that they had not been authorized by Charles II. Maryland, New York, New Jersey and Connecticut also produced coins during this period.

Norway was ceded by Denmark to Sweden in 1814, but resistance from Norwegian nationalists led to its rule as a separate kingdom under the Swedish crown until 1905, when it became a wholly independent sovereign state under Haakon VII, a Danish prince. Ties between the Scandinavian countries were strengthened by the adoption of a common currency based on the krona of 100 öre in 1875.

Below: Russian coinage of 1757 bore the arms of its conquered Baltic kingdoms, Livonia and Estonia.

THE LOW COUNTRIES

Belgium, the Netherlands and Luxembourg are another obvious choice for the subject of a group collection. Today they are separate countries, but they have a common history going back thousands of years to the time when they were settled by the Belgae, a Celtic people.

In the Middle Ages they formed the core of the duchy of Burgundy, which fell under Habsburg rule in the 1490s. The northern part broke away in the 1570s to form the United Provinces (now Holland) while the south became the Austrian Netherlands. By the Congress of Vienna (1815) the whole of the Netherlands was united under the king of Holland, but Belgium seceded in 1830 and Luxembourg was separated from Holland in 1890. Ties remained close and in 1945 they formed a commercial union (Benelux), a forerunner of, and model for, the European Union. Belgium and Luxembourg have had similar currencies (both struck at Brussels) and all three have issued coins in similar designs to commemorate events of common interest.

IMPERIAL COINS

The former territories of the French, Portuguese and British colonial empires are areas with strong political links. The French and Portuguese tended to use uniform motifs for their dependent territories, whereas apart from the profile of the reigning monarch, coins of the dominions and colonies of the British Empire, and later of the Commonwealth, were quite distinctive in their reverse types.

Then there are the colonies that federated. They would have enjoyed their own coins prior to uniting, and thus the colonial coinage can be collected as a separate entity, with or without the coins of the united country. There are quite a number of instances of this, the coins in each case varying considerably in scarcity and expense. At one end of the scale there are the coins of the American colonies produced in Massachusetts (1652), Maryland (1659) and New Jersey (1682), followed by the "Rosa Americana" series struck by William Wood at Bath in the early 18th century. Even after the Declaration of Independence in 1776, distinctive coins were circulating in Connecticut, Massachusetts, New Hampshire, New Jersey, New York and Vermont. Some of them were very similar to their British counterparts, with Britannia on the reverse but replacing the effigy of George III with George Washington or a Native American. From 1776 onward there were also various attempts at federal issues, such as the "Nova Constellatio" coppers and the "Fugio" cents, before the emergence of the Federal coinage in 1792. If the numerous tokens that also circulated in the late 18th century were also included, this would be a formidable group indeed.

A similar pattern obtained in British North America, where local issues, mainly bank tokens, were produced in Upper and Lower Canada (modern Ontario and Quebec), New Brunswick, Nova Scotia and Prince Edward Island, before the Confederation in 1867. Prince Edward Island continued to issue its own coins until it joined the Confederation in 1873; Newfoundland had its own coins, until 1947.

Above (clockwise from top left): United Provinces klippe, cut peso from Curaçao, gulden of the Dutch West Indies and thaler of the Austrian Netherlands.

Above: A Dutch coin weight being used in the Caribbean. The Dutch economy was boosted by its involvement in the sugar and tobacco plantations there.

RELIGIOUS SYMBOLISM

Just as coins of the Islamic world conformed in design to the belief systems of that religion, across Christendom coins used a common Christian imagery, sometimes in a bid to convert pagans to Christianity and, later, Catholics to Protestantism.

Christian iconography was prevalent on Byzantine coinage, while in north-western Europe subtle religious symbols appeared on coins in the territories subject to Anglo-Saxon influence. In Scandinavia, prior to the Viking Age, Harald Bluetooth employed Christian symbols on coins as a part of his efforts to convert the Danes. A handful of very rare coins produced around the first millennium depict brooding symbols of divine judgment, such as the hand of God on the English coins of Aelthelred. Nordic and Anglo-Saxon coins were again united in Christian symbolism by the imperial coins of King Canute, which featured the crucifix. This ubiquitous religious icon dominated the "Long-cross" and "Short-cross" pennies that circulated in Britain for centuries.

In later medieval times, Christian imagery was employed to highly picturesque effect on the coins of the great city states of the Habsburg Empire, and also on Italian coins such as those of Venice and the Papacy in Rome.

COLLECTING BY MINT

As an alternative to collecting coins of a particular country, a number of collectors are now examining some interesting and challenging alternatives. Such lateral thinking allows you to cut across national frontiers and find common factors to shape a collection. An obvious one is to study and collect the products of a particular mint. In most cases the larger mints (such as those operated under the US Treasury Department) produce coins only for their own country, or operate on such a global scale that the field would be far too wide, but others make interesting subjects for collections. Some mints have gained contracts to produce coins for territories too small to have their own national mint.

Above: Coins minted by royalist factions during the English Civil War had their own inscriptions, ranging from monograms such as "BR" on coins of the Bristol Mint (top), to motifs such as Oxford plumes on coins of that city (middle) and a lion of York (bottom).

COLLECTING BY MINT-MARK

Collecting coins according to mint can stretch back to the time of the Roman Empire. Many collectors of classical coins, for example, concentrate on the imperial coins struck at the Roman mints in Alexandria, Carthage, Serdica, Constantinople or western Europe. All are clearly identifiable by their mint-marks and inscriptions.

At the other end of the spectrum you could concentrate on the coins that emanated from a particular mint in a country where several mints were in simultaneous operation. This might, for example, mean confining your interest to coins bearing the S mark of San Francisco, the aqueduct mark of Segovia in Spain, or the letters A or D that identify coins from Berlin or Munich respectively.

During the English Civil War the Parliamentary forces controlled the mint at the Tower of London. This meant that the Royalists were obliged to rely on various temporary mints established at Aberystwyth, Shrewsbury or Oxford and later mints in a few pockets of resistance and Royalist strongholds such as Chester, Exeter, Truro and York. Identifiable coins from these places are much sought after by those occupied in collecting the antiquities of their own town or county, quite apart from their general numismatic interest.

Below: Imperial Roman coins bearing the mint-marks of Nikomedia (SMN), in what is now Turkey, and Treverorum (TROBS), now Trier in Germany.

Above: The Birmingham Mint was established in 1860 by Matthew Boulton. It still produces coinage, tokens and medals – like this commemorative issue for the mint itself – for the international numismatic market.

PRIVATE MINTS

This leaves the private mints, which, not being tied to national contracts, offer their services to any country or issuing authority that cares to use them. At one time the Birmingham Mint, the successor to Boulton & Watt's Soho Mint, later known as the Heaton Mint, struck coins for well over a hundred governments from Afghanistan (1886) to Zambia (1968). The company produced the first issues of many countries, from Chile in 1851 and

Perth Mint

The Perth Mint remained under the jurisdiction of the Royal Mint until 1970, where it was transferred to the authority of the Government of Western Australia. Today the mint still operates from its original building, constructed from limestone extracted from the offshore Western Australian island of Rottnest, and it is one of the oldest mints in the world to do so.

Above: Regional mint-marks on Spanish coins include the letters S for Seville (top), M for Madrid (middle) and B for Barcelona (bottom).

Bulgaria in 1881 to the emergent states of the former British Empire in the 1950s and 1960s. Many of these coins bore the mint-mark H, including some British pennies subcontracted by the Royal Mint, but most were unmarked. Fortunately, the comprehensive records of this mint have documented every coin struck there. In the 1980s, it was still producing coins under subcontract from the Royal Mint, but nowadays its numismatic output is confined to

Below: The Royal Canadian Mint produces coins for the native country and other territories around the world. Like the Perth Mint, it is also involved in refining gold for coinage.

tokens and medals: the company has diversified into die-stamping and forging radiator grills for cars and casings for microwave ovens, among many other products.

The Franklin Mint of Philadelphia was founded by Joseph Segel in 1965 and a decade later was boasting that it was the largest private mint in the world. It made its business originally when the silver dollar vanished from the scene and the gambling casinos of Nevada urgently needed a substitute. Dollar-sized pieces were struck in an alloy called franklinium, which resembled silver, and in 1969 the firm got its first coinage contract. Eventually it struck coins for the Bahamas, Barbados, Belize, the British Virgin Islands, Jamaica, Panama, Trinidad and Tobago and Tunisia, but by 1975 it had largely switched to other areas including a wide range of collectables, from limited edition books to costume dolls.

PROLIFIC MINTS

The role of leading private mint then passed to a company founded by Ernest Pobjoy after World War II but which could trace its origins in die-sinking and medal-striking back to Birmingham in the late 17th century. In its early years this family firm made its reputation in the manufacture of badges, regalia and Masonic jewels, but with the development of automats and slot machines it developed a business

Above: The stunning limestone colonnaded building that houses the Perth Mint has stood on Hay Street in the east of the city since 1899.

in tokens of all kinds. These may not be coins of the realm but they must be struck to a very precise specification for use in slot machines, and it was the development of this technology that placed Pobjoy at the forefront of the burgeoning medal market in the 1960s, notably producing the sets commemorating Sir Winston Churchill (1965) and the Apollo moon landing (1969).

Another key player in the market for bullion coins and collectable editions is the Perth Mint in Western Australia. Originally a branch of the Royal Mint, it went into operation in 1899, two years before Australia's five states, which had previously functioned as separate colonies of the British Empire, were federated. The Perth Mint was established by the Australian government in response to the need to convert nationally mined gold into real currency that could be exchanged within the Western territory. During its 100 years of operation, the mint has been instrumental both in the refinement of gold into ingots and in minting circulating coins. Its refining wing was merged with a select group of private companies in the late 1990s, and this now operates separately from the state-run mint, which continues to pioneer interesting coins.

COLLECTING BY PERIOD

Focusing on the coins of a particular era presents the collector with a great opportunity to explore historical interests. There are many different options for collecting by period. You can collect the coins of a particular reign or political regime, or you can study coins belonging to several countries involved in a religious, political or monetary upheaval, such as the countries affected by colonial ambition or religious crusades; the 20th-century victims of Nazi aggression; the effects of high inflation on the coins of Central Europe after World War I, or the economic struggles of Latin American countries in more recent years.

PERIOD OF OFFICE

You might pick on the coins that were issued during the term of office of a particular head of state. The coins struck by the US Mint and its branches lend themselves well to this approach.

You could consider the variations in coinage that appeared during the periods of office of certain presidents, such as James Madison (1809–17) or Andrew Jackson (1829–37). Even the brief presidency of Zachary Taylor (1849–50) is worth considering, as a lot of changes took place in that period. The two terms of Ulysses S. Grant (1869–77) were also extremely eventful, not least because the American economy was beginning to recover and expand in the aftermath of the Civil War, and this is reflected in coinage.

Undoubtedly, the most prolific coinage, in terms of different denominations, new types, dates and mintmarks, was the record presidency of Franklin D. Roosevelt (1932–45), whose four terms spanned the Depression years and World War II. A mark of the respect in which he was held was the prompt change of the dime soon after his death. The choice of this coin was singularly appropriate as Roosevelt, himself a victim of polio, inaugurated the March of Dimes, a nationwide fundraising campaign to combat polio and care for its victims.

Below: Imperial coins of George V produced for Southern Rhodesia (top), Canada (middle) and Cyprus (bottom).

Above: US presidents (clockwise from top left) Grant, Lincoln, Eisenhower, Roosevelt and Washington.

FAO Coins

The Food and Agricultural Organization, an agency of the United Nations, has orchestrated a long-running series of coins, bearing its initials and the slogan "Food For All". Most were issued by Third World countries and some issues concentrated on family planning or ecological matters.

REGAL COINS

The monarchical approach can offer even greater scope, for kings and queens have often reigned for very long periods and in some cases coins bearing their effigies were issued in overseas colonies and dominions, as well as in their own country.

It would probably be well-nigh impossible to collect all the coins that bear one or other of the effigies of Elizabeth II, which, introduced in 1953, have now been around for more than half a century. During this long period many colonies and protectorates that had quite happily got by with coins of the mother country attained independence and introduced coins of their own. While many of these territories are now republics whose coins portray their own presidents, as head of the Commonwealth the Queen's portrait may still be found not only on the current coins of the "old dominions" such as Australia, Canada and New Zealand, but also on those of many other, newer countries, from Antigua and Ascension to Tuvalu and Zambia.

ECONOMIC UPHEAVAL

The coinage of the world in modern times (which, in the numismatic sense, began with the 16th century) was relatively stable until World War I. When war broke out in August 1914, Britain hastily withdrew gold coins from circulation and introduced Treasury notes as a temporary measure. Like income tax (a temporary measure at the time of the Napoleonic Wars), this expedient became permanent and gold has never circulated in Britain since.

This did not end the production of gold sovereigns, for they were still required overseas, but at certain periods in Britain it was illegal to possess more than two examples of the same gold coin (this concession enabled bona fide collectors to keep examples showing both obverse and reverse side by side), and during the early 1970s it was illegal for unauthorized persons to hold gold coins of any kind. Other countries have placed similar restrictions on gold at various times. Ironically, there are probably more gold coins being minted than ever before, as well as a plethora of gold bullion pieces, though none sees general circulation owing to the high (and fluctuating) value of gold.

Below: Crusader coins include a 12th-century George and Dragon copper follis of Antioch (top), a 13th-century Aleppo dirham with a star motif imitating Ayyubid design (middle) and a silver gros of Bohemond VI, struck in Tripoli.

Above: American troops arrive in Germany at the close of World War I.

Below: The 10 pfennig coin of Duren, one of many German towns that issued local coins during and just after World War I. Due to inflation, these coins had a very short life and were replaced by Notgeld (emergency paper money).

While a collection of gold coins can illustrate the vagaries of monetary practice, a popular aspect of numismatics is concerned with the rise of inflation and its impact on coinage. Again, this was largely a product of World War I, although it began with people hoarding silver and gold coins. Even base metal coins disappeared from circulation, giving rise to the local tokens described as "money of necessity". The war's immediate effect on coins, however, was the replacement of bronze and brass (required for the manufacture of shell cases) by zinc, iron or steel. This expedient was resuscitated in World War II, particularly in countries under Nazi occupation (which themselves would be an interesting subject for a coin collection).

Inflation at other times has led to frequent changes in the coinage of such countries as Iceland and Israel. It was a chronic problem in Latin American countries, and although it can be spectacularly illustrated with the colourful and prolific banknotes of the period it can also be traced in the debasement and diminution of the coins.

CRUSADER COINS

The coinage of occupied Europe in both World Wars is a good subject, with a wealth of readily accessible material for study, but many centuries earlier there was another period that resulted in some fascinating coins. In spring 1095 the Byzantine emperor Alexius I Comnenus appealed to Pope Urban II to raise an army to liberate the Holy Land from the clutches of Islam. Thus began the extraordinary but poorly understood period in history known as the Crusades.

The Crusader coins mirrored their European contemporaries but were strongly influenced by Byzantine and Islamic models. Thus, the Kingdom of Jerusalem produced a lengthy series of gold bezants, silver deniers and billon obols, while the Principality of Antioch struck copper folles and billon deniers from 1100 to 1268. The County of Tripoli (1095–1289) had gold bezants, silver gros, billon deniers and copper obols, as well as drachmae and half drachmae in the 13th century. Copper coins of various sizes were issued at Edessa between 1098 and the mid-12th century, mainly in the names of successive kings of Jerusalem, although Tancred of Sicily, Prince of Antioch, struck coins in 1104.

Asssociated with the coins of these Crusader states were the Frankish coins in Cyprus, which, nominally part of the Byzantine Empire, was a separate fiefdom carved out by Guy de Lusignan in 1192, after he was deposed from the throne of Jerusalem. His successor, Aimery de Lusignan, declared himself king in 1197, and from then until 1324 monarchs were styled as Kings of Cyprus and Jerusalem. In addition to coins in copper (of which there was a natural abundance), the rulers of Cyprus struck "white bezants" in 8 carat gold. Also in this category are the coins of the Latin Empire of Constantinople itself (1204–61).

COLLECTING BY DENOMINATION

A possible departure from the tradition of collecting coins by country or period is to group them according to their denomination or face value. When focusing on coins of a particular size or type within a country, this approach is basically an extension of one-country specialization, but it becomes infinitely more varied and interesting to trace the development and spread of one kind of coin across a continent or, indeed, the entire world.

You can concentrate on "minors" such as cents and farthings, or major coins such as dollars and crowns. Some denominations have had a particularly long history, providing scope for discussion of changes to profile and value.

BUILDING A DOLLAR-THEMED COLLECTION

The dollar – still the world's most popular denomination and the currency of choice in many countries – is a very well-travelled example. Its early history, in fierce competition with other trade currencies, was beset with difficulties and false starts.

Below: A collection of US dollars might be organized around those featuring Native Americans (Missouri centennial half dollar of 1921, top, and 1908 Indian head gold eagle, middle left), or portraits of Liberty in profile (1795 dollar, middle right), seated (1862 half dollar, bottom left) or standing (1908 gold 20 dollars, bottom right).

COLLECTING SILVER DOLLARS

Over the years there were many types of silver dollar, from the original Liberty heads with flowing hair or draped bust and heraldic eagle to the seated Liberty types whose eagle reverse is found with or without a motto. Production of ordinary dollars ceased in 1873, but trade dollars with a seated Liberty facing left and an eagle that also looked the other way filled the gap. Ordinary dollars were resumed in 1878 and continued until 1935. Production was then suspended as the silver dollar's place had been taken by the silver certificate. Coins of this type dated 1964 were struck at Denver but were never issued, and every example is believed to have been destroyed.

When dollar coins of the same diameter were revived in 1971, they were struck in .400 silver in uncirculated and proof versions, but those intended for general circulation had a copper core and a cupro-nickel cladding. Too large for everyday use, the dollar was reduced in size and re-emerged in 1979 as a 12-sided coin. In 2000 this was replaced by a larger, circular coin in a gold-coloured alloy portraying Sacagawea, the Indian guide to the Lewis and Clark Expedition.

MAKING ITS MARK

Prior to the foundation of the German Empire, in 1871, the mark existed only as money of account. It derived from the fine mark of Cologne, an expression of bullion that was widely accepted in the vast conglomeration of German states. It took several years to replace the thaler of 32 groschen used in the northern states, and the gulden of 90 kreuzer prevalent in the southern states, with a single monetary system based on the Reichsmark of 100 pfennige. A measure of compromise was

Above: The history of the German mark can be explored in the state coinage of Saxony from 1903 (top), coins of the Third Reich (middle) and the currency of East Germany, 1971 (bottom).

Left: The German mark began as a unit used only in money of account. This 19th-century German coin weight would have been used to determine weight.

reflected in the minting of 2 and 3 mark coins, equivalent to the obsolete gulden and thaler respectively, which continued until 1939.

The mark was a silver coin from its inception, in 1873, until 1916. It vanished from circulation during World War I and was engulfed by inflation in the immediate post-war period. In 1924–5 it re-emerged inscribed "1 Mark", swiftly followed by silver coins of 1925–7 inscribed "1 Reichsmark". From 1933 to 1939 the coin was struck in nickel. When it re-emerged in 1950 it was inscribed "1 Deutschemark".

Cupro-nickel coins with the inscription "Bundersrepublik Deutschland" (Federal Republic of Germany) on the obverse and the reverse showing the

Frequently Changing Designs

While most British coins in everyday use have had unchanged reverse motifs since decimalization in 1971, an exception is the pound coin, which has had a different reverse each year since its inception in 1983. The royal arms (1983) were followed by floral emblems of the four countries comprising the United Kingdom (1984–7), then heraldic motifs and, most recently, landmark bridges of Scotland (Forth railway bridge), Northern Ireland (Belfast–Dublin Railway), Wales (Menai Bridge) and England (Gateshead Millennium Bridge). Of these four architectural giants, the first three were built at various points during the 19th century, whereas the latter, which crosses the River Tyne in Newcastle, opened in 2000 and quickly became the pride of this northerly city.

Left: Pattern obverses of the recent series of pound coins, paired with their pictorial reverses. From left: the famous transport bridges of Scotland, Northern Ireland, Wales and England.

Above: A "basic currency unit" collection centred on the British farthing might include a tin farthing issue of William and Mary (top) and the many imitative tokens (bottom).

Above: The Greek drachma was an ancient currency unit, revived soon after Greece won its independence from Turkey.

value flanked by oak leaves, continued until the advent of the euro in 2001. With annual issues from up to six different mints, identifiable by a code letter, the major types of the mark would form a very large collection.

By contrast, coins with a very similar reverse, but struck in aluminium with the emblem of the German Democratic Republic on the obverse, were not adopted until 1956 and were very sporadically struck thereafter, reflecting the political division and economic disparity of the German states. The "Ostmark" disappeared when Germany was reunited in 1990. Both republics were prolific producers of 2, 5 and 10 mark coins for commemorative and special issues.

BASIC CURRENCY UNITS

Not everyone can afford to collect large, handsome silver dollars and crowns, and many numismatists focus on other, smaller denominations.

In England the "splendid shilling" of 12 pence sterling began with the testoon of Henry VII and survives today as the 5 pence in the decimal series, but it has undergone many changes of design, weight and composition over the centuries, as have its counterparts in the Commonwealth. Even the cent, usually the smallest coin in a currency range, offers immense scope, from humble US pennies to the small bronze, steel or aluminium coins of many countries. Other minor issues include the öre coins of Scandinavia or the 1 and 5 centime coins of France. The humble pfennig of Germany was successively struck in copper, aluminium, bronze, zinc, bronze-clad steel and latterly copper-plated steel, reflecting the political and economic upheavals of the 20th century.

Such coins may have little or no spending power alone, but they are vital in making up odd amounts in everyday transactions. British numismatists have a special affection for the farthing (originally the fourth part of a penny). Redundant by 1956, many have survived in generally fine condition because people who got them in change tended to hoard them in jars. Similar hoarding of bronze cents in the USA caused a currency crisis in 1982 when the price of copper rose sharply, and the US Treasury was compelled to replace bronze by a zinc alloy.

Below: Interesting and collectable ephemera often accompanies the introduction of a new denomination coin.

COLLECTING PICTORIAL COINS

While coin obverses have, traditionally, been reserved for portraits – either allegorical or symbolic figures or lifelike effigies of rulers – pictorial reverses have predominated on coins since the very earliest currencies. The splendid silver coins of 16th century Europe – guldengroschen and thaler – stimulated the development of sophisticated pictorial designs by virtue of their large size, and numismatic pictorialism may be said to have attained perfection during the 20th century.

Landmarks of national or religious significance featured on ancient coins and on some of the beautiful city coinage of medieval trading centres, and continue to be commemorated on some of the world's most recent issues. Mythical creatures such as winged deities or dragons have also featured heavily, due to their links with national folklore and identity. Animals – once symbolic of trade and economic strength – remain a popular pictorial theme, though in a world economy that relies more on mechanization than livestock they are now likely to represent a topic such as conservation. Since the 1930s, the fashion for pictorials has become increasingly linked with commemoratives and coins produced for the collectors' market.

Below: A cock and a crab on an ancient Sicilian coin (top), and images of a heraldic bear and lion on medieval coins of Germany and Zealand (bottom).

Above: Many Roman coins feature allegorical figures or landmarks (clockwise from top left): an allegorical depiction of the Tigris and Euphrates with Armenia; the Ara Pacis; a personification of "City" carrying two temples; the market on Caelian Hill.

TWO POSSIBLE APPROACHES

Two recent books, R.G. Penn's *Aspects of Medicine on Ancient Greek and Roman Coins* (Spink & Son, London, 1994) and Marvin Tameanko's *Monumental Coins: Buildings & Structures on Ancient Coinage* (Krause, Iola, 1999), explore two distinct branches of thematic coin-collecting. Tameanko, an architect, has concentrated on coins, mostly from Imperial Rome, that show identifiable buildings, such as temples, shrines, forts and triumphal arches, or engineering structures such as roadways, aqueducts and harbours. His book classifies more than 600 classical coins, featuring such landmarks as the Temple in Jerusalem, the Colosseum and the Acropolis. Two of the Seven Wonders of the World appear: the Pharos of Alexandria (the world's first lighthouse) and the Mausoleum of Halicarnassus, but it is strange that the Hellenistic kingdom of Egypt never depicted the Pyramids or the Sphinx on its coins.

Penn, a doctor of medicine, has adopted a rather different approach and used pictorial coins to illustrate the origins and development of medicine in the ancient world. Certain Greek coins portray Hippocrates and Asklepios (Aesculapius), the real and mythological fathers of medicine, and coins with mythological subjects that have a bearing on the ancient perception of illness and cures. Many coins of both Greek and Roman periods depict medicinal plants. There are also coins advocating sanitation, depicting the goddess Hygeia, healing springs and aqueducts, as well as the Cloaca Maxima (the great Roman sewer) and even Cloacina, goddess of the sewers.

Both these writers have brought to bear their professional expertise to write about their chosen coins. In the same way, many collectors develop a thematic collection that reflects their professional or recreational interests, giving numismatics a new dimension.

OTHER CLASSICAL SUBJECTS

Because so many Greek coins do not bear an inscription identifying their origin, there are books that catalogue them according to their subject-matter, and this has stimulated interest in collecting them in this manner. *Greek Coin Types and Their Identification* by Richard J. Plant (Spink & Son, 1979) is a notable example of this genre. While it was primarily intended as an

Below: Animals are closely linked with perceptions of national identity, and continue to be a popular pictorial subject on modern coins.

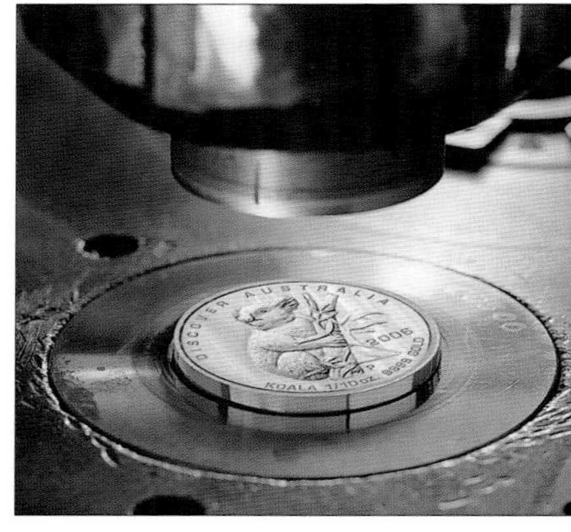

aid to identification, it serves as a very useful basis for a thematic collection. In it you can see at a glance the 116 coins showing Nike, the winged goddess of victory, or the numerous pieces that show helmeted warriors. The pantheon of Greek deities and associated heroes is set out clearly, from Aphrodite and Artemis to Zeus himself.

If animals are your choice, you can find coins showing animals fighting or feeding their young. In antiquity, bulls, either whole or in part, were a popular subject, perhaps an allusion to the value of cattle in the earliest barter economy, but dogs, wolves, sheep and goats are not far behind. Horses were a major subject, as were men on horseback or driving chariots and, of course, Pegasus the winged horse of mythology.

Lions, elephants, tigers and panthers form a veritable numismatic menagerie, while mythical beasts, such as the sphinx and the griffin, are also prominent. Eagles perching or in flight are a colossal subject, rivalling images of lions on coinage right down to the present day. Serpents, dolphins and fishes abound, as well as familiar flora.

Coins That Tell a Story

Several brass denarii of Vespasian and his son Titus have a reverse showing a date palm beneath which a woman sits weeping. To the left of the tree stands the emperor in armour, or a man with his hands tied behind his back – a captive taken in AD 70 when Titus suppressed a Jewish revolt, sacking Jerusalem and destroying the Temple. The sorrowful woman is an allegory for *Judaea capta* (captured) or *devicta* (defeated).

Above (clockwise from top-left): Coins have personified Africa, Helvetica, and Britannia both standing (middle) and seated (bottom), in female form.

MODERN PICTORIAL THEMES

The trend towards more pictorial reverses, which gathered momentum in the 1930s, yielded a good number of coins showing all kinds of shipping, from outrigger canoes to ocean-going liners. Although Germany struck some coins showing the Zeppelin airships, aviation as a theme only took off in 1983 with the celebration of the bicentenary of the first manned balloon flights; it received a tremendous boost in 2000–2, when many coins used the centenary of powered aircraft as an opportunity to show their development from the original Wright Flyer to Concorde. Both warships and military aircraft have been prominent in very recent years, on coins commemorating the military contingents fighting in World Wars and other conflicts.

Many contemporary coins are devoted to animals. Whereas earlier coins in this category merely showed them as typical examples of the fauna of a particular country, today the trend is didactic, highlighting species under threat of extinction. The People's Republic of China even launched its gold bullion series with motifs showing the giant panda, the elusive creature that has become the symbol of the World Wide Fund for Nature.

Above: A stunning medieval bishopric thaler of Münster (top), a landmark on a Turkish million lira coin and a temple on a Thai coin of Rama V.

Many pictorial coins are now issued in long thematic sets, which makes this kind of collecting all too easy. There is much more fun to be had in poring over coin catalogues, seeking out stray items on your favourite theme that will fit into your collection.

Above: This Iranian 1 rial coin is part of a series depicting mosques.

Below: A set of FAO coins issued by North Korea in 2002, depicting various modes of transport by land, sea and air.

COLLECTING PURPOSE OF ISSUE COINS

A major branch of thematic collecting is devoted to coins issued by several countries more or less simultaneously to celebrate a major anniversary of an event or personality of worldwide interest, or to publicize a contemporary event of global importance. These events are often the subject of colourful coins aimed at the collectors' market. The phenomenon of simultaneous or joint issues is relatively new, although there are some topics that, by their cyclical nature, have been the subject of coins from many countries at different times.

COMMEMORATIVES FOR COMMON PURPOSES

Philatelists describe issues by several countries celebrating the same event as omnibus issues. In numismatic terms the earliest instance of this occurred in 1617. The Thirty Years War, which split Europe on religious lines, was about to erupt when several states in Germany, Austria and Switzerland issued silver coins to celebrate the centenary of Martin Luther's Wittenberg Declaration, which launched the Reformation. Similar issues took place in 1717 and 1817. Even at the height of World War I, Saxony managed to issue a silver 3 mark coin in 1917 under the auspices of the German Empire, but only 100 coins were struck, making this quatercentennial coin the key issue in any collection devoted to the Reformation. Sri Lanka marked 2500 years of Buddhism in 1957 with a set of coins.

BIRTHS, MARRIAGES AND DEATHS

Diana, Princess of Wales, was not the first international figure to be remembered by coins of more than one country. That honour went to John F. Kennedy, who not only replaced Benjamin Franklin on the American half dollar but was also portrayed on a silver 5 riyal coin issued by Sharjah, a remarkable feat since this Gulf sheikhdom had never issued any coins previously and by this gesture flew in the face of the Islamic ban on human representation in any form. The precedent was soon followed by other Gulf States, which produced coins portraying the late President Nasser of Egypt. The portrayal of famous persons, either soon after their death (as in the case of Pope John Paul II) or on a major anniversary, such as a centenary, has now become commonplace.

Above: Austria marked the bicentenary of Mozart's birth with this 1956 coin.

SPORTING EVENTS

Arguably the most important of all events in the numismatic calendar are those pertaining to sports. If shooting is counted as a sport, some of the earliest coins on this theme are those produced in the German states and Switzerland from 1590 onward, as prizes for annual shooting contests. They endured longest in Switzerland, where silver 5 francs and gold 100 francs were struck on behalf of various cantons as late as 1939, Lucerne being the last canton to issue them.

However, the Olympic Games tower over all other sporting events. As long ago as 510 BC distinctive coins for the Games were struck by Elis, the host state. By 480 BC coins showing the winged figure of Nike (Victory) alluded to the athletes who won the events. It is believed that the beautiful large decadrachms of Syracuse dating from about 465 BC were intended as prizes for athletes at the Demareteian Games.

The modern Olympic Games were inaugurated at Athens in 1896, but it was not until they were held in Helsinki that Finland produced special coins in 1951–2 showing the Olympic rings. Since then it has become axiomatic that coins marking the Games are released by the host country, often in lengthy series. Since the 1970s, special coins have also been released by many of the participating countries as well, with separate issues for the Winter Games and Paralympics.

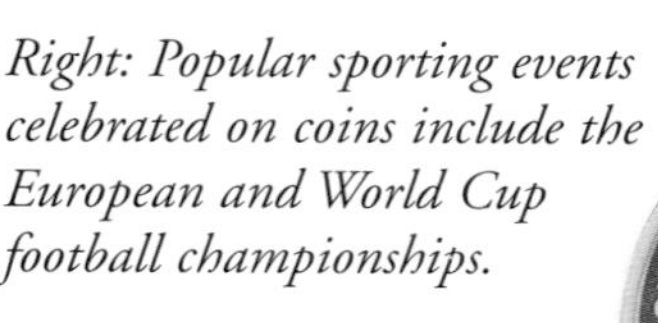

Right: Popular sporting events celebrated on coins include the European and World Cup football championships.

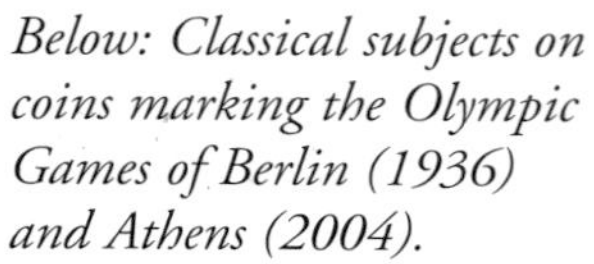

Below: Classical subjects on coins marking the Olympic Games of Berlin (1936) and Athens (2004).

Left: Silver coins from the Isle of Man celebrate British royal family events; a multicoloured memorial issue for Pope John Paul II was produced in 2005.

MILITARY ANNIVERSARIES

The end of World War II, in 1945, did not trigger off any celebratory coins for victory or peace, but in recent years the 50th and 60th anniversaries of D-Day and VE Day have precipitated widespread issues, mainly of dollar-sized coins, while coins have also marked the anniversaries of liberation, the Battle of Britain and other campaigns or individual battles. This has become a formidable subject that seems likely to prompt new issues every few years.

The nostalgia has now begun to extend to the events and anniversaries of World War I and other conflicts. Both Australia and New Zealand have issued coins to mark anniversaries of the ANZAC involvement in the ill-fated Gallipoli campaign of 1915. Czechoslovakia (and now both the Czech Republic and Slovakia), as well as Poland and the former Soviet Union, have produced a number of coins marking battles and campaigns of World War II.

ANNUAL COINS

Special coins celebrating Christmas began to appear in the 1970s but have been confined to the Isle of Man and Tonga, issuing genre and religious subjects respectively. An exception to this, however, occurred in 2000 when many countries marked the end of the second millennium with special coins.

Of much wider popularity are the coins that celebrate the lunar New Year and have reverse motifs depicting the animals of the Chinese zodiac. These coins originated in China, Hong Kong and Macao, but the practice has since spread to other parts of the world. Struck in silver or gold as well as base metal, they are often exchanged as New Year gifts.

Lunar New Year

An Australian silver bullion coin featuring a golden retriever was struck by the Perth Mint to celebrate the Year of the Dog (February 2006). The ideogram for the year appears at the top with the date at the side and the weight and fineness of the silver at the foot. The presentation set included a silver-plated pin of a matching design.

Below: This pattern 140 ecu coin from the Isle of Man, showing a Viking ship, was produced when the ecu seemed to be the likely European coin, though later the euro was adopted instead.

Below: A crown from the Isle of Man ingeniously celebrating the Millennium with the centuries from 1000 to 2000 around the edge and a clock ticking away the seconds to the Millennium.

Below: Many German states, such as Mecklenburg-Schwerim (top), produced coins for royal weddings. A porcelain issue (bottom) produced in Germany to mark the Occupation of Singapore.

COLLECTING SERVICE TOKENS

We have already seen how "token" coinage was issued as a replacement for legitimate currency during periods where the latter was in short supply. However, tokens also exist that do not have a cash value, but nevertheless have a real worth in so far as they represent a specific service and are used in exchange for that service. In some cases they also represent value by being expressed in certain small commodities. This aspect of tokens was once neglected but they are now avidly collected and studied, often as an adjunct to the study of local history.

Below: An Australian brass token for use in amusement centres and a Canadian token giving a humorous spin on the practice of tossing a coin.

Below and right: A scene in a German brothel in 1916, and an "All Night Token" from Prescott, Arizona, for a night at Kate's Place on Whiskey Row.

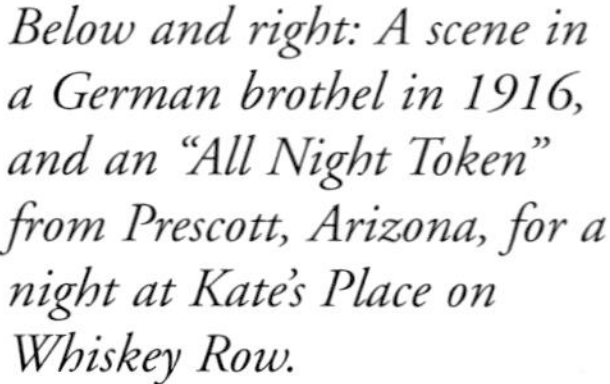

Above: Numbered Industrial Surveys security token with police telephone number and instructions to the finder to return it to the nearest police station.

Below: Replicas of pre-decimal British coins used in the souvenir shop at Ironbridge Gorge, England.

One of the main reasons for these tokens is security; as they have no cash value, they cannot be spent and therefore do not present any temptation to would-be thieves.

BROTHEL TOKENS

Tokens exchangeable for services date from Roman times. The most notorious were those known as *spintriae*, denounced by the first-century poet Martial as "*lasciva numismata*", which scholars regard as brothel tokens or tickets of admission to spectacles of the grossest indecency, such as the Floralia, a licentious festival celebrated by prostitutes in honour of the goddess Flora. They were struck in brass and bore erotic motifs and Roman numerals. The largest hoard was discovered at Capraea, where the lecherous Emperor Tiberius held his orgies.

Brothel tokens, often with scenes of copulation as well as hearts and cupids, were also produced in Europe and the USA in the 19th and early 20th centuries, with naïve inscriptions such as "Good for a Night at Kate's Place".

ADMISSION TOKENS

Tokens in brass, silver or ivory were given to actors in the 18th and 19th centuries as complimentary tickets for use by their friends, while tokens valid for any performance during the season of a particular play were made of pewter, copper or brass and sold to patrons of the theatre. Special tokens, often in silver, were issued to those who subscribed to an entire season, or to shareholders and directors of a theatre company. They often had a panel or cartouche where the name of the patron and a box or seat number could be engraved.

Metallic admission tickets were also struck for the pleasure gardens such as Ranelagh or Vauxhall in 18th-century London. The idea was taken up by the Tivoli Gardens in Copenhagen and has extended in recent years to many other theme parks and tourist attractions. In this category may be included replicas of obsolete British coins (with contemporary dates) used at Ironbridge, Shropshire, birthplace of the Industrial Revolution, in the shops on the site, which charge old prices.

MILK TOKENS

Relics of an era when milk was delivered to doorsteps in glass bottles are the milk tokens used in Britain, Australia and New Zealand. These tokens, in various metals or coloured plastic, solved a problem that caused inconvenience and irritation to householders and milkmen alike – the theft of coins put in the empty bottles in payment for the next delivery. A petty thief raiding a whole row of doorsteps at night could

Below: A 25 øre token from a Danish amusement park.

net a tidy sum for a night's work. The most desirable tokens bear the name of the town and dairy (an example from St Kilda, Victoria, recently sold online for $60), but usually they are inscribed or stamped with the initials of the dairy or even the individual milkman, with numerals indicating the number of pints. Now that milk comes in disposable cartons, these tokens are a thing of the past – and very collectable.

TOKENS FOR SLOT MACHINES

Coin-operated public pay-phones were another tempting target for the street bandit and the cost of repairing the damaged equipment induced the authorities in many countries (mainly in continental Europe and Asia) to adopt a system whereby the public purchased tokens from a post office or tobacconist's kiosk. As these could not be exchanged for coins, there was no point in breaking into the machines to steal them. Furthermore, the actual sale price could be varied or increased without the expense of altering the slot machines. Similar tokens were later devised for other machinery that would normally have been activated by a coin in the slot, from parking meters to car-washing and laundry facilities.

Below: Transport tokens from Dunedin, New Zealand (top), and Paris (1921, middle), and a range of American bus or subway tokens (bottom).

Tobacco and Beer Tokens

These brass tokens advertising Samson cigarette tobacco (1987) and Hofmeister Lager not only promoted the products but also represented a small discount off the next purchase.

GAMING TOKENS

Called jetons (from the French *jeter*, "to throw") or counters, gaming tokens have been in existence since the 15th century. They are used as money substitutes in games of chance, although they originated as the metal discs used in medieval accountancy on a chequerboard or counting table (the "exchequer"). Brass counters with an imitation of the heraldic device of so-called Spade guineas, and with the royal titles replaced by such slogans as "In memory of the good old days" were used in early 19th-century Britain.

Gambling chips afford security to casinos as they have no real value until converted into cash. Although most modern chips are made in coloured plastic they may also be found in aluminium, brass or cupro-nickel. Small tokens, also known as pub checks, have been used for games of chance in public houses and entertainment arcades.

TRANSPORT TOKENS

In 1549, metal tokens were adopted at Regensburg to control bridge crossings and to represent a fee levied on those who wished to enter a walled town after the gates were closed for the night. The system spread to the USA in the 1790s, and Pennsylvania was the first state to introduce tollgate tokens on the turnpike highways.

In the 19th century the use of tokens extended to public transport of all kinds, from ferries to trams, buses and

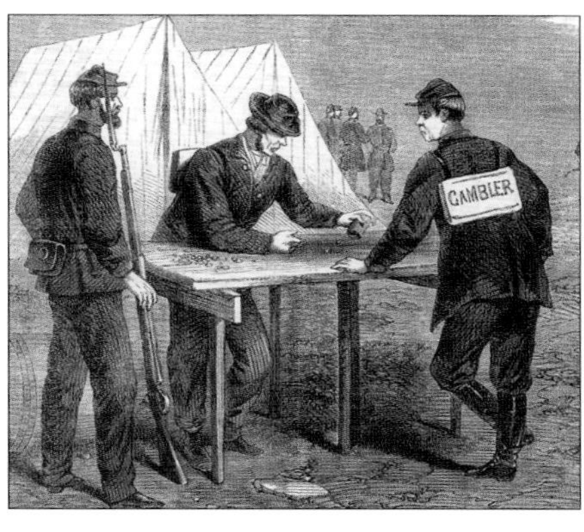

Above: American Civil War soldiers being punished for gambling.

Below: Gambling tokens from the West Point Casino, Tasmania (1974) and the Palm Beach Club, London (1968).

subway systems. They were often given to employees of post offices or other public utilities, enabling them to travel free on company or municipal business. Most bear a civic or corporate emblem, but many modern examples feature vehicles. Associated with them are the tokens used at public lavatories or restrooms in bus and railway stations, where they are given only to bona fide passengers on presentation of a travel ticket. There are also numerous checks, tokens and tallies formerly used by railway companies, coal mines and market traders. Usually utilitarian in design, they are actively collected for their historical interest.

Below: A bronze sugar estate token of Mauritius with the head of Victoria.

COLLECTING COIN LOOKALIKES

Sooner or later every collector acquires one or more puzzle pieces, which look like coins and may even have a name or value inscribed on them but cannot be located in any of the standard catalogues. It seems obvious that such pieces must have had a valid reason for their existence, otherwise why would anyone have gone to all that trouble and expense to manufacture them?

BOGUS COINS

Imitation Spade guineas made of brass instead of gold have already been mentioned. They bore the profile of George III on one side and the royal arms in a spade-shaped shield on the other. Anyone who could read the motto inscribed on the coins – "In memory of the good old days" – would have no problem recognizing these pieces for gaming counters, but trouble arose when unscrupulous people passed them off as real gold guineas (worth 21 shillings, or £1.05) on unsuspecting (and illiterate) members of the public.

In the same category comes a brass piece that very closely resembles the gold sovereign current in the 1830s, with the monarch's effigy on the obverse and a reverse motif which, at first glance, might be mistaken for St George and the Dragon but which actually shows a crowned horseman. In place of the usual inscription are the words "To Hanover", which provide the clue to the identify of this piece. Under Salic Law, which insisted that a male heir must always take precedence,

Below: Plastic play money from Hong Kong of the kind often used to teach children about different denominations.

Above: The obverse and reverse of mid-Victorian model coins struck by Joseph Moore of Birmingham, forerunners of today's bimetallic coins.

Queen Victoria could not succeed to the Hanoverian throne and her place was taken by her unpopular uncle, Prince George, Duke of Cumberland. It is believed that the "Cumberland Jack", as it is commonly known, was produced as a satirical piece, but it was often passed off as a genuine sovereign on the public.

MODEL COINS

At various times in 19th-century Britain the question of reducing the size and weight of the cumbersome copper or bronze coins was debated. The government was always reluctant to take such steps, clinging to the notion that even base metal coins should have an intrinsic metal value that was fairly close to the face value. It took well over a century for the authorities to abandon this notion and introduce the decimal coinage in small sizes, which weighed a fraction of their £sd predecessors.

As a possible solution to the problem, however, Joseph Moore, a Birmingham die-sinker and token manufacturer, produced a model coinage consisting of tiny bronze coins with a plug of silver in the centre. These model coins, portraying Queen Victoria, were intended to improve the coinage in general, as well as providing pieces whose intrinsic worth was the same as their circulating value. Similar bimetallic model coins were produced by Harry Hyams. These had a brass centre in a bronze surround, and ranged from the crown of 5 shillings (about the size of the modern 2 pence coin) to the halfpenny.

A tiny bronze coin was produced in 1887, with Victoria's profile on one side and St George and the Dragon on the other. The inscription "Jubilee Model Half Farthing" indicates its commemorative nature. Another such item is the diminutive silver piece portraying the infant Prince of Wales (later Edward VII), which was struck as a toy coin shortly after his birth in 1841. Model and miniature coins of this sort were popular as novelties in Christmas crackers during the 19th century.

Very tiny replicas of American coins are sold as souvenirs in the USA. At the other end of the spectrum are gigantic replica coins, often in the form of money-boxes or paperweights.

Spoof Coin

From 1966 until his death in 1987 Leonard Joseph Matchan was lessee of the tiny island of Brecqhou in the Channel Islands. As well as issuing stamps for a local postal service to Sark he created this spoof bronze coin, denominated "one knacker". As it was clearly never intended to be taken seriously, it did not render him liable to prosecution, unlike the owner of Lundy Island, whose coins of 1929 got him into trouble with the law and had to be withdrawn.

Above: "Fantasy" Tibetan coins include this restrike of a quarter rupee by the Shanghai Mint (top) and a Sichuan fantasy dollar (bottom).

PLAY MONEY

Tiny replicas of current coins are produced in many countries for use as toy shop or dolls' money. Long ignored by numismatists, these pieces were sought out by collectors of dolls' house furniture and the like, but have now attracted the attention of coin collectors as well. Actual-size toy money, for teaching children arithmetic and the basics of shopping, is also collectable.

During the transitional period from sterling to decimal currency in Britain (1968–71) many types of instructional money were produced, in plastic, metal or stout card, and these are now keenly collected as mementos of the greatest currency reform in Britain since Roman times. They were surpassed, however, by the instructional kits produced in the 12 European countries that adopted the euro in 2002. In many instances the kits, which included imitation coins, were supplied to every household.

Below: The publicity campaign that preceded British decimalization was aimed at businesses as well as the public, with measures taken, such as the release of 'play' coins, to ease the passing of the old currency system. In the event, the reforms were implemented within weeks.

FANTASY COINS

In 1925 a businessman, Martin Coles Harman, purchased Lundy, an island in the Bristol Channel, and proceeded to issue his own stamps. In 1929 he went so far as to issue his own coins, with his profile on one side and a puffin on the other. Because they were in the same metal, size and weight as the contemporary British penny and halfpenny, Harman was prosecuted under the Coinage Act of 1870, convicted and fined £5. The coins were withdrawn, but the dies were later used for an issue dated 1965, raising funds to preserve the island as a nature sanctuary.

In 1976, the self-styled Prince Leonard of the Hutt River Province (actually a sheep range in Western Australia) issued coins, from the aluminium 5 cents to the gold $100, which gained catalogue status, but not for long.

In Asia, the number of forged countermarks on Sichuan rupees and Tibetan coins during the early 20th century is such that a leading expert on Chinese coinage, Wolfgang Bertsch, self-published an entire volume dedicated to *Tibetan Fake Coins and Fantasy Countermarks* in 2003.

ELONGATES

Not really a coin lookalike but a novel way of converting a coin into a tourist souvenir or advertising piece, the elongate was invented by the American, Frank Brazzell, who also produced the machines to create them. The coin is placed between two rollers, on one of which is engraved a motif. When the handle is turned the coin emerges in an elongated shape with the original obverse and reverse removed and a new image on one side. Thousands have been produced in the USA. Often termed elongate or 'flat' pennies, they feature a broad range of subjects, from publicity for local businesses to whole series on dinosaurs or baseball heroes. The idea eventually took root in Britain in 1981, when the law forbidding the defacement of coins was repealed. Elongates are now also popular souvenirs in France, Germany and other European countries, and often feature famous landmarks.

Above and left: A 2 euro plastic token and a German elongate from a 5 pfennig coin, as a souvenir of St Bartholomä's Church on the Königssee.

Below: A cased set of miniature replicas of American coins.

COLLECTING ERRORS AND VARIETIES

Serious collectors love to acquire items that are in some way off the beaten track or out of the ordinary. They look out for subtle differences in apparently similar coins, as well as various types of errors that arise in the course of manufacture but somehow get into general circulation, and sundry oddities such as coins hastily withdrawn from circulation because of a mistake in design.

Above: A cupro-nickel 1 baht coin of Thailand, with the design struck approximately 10 per cent off-centre.

Above: Victorian Shield-back sovereigns bearing die variation marks 36 and 52.

DIE VARIATIONS

Right back in the days of the earliest hammered coinage, it soon became apparent that both the hammer and the anvil were liable to show signs of wear after the first few hundred coins had been struck. In many cases the designs engraved on the parts that actually struck the blanks could be sharpened up by re-engraving all or part of the surface. No matter how carefully this was done it gave rise to slight changes in the appearance of the coins.

As one side tended to wear out sooner than the other, scholars have often been able to trace the sequence of production by the combination of obverse and reverse impressions during the production of a particular coin. Hoards can often be a good source of large quantities of coins for such detailed studies.

This phenomenon is by no means confined to hammered coinage. Modern coins are produced in their millions, entailing the production of hundreds of dies. Theoretically, they should be identical but, inevitably, variations large and small tend to creep in. Sometimes these variations are quite deliberate, a prime example being the British gold sovereigns with shield reverse from 1863 to 1874, which bear tiny numbers engraved between the rose at the foot of the design and the knot tying the two laurel branches. All Shield-back sovereigns in this period should have a number ranging from 1 to 123 (though far fewer numbers were used in many years, while others may exist but have not yet been recorded). Some sovereigns of 1863 were issued without die numbers before the scheme started, and the same is true of 1874 coins after the practice was abandoned, but coins dated 1872 without die numbers are not uncommon. Conversely, a few sovereigns of 1863 have been discovered with the tiny numerals 827 impressed on the truncation of Queen Victoria's neck. Michael Marsh, the recognized authority on the gold sovereign, has recorded two examples with the die number 22 on the reverse and four without the die number, making the 827 coin one of the greatest rarities of British coinage.

Left: This mis-struck Indian rupee of 1984 makes a curious sight, with its design around 75% off-centre.

Much more common are coins in the American series with the last digit of the date overstruck, a practice of the US Mint in the 19th century to change the date in line with federal law, which required coins to bear the actual year of striking. American coins also exhibit such die variations as large or small numerals. The coins of most countries feature die variants, ranging from slight changes in the actual design (such as the high and low horizons on British pennies) to the number of serrations in the edge, or the number of beads in the border of the rim.

ERRORS

Accidents in manufacture give rise to some peculiar errors. A "brockage" is a coin with only one design, normal on one side and appearing incuse on the other. This occurs when a coin already struck adheres to the die and strikes the next blank to pass through the press. "Clash marks" are mirror-image traces on a coin struck by a pair of dies that have been damaged by having been struck together without a blank between them. Other mis-strikes occur

Below: Tibetan local government issues struck using different dies.

Above: A curved clip on a Sudanese 10 ghirsh coin of 1980.

Right: A British 10 pence struck by the Royal Mint in the scalloped collar of the Hong Kong $2, one of a batch shipped out to the colony, where the error was discovered.

when the dies are not properly aligned, and the design on one or both sides of the coin appears to be off-centre.

Such errors are ephemeral and are usually of little more than curiosity value. Much more interesting and desirable are hybrid coins, known to collectors as "mules", in which the obverse is not matched with its regular or official reverse. Mules have been recorded from Roman times, the obverse referring to one emperor and the reverse referring to a predecessor or another member of the imperial family. Accidental mules in recent times have resulted from the mixing of dies at mints where coins of several countries are being struck. This gives rise to such famous mules as the Coronation anniversary crowns with Ascension and Isle of Man dies, or 2 cent coins with Bahamas and New Zealand dies. Restrikes of rare American coins have been detected in which the dated die has been paired with the wrong reverse, such as the 1860 restrike of the rare large cent of 1804.

Sometimes the wrong collar is used, the most spectacular examples being British 10 pence coins with a scalloped edge, which actually got into circulation in Hong Kong as $2 coins before the error was detected.

COUNTERMARKS

There have been many occasions on which marks have been applied to coins after they were issued, analogous to overprints on stamps. This is a normal procedure in cases where the value of the original coin has to be changed, and it was a widespread practice in Britain in 1800–4, when Spanish and other foreign coins were stamped with the effigy of George III to pass current for 5 shillings. The Bank of England even overstruck Spanish coins with a new obverse and Britannia on the reverse, but traces of the original design usually showed through.

Unofficial countermarks make an unusual sideline. Although it was a serious offence to deface coin of the realm it was common practice to engrave or strike pennies with a lover's initials. In some cases more elaborate motifs, such as entwined hearts, were stamped. In Northern Ireland, many British and Irish coins of recent years have been countermarked by the IRA, UDA, UVF and other paramilitary factions, a curious memento of the "Troubles".

Above: Mules, pairing Italian and Russian rulers from a 20 lira coin of 1863 and 20 kopeks of 1867 (top) and colonial issues for Sierra Leone (obverse, bottom left) and Macao (right), mistakenly paired in the 1790s.

A particularly large and fascinating group consists of Spanish coins, or more often pieces of them, countermarked with values and the initials of various islands in the Caribbean, officially authorized as currency there, mainly in the 18th and early 19th centuries, before the introduction of a more regular coinage.

Below: Pennies of George III and George V with engraved or punch-marked letters, perhaps intended as love tokens. One has the incuse stamp of a broad arrow, an official government mark but here applied quite illegally.

Countermarked Dollars

At the end of the 18th century there was a severe shortage of silver coins in Britain. A large quantity of Spanish-American dollars (8 reales) had been captured and these were pressed into service, circulating as 5 shilling pieces and officially authorized by means of a countermark consisting of the bust of George III in an oval, or later octagonal, frame.

COLLECTING PATTERNS, PROOFS AND EPHEMERA

Serious numismatists are not content with the coins that actually circulate, but also seek out pieces that trace the development of a coin from the earliest concept to the finished article, as well as the various versions produced by mints to supply the collectors' market, and even the packaging and promotional material associated with each new issue.

PATTERNS

Pieces resembling coins, prepared by the mint to the specifications of a new design or on the authorization of the coin-issuing authority, but differing in some respect from the coin that actually reaches the general public, are known as patterns. This category also includes pieces produced by mints when tendering for a coinage contract – an actual piece of metal being a much more effective sales tool than a sketch or a photograph.

Patterns may differ from the final coins as issued in the type or quality of metal used, but more often than not they differ in details of the design. Sometimes these differences may be quite minor, such as the addition of some small detail, but they may be quite radical, or show entirely different motifs to those used for the issued coins. Patterns, especially if they exist in a sequence, are of particular use in illustrating the evolution of the coin.

Allied to them are the test pieces that occur when a new die is being tried out prior to going into actual production. These have a superficial resemblance to coins, in that they are usually struck on blanks of the correct weight and size, but the impression may vary from a mere ghostly outline to a nearly perfect image as the minter adjusts the machinery. Many test pieces, however, are known in lead or some other soft metal, pulled as the engraving of the dies is in progress, in order to make sure that no mistakes have arisen.

PROOFS

The die test pieces were, in fact, the true origin of proofs, but by the 19th century it had become standard mint practice to make impressions of coins on specially polished blanks for presentation purposes, and in more recent years this has become just another medium for selling coins to collectors.

Above: A 17th-century Christiania pattern silver strike of a gold coin.

Left: A pattern produced by VDM (a German manufacturer of coin blanks), with a reverse depicting the fortress of Altena, where the company is located.

The practice has now reached the point at which many deluxe coins are released only in proof form. They are undeniably very handsome but some purists are interested only in coins that actually get into general use, and some catalogues classify proofs of this kind as "non-circulating legal tender" (NCLT). One suspects that many of these beautiful pieces have never been accorded legal tender status.

PIEDFORTS

Derived from the French for "heavy or strong foot", the term "piedfort" denotes a coin struck with normal dies but on a blank of a much greater thickness than usual. The practice originated in France in the 15th century, when gold coins of twice or three times the normal thickness were struck for presentation to royalty, courtiers and foreign dignitaries. It spread to England in the reign of Henry VII. Examples of the gold sovereign, introduced in 1489, are known in double or treble weights. So far, only one of each has been recorded, and it is assumed that the king intended them as presentation pieces rather than high-value coins for general circulation.

This practice, long dormant, has been revived by the Royal Mint in recent years. The 50 pence coin, normally struck in cupro-nickel, was

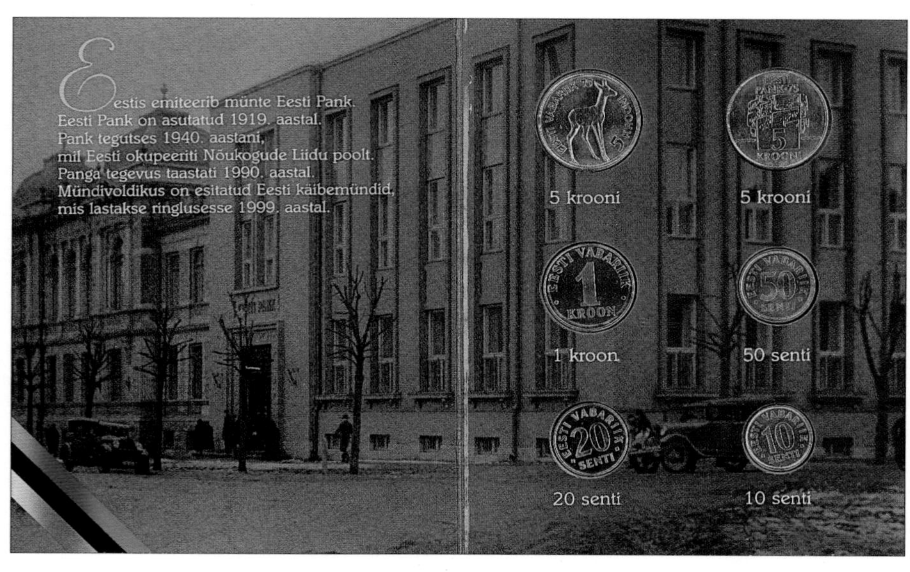

Below: A presentation folder from Estonia with a proof set of coins encased, 1999.

PNCs

Philanumismatic covers (PNCs) combine philately and numismatics and consist of a souvenir cover with stamps and a postmark as well as a coin encapsulated at the side, the coin and stamp being appropriate to each other.

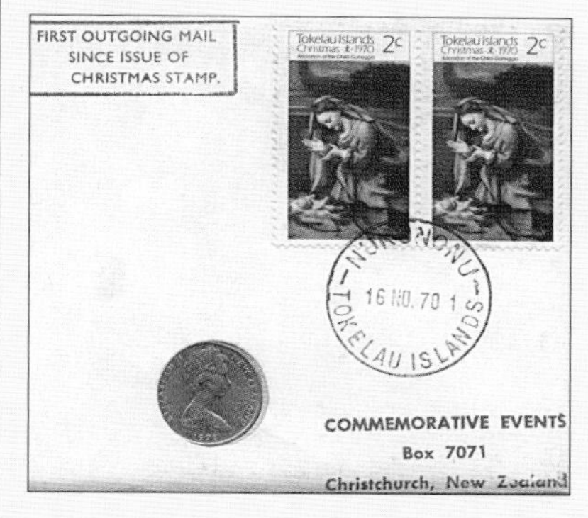

released in 1973 as a silver piedfort but only about 20 pieces were produced and they now command four-figure prices. Even the small 20 pence coin, introduced in 1982, was issued as a piedfort silver proof and this is now standard practice for pound coins (whose designs are changed each year) and commemorative 50 pence coins.

PACKAGING

Traditionally, proofs and year sets were tastefully packaged in leather cases lined with blue satin or plush. While this is still the case for the more expensive items, most mints have resorted to other forms of packaging, which are not only cheaper but more eye-catching. The vogue developed in the 1960s when year sets became fashionable. In this era rigid plastic cases were adopted, the coins within them being inserted into stout cards printed with the national arms and salient details. In other examples the coins were merely encapsulated in thin plastic envelopes, although in some cases these were then inserted in paper envelopes with stiffener cards bearing descriptions of the coins. The current trend is towards much brighter, more colourful coin folders, which can be housed intact in coin albums. Different forms of packaging are often used, distinguishing between simple sets of circulating coins, sets in a superior finish but still in base metal, and the deluxe proofs in precious metals.

Below: A Dutch bronze pattern coin of William III tendering two possible reverse designs.

Two other recent developments seek to draw the sister hobbies of philately and numismatics closer together. Both originated in Germany, where coins and stamps have long been collected by the same people. The first is the philanumismatic cover, examples of which are now produced all over the world, while the second is the *Numisblatt*, which has so far made little headway beyond the country of origin. It consists of a stiff colour-printed card bearing stamps with special cancellations, with a coin encapsulated for good measure. *Numisblätter* are very similar to PNCs but are generally much larger and more decorative.

EPHEMERA

Serious collectors also watch out for the various pieces of ephemera associated with coins. These range from press cuttings and leaflets about new or forthcoming issues to mini-posters used by banks. Coins incorporated in premium giveaways or advertising gimmicks are also worth considering. Even chocolate packaged in metal foil stamped to resemble coins is collectable – assuming you can withstand the temptation to eat the contents.

Acts of Congress or other parliamentary bodies authorizing coins, as well as government reports on proposed changes, are also eminently collectable. Photographs and the original artists' thumbnail sketches reflecting the initial design concept for a coin are very desirable but are understandably rare. Such items are keenly fought over when they occasionally appear in the auction rooms.

Above: A piedfort silver jeton depicting the assassination of William of Orange in 1584 (top) and a gold coronation jeton of Moscow.

Below: Collectable ephemera might even include hand-held beam balances and brass coin weights; such pocket balances were a must in the days of coin-clipping to check that coins were of full weight.

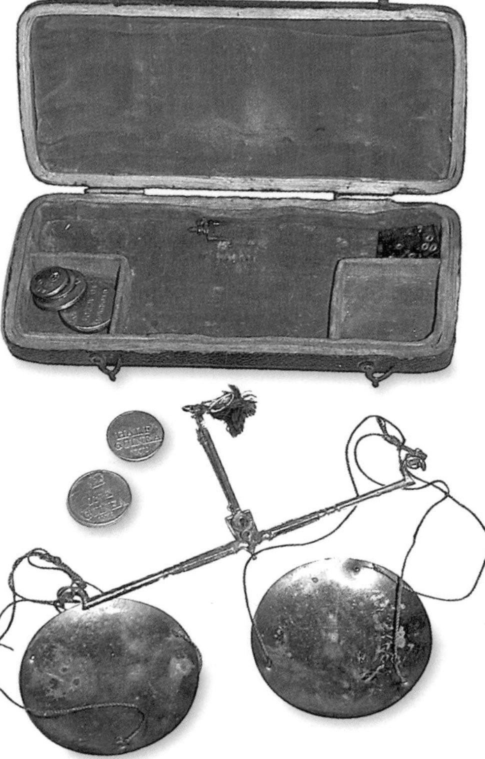

BUYING AND SELLING COINS

Although it is possible to form a collection from coins picked up in change or in the course of foreign travel, sooner or later you are more likely to want to start planning acquisitions in order to add to your collection in a meaningful way. There are several ways of acquiring new specimens: by exchange with fellow collectors, from dealers and by bidding at auction.

COIN CLUBS

All collectors inevitably accumulate material that is surplus to their requirements: such coins can very often be exchanged with fellow enthusiasts and new items added to the collection in return. If you are at all serious about your hobby, you will want to subscribe to a periodical devoted to the subject, and through it you can make contact with others through the small ads. You can also place an advertisement yourself stating what you have to offer and what you are looking for in exchange.

Most towns of any size have a coin club or numismatic society. Joining such a club gives you the chance to meet other collectors and swap coins. Your public library or museum will have information on clubs in the area, as will coin collectors' magazines. Many countries have a national numismatic society, perhaps with a website, which may be able to advise on local societies. Failing this, try an internet search.

Some clubs set aside time before or after each meeting for swapping, and in many cases one or more dealers will be in attendance. Others confine this activity to auctions once or twice a year. Apart from the chance to add to your collection, a coin club is the ideal venue to broaden your interests and improve your knowledge of coins.

Many of the larger numismatic societies host regular exhibitions and talks, and will be able to advise on the programme of events for the coming months. Some have extensive libraries of coins and other research facilities open to the public, or to members.

Fairs and Forums

National societies such as the American Numismatic Assocation are extremely active at local level, organizing events ranging from coin marts to seminars on the role of coins in education and research. These occasions offer collectors a great opportunity to interact.

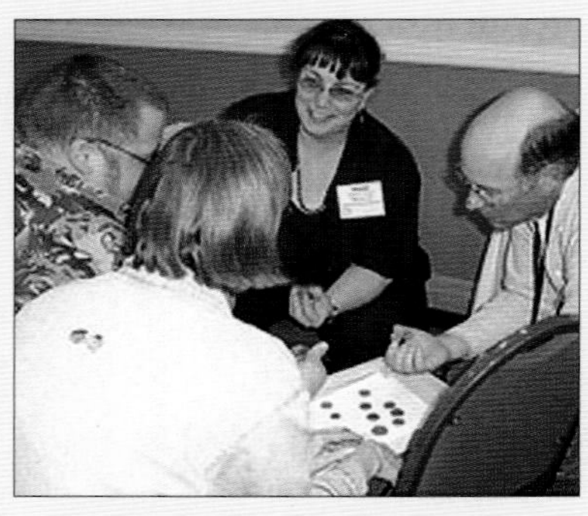

BUYING FROM DEALERS

A measure of how the hobby has grown in recent years is the increasing number of coin dealers operating in many European countries and elsewhere in the world, while the USA (which always had many more coin dealers than other countries) has retained its position in this respect.

Many dealers regularly take classified advertisements in coin magazines and are also fully listed in the various coin yearbooks and trade directories. A number of websites provide details of dealers who specialize in the coins of a particular country, region, period, denomination, or theme. The fact that the majority of dealers – from international companies specializing in tax-free gold to smaller-scale collectors offering information on their speciality and the opportunity to buy – now operate over the web means that the location of an outlet is much less important than in the past. As a result, it's possible to view images of and information about, and

Home > ANA Club

Join a Coin Club!

Club Directory

Are you interested in discovering and exploring the world of money with other people who share your interest? Then, join a coin club! There are over 500 ANA member coin clubs in the United States and other countries.

Local Coin Clubs

Most cities and towns have a local "home town" coin club and you are invited to attend and share the camaraderie! Generally, clubs meet once or twice a month in a bank, library, school, church or other public building. Some clubs meet at a restaurant and the meeting includes dinner, but they are the exception. Local clubs commonly take the name of their town like the West Chester, Long Beach or Colorado Springs Coin Clubs.

Above: National numismatic bodies often promote clubs at local level and offer searchable, on-line directories.

purchase, coins from anywhere in the world, greatly increasing the possibilities for making new acquisitions.

BOURSES AND FAIRS

These radical changes in trading practice, combined with high overheads, have meant that the number of actual coin shops has dwindled, but at the same time buying coins by mail order has escalated dramatically and many dealers now send out regular lists to their clients. In addition, there are now many bourses, fairs and dealer circuits, giving collectors and dealers frequent opportunities to meet face to face.

Below: You may be fortunate enough to live in a town with a local coin shop, where you can purchase coins and kit.

Annual fairs such as Coinex in London and the American Numismatic Association (ANA) World's Fair of Money or National Money Show provide opportunities for hundreds of collectors to exhibit and sell their wares. The United States is again the leader in this field, regularly hosting 10–20 high-profile coin shows per year in as many different states. The advantages of buying coins face to face or over the counter are obvious: you can examine the dealer's stock and be satisfied as to its condition before you buy.

AUCTIONS

The most important source of coins nowadays is the auction. Many of the finest collections and rarest coins are disposed of by auction, but this is also the place where bargains are to be found, and it may be the best method of buying a small collection intact to form the basis of a larger one.

London and New York continue to dominate the auction scene, with the largest and most prestigious salerooms, but there is also an increasing number of smaller auctions in provincial towns and cities. Much of the bidding at coin auctions is done by post, but there are so many pitfalls about buying in this way that it is advisable to get a coin dealer to bid on your behalf. Most dealers will do this for a small commission – it's simply a case of contacting a few to judge who can best work within the criteria you set. Most auction houses now add a buyer's premium to the sale price and this, with tax where applicable, can add considerably to the amount you have to pay. The general advice is, set your limit and stick to it.

SELLING COINS

Most collectors over-value their coins. Consequently, when they come to sell their collections, they are rapidly disillusioned and think that dealers are trying to cheat them. There have also been times when coins were subject to speculation, usually when the stock market is low and traditional forms of investment are showing a poor yield. There are many horror stories of investors who burned their fingers at this end of the market. However, you should have confidence in those dealers who belong to a reputable trade association; you will find the appropriate logo in their display advertisements. You should remember that there is often quite a difference between a dealer's buying and selling prices – after all, dealers have to make a living and cover their overheads.

Some coins are in greater demand than others and it may be that your collection consists of material of which there is a more than adequate supply chasing a smaller demand. Condition is the biggest problem, as collectors – even very experienced ones – are sometimes over-optimistic about the state of their treasures. Dealers, who are handling coins every day, develop a keen eye for condition and are quick to spot the flaws and blemishes that collectors often overlook, but which materially affect the value of coins.

Dealers will at least make you an offer for spot cash, and such transactions are swift. Selling by auction may net you a higher return in the long run, but several months can elapse between consigning coins to the saleroom and the actual auction, with a further wait for the proceeds, less the auctioneer's commission. In fact, despite the existence of dealers and auctioneers, and the rapid growth of on-line trading, many collectors still prefer the long-established method of selling direct to other collectors. Most clubs provide opportunities for this, and even arrange meetings for buying.

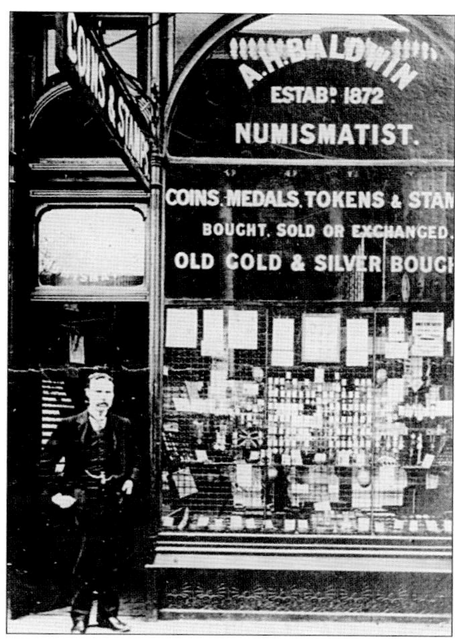

Above: World coin and medal dealer Baldwin's was established by the English numismatist Arthur Henry Baldwin in 1901. He began by selling coins from his home in Plumstead, London, before setting up shop with his three sons.

Right: While expensive gold coins might be out of your reach, investing sparingly in a few choice, popular collectables will always reap returns in the long run.

ON-LINE NUMISMATICS

The IT revolution has changed everyone's life in many different ways, so it is not surprising that it has also had a major impact on numismatics, bringing fellow collectors closer together, offering an unrivalled tool for research and, above all, for buying and selling coins on-line. Home computers with broadband connections are becoming increasingly commonplace. Indeed, the time is not far off when these facilities will be as accessible to the public as is the telephone or television today.

DEALERS' WEBSITES

Only a few years ago, websites set up by coin dealers were more or less a complete novelty. Only about a dozen dealers and auctioneers in Britain offered this facility, and, it must be admitted, their sites were decidedly patchy. All that has changed. Every coin dealer is now on-line – he or she could not survive in the numismatic trade otherwise – and their web pages are generally highly professional and easy to follow, usually with excellent links. You can view coins on screen in great detail, and buy in seconds with a click of a mouse.

Below: Part of the fun of round-the-clock on-line bidding is waiting to see whether you have been successful.

SEARCHING FOR COINS

Type the word "coins" into an internet search engine, for example, and you might be confronted with no fewer than 20 million different options. It would of course take many years to browse through these: the term is just far too vague. More useful, though still very general, search terms might include "old coins", "US coins", "rare coins" or "gold coins".

As a rule, global search engines will push larger or sponsored sites to the fore, which is likely to include wholesalers advertising a vast range of goods besides coins, such as Amazon or Yahoo Shopping. National mints also compete for collector's attentions, as well as the tourist market, many with sites offering a digital 'tour' through the mint, and the chance to buy the latest issues.

To narrow down the search, you can try a more specific subject. Keying in "Crusader coins", which is a relatively esoteric topic, might still bring up as many as 47,000 sites. A refined search for the coinage of Baldwin II, King of Jerusalem, will pull up far fewer sites, so the chances are that you would be able to find out everything you would ever need to know on that topic.

Naturally, as with any internet search, you need to be discriminating about what you find and verify its reliability (which is often possible by cross-checking factual material with other websites), but there is now a great deal of high quality numismatic information on the internet.

CONTACTING OTHERS

CoinTalk, the discussion forum that is likely to pop up near the top of any numismatic search, is designed as a non-esoteric medium for debate "where Numismatists, Collectors, Dealers and Novices [can] gather to discuss Coins". As soon as you open this site you are confronted with a bewildering array of choices. On the left side are links to a large number of dealers' websites, including "a comprehensive A to Z to reputable coin dealers" provided by www.shopperuk.com, which, in turn, opens up a whole world of reputable coin traders.

To get into the forum itself, you have to register, but this takes only a few minutes and you are then free to join in the discussion on any coin topic imaginable. Typical topics under discussion include "What's it worth?" (a perennial question), errors on coins, ancient coins, US coins, world coins, and so on. In other words, it is a worldwide network of fellow enthusiasts. Topics of discussion such as "Variety Nickels" might drawn in hundreds of threads and posts as collectors discuss the minutiae of dates, mint-marks and die variants in this ever-popular American coin. Coin forums are also an excellent place to post an advertisement about hard-to-find coins – you are certain to have a response from a collector somewhere in the world who has recently made a similar purchase, or who knows of a specialist dealer. The numismatic grapevine is a valuable entity for collectors seeking to make new acquisitions or simply to learn more and, though still in its infancy, the potential for growth is huge.

Above: Powerful digital cameras enable razor-sharp images of coins to be posted to dealers' websites. If you are hoping to sell your own coins in this way, remember that sharp images bolster confidence among collectors.

BUYING ON-LINE

As noted previously, most coin dealers now maintain websites, with detailed descriptions and high-resolution images allowing you to make purchases safely from anywhere in the world.

There are also many on-line auction sites on the internet, but the largest and best-known is eBay, where many of the coins on sale are offered by collectors themselves. This is often the medium of choice for buyers and sellers alike, because of the breadth of the audience it attracts and because, despite its ever-growing scope, it remains dedicated to secure shopping. Refining your bidding technique is part of the fun; rather like a gambler, it is often wise not to show your hand and place a serious bid until the final stages of the auction.

The larger auction sites usually offer a facility whereby you can view an enlarged picture in which any knocks and scratches would soon be apparent. Some collectors tell salutary tales about images being doctored and sharpened up, so that a coin that appears on screen as "brilliant uncirculated" turns out to be no more than about "very fine", but this does not seem to be the general experience. Moreover, security is tightening. Ebay's "Code of Conduct for Selling Coins and Paper Money", published on its website and created in conjunction with leading numismatic bodies such as the ANA, aims to stamp out the passing off of reproductions and copies as the genuine article by effectively blackballing any unscrupulous sellers who do so.

The biggest problem with the global nature of online auctions can be that, for a particular coin you are interested in, the closing time may be 3.30 p.m. on the other side of the world, which happens to be the middle of the night where you are. You can either leave a high bid, in the hope that you outbid rival bidders, or set your alarm clock and follow the actual bidding to a nail-biting conclusion in the small hours.

When buying coins in your own country, you can usually send a personal cheque through the post, but the use of PayPal is pretty well mandatory for purchases from abroad. It is easy to register, and thereafter purchases in American or Australian dollars, euros, or any other currency are automatically translated into your own and debited to your credit card – a painless and very fast process.

COIN PROFILES

Vendors' descriptions on auction sites are not always as helpful as they might be. Some wax lyrical about the origins of the coins but omit the important details. Larger sites do try to steer would-be sellers in the right direction by including essential questions about the item(s) as part of the formulation of an on-line profile or account. Ultimately, however, the success of a transaction largely comes down to the buyer having a clear idea of what they want, and confidence in the sale. In this respect, it is very important that on-line vendors scan the coins intended for sale at as high a resolution as possible. Serious, potential buyers will be frustrated by images scanned at 100dpi or less, as these make it impossible to judge whether the coins on offer really live up to their professed grading.

International marketplace

Described as the world's on-line marketplace, eBay was founded in 1995 by Pierre Omidyar of Echo Bay, California, who was convinced that the internet could be used as a tool for buying and selling. The site has revolutionized the coin trade, with about 300,000 lots of coins of all periods and countries on offer at any moment.

376
JULIO-CLAUDIAN DYNASTY
Issues of Claudius in honour of his deceased sister-in-law Agrippina Senior
(† AD 33)
1906 Brass sestertius.
BRITANNICUS
See also nos. 1869–70 and 1907.
AGRIPPINA JUNIOR
LARGE CENTS
1829-1837
Medium letters
note letter spacing.
1837-1839
Small letters;
note letter spacing.
1837, All kinds 5,558,
1837, Plain Cord,
Medium Letters
1837, Plain Cord,
Small Letters
1837, Head of 1838 ....
1838 6,370,200

WORLD DIRECTORY OF COINS

This is a comprehensive historical survey of coins across the whole world, from antiquity to the present day. Each section delves into the coins of a particular continent and, within these parameters, the coins of individual countries, or a group of nations that are related politically or geographically. Coins often chart interesting developments, among them the establishment and subsequent break-up of empires, the fight for supremacy among dynastic rulers, the arrival of religious or political doctrines from foreign lands, or the changing economic fortunes of once-prosperous, but later war-ravaged, nations. In the modern age, coins reflect the efforts of new republics to wrest themselves free of colonial power, or the rise and fall of Communism in the Soviet Union, Czechoslovakia and Yugoslavia. There are denominations that have become influential via foreign trade, or currencies born of economic unions among impoverished nations in Africa and South America. There are coins made of the precious metals favoured in centuries past, but gradually replaced by cheaper alloys. Each continental section includes a thematic feature with coins that reflect the culture, art or history of a particular region, and these offer rational options for building superior global collections.

Left: Piecing together the identity of your coins is one of the most enjoyable parts of the hobby. Above, left to right: iconic silver coinage of newly-independent Mexico, gold trading ducat of Habsburg Hungary, the first 'struck' copper coinage of the central Chinese mint.

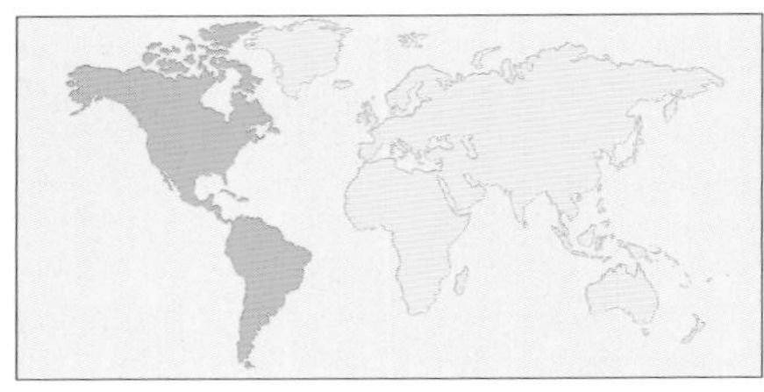

AMERICA

The earliest coinage consisted of crude pesos struck in the Spanish colonies from locally mined silver. The *peso a ocho reales* (8 real piece) later became the standard currency medium throughout the French and British colonies in North America and laid the foundation for the dollar system.

CANADA

One of the world's largest countries, Canada was colonized by the French after 1534. Although John Cabot discovered Newfoundland in 1497, it was not annexed by England until 1583, and no attempt was made to colonize it until 1610. Britain formally acquired Hudson's Bay, Newfoundland and Nova Scotia in 1713 and gained control of New France in 1763 after a decisive victory at Quebec in 1759. The early colonists used French, English, Spanish or Dutch coins, but suffered frequent shortages of money from France and resorted to using playing cards, stamped locally. In 1670 silver coins denominated in sols were struck at the Paris Mint, specifically for use in New France, but were unpopular as they could not be used to buy supplies from France. A second attempt to provide a purely local coinage was made in 1721, when the mint at La Rochelle struck copper deniers, but they were no more successful. The British colonies were supplied with gold and silver coins from England, but subsidiary coinage was in the form of tokens struck by the major banks. Federal coinage was adopted in 1870, following the Confederation of Canada in 1867. New Brunswick, Nova Scotia and Prince Edward Island issued copper or bronze coins before joining the Confederation in 1873, while Newfoundland had its own coins until 1949, when it joined Canada.

Left: The dollar of 1982, celebrating the 125th anniversary of Confederation, reproduces the painting entitled The Fathers of Confederation *by Robert Harris, showing delegates at the Quebec Conference of 1864, which led to the unification of the colonies in British North America.*

BANK TOKENS

From 1800 the chronic shortage of coins from Europe led tradesmen to issue copper tokens, but these were gradually suppressed from 1835 and replaced by copper or bronze tokens issued by the major banks. The first of these were the Bouquet Sous of the Bank of Montreal [1–2], followed by issues in Quebec showing the bank emblem with a farmer or bank building on the reverse [3], though the last issue had the farmer on the obverse and an allegorical scene on the reverse [4]. The Bank of Upper Canada (now Ontario) struck pennies and halfpence in 1850–7, with St George and the Dragon on one side and the bank's arms on the other [5–6]. The tokens were withdrawn in 1858, when bronze cents were introduced for the whole province of Canada.

PROVINCIAL COINAGE

Copper or bronze halfpence and pennies were issued by the Maritime Provinces before they joined the Confederation. New Brunswick had coins showing Queen Victoria on the obverse [7] and a shipping scene on the reverse, while Nova Scotia had coins featuring a Scottish thistle on one side and busts of George IV or Victoria on the other [8]. Both colonies also struck cents in the 1860s. Prince Edward Island produced only a single coin, a cent of 1871 [9–10], before joining the Confederation in 1873, but Newfoundland [11–12] had its own coins until 1949.

DEFINITIVES

The coins of the Confederation bear the effigy of the reigning monarch to this day. Prior to 1935 the reverses showed the value in words, set within a wreath and surmounted by a crown, but in 1920 a small cent was adopted with maple leaves flanking the value; two years later the nickel 5 cents replaced the tiny silver coin [13]. In 1937 a pictorial series was adopted: the reverses showing maple leaves (1 cent), beaver (5 cents), the schooner *Bluenose* (10 cents), caribou (25 cents) and national arms (50 cents) continue to this day [14–18]. The silver dollar first appeared in 1935, celebrating the silver jubilee of George V, and its motif of a Voyageur canoe was retained until 1987, when it was replaced by a circulating coin in aureate-bronze plated nickel depicting a loon [19]. A bimetallic $2 coin showing a polar bear was added in 1996 [20]. Gold coins began with a Canadian version of the British sovereign (1908–19) alongside $5 and $10 coins (1912–14). Gold bullion coins in the Maple Leaf series have appeared since 1983.

BULLION COINS

Canada is one of the world's leading producers of precious metals, and this inspired the development of the Maple Leaf in 1979, a coin containing a troy ounce of pure gold, originally struck to a fineness of .999. The reverse featured the national emblem, hence its name. The legal tender value of $50 appeared on the obverse. Since 1983 this coin has been struck in .9999 fine – "four nines gold" – which appears alongside the maple leaf. In addition to smaller gold coins, Canada has also produced platinum bullion coins since 1988.

From Barter to Beaver

Relics of the days when Canada's chief industry was fur trapping are the coins struck by the Hudson's Bay Company. These brass pieces, with the arms of the company on the obverse, had a cryptic reverse showing ligated H B over E M, then 1 or a fraction, with N B at the foot. The last initials were actually an error for M B ("made beaver") and denoted a value in terms of prime beaver pelts, which were highly prized for men's hats.

COMMEMORATIVE COINS

From 1935 the silver dollar was the preferred medium for commemorative coins, but since 1943 Canada has also produced many as base-metal circulating coins, beginning with the 5 cent coins in tombac brass or chromium-plated steel instead of nickel (which was required for the war effort). These substitutes featured the V-sign and had a victory slogan in Morse code around the rim [21–22]. The bicentennial of the nickel industry (1951) resulted in a special 5 cent coin, and this set the precedent for the entire series from 1 cent to $1, with motifs and double dates to celebrate the centennial of Confederation (1967).

More recently, 5 and 25 cent coins [23] have often been used as commemoratives, notably the 1992 series of provincial quarters [24] to mark the 125th anniversary. Special issues have proliferated since the 1970s, notably the series for the Montreal Olympics (1973–6) and the Calgary Winter Games (1985–7) [25–26], and the 150th anniversary of Toronto [27]. Gold and platinum have also been used in recent years for coins in thematic sets featuring Canadian wildlife.

16 17 18 19 20 21 22 23 24 25 26 27

UNITED STATES DEFINITIVES

Although the Continental Congress of 1777 resolved to establish a national mint, it was not until 1792 that the first mint was opened in Philadelphia. Up to that time the currency was chaotic, with base-metal subsidiary coins valued in pence or halfpence and silver based on the Spanish dollar. In common parlance the Spanish real was known as a "bit", and a quarter dollar was known as a "two-bit coin", a term still used to signify 25 cents. From the outset however, the infant United States adopted a decimal system (following the examples of Russia and France), although the original 10 cent piece soon changed its name from "disme" to "dime". An interesting feature of United States coins is the inclusion of initials denoting the various branch mints, which were set up to refine and coin gold and silver mined locally. This practice survives to this day, although most US coins are now confined to base alloys.

Left: Among the prototypes for a distinctive American coinage were the coins that have acquired the nickname of Fugio Cents, from the Latin word meaning "I fly" inscribed over a sundial. This reminder that time flies and the more trenchant legend "Mind Your Business" are believed to have been suggested by Benjamin Franklin. The reverse shows 13 rings, symbolizing the original states.

STATES OF THE CONFEDERATION

From the Declaration of Independence in 1776 until the introduction of a federal coinage in 1792, it was left to individual states to produce subsidiary coins. Massachusetts struck cents and half cents depicting a Native American and the eagle [1–2], but others, notably Connecticut, New Hampshire, New York and Vermont, imitated British and Irish coins, often with busts of George Washington laureated in the Roman manner and looking suspiciously like George III [3]. Even the seated Britannia was only slightly modified for many of the reverses.

EARLY COINS

The first coins consisted of cents and half cents, followed by silver dollars [5–6], half dollars [7–8] and half dimes (5 cents) in 1794, and the dime [11–12] and quarter dollar [13] in 1795. The half cent vanished in 1857 when the size of the cent was considerably reduced [4]. The remaining six denominations have continued ever since, although now for all practical purposes only the coins from 1–25 cents generally circulate. Some odd values have been struck from time to time, including the bronze 2 cents (1864–73) [14–15], the silver 3 cents with a shield in a star (1851–73) [16] and a larger piece in nickel with a head of Liberty and the value in Roman numerals (1865–89) [17–18]. Between 1875 and 1878, 20 cent coins appeared briefly, showing a seated figure of Liberty on the obverse and an eagle on the reverse.

The silver half dime, with the seated Liberty on one side [9] and the value in words on the other [10], continued until 1873 but was challenged in 1866 by a larger coin minted in nickel with a shield obverse and the value in numerals on the reverse. Both coins circulated side by side for several years and the latter acquired the nickname – nickel – by which it is still commonly known today, even though the circulating "silver" coins (dimes, quarters and half dollars) have been produced in a similar alloy since 1964.

The mid-19th century gold rush had a massive impact on US coinage, reflected by the dominance of gold in the eagle ($10), the double eagle ($20) [21–22] and its subdivisions of half ($5) and quarter ($2.50), deriving its name from the reverse motifs, which showed an American eagle in various guises, either heraldic or flying [19–20] or even walking. As if this were not sufficient, the 19th century saw tiny gold dollars as well as $2, $3, $4 and $50 denominations, though some of these were intended for commemorative purposes. Following the California gold rush of 1849, gold coins of 50 cents or $1 were struck locally in addition to the federal gold dollars. Many of these tiny coins were octagonal in shape and fairly basic in design [23].

MODERN COINS

Although the figure or profile of Liberty dominated American coins for many years, there were some attempts to replace her with other motifs. When the size of the cent was reduced in 1857 Liberty was replaced by a flying eagle, followed two years later by the head of a Native American wearing a war bonnet [30]. This motif continued until 1909, when it was replaced by a bust of Abraham Lincoln, marking the centenary of his birth [24]. Almost a century later it is still in use, second only to the world's longest-running coin design – Pistrucci's St George and the Dragon on the British gold coins. In 1943 cents were struck in zinc-coated steel [24–25]. In 1959, on Lincoln's 150th anniversary, the ears of wheat [25–26] were replaced by a Lincoln Memorial reverse [27–28].

The Indian Head Penny, as it is commonly known, inspired the changes made to the nickel in 1913,

Above: The profile of Dwight D. Eisenhower on the dollar of 1971.

When Precious Metal Replaced Base Alloy

Between 1942 and 1945 the nickel was actually struck in silver. It may not be a precious metal but nickel was vital to the war effort, hence its replacement by coins containing 35 per cent silver alloyed with copper and manganese. To distinguish the silver from the nickel coins a mintmark was placed above the dome on the reverse; these marks included a P – the first (and for many years the only) time the coins from the main mint at Philadelphia had been thus distinguished.

when pictorial motifs were used for both sides. James Earle Fraser produced the head of a Native American chief based on profiles of John Tree, Iron Tail and Two Moon, but the "buffalo" on the reverse (which gives this coin its nickname) was actually Black Diamond, the American bison in the New York Zoo. In 1938 it was replaced by designs portraying Thomas Jefferson (obverse) and his home, Monticello (reverse). Nostalgia being what it is, the Buffalo reverse was revived in 2005.

George Washington [29] replaced Liberty on the quarter in 1932, the bicentenary of his birth, while Franklin D. Roosevelt was the first president to receive this honour barely months after his death [31]. Similarly, Kennedy (1964) and Eisenhower (1971) appeared on the half dollar and dollar, the former replacing Benjamin Franklin and the Liberty Bell, which had graced the half dollar since 1948.

AMERICAN COMMEMORATIVE AND SPECIAL ISSUES

Although the United States was one of the first countries to produce commemorative coins (1893), this practice was overdone in the 1920s and 1930s to such an extent that it was virtually abandoned in 1938. No fewer than 48 different half dollars were produced in this first period, but with variants in date and mint-mark the total rose to 142, which collectors eventually protested at as being excessive. In the same period there was one quarter and one silver dollar, plus a pair of quarter eagles and two massive $50 gold coins. Apart from three circulating, double-dated coins celebrating the bicentenary of the Declaration of Independence (1976), commemoratives were not generally revived until 1982. Output since then has far exceeded that of the first period.

Left: The United States struck a number of gold commemoratives for the Pan-Pacific Exposition in 1915, marking the opening of the Panama Canal. Many, like these half-dollar coins, had typically ornate designs. Among the most collectable, however, are the gold $50 coins struck at San Francisco in 1915, which circulated in circular and octagonal versions [1–4].

EARLIEST COMMEMORATIVES

The first half dollars appeared in 1892 to celebrate the 400th anniversary of Columbus's voyage to America, as well as to publicize (and help finance) the Columbian Exposition in Chicago. This opened in 1893, hence coins of both dates were issued [7–8]. The half dollar bears the bust of Columbus on one side and on the other his flagship *Santa Maria* above the twin globes representing the hemispheres. The Ladies Committee of the Exposition pressed for a coin of their own, resulting in the silver quarter portraying Queen Isabella. Tiny gold dollars were struck between 1903 and 1922 to mark the centenaries of the Louisiana Purchase and the birth of Ulysses Grant [5–6]. William McKinley, assassinated in 1901, had the unusual distinction of appearing on one of the Louisiana coins of 1903 as well as coins of 1916–17 with his memorial on the reverse. The last of these tiny pieces marked the inauguration of Grant's memorial. Gold quarter eagles appeared in 1915 for the Pan-Pacific Exposition celebrating the completion of the Panama Canal, and in 1926 for the 150th anniversary of Philadelphia as the cradle of the Revolution. A silver dollar bearing the conjoined profiles of Washington and Lafayette appeared in 1900.

SILVER HALF DOLLARS

A silver half dollar was included in the set of 1915 marking the Pan-Pacific Exposition, but no further commemoratives of this denomination appeared until 1918, when the centennial of the state of Illinois was marked by a coin portraying Lincoln and an eagle [12–13]. Two years later the tercentenary of the Pilgrim Fathers was marked by coins showing a Pilgrim (obverse) and the *Mayflower* (reverse). In the same year a coin celebrated the state of Maine, with its arms on the obverse and the value on the reverse, establishing the precedent for several others commemorating statehood anniversaries [14–17]. Native Americans featured on the reverse of the Missouri Centennial half dollar in 1921 (with frontiersman) [18–19], and on the obverse of the Oregon Trail memorial in 1926 (with covered wagon on reverse)

The Spirit of '76

Although the definitive obverses were retained in 1976, the quarter, half and dollar bore the double date 1776–1996, with entirely new motifs on the reverse. A drummer boy of the Continental Army and Independence Hall, Philadelphia, graced the quarter and half respectively, while the dollar featured the Liberty Bell with a full Moon in the background, alluding to the recent Apollo missions.

[20–21]. Ulysses Grant was again commemorated on a half dollar of 1922 [10–11]. In the early years the events honoured were relatively important and included the Huguenot-Walloon tercentenary (1924) and the 150th anniversary of Cook's landing in Hawaii (1928), but by 1930 the pace of issues was escalating as the importance of the events diminished: even individual towns petitioned Congress for coins to mark their anniversaries. This reached its nadir in 1936, when no fewer than 16 coins appeared, celebrating the centenary of Bridgeport, Connecticut, the opening of the Bay Bridge linking San Francisco and Oakland, and even the opening of the Cincinnati Music Center [22–23]. More portentously, a silver half dollar was struck in preparation for the 75th anniversary of the Battle of Gettysburg in 1938. It featured conjoined busts on the obverse, plus two shields flanking a fasces (the ancient Roman symbol for authority and power over life and death) on the reverse.

Not only were these issues too frequent, but rumours of manipulation and speculation brought the programme into disrepute. Nevertheless, they are handsome examples of the numismatic art, and most are now quite expensive because the average mintage was very small. The post-World War II exceptions, honouring Booker T. Washington and George Washington Carver, were produced in plentiful quantities on a nationwide basis, and were even reissued in subsequent years to satisfy public demand.

MODERN COMMEMORATIVES

After a gap of almost three decades commemorative half dollars resumed in 1982, to mark the 250th anniversary of the birth of George Washington. Since then, they have been used sparingly, for the centenary of the Statue of Liberty, the bicentenary of Congress, Mount Rushmore's golden jubilee, the 450th anniversary of Columbus, the Bill of Rights and World War II.

The shape of things to come was manifest in the coins launched in 1983 for the forthcoming Olympic Games in Los Angeles, followed by coins for the 1994 World Cup soccer championship, hosted by the USA and, more recently, the Centennial Olympic Games in Atlanta. The last were celebrated by no fewer than six gold $5, ten silver dollars and six cupro-nickel half dollars [24–27]. Apart from these Olympic coins, half dollars have not been issued since 1996. The preferred denomination is the silver dollar, retaining its traditional size and weight.

Modern commemorative issues are much more prolific than the pre-war half dollars but tend to be restricted to events and personalities of national or international importance. Particularly poignant are the 1994 coins honouring US prisoners of war and Vietnam veterans. By contrast, the USA is now following Canada's example, with low-value circulating commemoratives [9].

16 17 18 19 20 21 22 23 24 25 26 27

THE STATE QUARTERS OF 1999–2008

Certain American coins, notably the commemorative half dollars of the early 20th century, alluded to particular states, but this was haphazard and piecemeal. Conversely, even individual towns and cities have been honoured solely because they petitioned Congress for a coin marking their jubilee or centenary. Every state of the Union is honoured equally for the first time in the ten-year celebration that began in 1999 and continues at the rate of five coins a year.

HOW IT ALL BEGAN

Although the 13 colonies declared their independence in 1776 and fought a long and bitter war to secure their freedom in 1783, a federal constitution was not finally drawn up until 1787 and then had to be ratified by each state. The first to do so was Delaware, on December 7, 1787. Pennsylvania followed five days later, and then New Jersey on December 18. Georgia ratified the Constitution on January 2, 1788, and Connecticut a week later. These five states were therefore selected for depiction on the quarter dollars released in 1999.

On December 1, 1997, President Clinton signed Public Law 105–124 (the 60 States Commemorative Coin Program Act), authorizing the United States Mint to celebrate each state with a special coin. The general circulating versions of the five coins issued each year have a copper core and a cupro-nickel cladding. They are struck at Philadelphia and Denver, identified by the P or D mint-marks below the motto on the obverse. Proof versions of each coin are struck at the mint in San Francisco and bear the S mint-mark.

The quarter was chosen for this ambitious series because it is the most widely circulated coin, as well as the largest of the four coins in everyday use. The US Mint invited the governors of each state to submit suggestions for the designs on the reverse of each coin. These were considered by the Mint, the Citizens' Commemorative Coin Advisory Committee and the Commission of Fine Arts. They were then sent to the Secretary of the Treasury for final review and approval.

No other quarters are being struck during this ten-year period. Five quarters are being released each year, in the order in which the states ratified the Constitution or attained statehood.

Below (clockwise from top-left): state and keystone (PA), Charter Oak (CT), statutory George Washington obverse used for all quarters, Delaware River crossing (NJ), Caesar Rodney (DE).

Above (clockwise from top-left): Jamestown (VA), young Abraham Lincoln (IL), Helen Keller (AL), Kitty Hawk (NC), Gateway to Discovery (FL), pelican (LA), space odyssey (OH).

DIVERSITY OF SUBJECTS

Obviously, when there is only a fairly limited amount of space for a motif, the choice of subject is very important. What is intriguing is the wide range of subject matter depicted on these coins, reflecting different outlooks and attitudes across the United States.

The designs for the first coins, issued on behalf of the states that were quick to ratify the new Constitution, have adopted a historical approach. Delaware chose a figure on horseback, Caesar Rodney, who, like the much more famous Paul Revere, made a midnight ride of 130km/80 miles in a thunderstorm on July 1, 1776, to break the deadlock in the Delaware vote for independence. A major-general in the Delaware militia, he held more public offices than anyone else in a career spanning 40 years. Connecticut chose its Charter Oak, but the most dramatic motif is to be found on the New Jersey quarter, with the caption "Crossroads of the Revolution" below the image of Washington crossing the Delaware to defeat the British at Trenton, the turning point in the war. A Minuteman – a member of the colonial militia, who fought the British from the outset, appears on the Massachusetts coin.

Above: Many states have chosen famous landmarks. Mount Rushmore appears on the South Dakota quarter.

HISTORIC EVENTS AND PERSONALITIES

Some of the states formerly ranked among the earliest colonies allude to events of another era. Virginia shows ships at Jamestown, which celebrates its 400th anniversary in 2007. By contrast, others have selected events and celebrities of much more recent vintage, ranging from a young Abraham Lincoln (Illinois) to Helen Keller (Alabama), who overcame both deafness and blindness to teach others. Appropriately the coin also bears her name in Braille. Ohio alludes to its role as the birthplace of aviation pioneers with an astronaut, John Glenn, in a spacesuit and the *Wright Flyer*. The latter is also featured on the coin from North Carolina, where the first flight actually took place near Kitty Hawk in December 1903.

Guitars and a trumpet celebrate the musical heritage of Tennessee, an oblique reference to jazz pioneer W.C. Handy and, of course, Elvis Presley. Florida has the slogan "Gateway to Discovery", contrasting a Spanish galleon with the Columbia Shuttle.

LANDMARKS

Some state quarters have picked an outstanding landmark. The strange geological feature aptly named the Old Man of the Mountain is shown on the coin from New Hampshire, while the Statue of Liberty was an obvious choice for New York. Other manmade features that appear include the most easterly lighthouse (Maine) and the dome of the state capitol (Maryland). Missouri has chosen the great arch at St Louis in the background to a scene showing the Corps of Discovery, led by Lewis and Clark, setting off on their expedition in 1804.

MAPS AND SPECIALITIES

Many of the designs incorporate a map of the state, often with the state bird such as the pelican (Louisiana), the great Carolina wren (South Carolina) or a loon on one of the 10,000 lakes of Minnesota. Arkansas features the mockingbird, an ear of corn and a diamond, alluding to the fact that it is the only state where diamonds are mined. Pennsylvania includes an allegorical statue with the caption "Virtue Liberty Independence", while Texas has the lone star and Georgia has a peach. Other states omit the map and concentrate on what they are best known for: cattle and corn (Wisconsin), sailing (Rhode Island), magnolias (Mississippi), breeding horses (Kentucky) and car racing (Indiana).

By the time the series is completed in 2008, with coins representing New Mexico and Arizona, which gained statehood in 1912, and Alaska and Hawaii, which attained that status in 1959, collectors worldwide will have a better picture of the various maps, birds, landmarks and achievements that characterize each State of the Union.

Above (clockwise from top-left): Old Man of the Mountain (NH), Statue of Liberty (NY), Pemaquid Point (ME), Lewis and Clarke (MO), Statehouse Dome (MD).

Below (clockwise from top-left): Camel's Hump (VT), musical heritage (TN), Great Lakes (MI), Minuteman (MA).

Below (clockwise from top-left): First Flight (NC), Lone Star (TX), cattle and cheese (WI), peach (GA).

Below (clockwise from top-left): Ocean State (RI), magnolia (MS), Indy Car Races (IN), thoroughbred (KY).

BAHAMAS, BERMUDA AND WEST INDIES

Contrary to popular belief, the Bahamas and Bermuda are not in the West Indies but lie in the North Atlantic rather than the Caribbean. Barbados was regarded as one of the Windward Islands but lies well to the east of the archipelago, while Trinidad and Tobago are at the southern end of the islands, off the coast of South America. In the 17th and 18th centuries, throughout the Caribbean, extensive use was made of Spanish, French and British coins, cut into pieces and countermarked for local circulation.

Left: The earliest coinage in this area consisted of the Hogge Money of Bermuda, produced in 1616 and so called on account of the image of a pig on the reverse, alluding to the wild hogs that succoured shipwrecked mariners. The image has been used on the reverse of 1 cent coins since their inception in 1970.

BAHAMAS

The Commonwealth of the Bahamas is an archipelago of about 3000 islands, cays, rocks and reefs east of Florida. The Bahamas have the distinction of being the first land sighted by Columbus in 1492, but they were colonized by the English in 1626 and, although they attained full independence in 1973, the British monarch remains the head of state.

A penny with the effigy of George III and the colony's badge was struck at Birmingham in 1806–7. British coins were legal tender until 1966, when distinctive coins from 1 cent to $5 were adopted with the bust of Elizabeth II on the obverse and images of island fauna and flora on the reverse [1–2]. The Bahamian sloop (25 cents) and blue marlin (50 cents) allude to the main tourist attractions. The same reverses were retained for a new series in 1974, with the arms of the Bahamas replacing the Queen's effigy [3–4]. The original series was struck at the Royal Mint; from 1974 to 1985 they were produced by the Franklin Mint and are now produced by the Royal Canadian Mint. Small gold coins marked the adoption of the new constitution (1967) while cupro-nickel or silver commemoratives have appeared since 1974, notably celebrating anniversaries of the arrival of Columbus.

BARBADOS

Although the island was discovered and named by the Portuguese in 1563, it was not settled until 1627. It remained in British hands from then until it achieved independence in 1966, Elizabeth II continuing as head of state.

Countermarked Spanish silver (1791–9) and copper tokens with a Negro head obverse and Neptune reverse (1788–92) [5–6] were followed by mainly British coins. Coins of the British Caribbean Territories (Eastern Group) were in use from 1955 to 1973, when a distinctive series from 1 cent to $5 was introduced [7–9], with the arms of the island (obverse) and landmarks, birds and fishes (reverse). Double-dated versions appeared in 1976 to mark the tenth anniversary of independence. Gold coins since 1975 and $10, $20 and $50 silver coins since 1981 have been struck as commemoratives, and they include the world's first cricket coin (1991).

BERMUDA

The "still-vex'd Bermoothes" of Shakespeare's *The Tempest*, the island was settled involuntarily when a shipload of British colonists bound for Virginia was wrecked there in 1609. The settlement became permanent in 1612. Apart from the crude Hogge Money (in denominations of 2, 3, 6 and 12 pence), Bermuda had a token coinage from 1793 [10–11] until 1842, when British coins became legal tender.

Bermuda abandoned sterling [12–13] in 1970 and adopted the dollar of 100 cents. Birds, fish and flowers form the subjects of the reverses, while various effigies of Elizabeth II have appeared on the obverse [14–18]. A brass $5 coin was added in 1983 for general circulation. A series of 25 cent coins appeared in 1984, with the arms of Bermuda or its ten parishes on the reverse, to celebrate the 375th anniversary of the colony. Large silver (and latterly cupro-nickel) dollars have served as a commemorative medium since 1970 while higher values ($2, $5 and $25) have been produced for the same purpose since 1975. Gold coins from $10 to $250 have also been issued for special events and anniversaries.

The Bermuda Triangle

Since 1996 Bermuda has produced coins to publicize the great mystery of navigation known as the Bermuda Triangle. The coins have, appropriately, three sides and are denominated as $3 or a multiple. The first coins ($3, $6 and $30) showed a map, a compass and a sinking ship; later issues have featured specific ships, such as the *Sea Venture*, wrecked in 1609, and the *Deliverance*, built by the survivors.

TRINIDAD AND TOBAGO

Discovered by Columbus in 1498, these islands were colonized by the French and Dutch but captured by the British in 1797 and formally annexed in 1814. Originally administered as separate colonies, they merged in 1888. They formed part of the British West Indies Federation until 1962, when they became an independent state, adopting a republican constitution in 1976.

Spanish, French or British countermarked or cut coins circulated in Tobago (1798) and Trinidad (1804 and 1811 respectively), followed in 1825 by British coins, which were replaced in 1955 by those of the East Caribbean. Distinctive coinage (1–50 cents) was adopted in 1966, with numerals of value on one side and the republic's arms on the other [19–20]. Higher denominations consist of $1 (1969), $5 (1971) and $10 (1976) in base metals, with silver and gold coins in higher values for commemoratives. Pictorial motifs were substituted from 1974 onwards, many featuring Caribbean landmarks, fauna and flora [21–24] but also giving prominence to cultural heritage, such as the steel bands for which Trinidad is world famous.

NETHERLANDS ANTILLES

These islands, forming part of the Kingdom of the Netherlands, comprised two groups: Aruba, Bonaire and Curaçao near the coast of Venezuela, and St Eustatius, Saba and part of St Martin south-east of Puerto Rico. Aruba became a separate state in 1986.

A general issue of coins for the Dutch West Indies appeared in 1794. Copper cents and silver stuivers were issued at Curaçao in the name of the Batavian Republic (1799–1803) and later, stuivers and reaals, often cut into segments under the Dutch kingdom. Cut or countermarked Spanish coins were used during the British occupation (1807–16) and after the restoration of Dutch rule, until 1821, when coins specifically minted for Curaçao were resumed.

Modern coins date from World War II, when the islands were cut off from Holland while it was under German occupation. These coins were similar to their Dutch counterparts, but with "Curaçao" inscribed on the reverse [25–27]. Distinctive coins inscribed "Nederlandse Antillen" have been in use since 1952, with a separate series for Aruba since 1986 [28–31].

CUBA, HISPANIOLA AND JAMAICA

The three largest islands of the Caribbean lie in its northernmost part, south of Florida and the Bahamas. Spanish-speaking Cuba is the largest and most westerly of the group. To the east lies the island of Hispaniola, the western third constituting the French-speaking Republic of Haiti and the remaining two-thirds the Spanish-speaking Dominican Republic. South of Cuba lies Jamaica, which is English-speaking and now a republic within the British Commonwealth. Associated with Jamaica are the Cayman Islands and the Turks and Caicos Islands, which were formerly its dependencies.

Left: Jamaica remained within the sterling area until 1969, and in this period produced its first commemorative coin, a crown-sized 5 shillings to celebrate its hosting of the 1966 Commonwealth Games.

CUBA

Reached by Columbus in 1492 and settled by the Spaniards in the early 1500s, Cuba remained a Spanish colony until 1898. The island was captured by the United States during the Spanish-American War and granted independence in 1902. The dictatorship of Fulgencio Batista was overthrown in 1959 by Fidel Castro, who instituted a communist regime. Although trade sanctions are still imposed by the USA, Cuba has become a popular tourist resort in recent years.

Distinctive coins based on the peso of 100 centavos were introduced in 1915, with an armorial obverse and a five-pointed star inscribed "Patria y Libertad" ("Fatherland and Liberty") on the reverse [1–2]. The Castro regime retained these motifs but changed the motto to "Patria o Muerte" ("Fatherland or Death") on some of the coins. In 1915 dollar-sized silver pesos were accompanied by a tiny gold coin portraying the martyr José Marti. Silver pesos ceased in 1939 but since 1977 smaller cupro-nickel coins have been extensively used as a vehicle for commemoration: by 2004 there had been well over 400 different issues [3–8]. Since 1975, 5 and 10 pesos have been almost as prolific, with even larger denominations in silver or gold.

HAITI

Hispaniola ("Little Spain") was, like Cuba, claimed by Columbus on his first voyage and colonized by Spain, but in the early 17th century the western district was taken over by French pirates, who ceded it to France in 1697. The coffee and sugar plantations worked by slaves imported from Africa made Saint-Domingue one of France's richest colonies, but a slave rebellion led by Henri Christophe led to the creation of the Republic of Haiti in 1804, the oldest Negro republic in the world and (second only to the USA) the oldest republic in the western hemisphere.

Countermarked French, Spanish and Portuguese coins circulated in the 18th century, followed by a local coinage denominated in escalins. Coins in deniers and sols, introduced in 1807, were rapidly superseded by a decimal system based on the gourde of 100 centimes, a currency that continues to this day. Circulating coins have the arms on one side and Liberty (1881–94), followed by profiles of historic figures (since 1904) on the other. Apart from the circulating coins from 1 centime to 1 gourde in nickel- or brass-plated steel [9], Haiti has issued many gold and silver commemoratives since 1971.

DOMINICAN REPUBLIC

The larger part of Hispaniola, which the Spaniards called Santo Domingo, remained under their control until 1822, when the Haitians invaded it. They occupied the entire island until 1844. In that year Juan Pablo Duarte raised a revolt and drove out the invaders, establishing the independent Dominican Republic. It voluntarily submitted to Spain from 1861 to 1866 but has been independent ever since.

A Spanish mint was established at Santo Domingo in 1542 and struck silver and copper coins. Distinctive coins appeared in 1814–21 under the name of Fernando VII. Copper or brass quarter reales of 1844–8 were struck, but no other distinctive coinage emerged until 1877, when the peso of 100 centavos was adopted. The earliest coins were non-figural, with the date on one side and the value on the other, but an armorial design was introduced in 1937 [10–16], with a palm tree or native American head on the other side. Numerous commemoratives, in gold, silver or platinum, have appeared in more recent years.

Colourful Coins

In 1994 Cuba became one of the first countries in the world to issue coins with a multicoloured surface. While the arms of the republic appeared in plain silver on the obverse, the reverse featured Caribbean fauna in full colour. The following year a similar series portrayed pirates of the Caribbean.

JAMAICA

Columbus reached Jamaica in 1494 and it was colonized by Spain in 1509 but captured by Britain in 1655. It joined the West Indies Federation in 1958 but seceded in 1961, gaining full independence a year later. Cut or countermarked coins were in circulation in the 18th century, followed by the coins of the British West Indies in 1822. Sterling was introduced in 1834, represented by silver coins of small denominations. Cupro-nickel coins were introduced in 1869 with the effigy of the monarch (obverse) and colonial arms (reverse); these continued until 1969 [17–22]. The dollar was adopted in 1969; the arms moved to the obverse [23, 29] and pictorial motifs (fauna and flora) occupied the reverse of the cents [24], while Sir Alexander Bustamente, the first prime minister, was portrayed on the dollar [25]. Subsequently, other political figures were depicted [26–28, 30]. Since the 1990s inflation has led to a great reduction in the size of coins and the introduction of higher denominations for general circulation. Silver and gold commemoratives, up to $500, have also been produced.

FORMER JAMAICAN DEPENDENCIES

The Cayman Islands west of Jamaica and the Turks and Caicos group to the north-east were formerly Spanish but ceded to Britain in 1670 and 1799 respectively. The latter group was long a dependency of the Bahamas, then briefly a separate colony, before becoming a dependency of Jamaica in 1873. Jamaican coinage was used in both groups until 1959, when they joined the West Indies Federation. Distinctive coins have been issued by the Cayman Islands since 1972 [31–32, 34–35] and the Turks and Caicos Islands since 1969 [33], but both groups prefer US coinage in general circulation.

EAST CARIBBEAN

Columbus laid claim to the smaller islands of the east Caribbean during his second and subsequent voyages, and they were originally colonized by Spain but were frequently fought over by France and Britain in the 17th and 18th centuries, before finally coming under permanent British control. These crown colonies joined together in 1958 to form the West Indies Federation, but when that broke up they were granted associate statehood, with self-government, as a prelude to full independence within the British Commonwealth. They used British currency until 1955, when the coinage of the British East Caribbean Territories was introduced, followed by that of the East Caribbean Territories in 1980.

Left: The first coins inscribed for each territory of the British East Caribbean were the $4 coins of 1970, which formed part of the Food for All programme instituted by the United Nations Food and Agriculture Organization. These coins had standard obverse and reverse, depicting the East Caribbean arms [11] and bananas respectively, but individual names were inscribed below the arms.

The standard issues of the British East Caribbean Territories had a crowned bust of Elizabeth II on the obverse, and numerals (low values), Columbus's flagship the *Santa Maria* (5, 10 and 25 cents) or Neptune driving a sea chariot (50 cents) on the reverse [1–6]. The coins of the East Caribbean Territories bear the Machin bust of Queen Elizabeth and laureated numerals (1, 2 and 5 cents) and the *Santa Maria* (10 and 25 cents and $1) [7–10].

ANTIGUA AND BARBUDA

At the eastern end of the Leeward Islands, Antigua and its dependency of Barbuda achieved self-government in 1967 and became a wholly independent member of the Commonwealth in 1981, with the British monarch as head of state. Although copper token farthings, some struck in the Bahamas, were issued in the mid-19th century, the first distinctive coins appeared in 1982 to mark the 250th anniversary of George Washington's birth; they comprised three $30 silver proofs showing scenes of the American Revolutionary War. A $10 coin appeared in 1985 to celebrate Queen Elizabeth's visit, while more recent coins have focused on Caribbean wildlife.

DOMINICA

Lying in the Windward Islands, Dominica was confirmed as a British possession in 1805 and at that time had a curious currency consisting of rings, dumps or fragments of Spanish coins denominated in bits. Spanish dollars had a crenellated piece cut out of the centre to form the moco (1½ bits) [12] while the rest was tariffed at 11 or 16 bits according to size and weight.

Dominica was granted associated statehood in 1967 and became wholly independent in 1978. Coins were issued in 1970 to mark the signing of an agreement among 18 Caribbean states, to promote economic development in the region [11], and $10 coin, released that year to celebrate independence, featured carnival dancers. The relatively few commemoratives include those for royal and papal visits and the Middle East peace brokered by Bill Clinton (1979).

ST KITTS AND NEVIS

Though colonized by Sir Thomas Warner in 1623, St Christopher (usually known as St Kitts) became a permanent British possession in 1783. Billon French deniers were countermarked SK and issued in 1801. Known

Coins on Coins

In 2004 the British Virgin Islands issued a pair of coins, denominated $1 (cupro-nickel) or $10 (sterling silver), to mark the Athens Olympic Games, featuring athletes from the ancient Games on the reverse. As well as scenes of runners and a chariot race alongside striking bronze busts, they bore facsimiles of ancient Greek coins, an Athenian owl and a coin showing a head of Zeus with Nike, goddess of victory.

colloquially as Black Dogs, and used as small change, they were withdrawn from St Kitts in 1849 and Nevis in 1858 [13]. Spanish silver dollars cut into eighths were countermarked S for circulation in St Kitts. More recently, it has issued a few coins marking a royal visit, bicentenaries of battles and anniversaries of independence [14–15].

Its former dependency of Anguilla seceded in 1967, countermarking various dollar-sized coins of Mexico, Peru and the Yemen to assert its independence. It was taken under direct British control in 1971 and accorded autonomy in 1976. In recent years, a few coins, including tiny $5 gold pieces, have featured local landmarks.

VIRGIN ISLANDS

Cut and countermarked Mexican coins were used in Tortola in the British Virgin Islands [16–17] in the late 18th century, although the circulation of countermarked Spanish and French coins was not authorized until 1801. More recently, the islands have preferred US coinage, which continues to circulate freely, although distinctive coins from 1 cent to $1 were issued in 1973 with Elizabeth II's profile (obverse) and fauna and flora (reverse). Gold $100 coins were added in 1975, mostly encapsulated in philanumismatic covers. Since 1977 the islands have produced many commemoratives in denominations from $5 upwards [18–21]. Loyalty to the British crown is reflected in numerous coins marking the Queen's coronation, birthdays, jubilees, and anniversaries; others have honoured the Queen Mother, Princess Diana and, most recently, the marriage of Prince Charles and Camilla Parker-Bowles. Dollar-sized silver coins are also now produced in thematic sets.

OTHER ISLANDS

Fragments of Spanish coins countermarked G were current in the much fought-over island of Grenada, finally ceded to Britain in 1783. Since 1985 the very few commemoratives that have appeared have marked the Queen's visit and featured wildlife.

St Lucia, reached by Columbus in 1502, was subject to similar territorial ambition until Britain gained permanent possession in 1814. It had an assortment of escalins, sous and livres, countermarked on Spanish silver [22]. The handful of commemoratives since 1986 include coins for papal and royal visits, the bicentenary of the Battle of the Saints and the Commonwealth Finance Ministers' Meeting (1986). St Vincent has followed the same pattern, using bits and holey dollars in the early 19th century but issuing even fewer commemoratives since 1985.

17

18

19

20

21

22

MEXICO

The United States of Mexico, to give it its full name, is one of the largest and most populous countries in the western hemisphere, third after the USA and Brazil. Boasting a civilization stretching back to pre-Christian times, it was the centre of the mighty Aztec empire, which survived until 1521 when it was subjugated by Hernando Cortez at the head of a small band of Spanish conquistadors. For three centuries Mexico was at the heart of the Spanish Empire and was known as New Spain. It became a republic in 1823 and has experienced frequent periods of economic instability since that time, reflected in attempts to reform and revalue its currency.

Below: Coins from the colonial period of Mexico's history are relatively easy to come by. This gold 8 escudo piece of 1802 is engraved with a bust of Charles IV of Spain on the obverse and, on the reverse, the regal arms surmounted by a crown and surrounded by the collar and badge of the Order of the Golden Fleece. It was struck at the height of Spanish colonial power, before Spain was hard hit by the Napoleonic Wars.

INDEPENDENCE

A mint was established at Mexico City as early as 1536 and coined Spanish currency until 1811. Coins were often roughly cut from bars and crudely stamped [1–2]. Numerous other mints were opened in the ensuing centuries, producing a vast range of silver and gold coins. Latterly, large coins such as the silver 8 reales [3–4] and gold 8 escudos [5–6] were well struck.

On September 18, 1810, Father Miguel Hidalgo raised the cry of independence, though more than a decade elapsed before it was accomplished by General Agustín de Itúrbide. He proclaimed himself emperor in 1822 but was deposed a year later and a republic instituted [7]. During this turbulent time temporary mints functioned at San Felipe de Chihuahua and Durango, and royalist coins were frequently countermarked by the rebels. The chronic instability of Mexico from then until 1867 saw frequent changes of dictators as well as the rise and subsequent decline of a second emperor, the luckless Austrian Maximilian. It was one year prior to Maximilian's rule that the first decimal coinage, based on the peso of 100 centavos, was introduced (in 1863), paving the way for a republican series of 1869. Under Benito Juárez (president until 1872) liberal democracy was briefly established, but by the end of the century Mexico was under the iron grip of Porfirio Díaz. In this period, the old silver 8 reales coinage was revived (1873–98) [11], yet Díaz's government also introduced the sweeping reforms of 1905, which corrected the balance between gold and silver. Díaz was overthrown in 1911, but this precipitated a wave of revolutions that lasted until 1917. During its first century of independence Mexico was kept afloat by its extraordinary mineral wealth, reflected in the abundance of coinage and a bewildering array of mint-marks as coin production devolved on individual states. No fewer than 14 mints functioned, from Alamos to Zacatecas.

CIVIL WARS

The overthrow of Díaz brought Francisco Madero to power, but he was murdered in 1913. His death triggered civil war. The Constitutionalists were led by Pancho Villa and Emiliano Zapata in opposition to Victoriano Huerta. Other guerrilla leaders, such as Venustiano Carranza and Alvaro Obregón, jostled for the presidency and the country was in turmoil until Carranza emerged as president in 1916 and eventually forced through a constitution acceptable to most factions.

During this period of turbulence separate issues of coins were made in the Mexican states of Aguascalientes, Chihuahua, Durango, Guerrero, Jalisco, Estado de Mexico, Morelos, Oaxaca, Puebla and Sinaloa, and in many cases separate issues appeared in towns and cities within these states. The coins ranged from the crudely cast pieces of Buelna and Carrasco and the rectangular pieces of Oaxaca to coins of Duranga inscribed "Muera Huerta" ("Death to Huerta").

UNITED STATES OF MEXICO

Up to 1905 coins bore the legend "Republica Mexicana" but since then "Estados Unidos Mexicanos" has been preferred [8]. Considering the number of mints functioning in the country, it seems ironic that Mexico has sometimes relied on the Birmingham Mint (1909–14) and the Royal Canadian Mint in more recent years.

Not only has a wide range of different metals and alloys been used, especially in the subsidiary coinage (bronze, brass, stainless steel, nickel and cupro-nickel of varying composition) [9–10], but Mexico also holds the record of striking pesos in the greatest range of finenesses, from almost pure silver to a mere .100 fine [12–15].

Decline and Fall

The silver peso serves as a barometer for the decline of the Mexican economy in the course of the 20th century. The Cabalitos of 1903–14 were minted in .903 silver, while the Sunray pesos were struck in .800 silver (1918–19), then in .720 silver (1920–45). Thereafter the fineness of the silver was reduced to .500 (1947–9), .300 (1950) and finally .100 (1957–67). It was not until 1970 that Mexico at last admitted defeat and substituted cupro-nickel (1970–83) and stainless steel (1984–87).

PICTORIAL MOTIFS

Most coins in the period up to the 1940s had an obverse showing an eagle and serpent and a reverse showing a radiate Cap of Liberty, with wreathed numerals on the lower denominations. The exceptions were the pesos of 1910–14, nicknamed Cabalitos for their depiction of a horseman. A pictorial approach was generally inaugurated in 1943, when a large bronze 20 centavos was introduced with a view of Chichen Itza on the reverse [14]. Portrait reverses were produced from 1950 and, for the next three decades, bore historical figures ranging from Cuauhtémoc (the last Aztec emperor) [15] to José Morelos, leader of the war of independence [16], Hidalgo [17] and Madero. In the same period, the smallest coins featured a corn cob, symbolic of the agrarian economy. The 5 peso coins became a popular medium for commemoratives marking the anniversaries of major celebrities.

CONTEMPORARY COINAGE

Mexico's periods of inflation in the 1980s were reflected in frequent changes of coinage as major denominations shrunk in size and fineness, while ever-higher values were required for everyday use. In an attempt to maintain some kind of ratio of weight to value, it ended up with some very large coins, notably the massive brass 1000 pesos of 1988–92 and the cupro-nickel 5000 pesos of 1988 [18–21].

8
9 10
11
12 13
14 15
16 17
18 19
20 21

CENTRAL AMERICA

The Caribbean coast of Central America was sighted by Columbus during his last voyage (1502). Panama was explored by Vasco de Balboa in 1513 and settled in 1519, but the territories to the north were not conquered until 1522–3. Of the seven Central American countries, six were under Spanish rule while the seventh was a British colony. In the colonial period silver coins, mainly from Mexico, were in use, with numerous provisional issues of countermarked pesos and the very crude pieces known as "cobs".

Left: Vasco Nuñez de Balboa (1475–1519) arrived in Central America in 1511 as a stowaway but within two years had established himself as leader of the Spanish settlement at Darien. He explored the surrounding region and was the first European to sight the Pacific Ocean. Balboa lost his head (literally) after a disagreement with the new Spanish governor, but he gives his name to the unit of currency in Panama and appears on many of its coins.

CENTRAL AMERICAN REPUBLIC

The region threw off the Spanish yoke in 1821 and formed the Republic of Central America, with coins featuring the Tree of Liberty [1] and five mountain peaks [2], but by the mid-19th century Costa Rica, El Salvador, Guatemala, Honduras and Nicaragua were separate republics. Coins in a common design showing five peaks but inscribed with the name of each state were issued in this period.

COSTA RICA

Decimal currency based on the peso of 100 centavos was adopted in 1865 [3–4]. The peso was replaced in 1896 by the colon (named after Columbus) of 100 centimos, the coins of this series having an armorial obverse [6–8] but the value on the reverse. Costa Rica lives up to its name ("rich coast") by being the most prosperous and stable in Central America. A nickel 10 colon piece celebrated the 25th anniversary of the Central Bank (1975) [5], presaging some large, handsome commemoratives in silver or gold.

GUATEMALA

A mint was established at Antigua Guatemala in 1731 and moved to Nueva Guatemala in 1776, striking coins in the Spanish colonial style [9–10]. Guatemala, the most northerly of the Central American group, was briefly absorbed by the Mexican Empire of Itúrbide (1822–3) before joining the Central American federation. Its secession in 1839 hastened the break-up of the union.

It was only in 1859 that a distinctive coinage was adopted, based on the real, with an obverse of three peaks and the value on the reverse for the low values; the higher values featured an allegorical figure or a profile of Rafael Carrera, founder of the republic. A new style of arms (1892) incorporated a quetzal, the national bird, and when the currency was reformed by the dictator Trujillo in 1924 the quetzal of 100 centavos was introduced. An armorial obverse and a reverse bust of Fray Bartolome de las Casas (who introduced Christianity and defended the rights of the indigenous people against the ruling regime) appeared on the centavo [11–12], but the higher value reverses bore a quetzal or a Mayan monolith [13–14].

HONDURAS

The earliest coin was an 8-reales minted at Tegucigalpa in 1813, while the entire region was under Mexican control. As the union disintegrated there were some local issues, superseded by the series of 1869–70. The first decimal coins (1879) had a pyramid emblem on the obverse and the value on the reverse [26]. Like the others, Honduras abandoned the peso (with its connotations of colonial rule) in 1931 and adopted a distinctive unit, the lempira, named after an Indian chief whose exploits against the Spanish were legendary. Lempira himself was portrayed on the obverse of the higher values [16, 19], with the arms on the reverse [15, 20]. On the smaller coins the arms occupied the obverse and the value appeared on the reverse [17–18].

NICARAGUA

This republic got by with Spanish pesos and the coins of its neighbours until 1878, when it acquired its own coinage, struck by the Heaton Mint of Birmingham, although the full range, from the half centavo to the cordoba [21–24], was not completed until 1912. The unit was named in honour of Francisco Fernandez de Cordoba who explored the area (1515–24). After the earthquake disaster of 1975 Nicaragua produced a silver 20 cordoba coin to raise funds for the victims, a very early example of a charity coin.

EL SALVADOR

Apart from an interesting issue of 1828–35, when the federation was collapsing, inscribed "For the freedom of Salvador", Central American federation reales and countermarked Spanish coins served El Salvador until 1889, when the peso of 100 centavos was adopted. While silver pesos and half pesos showing the flag or a bust of Columbus, and a gold series with the head of Liberty, were struck in San Salvador, some centavo denominations, in cupro-nickel, were produced by Heaton. In 1920 the colon replaced the peso as the unit of currency. Armorial obverses have alternated with a profile of Francisco Morazan, hero of the struggle for liberation and president of the Central American Republic from 1829 to 1840 [25]. Gold coins were revived in 1971, the prelude to many special issues of recent years [29–32].

PANAMA

After seceding from Colombia in 1903, Panama adopted the balboa of 100 centesimos [26–27], although an actual 1 balboa coin did not appear until 1947 [28]. Balboa himself has dominated the obverse of the coins since their inception; other historical figures have appeared since 1975. Panama has the distinction of producing both the region's smallest and (until recently) largest coins – the tiny silver 2 centesimos or "Panama pill" and the giant 20 balboas portraying Simon Bolivar.

Below: Panama's silver 20 balboas was the largest coin in the world when it was issued in 1971, with a diameter of 61mm/2½in.

Country Named After a Town

British Honduras was settled by sailors shipwrecked in 1638 and later became the haunt of buccaneers who founded Belize, a town allegedly named after a pirate called Wallace. The country took the name of Belize in 1973 when it became independent. Coins portraying the reigning monarch were introduced in 1885, and since 1973 have had pictorial reverses.

COLOMBIA, ECUADOR AND VENEZUELA

Columbus reached the Atlantic coasts of Colombia and Venezuela in 1498 but no Spanish settlement took place there until the mid-16th century. These three countries in the north-east of South America originally formed the vice-royalty of New Granada, but revolted against Spanish rule in 1811. Although they achieved their independence in 1821, Spain did not recognize it until 1845. Initially the three countries united to form Greater Colombia or the Granadine Confederation, striking reales or using countermarked Spanish pieces, with numerous local issues during the war of independence. When the confederation disintegrated in 1830 each country went its own way. Panama seceded from Colombia in 1903, having used the coins of that country up to that time.

Below: Simon Bolivar (right), born at Caracas, Venezuela, in 1783, led the 1911 revolt against Spanish rule and is the great national hero of Colombia, Ecuador and Venezuela as well as Peru and Bolivia. The last of these was named in his honour, and from this derived the currency unit, the boliviano, while the Colombian state of Bolivar also perpetuates his memory. In his native land his name was given to the unit of currency, while that of his lieutenant, Antonio Sucre (left), was used for the currency unit in Ecuador.

VENEZUELA

Bolivar's homeland issued reales until the 1860s, although a reformed currency, based on the venezolano of 100 centavos, was in parallel use from1873 to 1879, when it was replaced by the bolivar of 100 centimos. Early coins bore the head of Liberty, but since 1874 Simon Bolivar the Liberator has been portrayed instead [1], with a heraldic shield on the reverse [2–6]. Since 1975 a number of large gold or silver coins have commemorated historic events and personalities or appeared in sets highlighting nature conservation and other worthy causes.

ECUADOR

Francisco Pizarro penetrated the north-west Pacific coast of South America in 1526, and within a decade Ecuador had been pacified by Sebastian de Benalcazar, who founded Quito in 1534. Revolts against Spain were crushed in 1810 and 1812 and it was not until 1822 that Ecuador was liberated by Antonio Sucre.

Distinctive coins date from 1833 and were originally inscribed "Ecuador in Colombia", but "Republica del Ecuador" was substituted in 1837. The head of Liberty [7] and the sunrise over twin peaks were the main features of the early issues [8]. Decimal coinage based on the sucre of 10 decimos or 100 centavos was adopted in 1872, the obverses showing an elaborate coat of arms with the wreathed value in words on the reverse – a design that has endured for decades [9–11]. The effigy of Sucre appeared in 1884 and has dominated the higher values ever since [12], although pictorial designs still featured on the lower values [13–14]. Unusually, some coins of Ecuador include the word "Mexico" at the foot of the reverse to denote the place of minting [15]. Since 1988 nickel-clad

Leper Coins

Special coins were produced by Colombia from 1901 onward for the use of patients in the government-managed leper colonies at Agua de Dios, Cano de Loro and Contratacion. The standard obverse bore the name of the country with "Lazareto" across the middle. The coins, ranging from 1 centavo to 10 pesos, continued in use until the leper colonies were shut down in 1959. Venezuela also issued distinctive coins between 1913 and 1936 for each of its leper colonies at Maracaibo, Providencia and Cabo Blanco, and Panama produced coins for its leper colony at Palo Seco in 1907.

steel coins of Ecuador have matched a new armorial obverse [16] to images of the independence memorial [17] or indigenous sculpture and artefacts. Very few commemoratives have so far appeared, notably the series of 1991 for the Columbus quincentenary.

COLOMBIA

If the coinage of Ecuador and Venezuela has been relatively straightforward, that of Colombia has been exceedingly complex, reflecting turbulent times and periods of rampant inflation. A mint was opened at Bogota in the 1620s, striking silver pesos and also, from 1756, gold coins such as the beautiful 8 escudos portraying Charles III [18] with the crowned royal arms of Spain on the reverse [19], struck at the Bogota Mint in 1785. A subsidiary mint producing silver also functioned at Popayan from 1729. Spanish royalists and republican rebels struck coins in areas under their control during the prolonged wars of independence, the former at Popayan and Santa Marta and the latter in Cartagena and Cundinamarca. A national coinage of escudos and reales appeared in 1820, richly symbolic with flowers, cornucopiae and doves of peace as well as the obligatory head of Liberty.

The first attempt to decimalize the currency (1847) yielded the peso of 10 reales or decimos. These coins continued the previous symbols but had the value on the reverse. The peso of 100 centavos was adopted in 1872, Liberty heads and arms or symbols providing the motifs, with profiles of Bolivar and other national figures more prominent from 1912 [20–22]. Bronze (and later copper-clad steel) subsidiary coins were introduced in 1962 with a wreathed Cap of Liberty on the obverse and a numeral of value flanked by flowers and a cornucopia on the reverse. Higher denominations with armorial motifs were struck in brass [24] while bimetallic high values were adopted in 1993 [23]. Recently, inflation has necessitated base-metal coins up to 5000 pesos. These have the value on one side and motifs derived from indigenous art on the other [25–26].

Special issues began in 1968, with cupro-nickel 5 pesos and gold 100 pesos to mark the Eucharistic Congress, while a 5 pesos of 1971 celebrated the Pan-American Games. The relatively few commemoratives issued since have mostly been of very high denominations (500, 1000, 1500 or 2000 pesos), struck in gold.

Colombia was rent by civil wars in the early 20th century, and the territory of Panama seceded with the connivance of the USA. In that period uniface coins of 10, 20 and 50 centavos were struck from thin sheets of brass at Santander under the command of General Ramon Gonzales Valencia. In the immediate postwar years the paper currency depreciated to the point at which a paper peso was worth no more than a centavo in silver coinage; 1, 2 and 5 peso cupro-nickel coins of 1907–16 are inscribed "P/M" below the value on the reverse, signifying "*papel moneda*" (paper money).

BRAZIL AND GUYANA

The largest of the Latin American nations, Brazil was claimed by the Portuguese explorer Cabral in 1500, and settled by the inhabitants of that country, who imported their currency based on the real. By the late 16th century sugar was serving as a medium of currency, with cowries (known as *zombo* or *gimbombo*) as small change. From 1580 to 1640 Portugal was under Spanish rule, and Spanish silver pesos circulated, followed in 1643 by countermarked coins. Mints were opened at Bahia (1694) and Rio (1698), where the 4000 reis coin of João V was minted in 1719 [1–2], and struck in gold and silver. Guyana is the generic name for the region north of Brazil and east of Venezuela, colonized by the French and Dutch, and later the British: these territories are now a French overseas department, Surinam and Guyana respectively.

Left: In 1900 Brazil celebrated the 400th anniversary of Pedro Alvares Cabral's arrival on its shore with a very large 4000 reis silver coin, the obverse showing the Portuguese explorer setting foot on dry land, cap in hand, while the reverse showed the sunrise flanked by the arms of Portugal and Brazil in upright oval cartouches.

THE EMPIRE

Some of the world's most poignant coins are those struck at the Rio Mint portraying the Portuguese royal family in the late 18th century. Queen Maria I suffered from severe melancholia, which descended into madness following the death of her husband, Pedro III. Their conjoined profiles appeared on the gold peca of 1782 [3–4], but the widowed queen appeared alone on later coins [5–6]. Coins were struck in the name of João VI, who served as regent from 1799 to 1816, including a gold peca of 1811 [7–8].

When Napoleon's armies invaded the Iberian Peninsula the Portuguese royals fled to Brazil and set up court in Rio de Janeiro. After Portugal was liberated by Wellington's troops in 1811, the Prince Regent, who would later accede to the throne as João VI, returned to Lisbon, leaving his son Pedro as his viceroy, but in September 1822 Pedro declared Brazil a wholly independent empire and proclaimed himself emperor. His son succeeded in 1831 and, as Dom Pedro II, ruled wisely until 1889. The abolition of slavery caused great discontent among the landowning classes and led to a military coup, which abolished the empire and deposed the monarchy.

Imperial coinage had a crowned shield on the obverse and the value on the reverse [9–10]. A singular feature of the early period was the plethora of countermarked copper coins [11] as the government strove to impose a standard system, although it was not until the 1860s that the coinage was reformed. Portraits of the emperor, from boyhood to old age, were confined to gold and a few silver coins.

THE REPUBLIC

As in Spain, Portuguese currency was based on the real, but it became so depreciated that it was counted in large multiples known as reis (the plural of *real* in Portuguese). Even in imperial times the lowest denomination was 5 reis, while silver coins ran up to 2000 reis and gold from 5000 to 20,000 reis. Under the republic the lowest coin was the bronze 20 reis, the highest the gold 20,000 reis minted between 1889 and 1922. Latterly money was counted in

Revaluation

Inflation and depreciation are nothing new to Brazil. Between 1667 and 1683, when the value of money fell in relation to the intrinsic worth of coins, Portuguese gold coins of 1000, 2000 and 4000 reis were countermarked in Brazil and stamped with new values of 1100, 2200 and 4400 reais respectively.

milreis (1000 reis) and the banknotes ran up to 1,000,000 reis, known as a conto. Liberty and the numerals of value dominated the coinage [12–14] but during the dictatorship of Getulio Vargas (1938–42) his profile appeared on the obverse [15]. A few special issues of the inter-war period commemorated the 400th anniversary of settlement and honoured celebrated Brazilians.

CURRENCY REFORMS

Despite the greatest natural resources of any South American country, Brazil has been hard hit by economic and political instability from time to time, coupled with periods of high inflation. This led to a reform of the currency in 1942 when the outmoded milreis gave way to the cruzeiro of 100 centavos. A feature of this series was that a different portrait of a famous Brazilian was used for each value from 10 to 50 centavos, while a map of the country or the federal arms graced the higher values. In every case the value, denoted by large numerals, occupied the reverse.

Inflation in the 1950s led to changes from cupro-nickel to brass and latterly aluminium, notably the series of 1965. Two years later the currency was reformed, the cruzeiro novo being worth 1000 old cruzeiros. In this period occurred the avant-garde coins marking the 150th anniversary of independence [16–17]. The currency was again reformed in 1986 when the new cruzeiro was superseded by the cruzado of 100 centavos [18–22]. Like its predecessors, this series was struck in stainless steel but by 1989 had also depreciated: 1000 cruzados were worth one cruzado novo, which was again replaced by the cruzeiro a year later. In 1993, 1000 cruzeiros equalled one cruzeiro real, but in July 1994, 2750 of these equalled 1 real of 100 centavos. So far, the real (plural *reais*) has managed to hold steady [23–24].

GUYANA

To a large extent coins of the mother country were used in the British, Dutch and French parts of Guyana, although during World War II Dutch coins were struck at the US Mint with a P (Philadelphia) mint-mark for use in Surinam. Appropriately countermarked Spanish coins, holey dollars and dumps were used in Essequibo and Demerara following the British occupation of 1796, made permanent in 1814. In the British colonial period stuivers and guilders portrayed the reigning sovereign [25–26]. British silver groats (4 pence) were superseded by distinctive coins of the same value, augmenting ordinary British coins [27–30]. When the territory gained independence in 1967 the dollar of 100 cents was introduced. The coins had armorial and numeral motifs [31–32], which changed to pictorial reverses in 1976.

The coinage of Dutch Guiana began at Recife in 1645, with gold florins inscribed "Brasil" (the first numismatic use of the name), followed by silver in 1654. These coins were rectangular, with the "GWC" monogram of the Dutch West Indies Company. Distinctive coins were introduced in Surinam in 1962, with an armorial obverse and value reverse. The former Dutch Guiana attained independence in 1975, and celebrated its first anniversary with silver and gold coins.

BOLIVIA, CHILE AND PERU

The former Inca strongholds were absorbed by Spain's colonial empire in the 1530s. In 1543 silver was discovered in Bolivia at Potosi in the Cerro Rico, which contained the largest silver deposit then known. Pesos were crudely struck at Lima, Peru, from 1565 and at Potosi from 1575, exemplified by the 1723 cob 8 reales of Potosi [1–2], intended mainly as a convenient medium for shipping bullion rather than for local circulation. Although independence was declared in 1809–10 and secured by 1824, Spain made many later attempts to regain the territory and did not finally recognize its independence until 1879. Ironically, by that time relations between the states had deteriorated, leading to the Pacific War of 1879–83, which resulted in victory for Chile, and territorial losses for Bolivia and Peru.

Left: The Andean condor, in flight or, as shown here, alighting on a lofty peak, has long been a popular motif for the coins of the countries dominated by this great mountain range.

BOLIVIA

Known as Upper Peru in Spanish colonial times, the country declared its independence in 1809, following a revolt in La Paz. It was the first of the Spanish territories to do so, but 16 years elapsed before it was secured by Bolivar's crushing defeat of the last Spanish army in South America, at Maipu in 1824. The republic, established in August 1825, took its name from its liberator.

Distinctive coinage began in 1827 with the escudo of 2 pesos or 16 soles, portraying Simon Bolivar with a palm tree on the reverse or the sun rising over the Andes (on gold escudos) [3–4]. A tiny quarter sol was added in 1852, featuring a llama (obverse) and an Andean peak (reverse). The coinage was decimalized in 1864, based on the boliviano of 100 centecimos, replaced by centavos in 1878. Arms, eagle or mountain motifs replaced Bolivar's effigies while the reverse bore the value. This series continued until 1919, although by that date only the 5 and 10 centavo coins were still being struck.

Attempts to re-introduce coins in 1935–7 and 1951 were hampered by rampant inflation. A drastic currency reform in 1963 led to the introduction of the peso boliviano and coinage was resumed in 1965. The first commemoratives, in 1952, consisted of small gold coins celebrating the revolution of that year. By 1980 coins had disappeared from circulation, overtaken by inflation, but in 1987 a monetary reform, replacing 1,000,000 pesos with the new boliviano of 100 centavos, resulted in the first full range of coins in 80 years, with the arms (obverse) and value (reverse) [5–8]. A few special issues since then include the Ibero-American series of 10 boliviano coins and a 50 boliviano silver piece of 1998 for the 450th anniversary of La Paz.

CHILE

Coins were struck at Santiago from 1749 in the prevailing Spanish colonial styles; they included silver pesos and gold coins such as the handsome 8 escudo piece of Ferdinand VII minted in 1813 [9–10]. Following the revolution, distinctive coinage dated from 1817 and consisted of the peso inscribed "Chile Independent" with Santiago at the foot of a motif showing an erupting volcano. Other values from the tiny silver quart (quarter real) to the gold 6 escudos followed, but the peso of 100 centavos was adopted in 1835, with a star, condor or Liberty head (obverse) and value (reverse). Variations on these themes continued until 1942, when peso coins were introduced portraying Bernardo O'Higgins, dictator of Chile (1817–23). The peso was hard hit by inflation and by 1958 the condor or 10 pesos, originally a gold coin, was reduced to aluminium [11–12]. In 1960 the currency was reformed, introducing the escudo of 100 centesimos, with the centesimo worth 10 old pesos.

This series retained the flying condor obverse and value reverse, but since 1971 O'Higgins and other national heroes have been portrayed. In 1975 the coinage was again reformed, making the peso equal to 1000 old escudos. In this series the condor appeared in repose on the lower denominations [13–14], while O'Higgins graced the obverse [17] with a laureated value on the reverse [18]. Gold and silver coins showing a winged Victory appeared in 1976, originally celebrating the revolution of 1973, but the motif was subsequently extended to the base-metal coinage [15–16].

Tiny Gold

The peso was normally minted in silver, but from 1860 to 1873 Chile struck this denomination in 22 carat (.917 fine) gold, with the standing figure of Liberty on the obverse and a wreathed value on the reverse (see enlarged view, bottom). The tiny coin (14mm/⅝in diameter, top) proved unpopular and very few were struck after the production of silver pesos resumed in 1867.

PERU

Low-denomination copper coins appeared in 1822–3 as a prelude to a regular series in silver. The tiny silver quarter real of 1826–56 featured a llama, but the higher values had the standing figure of Liberty (obverse) and arms (reverse). Coins inscribed "Nor-Peruana" or "Repub. Sud-Peruana Confederacion" appeared in 1836–9 and reflected a short-lived confederation with Bolivia.

A decimal system based on the libra (pound) of 100 soles, 100 dineros or 1000 centavos was adopted in 1863. The 1 and 2 centavos were struck in bronze, with a sunburst obverse [21] and a wreathed value reverse [22], but higher denominations were minted in silver with the seated figure of Liberty on the obverse [19] and the national arms on the reverse [20]. The dinero was phased out in 1916, but the gold libra and fifth libra survived until 1969. The brass coins of 1935–65, from the half sol upwards, bore the name of the Central Reserve Bank and a promise to pay the bearer in gold soles [23]. The promise gave way to an image of a llama on coins of 1966–75 [24–25].

Like other Latin American countries, Peru was hard hit by inflation, resulting in base-metal coins up to 500 soles by 1985. The currency was reformed in that year and adopted the inti (the Inca word for "sun") of 1000 soles de oro, with the value or arms on one side and a bust of the national hero Admiral Grau on the other [26]. Brass coins from 1 to 50 centimos and cupro-nickel 1 and 5 intis were struck until 1988. Yet another reform in 1991 produced the nuevo sol, worth 1,000,000 intis, and a range of brass coins from 1 centimo to 5 nuevos soles [27–28]. The arms and value were enlivened by the inclusion of tiny birds on the reverse of the highest denominations, while the lower coins incorporated the value in Braille. Among the relatively few commemorative coins should be noted the series of 1965 celebrating the quatercentenary of the Lima Mint, the reverse reproducing a coin of 1565 [29].

ARGENTINA, PARAGUAY AND URUGUAY

Spanish penetration of the countries bordering the River Plate and its tributaries began in 1515, but settlement was very slow and there was little European development, due largely to the preservation of the indigenous people by the Jesuit missions, which were brutally suppressed in 1767–81. In the decades that followed opposition to the tyrannical rule of Spain escalated and fuelled the movement for independence in 1810–11. Argentina won its independence in 1816. Paraguay followed soon afterwards, but Uruguay was conquered by the Portuguese from Brazil and did not gain its independence, with help from Argentina, until 1830.

Left: Veinticinco de Mayo (May 25) is to Argentines what the Fourth of July is to Americans, commemorating the date on which independence was declared in 1810. The 150th anniversary was celebrated by this peso showing the Old Town Hall in Buenos Aires and the national arms.

ARGENTINA

Republica Argentina (literally "silver republic") owes its name and origin to the mineral wealth in the basin of the Rio de la Plate ("river of silver") and the earliest coins (1813–15) were given Spanish inscriptions signifying "Provinces of the River Plate". They consisted of gold escudos and silver soles and reales with a radiate sun obverse and arms reverse. Continual civil war resulted in separate issues of coins in the provinces of Buenos Aires, Cordoba, Entre Rios and La Rioja at various times until 1867, and it was not until 1881 that a national currency emerged, based on the peso of 100 centavos. Arms and the head of Liberty [1–4] provided the dominant motifs until 1962, but as inflation took hold the need for higher denominations in base metal resulted in some coins portraying historic figures or the sailing ship *Presidente Sarmiento* (5 pesos) and a gaucho (10 pesos) [5–6].

The first of many currency reforms took place in 1970, when the old peso became the new centavo. Coins from 1–50 centavos showed Liberty [8] with the value on the reverse [7]. Inflation led to the re-introduction of peso coins in 1974, the radiate sun being revived [9]. José de San Martin, the father of independence, and the naval commander Almirante Brown appeared on the 50 and 100 pesos brass-clad steel coins of 1980–81 [10–11]. In 1983 the peso argentino, worth 10,000 pesos, was introduced, followed by the austral, worth 1000 pesos argentinos (1985), and the peso of 10,000 australes (1992); the currency has been reasonably stable since then [12–13]. The austral coins included fauna on the low values – a respite from the sun and Liberty head. In recent years Argentina has also produced a number of commemoratives, mainly in base metal, for general circulation.

PARAGUAY

Apart from a copper half real showing a lion and the Cap of Liberty (1845) Paraguay had no coinage until 1870, when the peso of 100 centesimos was introduced. A radiate star in a wreath alternated with the lion emblem on the obverse, with the value on the reverse, apart from the large silver peso of 1889, which used both symbols. A new system, based on the guarani of 100 centimos, was adopted in 1944 and struck in aluminium (centimos) or stainless steel (1–50 guaranies), with brass-plated steel 100 guaranies since 1992. The guarani series has a mixture of allegory and portraiture on the obverse, notably the figure of a soldier alluding to the disastrous Chaco War with Bolivia of 1932–5 [14]. Paraguay had lost half its territory to Argentina, Uruguay and Brazil in the War of the Triple Alliance (1864–70) and was not minded to give up any more. The Chaco War, fought in a harsh terrain, claimed more lives through malaria than combat. It was a pyrrhic victory for Paraguay, which decimated the population and almost bankrupted the economy. The soldier appeared on Paraguayan coins and banknotes from 1975 onwards. By contrast, the 5 guarani coin portrayed a typical Paraguayan woman [17].

The higher denominations, in stainless steel or cupro-nickel zinc, featured landmarks on the reverse, such as the Acaray River hydroelectric dam [15], ancient ruins [19] and modern buildings. The obverses bore national figures, such as Generals Estigarribia, Garay [16] and Caballero [18], beginning in 1968 with a 10,000 guarani coin portraying General Alfredo Stroessner.

Paraguay embarked on a prolific programme of special issues struck in gold or silver. These have portrayed not only local heroes but also a staggering range of international celebrities (Goethe, Beethoven, Lincoln, Bismarck, Einstein, Garibaldi and Kennedy were among the earliest).

Conquering the Desert

The pacification of the interior of Argentina was not completed until 1879, when a military expedition was sent to Central Patagonia to subjugate the native peoples at the point of a lance. The centenary of the "conquest of the desert", as it is euphemistically known, was celebrated by this coin showing a lancer on horseback.

URUGUAY

Coinage in Uruguay was produced very sporadically in the 19th century, beginning with the copper 5 and 20 centesimos of 1840, followed in 1844 by the 40 centesimos and the silver peso. The copper 1, 2 and 4 centesimos appeared in 1869 and the silver 10 and 50 centesimos in 1870. The centesimos had a radiate sun obverse [20] and value reverse [21] but the peso had the republican arms. These types continued until 1953, when base-metal coins bore the national leader, José Artigas [22], previously portrayed in 1916–17. A brass 10 centesimo, issued in 1930 to celebrate the centenary of independence, had the head of Liberty (obverse) and a puma (reverse); it was re-issued in 1936 without the centenary inscription. A wide range of base alloys was used (bronze, cupro-nickel, aluminium-bronze or aluminium) for coins dated 1965, struck in very small quantities for the numismatic market.

Since the monetary reform of 1977, which exchanged 100 old pesos for one new one, aluminium or aluminium-bronze have been used for the circulating coins, with pictorial images and values on obverse and reverse respectively. The motifs were a curious mixture of the allegorical, such as the scales of justice on the 50 centesimo [23], and the agricultural, reflecting the importance of the cattle industry [24]. The nuevo peso denominations, however, featured José Artigas on the obverse [25–26]; Artigas was also the subject of a 5 nuevo peso coin issued in 1975 to celebrate the 150th anniversary of the revolutionary movement [27–28]. The currency was again reformed in 1993, when the peso uruguayano, worth 1000 nuevos pesos, was adopted. In recent years Uruguay has produced numerous medallic or bullion pieces in gold or silver [29–30]; they bear the revolutionary slogan "Libertad o Muerte" (Liberty or Death).

18 19 20 21 22 23 24 25 26 27 28 29 30

SOUTH ATLANTIC ISLANDS

The islands of the South Atlantic were some of the last outposts of the British Empire. Ordinary British coinage was largely used but in quite recent times distinctive sets in base alloys for general circulation have appeared. Since the 1970s they have also produced numerous commemorative or special issues. St Helena and its dependencies of Ascension and Tristan da Cunha were discovered by the Portuguese in 1501–2, while the Falkland Islands (named after Lord Falkland, Treasurer of the Navy) were discovered by John Davies in 1592. While St Helena (a staging post of the East India Company from 1659) was originally colonized by refugees from London after the Great Fire of 1666, Ascension and Tristan da Cunha were garrisoned in 1815 as a security precaution following the exile of Napoleon to St Helena.

Left: The Falklands, settled by Britain in 1833, have long been claimed by Argentina, resulting in the military invasion of April 1982 and the occupation of both the Falklands and its dependency, South Georgia. The South Atlantic War, which followed, led to the liberation of both island groups in mid-June. Crown-sized 50 pence in cupro-nickel, silver or gold celebrated the liberation and showed the arms of the colony superimposed on the Union Jack.

ST HELENA

Apart from a copper halfpenny of 1821 bearing the colonial arms [1–2], St Helena used coins of the East India Company and countermarked foreign coins until 1834, when British coinage was adopted exclusively for general circulation. In 1984, coins in the same weights and specifications as the British series were introduced with the names of both St Helena and Ascension inscribed on the obverse. The reverses feature South Atlantic fauna and flora.

In 1973, St Helena issued a crown-sized 25 pence in cupro-nickel or proof silver to celebrate the tercentenary of its return to British hands after a period of occupation by the Dutch [3–4]. A similar coin celebrated Elizabth II's silver jubilee in 1977 [5] and in 1978 the 25th anniversary of her coronation was likewise celebrated. Since then relatively few silver or gold coins have marked royal anniversaries and occasions. Crowns valued at the traditional 25 pence continued to be issued, both for St Helena alone [6–7] and with Ascension [8], although other crown values have also appeared. In 1984, a crown-sized 50 pence celebrated the 150th anniversary of St Helena as a crown colony.

ASCENSION

This island, which derives its name from its discovery on Ascension Day 1501, was occupied in 1815 to prevent any attempt by Bonapartists to free Napoleon from exile on St Helena. It acquired a strategic value in World War II and more recently has been an important staging post for communications and a NASA tracking station.

Apart from the joint issues with St Helena, a number of which depict flora and fauna [9–11], Ascension has had several crown-sized coins, generally complementing the issues of St Helena. The first distinctive coin marked the 25th anniversary of the coronation and

The Queen's Beasts

In 1978 the 25th anniversary of the coronation was marked by an omnibus issue of stamps in the various crown colonies and dependent territories. Their theme was the set of 12 heraldic animals known as the Queen's Beasts. The stamps showed a facing portrait of the Queen flanked on one side by one of the original beasts and on the other by a creature relevant to the particular country. St Helena and its dependencies of Ascension and Tristan da Cunha went further by issuing coins to mark the event and made philatelic and numismatic history by reproducing the stamp designs on the reverse of the coins.

includes the error in which the Ascension reverse was muled with an Isle of Man obverse. The coin issued for the royal golden wedding in 1997 featured an equestrian event at the Montreal Olympics. Other Ascension issues marked International Year of the Scout (1983) with a portrait of Lord Baden-Powell, and the nature conservation programme of the World Wide Fund for Nature (1998), for which frigate-birds and long-tailed tropicbirds were shown on a pair of coins.

TRISTAN DA CUNHA

One of the world's remotest islands, situated roughly midway between South America and West Africa, Tristan da Cunha was named in honour of the navigator who discovered it, and like Ascension, it was garrisoned in 1815–16, though most of the present population are the descendants of shipwrecked seamen.

Barter currency of cigarettes or potatoes continued in use until the 1950s, when South African coins were adopted, but the island switched to British money after it was resettled in 1963, following the volcanic eruption of 1961. No circulating coins have been produced but a handful of crown-sized 25 pence and later 50 pence have marked royal events [12–13]. The sole exception is the gold £2 of 1983 for the Year of the Scout.

FALKLAND ISLANDS

British coins used on the islands were superseded by a distinctive series in the same weights and specifications in 1974, with the Queen's bust (obverse) and fauna (reverse) [14–15], including a gold sovereign and half sovereign featuring a Romney Marsh ram. Special issues began with the silver jubilee crown (1977) but began to proliferate after the South Atlantic War, including a lengthy series of 1996 entitled Royal Heritage, featuring monarchs from Egbert of Wessex (802–39) to Victoria (1837–1901). Very large silver coins (65mm/2⅝in diameter) tariffed at £25 have also appeared in recent years.

SOUTH GEORGIA AND SOUTH SANDWICH ISLANDS

Until 1985 these sub-Antarctic islands were dependencies of the Falklands, but they were then constituted a separate crown colony. Ordinary British coins are in everyday use, but since 2000 crown-sized £2 coins in cupro-nickel or silver, with occasional higher denominations in gold, have marked historic anniversaries, mainly pertaining to the islands, although also acknowledging royal events [16–19].

12 13 14 15 16 17 18 19

EUROPE

With a coinage that dates back to the 6th century BC, Europe is responsible for the largest number of different coins – far more than the rest of the world put together. This is due primarily to the multiplicity of petty kingdoms and principalities in the Middle Ages, each striking its own coinage. Even after the emergence of nation states with centralized coinage systems, political and economic upheavals, and the growth of commemorative and special issues, resulted in a vast output in the past century alone.

WESTERN SCANDINAVIA

This group includes the most south-westerly of the Scandinavian countries, Denmark, together with its colonies or dependencies in the North Atlantic. Iceland became autonomous in 1918 and a wholly independent republic in 1944. The unit of currency since 1874 has been the krone (crown) of 100 øre, replacing the daler (dollar) and skilling (shilling) of earlier times.

Left: Danish currency was reformed and rationalized with the foundation of the Rigsbank in 1813; the rigsspeciedaler of 96 skilling was replaced by the rigsbankdaler of 96 rigsbank skilling. The rigsbankdaler was worth half a rigspeciedaler, while five of them were worth a speciedaler d'or. Currency changed again in 1854, when the rigsdaler of 96 rigsmont skilling was introduced. Gold coins were known by the ruler's name followed by d'or *("of gold"), such as the Christian d'or.*

DENMARK

The kingdom of Denmark emerged under Gorm the Old in the 10th century, and his descendants have reigned ever since. King Cnut (Canute) united the Norse lands and even ruled over England (1016–35). Harthacnut, son of Cnut, ruled Denmark while his father reigned in England, and struck coins derived from Anglo-Saxon models [1–2]. About 800 the Danes began striking silver deniers and later imitated English pennies. The first distinctive coins appeared about 995 and followed the northern European pattern. Typical cross-type coins were the pennies issued by Eric of Pomerania at Lund in the 14th century [3–4]. In 1522 the first large coins appeared under the name daler. By the 16th century, Danish currency was in total chaos, with more than 150 different coins in circulation in the reign of Christian IV, many of which bore the crowned bust of the monarch on the obverse [5] and a crown on the reverse [6]. A similar style was continued under his successor Christian V (1670–95), typified by fine portrait ducats [7–8] reflecting the growing importance of Denmark as a trading nation of world rank.

In the 19th century Denmark had a very complex monetary system based on the skilling, rigsbank skilling or rigsmont skilling as subdivisions of the rigspeciedaler, rigsbankdaler or rigsdaler. While the smaller coins featured a crowned monogram or shield, higher values portrayed the reigning monarch [9] with the value on the reverse [10].

DECIMAL COINAGE

On the formation of the Scandinavian Monetary Union the krone of 100 øre was introduced in 1874 and continued the style of the earliest coins, with a crowned monogram on the smallest denominations [11] and a royal effigy on the higher values [18], with the value on the reverse [12, 19]. Iron

Above: The obverses of Iceland show the four mythical guardians as supporters.

replaced bronze in 1918–19, and zinc, adopted as a wartime measure in 1942, continued in use until 1972. Coins with a central hole were first used in 1926 and continue today [13–17]. The silver krone denominations originally featured the monarch's portrait on the obverse with a crowned shield reverse, but when aluminium-bronze was substituted in 1924, a crowned monogram (obverse) and crown (reverse) were adopted. Coins since 1972 have borne two initials, identifying the mintmaster and the moneyer.

The relatively few commemorative coins mostly record royal birthdays, jubilees and weddings; a silver 10 krone (1972) simultaneously mourned the death of Frederik IX and celebrated the accession of Margrethe II.

ICELAND

The coins of Denmark circulated in Iceland, but after the constitutional change of 1918 distinctive coins began to appear from 1922. Many coins issued prior to 1944, when Iceland became an independent republic, bore the crowned monogram in the Danish style or a crowned shield flanked by the royal monogram (obverse) [20–21], while the country's name and value in Icelandic (eyrir, aurar, króna, kronur) distinguished the reverse [22–25]. From 1945 the crown and royal monogram were omitted from the shield [26–27]. A new version of the arms, flanked by the mythical guardians of Iceland, began with the aluminium-bronze krona values (1946). The 50th anniversary of sovereignty was marked in 1968 by a 50 kronur featuring the parliament building and this, minus the commemorative inscriptions, was retained as a definitive coin until 1980. The currency suffered severe inflation and was reformed in 1961, 10,000 old kronur being worth one new króna. In this series the guardian spirits, individually or together, graced the obverse [28], while the reverse motifs featured different species of fish and marine life [29–30]. The few commemoratives include a gold 500 kronur of 1961 for the 150th birthday of the independence leader Jon Sigurdsson, a set of three silver coins for the millenary of the Norse settlement (1974) and a gold 10,000 kronur for the millenary of Christianity (2000).

GREENLAND

Bronze or cupro-nickel tokens were produced by trading companies from 1875 to 1922, but Danish coins were otherwise used in this colony, politically regarded as part of Europe. Three coins (25 and 50 øre and 1 krone) were introduced in 1926 with crowned arms (obverse) [31] and a polar bear (reverse) [32]; a 5 krone coin was added in 1944. Since 1957 the krone has had the conjoined shields of Denmark and Greenland on the obverse [33] and a wreathed value on the reverse [34].

Wartime Occupation

Danish coins continued during the German occupation of Denmark, but Iceland, Greenland and the Faroes, occupied by the Allies, had coins supplied from Philadelphia or London, distinguished from their Danish contemporaries by the omission of the heart mint-mark of Copenhagen. A pattern coin showing a polar bear was struck in London for use in Iceland but was never generally released.

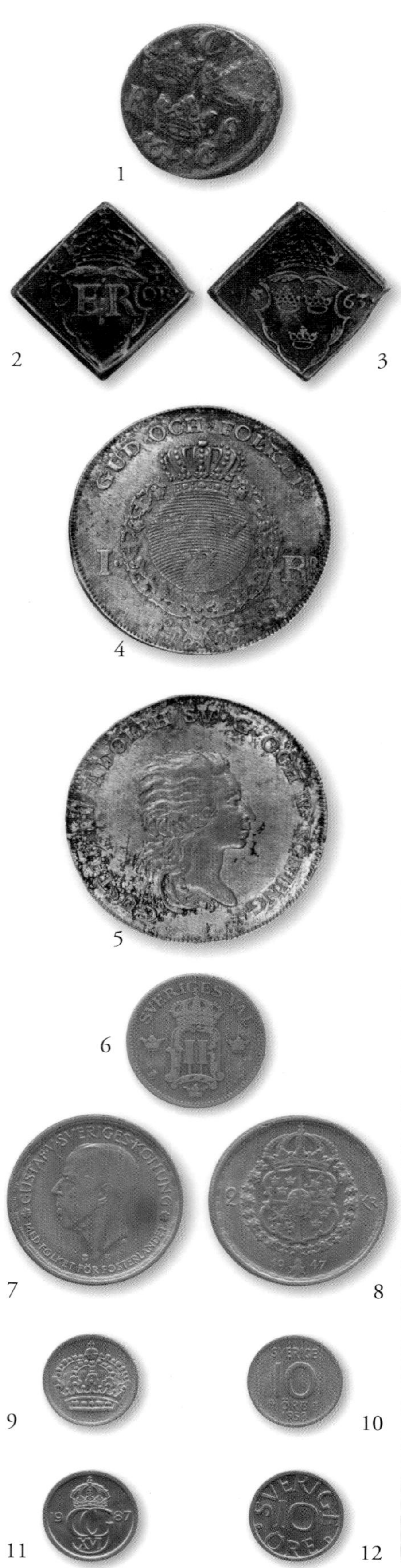

EASTERN SCANDINAVIA

The Scandinavian peninsula is occupied by Norway and Sweden, which were united under the personal rule of the Swedish kings from 1814 to 1905. The former Grand Duchy of Finland was under Swedish rule until 1809, when it was ceded to Russia. It gained its independence in 1917.

Left: Swedish copper was once mined in such abundance that monarchs such as Queen Christina (1632–54), pictured on these Swedish marks struck towards the end of her reign, sought methods of exporting an important product at a guaranteed price. To this end, plåtmynt *(plate money) – a currency based on copper – was adopted in 1643 and endured until 1768. The 10 daler piece weighed 19.75kg/44lb, and lower denominations of 1–8 daler were of proportionate size and weight. During the 125 years in which these large copper pieces were in circulation, Sweden established a number of mints close to the mines. This resulted in the most northerly mints in the world, at Kengis, Husa and Ljusendal, which functioned from 1644 to 1768. As in China, where cash proved too cumbersome, plåtmynt was unpopular and led to Sweden pioneering paper money as a substitute.*

SWEDEN

A wide range of coins, from Frankish deniers to Islamic dinars, has been found in coin hoards in Sweden, testifying to the prolific trade (or booty) of the Vikings in the early Middle Ages. In 995 King Olaf Skottkonung brought Anglo-Saxon moneyers to Sweden to strike coins at Sigtuna modelled on the English penny, and these continued until 1363, occurring in different weights according to where they were minted. The Swedish coinage was then standardized, with the örtug as the principal unit.

During the period of the Union of Kalmar, coins of the Danish type were used. Distinctive coinage reappeared in the 1520s under Gustav Vasa, who founded a dynasty that lasted until 1818 [1]. The daler and its subdivisions were introduced in 1534, followed by the mark and its öre subdivisions in 1536. Diamond-shaped coins called klippe [2–3] were issued by Erik XIV.

Like Denmark, Sweden had a very complex currency system in the 18th and 19th centuries. In 1776 the currency was reformed and the riksdaler of 48 skilling introduced [4–5]. From 1798 to 1830 the gold ducat was worth two speciedaler or riksdaler of 48 skilling. From 1830, 32 skilling banco equalled a riksdaler riksgalds, four of which equalled a riksdaler specie. From 1855 a riksdaler riksmynt was worth 25 öre, but when the Scandinavian Monetary Union was formed in 1874 the riksdaler was brought in line with the krona (plural *kronor*) of 100 öre. Lower denominations had a crowned monogram or effigy on the obverse, with the value on the reverse, often incorporating the triple crown emblem signifying the kingdom of the Swedes, Wends and Goths [6], whereas the krona values had an effigy (obverse) and arms (reverse).

The decimal coinage since 1874 has followed a similar pattern, the general principles remaining the same, even if the treatment of values, arms and portraits has varied over the years [7–12]. A conservative policy regarding special issues tended to confine them to royal occasions, but a more liberal attitude since 1980 has resulted in silver 50 or 100 kronor being struck for all manner of events, from the 350th anniversary of the Swedish colony in Delaware (1988) to the millenary of the Swedish Mint (1995).

Russian Colony

The Svalbard archipelago in the Arctic Ocean, of which Spitsbergen is the largest island, was annexed by Norway in 1920 on the basis that it was discovered by Norsemen in the 12th century, although it was first charted and named by Willem Barents in 1596. Its coal reserves led to the development of mines by American, Dutch and Scandinavian companies from 1904. Norwegian currency is used, but the Russian mines, established at Barentsburg in 1932, have had their own token coins, struck at the mint in Leningrad (now St Petersburg) and issued by Arktikugol, the state Arctic coal corporation. The series of 1946, of 10–50 kopeks, was non-pictorial, but a 1993 series of 25–100 roubles showed a polar bear atop the North Pole. The current set (1998), from 10 kopeks to 5 roubles, features walruses, a polar bear or a whale above the globe.

NORWAY

Distinctive coins first appeared in Norway in the late 10th century. While the country was under Danish rule, separate coins were struck from the 15th century [13–14]. A separate coinage also appeared in Norway under Swedish rule: it conformed to Swedish weights and specifications, but the obverse featured the crowned lion rampant shield of Norway [15]. The higher values portrayed the king on the obverse and relegated the Norwegian arms to the reverse. The decimal series featured the royal monogram on the reverse of the low values [16–17], and the king's effigy and arms on the higher values. In 1908 new types were introduced for the low values, with the crowned monogram of Haakon VII. The series with the monogram of Olaf V or his profile (1958) adopted pictorial reverses [18–20]. Coins of 50, 100, 200 kroner (silver) or 1500 kroner (gold) have been issued recently, mainly for sporting events.

FINLAND

The Finns were converted to Christianity in the 12th century and Finland became a Swedish duchy in 1284. Local issues, from about 1410, were followed by coins in the name of the Swedish king, struck intermittently at Åbo (Turku) from 1558 to 1801. Under Russian rule the markka, worth a quarter rouble, became the unit of currency, divided into 100 penniä, and coins bore the Tsar's monogram (low values) or the imperial double eagle (high values) with the value on the reverse. Following the abolition of the monarchy, coins with the double eagle (minus its crowns) were issued in 1917, but the series adopted by the Republic of Finland (Suomen Tasavalta) [21–26] bore the lion rampant of the Vasa kings until 1969, when an ornamental knot was substituted on the lowest values.

Since 1990 some pictorial elements have crept in. Previously, the 5 markkaa coins featured icebreakers, the ships *Varma* (1972–8) or *Urho* (1979–83). Special issues from 10 to 2000 markkaa have appeared in recent years, celebrating anniversaries of independence and a few historical figures. Finland produced the first coins marking the modern Olympics (1951–2) and sporting events, from the Lahti Games to the World Ski Championship, continue to predominate.

Above: The 5 markkaa of 1986 shows an unusual incuse treatment for numerals and inscriptions.

THE OLYMPIC GAMES

The great Panhellenic sporting festival known as the Olympic Games was in existence by 776 BC and continued to be held every four years until AD 393, when it was suppressed. The concept of a great sporting contest of athletes of all nations was revived in 1894 by Baron Pierre de Coubertin and the first modern Olympics were staged at Athens in 1896. The Games have been held every four years since then, except during the World Wars.

Special coins for the classical Games were issued by the tiny Greek state of Elis in the Peloponnese, in whose territory the athletic contest was held, but it was not until 1951–2 that coins were minted to celebrate the Games of the modern era, when Finland produced a silver 500 markkaa to publicize the Helsinki Games. No further Olympic coins were minted until 1964, when Japan produced 100 and 1000 yen coins for the Summer Games at Tokyo that year, and Austria issued a 50 schilling silver coin showing a ski-jumper, in honour of the Innsbruck Winter Games. In 1968, Mexico hosted the Summer Games and issued a 25 peso silver coin. Germany celebrated the Munich Olympics in 1972 by issuing six 10 mark coins, and in the same year Japan released a 100 yen coin for the Winter Games held at Sapporo.

Below: A set of four silver crowns issued by Gibraltar to mark the 1998 Winter Olympic Games in Japan, showing various winter sports.

For the Montreal Olympics in 1976 Canada produced seven sets, each comprising two $5 and $10 silver coins, topped by $100 gold coins in two different sizes and alloys, making a total of 30 coins. By contrast, Austria issued four 100 schilling coins featuring winter events for the Games at Innsbruck in 1976.

Up to that time Olympic coins had been confined to the countries hosting the Summer and Winter Games, but now coins began to appear elsewhere, and in many cases it has to be admitted that these supporting issues were often better designed and more visually attractive than those from the host countries. One example is the handsome crowns, in silver or cupro-nickel, produced by the Isle of Man for the Olympics from 1980 onward, a tradition maintained right down to the present time.

For the 1980 Summer Games in Moscow, the Soviet Union embarked on a lengthy series of coins, spread over the previous three years and struck

Above: A coin from Niue (top) to mark the admission of tennis to the Games in 1987 and an Olympic torchbearer and globe on a $50 coin of 1988 (bottom).

in silver, gold and platinum. Exceptionally, the USA, which hosted the Winter Games at Lake Placid that year, did not issue any commemorative coins. Four years later, however, when the same country hosted the Summer Games at Los Angeles, a 30-year embargo on commemorative coins was broken by the release of a silver dollar and a gold eagle ($10).

The 1984 Winter Olympics were staged in Sarajevo, and, to publicize the Games, Yugoslavia had begun issuing a series of 500 dinar silver coins at six-monthly intervals from 1982 onward, featuring various winter sports on

Timeless Classic

Benedetto Pistrucci's St George and the Dragon, featured on the gold coins of 1816–25, was revived in 1871 and has occupied the reverse of the gold coins ever since. It was also used for the silver crowns of 1818–23 and 1887–1902 and finally for the crown of 1951 marking the Festival of Britain. The model for St George was a waiter at Brunet's Hotel in Leicester Square, London.

EARLY TWENTIETH CENTURY

The coins of Edward VII followed the pattern of his predecessor, the standing Britannia motif of the florin being a notable concession to Art Nouveau (and inspiring the later Britannia bullion coins). A garlanded crown featured on the reverse of the George V crowns, but an Art Deco version of St George and the Dragon was used for the silver crown of 1935 for the silver jubilee [17]. Pictorial motifs were used on the low-value coins of George VI and Elizabeth II [20], while two different shillings (with English or Scottish heraldic lions) appeared in 1937 [18–19]. Few commemoratives appeared in this period, notably the crown honouring Sir Winston Churchill (1965).

DECIMAL COINAGE

Debated since the 1790s, British decimalization finally reached fruition in 1971. In the run-up to it several of the £sd series were not struck after 1967, while the first decimal coins appeared in 1968, the 5 and 10 new pence being struck in the same sizes as the shilling and florin. The half crown was withdrawn at the end of 1968 and in February 1971 the penny and threepence were superseded by the new ½, 1 and 2 pence coins [21]. In 1969 the 10 shilling note was replaced by the seven-sided 50 new pence. In 1982 the word "New" was dropped from the inscription and the small seven-sided 20 pence was introduced [24]. Two years later the halfpenny was discontinued.

The 50 pence was reduced in size in 1987, and the 5 and 10 pence were likewise reduced in 1990 and 1992 respectively. A nickel-brass circulating pound coin was introduced in 1983 and since its inception the reverse has changed annually [26]. Two pound coins were issued as commemoratives (1988–96) but a bimetallic coin of this value was added to the circulating series in 1997 [22]. The effigy of Queen Elizabeth has been changed four times. A bust by Mary Gillick was used for pre-decimal coinage [23], followed by effigies by Arnold Machin (1969), Raphael Maklouf (1988) [25] and Ian Rank-Broadley (1998). The crown was used for commemoratives and decimalized as 25 pence, but in 1990 it was revalued at £5. The 50 pence coin has often been used as a commemorative medium since 1973 [27].

Above: A crown released in 1981 to celebrate the wedding of the Prince of Wales and Lady Diana Spencer.

IRELAND AND OFFSHORE BRITISH ISLANDS

As well as the United Kingdom, there are four other countries in the British Isles that issue their own coins. The coins of Ireland issued before the Union of 1801 have already been discussed, but after 1928 the Irish Free State (now the Republic of Ireland) issued distinctive coins, while the Channel Islands (Guernsey and Jersey) and the Isle of Man each have a coinage history going back centuries.

Left: Guernsey released a square 10 shilling coin with rounded corners in 1966 to celebrate the 900th anniversary of the Norman Conquest of England, bearing the bust of William the Conqueror, Duke of Normandy. The Channel Islands are the last remnants of the Duchy governed by the British Crown.

JERSEY

Hoards of Armorican Celtic staters from 75–50 BC have been discovered in the Channel Islands, suggesting that they may even have been minted there.

Various bank tokens were issued between 1812 and 1831[1–2], but French currency circulated in Jersey until 1834, when the island switched to British money, and distinctive coins were adopted in 1841. Unfortunately, the money of account was the pre-Revolutionary French sol, tariffed at 520 to the pound. Jersey's largest coin was worth 2 sols – 1/260 of a pound or 1/13 of a shilling – hence the values on the early coins: 1/52 (farthing) [3–4], 1/26 (halfpenny) and 1/13 (penny). In 1877 the currency was brought into line with Britain and the coins revalued at 1/48, 1/24 and 1/12 of a shilling [5]. British coins served the higher values until 1957, when the quarter shilling (3 pence) was introduced. Since 1971 the decimal coinage has followed British standards.

GUERNSEY

French coins circulated in Guernsey for centuries, but halfpennies and farthings were imported from England from 1672 along with worn silver coins, which were not recalled until 1817. The vacuum was filled by a wide range of foreign coins and order was not restored until 1830, when the island introduced its own coinage based on the ancient French *double tournois*, hence "Double" on the Guernsey coins [6–9]. Copper, and later bronze, issues of 8 (penny), 4 (halfpenny), 2 (farthing) and 1 double (half farthing) bore the arms of the bailiwick and the value.

A cupro-nickel threepence featuring a cow appeared in 1958–66 and the square 10 shillings in 1966. Since 1971 the full range of coins has conformed to British standards, the arms occupying the obverse until 1977, when Elizabeth II's profile was substituted. Gold and silver commemoratives have been struck for Alderney, Guernsey's dependency, since 1989.

ISLE OF MAN

Silver pennies modelled on the Hiberno-Norse coins of Ireland, but with blundered inscriptions and a crude portrait, were struck about 1025–35, but otherwise Scottish, English and Irish coins and tokens circulated freely and included Murray's Pence – local tokens declared legal tender in 1673. Distinctive pennies and halfpennies date from 1709, issued under the authority of the Earls of Derby [10–11] and later the Dukes of Atholl [12–13] as Lords of Man, with their emblems. The island was transferred to the British Crown in 1765 but regal coinage was not issued until 1786, with the bust of George III [14–15]. No coins were struck from

Above: The Isle of Man's close ties with Scotland are reflected in the set of four crowns issued in 1996 to mark the bicentenary of the death of Robert Burns, Scotland's national poet.

1813 to 1839, when coppers portraying Victoria were released [16]. Island money was tariffed at 14 pence to the shilling, but the Manx government brought it into line with Britain in 1840 and from then until 1971 British coins circulated. A gold series of 1965 marked the bicentenary of the Revestment Act, while a crown of 1970 featured the tailless Manx cat [19].

Since 1971 the island has issued the full range of coins for general circulation. The reverses often bear the national three-legged emblem and its motto, "Quocunque Jeceris Stabit", which translates as "Whithersoever you throw it, it will stand" [17]. While generally conforming to British standards, the Isle of Man pioneered £1 (1978), £2 and £5 coins (1981) in virenium, a special base-metal alloy [20]. Since 1972 it has been one of the world's most prolific issuers of commemoratives [18] and special issues, often in long thematic sets [21–22].

IRELAND

The first coins, designed by the noted sculptor Percy Metcalfe, appeared in 1928 with a harp (obverse) and various birds and animals (reverse), earning the nickname the Barnyard Series [23–25, 27–28]. The obverse was modified in 1939 when "Eire" (Ireland) replaced "Saorstat Eireann" (Irish Free State). In 1966 the 50th anniversary of the Easter Rising was marked by a 10 shilling coin portraying Padriag Pearse and the statue of Cuchulainn. Ireland decimalized its currency at the same time as Britain, using the same specifications, but adopted distinctive nickel-bronze 20 pence (1986) and cupro-nickel pound coins (1990). The harp obverse was retained, as well as the horse, salmon and bull motifs on the 20, 10 and 5 pence [29–30], but Hiberno-Norse ornament graced the bronze coins [26], while the pound featured a stag and woodcock, formerly on the farthing, was promoted to the 50 pence. A 50 pence featuring the civic arms celebrated the Dublin millennium in 1998. The Millennium was marked by a pound coin depicting a galley surmounted by a cross, symbolizing the advent of Christianity in Ireland. Ireland adopted the euro in 2002, but medallic pattern ecus signalled the EEC Council Meeting in Dublin in 1990.

Portrait Gallery

One of the most spectacular coins of recent times was the crown released by the Isle of Man in 1987 to celebrate the bicentenary of the American Constitution. The reverse shows the Statue of Liberty surrounded by 11 portraits of US statesmen, from George Washington to Ronald Reagan.

BRITISH EUROPEAN TERRITORIES

Four Mediterranean countries with long and distinctive histories are grouped here because they came under British rule for many years and their modern coinage was therefore either closely linked to that of Britain or strongly influenced by it.

Left: The traditions of the Knights of St John of Jerusalem are continued to this day by the Sovereign Order of Malta, based in Rome. Since 1967 the Order has produced a large number of medallic pieces, denominated in scudi, illustrating the history of the Knights and raising funds for its charitable works.

CYPRUS

This island was of vital importance to Mediterranean cultures in the Bronze Age as the chief source of copper (from which the island derives its name); imitation cowhides cast in copper rank among the earliest forms of currency. In Greek classical times coins were struck at Amathus, Salamis, Paphos, Idalium and Citium. Typical of these coins was the silver of Evagoras II (361–351 BC) of Salamis [1–2] and Azbaal of Citium in the 5th century BC [5–6]. Coins of Alexander the Great were minted in Cyprus [3–4] from the 4th century BC.

Shown here is a Byzantine coin of Isaac the Usurper (1184–91), struck in Cyprus before he was overthrown [7–8]. Between 1192 and 1324, deniers, obols and gros were issued by the Crusader Guy de Lusignan and his descendants, such as Henry III, who struck large silver gros with facing portraits and cross motifs [9]. Distinctive coinage was revived in 1879 when Cyprus became a British protectorate. The Turkish piastre was tariffed at nine to the shilling, hence there were coins of 18, 9 and 4 piastres as well as smaller coins down to the bronze quarter piastre. These bore the effigy of the British monarch and the value or arms on the reverse. Latterly the reverse featured two lions passant gardant, the emblem of Richard the Lionheart, who seized Cyprus from the Byzantines in 1191.

Decimal currency based on the pound of 1000 mils was adopted in 1955, and pictorial reverses were then selected [10–11]. In 1960 Cyprus became an independent republic and introduced coins with the state emblem on the obverse [12]. The currency was reformed in 1983 and the pound of 100 cents adopted. A few commemoratives have appeared since 1976.

MALTA

Like Cyprus, Malta has a long numismatic history, its earliest coins being attributed to the Phoenicians in the 3rd century BC. Subsequently there was a limited (and very rare) coinage under Greek or Roman influence [13].

The Knights of St John of Jerusalem, having been driven out of Rhodes, occupied Malta from 1530 until they were expelled by Napoleon in 1798, and coins in various denominations from the tiny picciolo (72 to the penny) to the zechino (sequin, or third of a pound sterling) [14–15] were minted under successive Grand Masters from Villiers de l'Isle Adam (1533) to Count von Hompesch (1798) [16–17]. The French garrison produced siege coins in gold, silver and bronze during the British blockade of 1799–1800.

Ordinary British coins circulated from 1800 until 1972 but included third farthings (1827–1913), which corresponded to the copper grano. A decimal system based on the lira or

Gallantry Award

Throughout its long and turbulent history Malta was besieged many times, but its worst ordeal was the incessant bombardment from sea and air during World War II. The fortitude of the islanders was recognized in 1942, when George VI conferred the George Cross, the highest civilian gallantry award, on the island of Malta. Several definitive coins have borne the cross, while the 50th anniversary was celebrated by a £M5 coin featuring the cross and the citation.

pound of 100 cents or 1000 mils was adopted in 1972, with various motifs on the obverse and the value on the reverse [18–21]. In 1982 the tenth anniversary of decimalization was marked by distinctive obverses. An entirely new series with the national arms and pictorial reverses was adopted in 1991 [22–23].

A characteristic of Maltese coins is the use of different shapes – scalloped edges (mils) and octagons or decagons (25 and 50 cents). Gold and silver coins from £M1 to £M100 have appeared since 1972, beginning with a series depicting Maltese landmarks, and a set of 12 £M5 was issued in 1986 tracing the maritime history of the Knights of Malta.

IONIAN ISLANDS

This group of islands in the Adriatic, including Corfu, Cephalonia and Zante, were under Venetian rule until 1798, when they were seized by the French. They were later occupied by the British in 1809 and ceded to Greece in 1864. From 1819 [24–25] onward they had a series of copper obols and silver 30 lepta coins with the lion of St Mark on the obverse [26] and Britannia on the reverse [27].

GIBRALTAR

The Rock of Gibraltar, captured by Britain from Spain in 1704, used British and Spanish currency, although copper coins of half, one and two quarts appeared in 1842, with a profile of Queen Victoria (obverse) and the key and triple-tower emblem (reverse) [28–29]. Cupro-nickel crowns with the triple tower were issued from 1968 to 1970, mainly for use in casinos.

Gibraltar adopted decimal coinage the following year and switched to a crown-sized 25 new pence with a Barbary ape on the reverse. Otherwise there were no distinctive coins for general circulation until the 1988 series, conforming to British weights and specifications, with the Queen's effigy and pictorial reverses [30–31].

Apart from a set of gold £25, £50 and £100 coins in 1975 to celebrate the 250th anniversary of the introduction of sterling currency, commemoratives began with crowns for the Queen's silver wedding (1972) and silver jubilee (1977). Since 1988, however, commemorative and special issues have been very prolific, ranging from Christmas 50 pence coins to gold pieces marking the Japanese royal wedding (1993) and the centenary of Peter Rabbit (1994). The gold coins are denominated from the tiny 1/25 crown upwards. Gibraltar was also unique in adopting coins denominated in both sterling and ecus (1991), ranging from the cupro-nickel £2 (2.8 ecus) to the gold 140 ecus of 1996 [32–33].

Above: The reverse of the Gibraltar 50 pence shows the value surrounded by candytuft, the national flower.

BENELUX COUNTRIES

Belgium, the Netherlands and Luxembourg have a common history dating from the Middle Ages when they formed the duchy of Burgundy, which passed under Habsburg rule in 1494 and later became the Spanish Netherlands. To that period belongs the silver patagon of Charles II [1–2]. The Dutch revolted against Spanish rule in the 16th century, and Belgium later became the Austrian Netherlands. After 1815 the two countries were united under Prince William of Orange-Nassau, who reigned as King William I of the Netherlands and Grand Duke William of Luxembourg. Belgium seceded in 1830, and Luxembourg passed to a junior line of Orange-Nassau in 1890, when Queen Wilhelmina was barred from succession under Salic Law. Close ties resulted in the formation of Benelux in 1945, a fore-runner of the European Community.

Left: Francis I (1708–65), Duke of Lorraine and Holy Roman Emperor, whose arms appear on this silver coin struck in Brussels, ruled the Austrian Netherlands with his wife, Maria Theresia. Together they survived numerous disputes with their fellow European powers, including the bloody Seven Years War, during which the Habsburg heiress – rather than her husband – is remembered for her great courage and determination.

BELGIUM

The Celtic tribe known as the Belgae, who inhabited the region in pre-Christian times and struck the staters that formed the first coinage in Britain, gave their name to the country of Belgium. In the Middle Ages, apart from the prolific issues of the Duchy of Burgundy and later of the Spanish Netherlands, the rulers of Brabant [3–4], Hainault and Flanders [5–6] and the bishops of Liege all struck their own coins. Later, Spanish, French and Dutch coins were in use.

The Belgian provinces of the Netherlands broke away from Holland in 1830 and in 1831 elected Prince Leopold of Saxe-Coburg-Gotha as their king, shown here on a pattern 5 francs [7–8]. The country got off to a bad start with its first coin, the 5 centimes of 1831, which was erroneously dated 1811. Other denominations followed in 1832–3, based on the franc. Silver coins portrayed King Leopold with a wreathed value on the reverse. Coins were inscribed in French, but from 1894 both French ("Belgique") and Flemish ("Belgie") versions were produced. Later coins bore the country name in both languages [9] and from 1938 parallel sets had the French or Flemish name first.

Coins portraying a coal miner [10–11] appeared in 1953 and continued until the advent of the euro. Royal portraiture gradually returned to the franc coins from 1969, the reverse showing the date, denomination and country name in French or Flemish [12]. Since the centenary of independence (1930), commemorative coins have marked royal anniversaries and important events, the 20 francs often serving as a medium for precious gold commemoratives[13].

NETHERLANDS

After breaking free of Spain in the 1570s the seven United Provinces issued an enormous range of coins until 1608, when there was some attempt to rationalize the coinage, resulting in gold ducats, silver rijksdaalders [14–15], bronze stuivers and silver klippe double stuivers [16–17] or duits. The French struck coins in the name of Louis Bonaparte as King of Holland (1806–14), but following the establishment of the Kingdom of the Netherlands in 1815 coins based on the gulden of 100 cents were introduced. They continued to be minted at Brussels until 1830, when Belgium seceded, and since then have been struck at Utrecht.

Most Dutch coins have the monarch's profile on the obverse and a crown or the royal arms on the reverse [18–19]. During the long reign of Wilhelmina (1890–1948) five different portraits appeared [20–21], whereas a stylized profile of Queen Beatrix has been in use since 1982. Relatively few commemoratives have appeared since 1979, when the 400th anniversary of the Treaty of Utrecht was celebrated. They are chiefly noted for the avant-garde treatment of the Queen's portrait, at times verging on caricature.

LUXEMBOURG

Originally a county of the Carolingian Empire, Luxembourg became a duchy in 1354. Under the Holy Roman Empire, coins were minted at Antwerp, portraying successive Dukes of Luxembourg [22] with an armorial reverse [23]. The duchy passed under the rule of Burgundy, Spain, Austria and France from 1443 to 1815, when it was constituted a separate grand duchy under the personal rule of the King of the Netherlands.

Dutch and later Belgian currency was used, apart from bronze 2, 5 and 10 cent coins from 1854 to the end of the century, with an armorial obverse and value reverse [26–27]. They were superseded by cupro-nickel coins portraying Grand Duke Adolphe (1901) or William IV (1905–12) [24–25], but higher denominations were only gradually introduced from 1916. Later coins favoured an armorial obverse, the French name of the country being dropped from 1939 in favour of "Letzeburg", although French was later restored to the higher values. Like the Low Countries, Luxembourg was occupied by Germany in World War II; unlike Belgium and the Netherlands, the grand duchy was absorbed into the Third Reich and did not resume its own coinage until 1946. As in Belgium, the language problem has been solved since 1965 by reducing inscriptions to the bare minimum.

A few commemoratives have appeared since 1946, when the 600th anniversary of John the Blind was celebrated. In more recent years most have alluded to Luxembourg's position at the heart of the European Community. A 500 franc silver coin of 1994 marked the 50th anniversary of liberation and featured the US flag on the reverse.

Anepigraphic Coins

Political correctness in Belgium eventually led to the issue of trilingual coins, with the country name in French, Flemish and German (recognizing the inhabitants of Eupen, Malmedy and St Vith). Alternatively, however, many coins since 1969 have had an anepigraphic obverse with no inscription of any kind, the profile of the king being sufficient identification.

Above: Although modern Luxembourg coins have the denomination in French, the country name in the local German dialect, Letzeburg, has appeared below the arms on the obverse since the 1940s.

SWITZERLAND

The Swiss Confederation, consisting of 22 cantons or states located in the Alps, is unique politically, linguistically and culturally: a model of federal union bringing together people of French, German, Italian and Romansch languages and different religious and political backgrounds. The region was successively under the rule of Rome and the Holy Roman Empire, but in 1291 the elders of the remote valleys of Uri and Unterwalden joined forces with Schwyz (from which the modern country name is derived) to form an alliance while recognizing each other's rights to autonomy.

Left: William Tell, the celebrated crossbowman of Uri, saved his district from Austrian oppression. According to legend, he was forced to shoot an apple off his son's head but later he slew the Austrian governor and so triggered off the independence movement.

CANTONAL COINS

Each of the Swiss cantons issued its own coins in a bewildering array of denominations from the early 14th century onwards, including gold from 1411. Even after Swiss independence was briefly suppressed by the French from 1798–1803, when they created the Helvetic Republic (named after the Roman province of Helvetia), the cantons resumed their coinage and continued until 1850, when a federal system based on the franc (frank) of 100 centimes (rappen) was adopted.

The coins used in the individual cantons tended to reflect the currency of neighbouring countries. Thus, those in the Italian-speaking region favoured the franco or lira of 20 soldi or 240 denari (like the British £sd system), whereas the easterly cantons adopted the pfennig, thaler (typified by coins from Zurich [1–2] and Berne [5–6]), kreuzer and haller (heller) and the French-speaking cantons favoured deniers, quarts, sols [3–4], florins and pistols. In many cases the tiny rappen and batzen provided a basic unit, resulting in multiples in odd amounts, such as 21 batzen (Neuchatel) or 39 batzen (Vaud) to fit them into the franc or thaler systems. Most of these cantonal coins had an armorial obverse with the value on the reverse.

FEDERAL COINAGE

War between the cantons, mainly polarized on religious grounds, erupted in 1847, but after a brief campaign law and order were restored and the following year steps were taken to create a federal administration centred on Berne. The cantons agreed to give up their coinage privileges and a decimal system based on the franc was introduced throughout the country.

Probably on account of the confusing plethora of denominations and designs in the cantonal coinage, the federal authorities decided to strike coins that, from the outset, would be universally recognizable and acceptable. The lower denominations of the first series, introduced in 1850, had the name "Helvetia" on the obverse over a shield containing a Swiss cross, while the reverse had numerals within a wreath [9]. No notation of value was included to indicate rappen, centimes or centesimi. Silver coins [7–8] from the franc upwards had allegorical motifs on the obverse and the wreathed value and date on the reverse, although in this case the abbreviation "Fr." could be included to denote "francs", "franchi" or "franken".

The first change came in 1874–5, when a standing figure of Helvetia surrounded by 22 stars standardized the obverse of the 1 and 2 franc coins. In 1878 a female profile replaced the cross on the 5 and 10 rappen, followed by the 20 rappen in 1881 [10–11]. In these coins the country name was rendered in Latin "Confoederatio Helvetica". The seated figure on the 5 franc coin was replaced by a garlanded profile in 1888, with the cross on a shield flanked by the value on the reverse. This type continued until 1922, when the bust of William Tell (obverse) and modified shield (reverse) was introduced. The bronze subsidiary coins had a Swiss cross on the obverse and a wreathed value on the reverse [12–13]. Last, new designs were adopted for the 1 and 2 rappen coins in 1948, with a plain cross (obverse) and a numeral superimposed on an ear of corn (reverse) [14–15]. Apart from the replacement of silver by cupronickel in 1968, the Swiss coins have since remained unchanged [16–17].

Shooting Festival Coins

From the late 16th century many German states and free cities issued special coins that were given as prizes at shooting festivals. This tradition spread to Switzerland in 1842, and while it died out everywhere else it continued there until 1939. The coins, variously denominated 4 francs, 40 batzen or 5 francs, usually had armorial or allegorical motifs, with figures of marksmen or crossed rifles as popular images. These handsome silver coins, which were struck for the annual festivals at a different venue each year, were last regularly minted in 1885 but were sporadically revived in the 1930s.

COMMEMORATIVE ISSUES

Just as the permanent series has been very structured since its inception, so also the approach to commemorative and special issues has been very carefully orchestrated. Beginning in 1936, 5 franc coins were produced for special occasions [18–19], the first such coin publicizing the Confederation Armament Fund. The majority of coins have celebrated historic anniversaries or major current events and organizations, such as the Zurich Exhibition of 1939, the International Olympic Committee [20–21] and the Wine Festival of 1999 [22–23]. Since 1991, however, the chief medium for special issues has been the 20 franc denomination, usually confined to no more than two coins a year.

LIECHTENSTEIN

This tiny principality has had a lengthy association with Austria, whose currency it used until the end of World War I, augmented by the silver and gold vereinsthaler in the 19th century and similar coins in the kronen system from 1900, portraying the ruler (obverse) and princely arms (reverse).

In 1921 Leichtenstein entered a monetary union with Switzerland and adopted its coinage, followed by indigenous coinage of 100 rappen in 1924, portraying John II (1858–1929) or Franz I (1929–38). A series portraying Prince Francis Joseph II appeared in 1946. Since then there have been a few silver or gold commemoratives marking royal weddings, anniversaries [24–27] and the accession of Prince Hans Adam (1990) but Swiss coins are in everyday use.

GERMAN STATES

Within the boundaries of modern Germany there were hundreds of kingdoms, principalities, grand duchies, duchies, counties and free cities, which for almost 2000 years produced their own coins, ranging from Celtic and Roman provincial to the prolific Frankish and Saxon issues that preceded the medieval coinage. These coins range from the pilgrim denars of Cologne [1–2] to the regal issues of Otto III (982–1002) [3–4]. Although the number was greatly reduced as a result of mergers and territorial aggrandisement by the more powerful states such as Prussia [5–6] in the course of the 17th and 18th centuries, no fewer than 39 states were, nevertheless, still issuing coins by 1815. Even after the formation of the German Empire in 1871 many states reserved the right to strike coins with distinctive reverses, even if the obverse conformed to the imperial standard – a precedent followed by the European Union's common currency at the present day.

Below: Some of the most spectacular coins ever struck emanated from the Duchy of Brunswick and the Kingdom of Saxony, notably the great multiple thalers of the 17th and 18th centuries. Examples include the 1631 Purim thaler of Erfurt, with Hebrew inscription and radiate sign of Yahweh (left), and the 1661 thaler of the bishopric of Munster showing St Paul above a panoramic view of the city (right).

CURRENCY REFORM

Different systems of weights and measures as well as varying standards of gold and silver meant that each German state was a law unto itself, making interstate trade exceedingly complex. By the late 18th century this had been rationalized to some extent, with distinct patterns emerging in the northern and southern states, whose coinage was largely based on the thaler and kreuzer respectively. Thus, in the north, the thaler was worth 24 groschen, a groschen was worth 12 pfennige and 2 heller equalled a pfennig [7–8], but there was also the mariengroschen, worth 8 pfennige. Meanwhile, attempts to equate the gulden with the thaler resulted in a ratio of 2 gulden to one and a third thalers. In the southern states the kreuzer [9–10] was worth 4 pfennige or 8 heller, but 24 kreuzer Landmunze were equal in value to 20 kreuzer Conventionsmunze, while 120 Convention kreuzer equalled two Convention gulden or 1 Convention thaler ("Convention" refers to an agreement of 1753, which first tried to bring the states into line). A new agreement (1837) reduced the complexity further. In the north the thaler was now worth 30 groschen or 360 pfennige (as recently as the 1960s Germans habitually referred to the 10 pfennig coin as a groschen). In the south the sole unit was the kreuzer.

VARIETY OF SUBJECTS

Several states produced a local coinage for provinces and other administrative subdivisions. Thus the kingdom of Prussia [11–12] also produced a subsidiary coinage for the province of Brandenburg and, within that, coins for Brandenburg-Ansbach-Bayreuth. The most notable of the subdivisions arose in Brunswick, where the practice of dividing a territory among all the sons of the ruler, instead of leaving everything to the eldest son, created a fragmentation resulting in the issue of separate coins for Brunswick-Lüneberg [13–14], Brunswick-Grubenhagen and the numismatically very prolific Brunswick-Wolfenbuttel [15]. Separate coins were also produced by the free cities of Bremen, Hamburg [16–17] (such as the Standing Knight ducat), Hanover [18–19] and Lübeck; in these cases the civic arms replaced royal portraits [22–23].

In the 19th century some states were more apt to strike commemorative coins than others. The most prolific in this respect was Bavaria, which seems to have recorded every event with large silver coins, from the death of the scientific instrument makers Reichenbach and Fraunhofer (1826) to the opening of the steam railway (1836). Several coins featured the various royal orders of chivalry, anticipating the long thematic sets of the present day, and when there was no special occasion to celebrate Bavaria resorted to the magnificent thaler of 1828 entitled "Blessings of Heaven on the Royal Family" whose reverse portrayed the queen and her eight children [20–21].

Currency Chaos

Coins with values expressed in two ways were frequently issued by the German states. Anhalt-Dessau had coins with "3 pfennige" on one side and "120 Einen Mark" ("120 to one mark") on the other, whereas Anhalt-Zerbst had a coin inscribed "IV Groschen" (obverse) and "LXXX I F. Marck" (reverse) signifying "80 to one fine mark". The 5 kreuzer coins of Arenberg had "CCXL Eine Feine Marck" ("240 to the fine mark"). Conversely, thalers often had their value expressed in local currency, while Hanoverian coins were inscribed in two equivalent values (gutengroschen and mariengroschen) and had three different standards of gold and silver fineness.

MONETARY UNION

In 1857 the German states produced the prototype for a single currency, adopting the vereinsthaler ("union thaler") of a standard weight and fineness. Although this became the standard, the states continued to issue their local coins for small change, often attempting to fit them into the Verein system [24–25]. The unification of Germany under the hegemony of Prussia in 1871 did not lead to an immediate streamlining of coinage, and both the thaler and kreuzer systems continued for several years, in the northern and southern districts respectively, before they were replaced by the mark of 100 pfennige.

Although a standard imperial coinage was gradually introduced from 1873 onward, many of the states continued to issue their own gold and silver coins above 1 mark in value. These coins bore the imperial eagle on one side and, theoretically at least, were legal tender throughout the Reich, though the other side bore the portrait of the local ruler [26–27]. The coins consisted of 10 and 20 marks in gold and 2 and 5 marks in silver. Interestingly, many 3 mark coins were also produced, because this weight was in line with the obsolete thaler. As well as these high-value coins for general circulation many of the states issued commemoratives, mostly celebrating royal weddings and jubilees.

The state coins vanished shortly after the outbreak of World War I (as gold and silver disappeared from general circulation). The last of them appeared in Württemberg in 1916, to celebrate Wilhelm II's silver jubilee, and in Bavaria in 1918, to mark Ludwig III's golden wedding. The concept of a standard obverse with regional reverses has been adopted by the EC for its euro coinage in recent years.

15
16 17
18 19
20
21
22 23
24 25
26 27

GERMAN REICH

The First Reich was the empire created by Charlemagne in AD 800, uniting most of Christian western Europe. It eventually became the Holy Roman Empire, which was finally dissolved in 1806. The Second Reich was created by the victory of the German states over France in 1871 and was actually proclaimed in the Hall of Mirrors at Versailles. Although it ceased to be an empire in 1918 with the abolition of the monarchies, the term "Deutsches Reich" was retained by the Weimar Republic. In 1933, Adolf Hitler proclaimed the Third Reich, which was to last a thousand years before collapsing in 1945. Thus a unified German Reich existed for a total of only 75 years.

Left: Portrayed on the obverse of the 2 and 5 Reichsmark coins of 1936–9, Paul von Hindenburg (1847–1934) rose to the rank of field-marshal in the imperial army and was a national hero before becoming second (and last) president of the Weimar Republic. He appointed Hitler as chancellor in 1933.

THE EMPIRE

Nothing symbolized the unity of Germany more graphically than the coinage that was introduced in 1873. The obverse, devoid of any inscription, was dominated by the imperial eagle, while the reverse bore the inscription "Deutsches Reich" followed by the date with the value in the centre [1–2]. For all his vanity, Kaiser Wilhelm II never appeared on the imperial coinage (though he was portrayed on the Prussian coins); the imperial eagle alone would be depicted. This concept gives the coins of the German Empire their distinctive character and cohesion. In the early period (to 1889) the eagle was given a generous margin all round but from 1890 onward the size of the eagle was increased to fill the entire obverse of the coins [3–4]. During World War I bronze was replaced by aluminium for the pfennig, while silver coins disappeared after 1916.

Although the German Empire was dissolved in November 1918, its coinage survived for several years: the 5 and 10 pfennige, struck in iron from 1915, lasted until 1922, and the 50 pfennige, which had been discontinued in 1903, was revived in 1919, in aluminium rather than the original silver. In addition there were numerous local issues of subsidiary coinage, usually including the word *Kriegsgeld* (war money) in their inscriptions. Small-denomination tokens were also widely circulated in lieu of government issues from 1919 to 1921, but they omitted the word *Krieg*.

WEIMAR REPUBLIC

The Kaiser abdicated at the end of World War I and fled into exile in Holland, in November 1918. The other monarchies toppled in his wake. In 1919 a constitutional convention at Weimar in Thuringia proclaimed the republic would ever afterwards be known by this epithet.

Imperial coins continued until 1922 but they were soon engulfed in hyperinflation, which resulted in millions of marks being needed to buy a box of matches. Workers were paid daily and required wheelbarrows to cart away their wages in paper currency, which lost value overnight. In 1923, Hjalmar Schacht, president of the Reichsbank, performed the economic miracle of restoring the currency, introducing the Rentenmark of 100 Rentenpfennige, whose stability was vested in land [5–6]. Appropriately, the obverse types of this coinage depicted wheatsheaves or ears of wheat. By 1924 it was even possible to reintroduce the silver mark, and the following year a new currency, based on the Reichsmark of 100 Reichspfennige, was adopted. The wheat motifs were retained for the pfennigs [17–18] but from the outset the mark values bore a spread-eagle shorn of its imperial crown and breast shield [15–16].

Designs for coinage with the allegorical bust of Germania on one side and the republican eagle on the other were produced in 1926, but they were never put into production [9–10]. Coins of 3 mark value were issued from 1922 onward, both for general circulation and as a commemorative medium, a hangover from the thalers of an earlier period.

From 1925 onward, 5 mark coins and patterns were also produced to celebrate historic events and people, from the anniversary of the liberation of the Rhineland [7–8] to the pioneering global flights of the Graf Zeppelin in America [11–12] and Egypt [13–14], which also portrayed the zeppelin's commander, Dr Hugo Eckner.

Notgeld

The term *Notgeld*, meaning "emergency money", is usually associated with the prolific issues of paper produced in every German town and city during the hyperinflation of 1922–3, but there were also local coins, mostly struck in aluminium or bronze (sometimes plated to simulate gold). Red stoneware or white porcelain coins were produced at various potteries, notably the Meissen factory, whose coins circulated in Saxony. Unlike the earlier *Kriegsgeld* these pieces attained astronomical denominations, Westphalia producing coins up to 50 million marks in value.

THIRD REICH

Adolf Hitler was appointed Reichs Chancellor by President Paul von Hindenburg in January 1933, not because the Nazis seized power (as is commonly believed) but because at that time they represented the largest party in the Reichstag (the German parliament). The burning of the Reichstag building on February 27, allegedly by communists but actually by the Nazis themselves, gave Hitler the pretext for a general election, which was masterminded by Hermann Göring. Even so, this resulted in only a very slender majority for the Nazi party, but it was sufficient for Hitler to push through an enabling act in March 1933, allowing him to abolish all other political parties. This and the death of the aged president placed absolute power in Hitler's hands. Within weeks of his appointment, therefore, Adolf Hitler had transformed Germany into an absolute dictatorship.

A 4 Reichspfennig coin dated 1932 was struck at Berlin with a new obverse showing the Nazi eagle and swastika emblem – the date was clearly an error rather than an anticipation of Hitler's rise to power in January 1933. This became the standard obverse type for most of the coins issued until 1945 [19–23]. As in World War I, although a reasonable supply of coinage was maintained throughout World War II zinc was substituted in 1940 (1–10 pfennige) [24–25], while aluminium replaced nickel in the 50 pfennige, and the silver mark [26–27] and its multiples ceased to be produced after 1939.

Unlike the Weimar Republic, the Nazi state made very little use of commemorative coins. Among the few exceptions were the 5 mark coins struck for the 450th anniversary of Martin Luther in 1933 and the 175th anniversary of Friedrich Schiller in 1934. Another coin of 1934, showing the Potsdam Military Church, marked the first anniversary of Nazi rule. The same design, minus the date, "21 März 1933", was retained for the general issue of 1934 and 1935 [28–29].

13 14 15 16 17 18 19 20 21 22 23 24 25 26 27 28 29

POSTWAR GERMANY

Following its unconditional surrender to the Allies in May 1945, Germany was divided into American, British, French and Russian zones of occupation. The coins that circulated in these zones were either introduced or adapted by the occupying forces. By 1948, Germany had polarized between the three western zones and the five easterly provinces under Soviet control, leading to the establishment of the German Federal Republic (west) and the German Democratic Republic (east). Both East and West Germany adopted the Deutschemark as their currency, although they remained separate entities, subject to different exchange rates. The Deutschemark was also the name of the currency adopted by the unified Germany after the GDR ceased to exist in October 1990.

Left: The silver 5 Deutschemark coin, contrasting with the lightweight aluminium coins of East Germany, was widely regarded as the symbol of West Germany's economic miracle during the Cold War period. This anepigraphic obverse continued until 1974, but from 1975 to 2000 a more stylized eagle was used, with the year inscribed below it.

ALLIED OCCUPATION

A zinc 1 pfennig coin dated 1944 was struck at Munich, presumably in the following year, when the mint was under Allied control, as the eagle motif was divested of its swastika. This set the pattern for the zinc 1, 5 and 10 pfennig coins, which circulated in occupied Germany until 1948 [1].

France occupied the Saar in 1945 and effectively integrated this rich industrial province. West Germany campaigned incessantly for its return and in 1955 France undertook to retrocede the territory to Germany in 1957. French currency was in use until 1954, when coins denominated from 10 to 50 franken (on a par with the French franc), inscribed in German, were adopted as an interim measure. The aluminium-bronze coins showed arms on a background of factories and a coal mine [4–5], while a cupro-nickel 100 franken, issued in 1955, had a more elaborate version of the arms.

FEDERAL REPUBLIC

The Allied powers handed over civil government to the newly constituted Federal Republic in May 1949, but the split between East and West occurred a year earlier, when the currency was reformed and the Deutschemark (DM) was introduced. Coins of 1, 5 and 10 pfennige, in bronze- or brass-clad steel with oak leaves on the obverse, were originally inscribed "Bank Deutscher Lander" (Bank of the German Provinces) [2, 8], but from 1950 they bore the new country name "Bundesrepublik Deutschland" [13]. These inscriptions also appeared on the cupro-nickel 50 pfennige [9], whose reverse showed a girl planting a seedling, and the cupro-nickel 1 [12] and 2 DM featuring the German eagle [6–7]. The 5 DM was struck in silver and had the value on the obverse [3] and eagle on the anepigraphic reverse.

When cupro-nickel replaced silver in 1975 a more stylized design was adopted for the 5 DM. Like the earlier coins of Germany this series was struck at several mints, which were identified by the code letters A (Berlin), D (Munich), F (Stuttgart), G (Karlsruhe) and J (Hamburg).

From 1952 until 1986 the 5 DM [10–11] was the preferred coin for commemoratives, while 10 DM coins, first used to celebrate the Munich Olympics (1972), were used as commemoratives from 1987 until 2000, when the euro coinage was adopted.

Portrait Gallery

From 1957 onwards the 2 DM became more interesting as its reverse portrayed famous Germans. The physicist Max Planck was followed by a series of postwar politicians (clockwise from top left): President Theodor Heuss (dates of use 1970–87), Konrad Adenauer (1969–87), Chancellor Ludwig Erhard (1988–2000) and Dr Kurt Schumacher (1979–93). Also portrayed were Franz Joseph Strauss (1990–2000) and Willy Brandt, Mayor of West Berlin throughout the Cold War (1994–2000). As can be seen, these coins were often in simultaneous production and circulated widely.

DEMOCRATIC REPUBLIC

In the immediate postwar period the coins of the Bank of the German Provinces circulated in the Soviet zone, but economic disparity between the Soviet and Allied zones led to the currency reform of 1948, which recognized the difference between the money in East and West Germany. At this time distinctive coins began to appear in the Soviet zone. They comprised 1, 5 and 10 pfennige in aluminium and were simply inscribed "Deutschland" (Germany), with a numeral obverse and a reverse showing an ear of wheat superimposed on a cog wheel symbolizing industry and agriculture [14–17]. The German Democratic Republic was formally instituted in October 1949 and by 1952 coins bore the emblem of the new state – a hammer and compass on wheat ears – with the country name "Deutsche Demokratische Republik" [18]. The 1 pfennig coin was modified in 1960, the central design now appearing within a border with the legend running around the outside [19–20]. Attempts to introduce higher denominations led to a short-lived 50 pfennig coin (1950 and 1958) [25], although this did not become a regular issue until 1968, followed by the 20 pfennige in 1969 [23–24]. Similarly, 1 and 2 mark [26–27] coins were sporadically produced from 1956 but did not become regular issues until 1973–4. The 1 pfennig was reissued in 1979 and remained in circulation until the switch to West German currency in 1990.

A 5 mark coin showing the Brandenburg Gate was minted in 1971 [21–22] and then annually from 1979 to 1990, but this denomination was mainly used for commemoratives [30–31], beginning with the 125th anniversary of Robert Koch (1968). From 1966, when the 125th anniversary of the architect Karl Schinkel was celebrated, 10 and 20 mark coins [28–29] were also released.

UNIFIED GERMANY

Ironically, the last issue of the GDR was a cupro-nickel 20 mark coin for the opening of the Brandenburg Gate in 1990 – the landmark that, with the breaching of the Berlin Wall, effectively brought the Democratic Republic to an end. The five eastern provinces were formally admitted into the Federal Republic on October 3, 1990.

No change was necessary in the coinage, which was merely extended to the East [32]. However, in 1991 a 10 DM coin marked the bicentenary of the Brandenburg Gate with an inscription signifying "Symbol of German Unity". For 40 years the gate had been the symbol of a divided nation. The commemorative coins issued since then tended to reinforce the concept of unity and a common heritage.

AUSTRIA AND HUNGARY

These two countries of Central Europe were at the heart of the Habsburg dominions, and for centuries they were administered as a single state. In the 19th century the rising tide of nationalism led to the Ausgleich (compromise) of 1867, whereby Kaiser Franz Josef of Austria also became Kiralyi Ferenc Joszef of Hungary. Henceforth, distinctive coins appeared under the Dual Monarchy, denominated in krone (korona) and heller (filler) respectively. The collapse of the monarchy in 1918 led to the establishment of two quite separate countries which, despite the political turmoil of the later 20th century, have retained close cultural and economic ties.

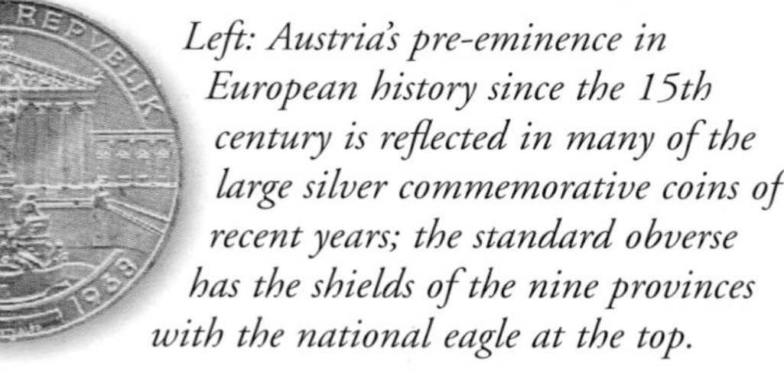

Left: Austria's pre-eminence in European history since the 15th century is reflected in many of the large silver commemorative coins of recent years; the standard obverse has the shields of the nine provinces with the national eagle at the top.

HABSBURG EMPIRE

Small silver coins known as *Wiener pfennige* (Vienna pennies), portraying the Dukes of Austria, were struck in the late Middle Ages, but the Habsburgs' outstanding contribution to numismatics was the development of large silver coins, the guldengroschen and the thaler [1–2] from the late 15th century, while gold ducats [3–4] ranked among the most popular trade coins until the early 20th century.

The circulating coinage of the Habsburg dominions was based on the thaler worth two gulden or 120 kreuzer [5–6], but the currency was decimalized in 1857 to the gulden or florin of 100 kreuzer, with the vereinsthaler worth 1 florin. These coins bore the bust of the emperor (obverse) and double-eagle emblem (reverse), but some of the smaller coins had the imperial arms (obverse) with a value (reverse). They were superseded by the krone of 100 heller in 1892, with arms and a value on the heller coins and the emperor's profile on the krone obverse and the imperial double eagle on the reverse [7–8].

Shooting festival 2 florin coins were struck in 1873 and 1879, while the opening of the Vienna–Trieste Railway in 1857 was marked by a double vereinsthaler. Both silver and gold coins celebrated the emperor's diamond jubilee (1908). The humble heller and the silver coins vanished after 1916, while iron or zinc alloys were used for the 2 and 10 heller of 1916–18.

Hungary was a major source of both gold and silver in the Middle Ages [18–19], most of it exported to Venice, hence the lengthy series of ducats and florins of the Kremnitz Mint from 1324 onward [20]. After 1526, however, Hungary was claimed by the Habsburgs and thereafter its coinage followed a similar pattern to that of Austria, but inscribed "krajczar" (kreuzer) [21–22] or "forint" (florin). The filler denominations of 1892–1914 featured the crown of St Stephen on the obverse, while the korona coins showed it on the reverse surmounting the value.

AUSTRIA

The krone continued as the unit of currency after World War I but rampant inflation reduced the 100 krone to a tiny bronze coin in 1923–4 [9]. Like Germany in the same period, Austria resorted to *Notgeld* paper money, but, upon the reformation of the currency in 1925 [10], introduced the schilling of 100 groschen. Coins were struck in bronze, cupro-nickel or silver up to the schilling for general circulation, but from 1928 silver 2 and 5 schilling or gold 25, 50 and 100 schilling coins were struck as commemoratives.

Austrian coins were suppressed in 1938, when the country was absorbed into the Third Reich. When distinctive coins resumed after World War II, aluminium or aluminium-bronze were used for the lower values and cupro-nickel for the schilling denominations in general circulation [11–14]. Like their pre-war counterparts, these coins had symbolic or pictorial motifs on the obverse and a numeral reverse. Commemoratives comprised base-metal 20 schilling coins (1982–2000) [15–17], silver 25, 50, 100, 200 and 500 schilling pieces (1955–2000) and gold 1000 schillings (1976–2000). In addition, gold 200 and 2000 schilling coins were struck annually from 1989 to 1999 in support of the Vienna Philharmonic Orchestra.

International Coin

The silver thaler portraying the Empress Maria Theresia, with the date frozen at 1780 (the year of her death), was struck at Vienna until 1937 and also after 1956 to satisfy demand from the Arab countries. It was struck in Milan and Venice in the 19th century, at Rome (1935–9) for use in Ethiopia, and at Paris (1935–57), London (1936–61), Brussels (1937–57), Bombay (1940–1) and Birmingham (1949–55), as well as Prague and Leningrad until 1975. It has been estimated than more than 800 million coins have been struck.

HUNGARY

Inflation hit Hungary in the aftermath of World War I, but it also suffered foreign invasion and the loss of much territory to its neighbours. A short-lived Soviet republic under Bela Kun was ruthlessly suppressed and Hungary became "a kingdom without a king, ruled by an admiral without a navy".

The currency was reformed in 1925 with the adoption of the pengo of 100 filler, and coins continued to feature the crown of St Stephen with a royal inscription. During World War II steel or zinc replaced bronze and cupro-nickel, while the pengo switched from silver to aluminium. A number of commemorative 2 and 5 pengo coins appeared from 1930, ranging from the silver coin of 1930 marking the tenth anniversary of Admiral Horthy as regent, to the aluminium coin of 1943 celebrating his 75th birthday.

After World War II Hungary suffered the worst inflation of any European country and the currency reform of 1946 restored the forint. The obverse inscriptions reflect postwar political changes: "Allami Valtopenz" (Provisional Government, 1945) "Koztarsasag" (Republic, 1946) [23–24], "Nepkoztarsasag" (People's Republic, 1950) [25–28] and "Koztarsasag" (Republic again since 1990) [30–31]. Most circulating coins under the communist regime were of aluminium, though the 2, 5 and 10 forint were in nickel alloys. The tenth anniversary of the forint was marked by a silver 10 forint in 1956, but 20, 25, 100 or 200 forint coins were the main commemorative medium [29].

CZECHOSLOVAKIA

Situated in the very heart of Europe, Czechoslovakia was formed at the end of World War I from the historic kingdom of Bohemia, with Moravia, Slovakia and Ruthenia, formerly part of the Habsburg dominions. Ethnically and linguistically Slavonic, these areas were administered under Austria or Hungary, which created an economic and political imbalance leading to dissolution in 1938–9 and again in 1993. The silver mines of Joachimsthal in Bohemia produced the raw material for the large coins that therefore came to be known as Joachimsthalers; the name was soon shortened to "thalers", from which the word "dollar" is derived.

Left: The Pragergroschen, which derived its name from the Latin inscription "Grossi Pragensis" *on the original version, was the first of the large coins to circulate in Europe. The coins were originally struck at Kuttenberg (Kutná Hora). The kingdom of Bohemia played a major role in European coinage, its mines producing both gold for the Pragergroschen of the 14th century and silver for the great thalers that were minted from 1519 onward.*

KINGDOM OF BOHEMIA

The early denars of Bohemia, struck at Prague in the 10th and 11th centuries, were a curious blend of Anglo-Saxon and German types, reflecting the commercial influences on this important duchy at the heart of Europe. In the 12th century, Bohemia produced bracteates in the German style. The discovery of silver at Kutna Hora in the late 13th century, and the establishment of a mint there in 1298, had a tremendous impact on European coinage thereafter [1].

In the 15th century the kingdom increasingly came under German domination, until in 1526 the throne was claimed by the Archduke of Austria. Thereafter, the Habsburgs ruled Bohemia until 1918, and the later coinage closely followed that of Austria and Hungary. The Prague Mint produced coins for the Habsburg Empire, including the famous Maria Theresia thaler of 1780.

FIRST REPUBLIC

The Czech lands of Bohemia, Moravia and part of Silesia were united with Slovakia and Ruthenia in October 1918 when the Habsburg monarchy collapsed. The coinage, introduced in 1921, was modelled on that of pre-war Austria and Hungary and comprised the koruna (plural *korun*) of 100 haleru. The obverse showed the lion of Bohemia, while numerals and quasi-symbolic motifs occupied the reverses [2–3]. Commemorative silver coins celebrated the tenth anniversary of the republic (1928) or mourned the death of Tomas Masaryk, the first president (1937) [8–9]. Gold ducats (known in Czech as *dukaty*) carried on a Habsburg tradition from 1923 to 1939 [4–5].

The dismemberment of the country began in 1938, when Czechoslovakia was forced to cede the Sudetenland to the Third Reich. Slovakia became a separate state and a fascist ally of Hitler. Carpatho-Ukraine was granted autonomy in March 1939 but was promptly seized by Hungary. At the end of the war, Ruthenia was briefly independent before it was absorbed by the USSR; it is now part of the Ukraine.

On March 15, 1939, Nazi Germany invaded what was left of the Czech lands and proclaimed the Reich Protectorate of Bohemia and Moravia.

Although the general appearance of the coins was similar to the Czech series, the wartime issues of Bohemia and Moravia bore the names of the protectorate in German and Czech.

POSTWAR CZECHOSLAVAKIA

The pre-war coinage was resumed in 1946 but with new reverse designs. It included several silver coins, commemorating the risings in Slovakia and Prague (1947–8), the 600th anniversary of the Charles University (1948) and the 30th anniversaries of independence (1948) and the Czech Communist Party (1951) [6–7].

In February 1948 the communists seized power and Czechoslovakia subsequently became a people's republic, then a socialist republic (1962) and finally the Czech and Slovak Federal Republic (1990) [16]. Within two years, however, the return to democracy led to a break-up, although ties between the Czech Republic and Slovakia have remained close. The coins of 1948–90 reflect the dichotomy between those in general circulation, which are mainly struck in aluminium or brass [10–11], and the prolific issues of silver commemorative coins, from 25 to 500 korun.

SLOVAKIA

Distinctive coins based on the koruna slovenska (Sk) of 100 halierov were struck at Kremnica from 1939 to 1945 [12–15]; zinc, bronze or aluminium was used for the lower values and cupro-nickel for the 50 halierov, and 1 and 2Sk. Despite wartime strictures, the Slovak state even produced a few silver coins marking anniversaries of independence and portraying Monsignor Joseph Tiso, the state president. Their obverse featured the double cross emblem, and this motif has also graced the coins of the republic since its restoration [22].

The present series was introduced in 1993 and has attractive scenic motifs in the background of the numerals on the reverse of the halierov coins [17–19], and images derived from ancient statuary on the koruna values [20–23]. Silver 100, 200, 500 and 2000Sk and gold 5000Sk coins have also been produced since 1993 to mark anniversaries of independence and pay tribute to famous Slovaks, as well as highlighting environmental problems and nature conservation.

Stalin's Birthday

A sad reflection on the extent to which postwar Czechoslovakia was in the grip of communism was the release of silver coins in 1948 to celebrate the 70th birthday of Joseph Stalin. The reverse featured the bust of the Soviet dictator, who was never portrayed on any Russian coins.

CZECH REPUBLIC

Coins for the Czech Republic were introduced in 1993: the 10, 20 and 50 halierov in aluminium, the 1, 2 and 5 koruna czech (Kc) in nickel-plated steel and the 10, 20 and 50Kc in copper- or brass-plated steel [26]. The top value is a bimetallic coin with a plated brass centre and a copper-plated outer ring. The series has a standard obverse showing the lion of Bohemia [28], while the reverse motifs blend large numerals with symbols (up to 2Kc) [24]. The higher values show the Charles Bridge in Prague (5Kc) [25], Brno Cathedral (10Kc) [27], the equestrian statue of St Wenceslas (20Kc) [29–30] and a panoramic view of Prague. It constitutes one of the most aesthetically pleasing series of modern times. Silver (200Kc) or gold (1000–10,000Kc) coins have provided a rich variety of commemorative or special issues in the same period, including a 2000Kc in gold and silver with a holographic inlay to celebrate the Millennium.

POLAND

In the late Middle Ages, Poland expanded dramatically: at the height of its powers it extended from the Baltic to the Black Sea, encompassing Lithuania, the Ukraine and Belarus, but it declined in the 18th century and between1772 and 1795 it was dismembered by Austria, Russia and Prussia. In 1807, Napoleon reconstituted much of the territory seized by Prussia as the Duchy of Warsaw, which briefly had its own coins portraying Friedrich August of Saxony, whom Napoleon installed as duke [6–7]. The duchy was overrun by Prussia and Russia in 1813 and partitioned between them in an arrangement ratified by the Congress of Versailles (1815), which also created the tiny republic of Cracow and granted the eastern lands to the Tsar as the so-called Congress Kingdom of Poland. The upheavals of World War I and the downfall of the three empires that had partitioned Poland enabled its reconstitution in 1917–18 as a republic.

Left: A 500 zloty coin of 1995 recalled the sufferings of Poland in World War II, when it was again partitioned, Nazi Germany taking the western provinces, including Warsaw, while the Soviet Union grabbed the rest – and retained most of it at the end of the war.

THE KINGDOM OF POLAND

The earliest coins emerged in the 12th century and consisted of bracteates [1–2] as well as small denars of a more orthodox appearance, such as the coin minted by Wladislaw II Wygnaniec [3]. The power and wealth of the medieval kingdom was reflected in the rich diversity of its coinage. This included the first coins with face-to-face portraits since Roman times (Charles I of Hungary and Elizabeth of Poland, 1308) and the coins of Sigismund I featuring the Golden Fleece (1601), after he was admitted as a member of that prestigious imperial order of chivalry. Under Sigismund III Vasa (1587–1632) the coins of Poland reflected Swedish influence, typified by the ort or 6 groschen [4–5].

The designs of the 17th and 18th centuries showed the influence of Germany, Spain and Italy. The coinage was exceedingly complex and included the szostak of 6 groszy and the tympf of 3 szostak, the polturak of 1 grosze or 3 poltura, and the gross of 2 poltura or 3 solidi or schillings. Under the Napoleonic Grand Duchy of Warsaw the basic unit was the talara or zloty (from the Polish word for gold) worth 30 groszy, though 6 zlotych made a reichsthaler and 8 a speciesthaler. The reconstituted kingdom of Poland (1815) rationalized the coinage in 1832 [8–9] and linked it to the Russian system, so that 10 zlotych were worth 1 rouble and 30 groszy were worth 15 kopeks. Under the Grand Duchy and later kingdoms, coins in copper or silver had an armorial obverse and the value in words, but Tsar, as king of Poland, appeared in profile on the higher silver and gold denominations. After 1841, Polish coinage was suppressed and replaced by Russian currency. A crowned eagle obverse and numeral reverse appeared on coins issued in the districts occupied by Austro-German forces in World War I, based on the marka of 100 fenigow.

FIRST REPUBLIC

Because of postwar inflation and the problems of integrating the mixture of Austrian, German and Russian currencies in different parts of Poland, it was not until 1923 that a unified coinage was introduced, based on the zloty of 100 groszy, with the eagle obverse and value reverse [10]. Certain denominations (20 and 50 groszy) had fixed dates and were even restruck during the Nazi occupation, bearing the original date of 1923 but in zinc and iron instead of bronze or nickel. The silver 2 zlotych dated 1924 was originally minted in Paris but was restruck with a fixed date in Birmingham, Philadelphia and the Royal Mint, London, identified by mint-marks. By contrast, from 1932, 2 zloty coins had their designs changed every two or three years [12–13]. A somewhat similar course was adopted with the large silver 5 zlotych, but this was also used as a commemorative medium, with coins for the centenary of the revolution of 1830 and Pilsudski's Rifle Corps (1934). A gold 20 zlotych of 1925 portrayed the medieval ruler Boleslaw I, but this denomination was later reserved for large silver commemoratives.

Free State

Danzig had been an important Polish seaport, constantly fought over from 1308 to 1919, when it was made a free state. Coins based on the mark and later the gulden of 100 pfennige were issued between 1923 and 1939, when Danzig was incorporated into Nazi Germany. Since 1946 it has been Polish again, under its original name of Gdansk.

POLAND RESTORED

The country was invaded from the west by Germany on September 1, 1939, and from the east by the Soviet Union two weeks later. On September 28 Poland was partitioned along the line of the River Bug. In July 1944 the Red Army began to advance into Nazi-held territory and a provisional government was established at Lublin. Postwar Poland lost its eastern provinces to the USSR but was compensated by a substantial part of pre-war Germany. A government of national unity was proclaimed but by 1948 had fallen under communist control.

Coins commenced again in 1949, with a modification of the pre-war types mainly struck in aluminium. The pre-war inscription "Rzeczpospolita Polska" (Polish Republic) continued until 1957 [11, 14], when similar coins with "Ludowa" added to the text belatedly signified the People's Republic. Coins of 2 and 5 zlotych were added to the series in 1958, also struck in aluminium, but were replaced by brass in 1975 [15], reverting to aluminium in reduced sizes in 1969. Higher values consisted of the cupro-nickel 10 zlotych (1959) [20–21], which went through radically different designs throughout the 1960s [16–19], and 20 zlotych (1973) [22–23]. Both originally had pictorial or symbolic reverses, replaced by plain numerals in 1984. The 10 and 20 zlotych were popular for a wide range of commemoratives, as were the 100 and 200 zlotych (silver) [24–25] and 500, 1000, 2000, 5000 and 10,000 zlotych (gold), although later cupro-nickel [28] and silver were used respectively. Inflation in the 1980s was reflected by astronomical values placed on many of the precious-metal commemoratives, culminating in the massive (70mm/2¾in) 200,000 zlotych coins of 1989 celebrating the tenth anniversary of the papacy of John Paul II.

Poland again became a free and democratic republic in 1990, reflected in the omission of "Ludowa" from the obverse inscriptions, though by that time the smallest denomination was 50 zlotych. The currency was reformed in January 1995, 10,000 old zlotych being equivalent to one new zloty. Brass (1, 2 and 5 groszy) and cupro-nickel (10 groszy to 1 zloty) coins appeared with various dates from 1990 [26–27, 29]. Bimetallic zlotych appeared from 1994.

14 15 16 17 18 19 20 21 22 23 24 25 26 27 28 29

BALTIC STATES

The republics of Estonia, Latvia and Lithuania have had a very chequered history. Estonia enjoyed less than 20 years of independence between the 13th century and 1918, while its neighbour Latvia fared little better. Both were conquered in turn by German military orders, Swedes, Poles and Russians, and were constantly fought over. By contrast, the Grand Duchy of Lithuania was a major power in the 14th and 15th centuries, extending from the Baltic to the Black Sea, but was united with Poland in 1569 through dynastic marriage, and shared Poland's fate. All three gained independence in 1918 and lost it in 1940 when they were absorbed by the USSR, re-emerging as sovereign nations in 1991.

Left: In 1989 one of the first acts of defiance against the Soviet regime was the linking of hands across the Baltic states to show the solidarity of Estonia, Latvia and Lithuania. The three states later created the road and rail link known as the Baltic Highway. The tenth anniversary was marked by this coin showing three pairs of hands.

LITHUANIA

The most southerly of the Baltic republics, Lithuania had an extensive medieval coinage based on the denier before falling under Polish rule [1]. It then used Polish or Russian coins, and it was not until 1925 that a distinctive coinage was re-introduced. The obverse showed a mounted knight, a revival of the medieval type alluding to the early 15th-century Grand Duke Vytautias.

The vagaries of Lithuanian grammar are reflected in the confusing forms of the denominations: 1 centas, 2 or 5 centai [2], 10, 20 or 50 centu [3], 1 litas, 2 litu, 5 litai and 10 litu in the pre-war series, struck at the Royal Mint in London. Unusually for the period, most of the coins were originally struck in aluminium-bronze (a brass alloy), but switched to bronze in 1936, when the 2 centai was added. The coins up to 5 litai had the value on the reverse with plants or flowers as minor ornament. Silver coins of 5 litai (1936) and 10 litu (1938) respectively portrayed Jonas Basanavicius, founder of the modern republic, and President Antanas Smetona, celebrating the 20th anniversary of independence. Both coins had an incuse inscription around the rim instead of the customary graining. The coinage re-introduced in 1991 retains the horseman obverse [4] with a more modern rendering of the values on the reverse [5]. Bimetallic versions of the 2 and 5 litai were introduced in 1998 [8–9]. Apart from a silver 5 litai of 1998 publicizing the work of UNICEF, commemorative and special issues consisted mainly of the cupro-nickel 10 litu and silver 50 litu from 1993 and 1995 onwards respectively, but in 2004 a cupro-nickel 1 litas coin was released to celebrate the 425th anniversary of the University of Vilnius [10–11]. The 75th anniversary of the national bank was celebrated in 1997 with 1 litas coins, struck not only in cupro-nickel for general circulation [7] but also as proofs in pure gold [6].

LATVIA

In medieval times the Latvian capital Riga had an important mint for the Teutonic Knights and later Sweden or Poland, but no distinctive coins appeared until Latvia became an independent republic. A coinage based on the lats of 100 santimu (centimes) was introduced in 1922, with the national arms and value, the exception being the 50 santimu, which had an allegorical reverse [12–13]. Silver coins of 1 lats (1924) and 2 lati (1926) had the national arms on the obverse [14] and a wreathed numeral of value on the reverse [15]. A dollar-sized silver 5 lati was added in 1929 and depicted a girl in national costume (obverse) and elaborate arms (reverse) The original 1 santims [16–17] of 1922–35 was followed in 1937 with a new design with revised arms (obverse) and wreathed numeral (reverse). No commemoratives were produced in this period.

Coins were revived in 1992 with modernized versions of the arms and numerals on obverse and reverse [18–19, 20–21]. In the higher denominations the reverses feature a salmon (1 lats) or a grazing cow (2 lati). Large 10 latu coins have marked anniversaries and publicized endangered wildlife since 1993, while a few gold coins have celebrated the declaration of independence and the Olympic Games. In 1999 a bi-metallic 2 lati anticipated the Millennium [22–23]. It married a cupro-nickel-zinc central circle with a cupro-nickel outer ring, the two parts of the coin united by the cloud design in the background.

A Chivalric State

Livonia, consisting of much of modern Estonia and Latvia, emerged in the 12th century as a Christian state ruled by the Knights of the Livonian Order. The people were of Finnic or Baltic race with a German ruling class. In 1561 Livonia was absorbed by the union of Poland and Lithuania but the northern portion fell to Sweden in 1620. The coinage of Livonia reflected its strong commercial ties to the Hanseatic League and Russia, hence this silver coin of 1597 tariffed at 96 kopeks. Russia captured Swedish Livonia in the course of the Great Northern War, which ended in 1721.

ESTONIA

Until 1721, when it passed to Russia, Estonia was under Swedish rule, yet the people managed to retain their distinctive language and culture. An independence movement developed in the early 20th century and, after the October Revolution, a republic was proclaimed in February 1918, although a state of war with the Bolsheviks continued until 1920.

Coins based on the kroon of 100 marka appeared in 1922 and reflect the influence of Germany and Finland. The standard obverse featured the three lions more commonly associated with England, but also, as here, the emblem of the Knights of the Sword, a crusading order that converted the Estonians to Christianity in the 14th century. The currency was changed in 1928 to the kroon of 100 senti, retaining variations on the armorial theme with the value on the reverse. The kroon values had pictorial reverses showing a Viking longship [24–25] or the fortress at Tompea [26–27], while commemorative coins marked the tercentenary of Tartu University (1932) and the Tenth Singing Festival (1933).

Estonia was occupied by Soviet troops in June 1940 and thereafter only Russian coins were in circulation. Independence was restated in August 1991, and subsequent coins have reprised the pre-war designs [31–33], with a range of commemoratives from the brass 5 krooni of 1993 marking the 75th anniversary of independence [28] and the 75th anniversary of the national bank in 1994 [29–30], to the gold 500 krooni of 1998 for the 80th anniversary. The preferred medium is the silver 10 and 100 krooni, marking the Olympic Games (1992 and 1996), bird conservation (1992) and independence anniversaries. In 1999, Estonia released a tiny gold coin tariffed at 15.65 krooni, the Estonian equivalent of the euro.

18 19 20 21 22 23 24 25 26 27 28 29 30 31 32 33

RUSSIA

Until the Middle Ages, Celtic, Roman, Anglo-Saxon, Viking and Byzantine coins circulated widely in what is now Russia, and gold Byzantine coins, such as the histamenon of Constantine VIII and Basil II (976–1025) were particularly popular [1–2]. Foreign coins and their imitations continued until the 11th century, when the earliest indigenous coins began to emerge in the Principality of Kiev, such as the cross and bust type struck by Prince Mstislav Vladimirovich [3–4]. Before Peter the Great modernized Russian coinage at the end of the 17th century, foreign gold and silver coins circulated extensively. They were often melted down and cast into ingots known as *grivny* (the name adopted as the unit of currency in the Ukraine). A half ingot was known as a rouble, from the Russian verb *rubit*, "to cut".

Left: The influence of the Byzantine Empire on the development of Russian coinage is shown clearly in the gold-plated coppers of John I Zimisces, ruler of Kievan Rus, in conscious imitation of the gold histamenon that circulated widely in medieval times.

TSARIST EMPIRE

Money of account was translated into actual coins from 1700, when Peter introduced the large silver rouble, often referred to as a "Jefimok" (from Jachymov or Joachimsthal in Bohemia where such large coins originated in 1519). The obverse bore the bust of the ruler [5] with the imperial double eagle on the reverse [6], and this became the standard from the start of the 18th century. The double eagle sometimes alternated with an armorial reverse [7–8], with the Tsar's monogram on the smallest coins, but in 1886 the profile of the Tsar was restored and the eagle relegated to the reverse. This style obtained in the gold and silver coins from then until the collapse of the monarchy in 1917.

The monetary system in the 18th and early 19th centuries was complex: each coin had a distinctive name inscribed on it, from the copper polushka (quarter kopek) and denga or denezhka (half kopek) to the grivna or grivnik (10 kopeks) [9–10], polupoltina (25 kopeks) [11–12], poltina (50 kopeks) and rouble; 10 roubles made an imperial or chervonetz. With such a vast country to supply with coins it is not surprising that production was spread across mints in St Petersburg, Ekaterinburg and Warsaw, as well as smaller units such as Souzan, Kolpina and Anninsk, which often confined their output to the copper coins used as small change.

From 1834 onward, the silver rouble was often used as a commemorative coin, mainly celebrating royal events. Russia also produced the world's first regular coinage struck in platinum, the 3, 6 and 12 roubles of 1828–45.

SOVIET UNION

The ill-fated Tsar Nicholas II was portrayed on the obverse of the coins from 1895 to 1915 [13–14], when the exigencies of World War I drove silver and gold out of circulation. The downfall of the monarchy, followed by the short-lived republic headed by Alexander Kerensky in 1917, and the October Revolution that brought Lenin and the communists to power, occurred at a time when the rouble was hard-hit by inflation. Monetary chaos was aggravated by the wave of civil wars and foreign interventionist campaigns.

In 1921 an attempt was made to reintroduce silver coins, from 10 kopeks to 1 rouble, and the gold chervonetz. These coins bore the hammer and sickle on the obverse, surrounded by the slogan "Workers of the world

Siberian Copper

The city of Ekaterinburg, named in honour of Catherine the Great, was the centre of the Siberian copper mining district. The Ekaterinburg Mint was geared up to refine and coin Siberian copper in 1725–7, and during Catherine's reign it produced very heavy copper coins similar in size to the *plåtmynt* of Sweden. Although much favoured by the monarch, these coins were far too cumbersome for everyday use and were extremely unpopular with the merchant classes for that reason. As a result, they were withdrawn after two years and melted down.

unite", with "RSFSR" at the foot signifying the Russian Soviet Federative Socialist Republic [15–16], which gave way to the Union of Soviet Socialist Republics in 1923. Coins bearing the Cyrillic "CCCP" (USSR) appeared from 1924. A legacy of tsarist times was the wide range of denominations, with coins of 1, 2, 3, 5, 10, 15, 20 and 50 kopeks. Silver was replaced by cupro-nickel in 1931 and a brass alloy of cupro-nickel-zinc in 1961, with subtly changed designs.

From 1965, when a rouble celebrated the 20th anniversary of the end of World War II, the Soviet Union produced numerous commemorative pieces in denominations of 1, 2, 3, 5, 10, 25, 50, 100 and 150 roubles, culminating in the platinum, gold and silver coins marking the 1980 Moscow Olympics. Typically these coins had an obverse showing the Soviet arms with the value in the exergue [17], with an image and commemorative inscription on the reverse [18].

As the Soviet Union began to fall apart in 1991, an issue of coins was made by the State Bank in denominations from 10 kopeks to 10 roubles, with a standard obverse showing the Moscow Kremlin and a reverse bearing the value between an ear of wheat and oak leaves for the lower denominations [21–22]. They were struck in copper-clad steel (10 kopeks) or cupro-nickel (50 kopeks and 1 rouble), while the higher values were bimetallic. The issue even included a pair of 5 rouble coins for wildlife conservation, depicting an owl or a mountain goat on the reverse, with the value on the obverse. The State Bank also produced special issues such as the series featuring gems of Russian classical architecture [19–20].

Above: Despite the negative experience of issuing very large and cumbersome copper pieces, Russia persevered with comparatively large copper coins, such as this 5 kopek of 1769, with the imperial double-headed eagle on one side and the crowned monogram of the Empress Catherine the Great on the other.

COMMONWEALTH OF INDEPENDENT STATES

The collapse of the communist regime in 1991 precipitated the dissolution of the Union of Soviet Socialist Republics. Mikhail Gorbachev attempted to hold the component republics together in a loose federation known as the Commonwealth of Independent States (CIS), but this concept was short-lived, as the various republics went their separate ways and even fought wars over disputed territory. Nevertheless it is convenient to survey the coins issued since 1992 under this heading. Outside Russia proper, indigenous coinage existed from the beginning of the Christian era in the Caucasus region, crude bronze pieces derived from Greek and Roman models being recorded from Georgia and quite sophisticated coinage in medieval Armenia, emulating the gold and silver of the Byzantine Empire. Although some of the states that briefly emerged in the early 1920s had their own paper money, none had distinctive coins until gaining independence in the 1990s.

Left: Levon, the Lion King of Armenia (1198–1226) allied himself to the Crusaders and married a Lusignan princess, founding a dynasty that expanded its territory in Asia Minor and was for some time a bastion of Christianity against Turkish aggression. Levon was a skilled diplomat, who forged alliances with the German emperors and Pope Celestine III. His westward orientation is reflected in his silver coins, such as this double tram showing him seated on the lion throne, holding the orb and sceptre, with the crowned lion in front of a patriarchal cross on the reverse.

RUSSIAN FEDERATION

By far the largest of the former Soviet republics is Russia, itself a federation of autonomous republics extending from the Baltic to the Pacific. It was hard hit by inflation when the USSR collapsed and a reform of 1992 led to the new rouble worth 10,000 old roubles. Brass-clad steel roubles were introduced that year, with the old double eagle emblem (minus imperial crowns) on the obverse [1–2] and the value on the reverse. Significantly, these and later coins were issued by authority of Bank Rossiya, the new state bank. Smaller coins, from 1 to 50 kopeks, featured St George and the dragon on the obverse [3–4]. The Soviet practice of issuing numerous commemorative coins has continued since 1992, including long thematic sets [5–7], such as the wildlife series of 1995–6. Some tiny 10 rouble gold coins have appeared since 1994.

CAUCASIAN REPUBLICS

As a once powerful kingdom geographically linked to Asia Minor and the Black Sea, Armenia's early coinage was subject to Greek, Roman and Byzantine influences. It struck its own coins from the 3rd century BC to the 16th century, but used Russian coins from 1801. Coins based on the dram (drachma) of 100 luma were introduced in 1994, with a double eagle obverse and value reverse [8–9]. A 5 dram silver coin of 1998, marking the fifth anniversary of the currency, reproduced banknotes on the reverse.

Azerbaijan's currency, based on the manta of 100 qapik, was launched in 1992 with symbols (obverse) and values (reverse) [10–11]. Gold and silver 50 manat appeared in 1996 to honour the national poet Mohammad Fuzuli.

In the 19th century, Georgian silver was mined for imperial Russian coins,

Return to Barter?

Tatarstan, an autonomous republic of the Russian Federation, declared its independence in February 1994. Since then, undated bronze coins with the state emblem on the obverse (top-right) have been introduced. These coins bear no inscibed value, but the smaller piece, which has ears of wheat on the reverse, is worth a kilogram of bread, while the larger coin, showing an oil well pump (bottom), is worth 10 litres of petrol (gasoline).

many bearing the Tiflis (Tbilisi) mintmark [12–13]. Independent Georgia's coinage consists of the lari of 100 thetri; coins from 1 to 20 thetri in stainless steel, and 50 thetri in brass, have a wheel symbol (obverse) and various animals (reverse) [14–16]. A 500 lari gold coin appeared in 1995 to celebrate the 50th anniversary of liberation from Fascism.

WESTERN REPUBLICS

The Ukraine almost rivals Russia in its prolific coinage since 1995. It began with coins of astronomical denominations, but in practice, everyday money consisted of paper and the cupro-nickel 200,000 karbovanetz and silver coins denominated in millions were purely commemorative. The currency was reformed in September 1996, the hryven of 100 kopiyok being worth 100,000 old karbovanetz. Aluminium, steel or brass coins featured the trident emblem and value [17–20]. Numerous commemoratives from 2 to 500 hryvni in silver or gold have been released.

Belarus (formerly Byelorussia or White Russia) has stuck to the rouble of 100 kapeek and has had commemorative gold, silver and cupro-nickel coins since 1996, while relying on small paper notes for everyday use.

Moldova lies next to Romania and has adopted the currency of that country, the leu of 100 bani, but unlike Romania its lei have not assumed astronomical proportions as a result of inflation. Aluminium coins from 1 to 50 bani [21–22] and clad steel leu and 5 lei pieces were introduced in 1992–3. A few silver 100 lei commemoratives have appeared since 1996.

CENTRAL ASIAN REPUBLICS

If the Ukraine and the Caucasian republics enjoyed a brief existence after World War I, the republics of Central Asia had no political existence before their creation by the USSR. Kyrgyzstan became a Union republic in 1936 and, so far, its only coins (since 1995) have been silver 10 som or gold 100 som commemoratives. Kazakhstan introduced circulating coins based on the tenga of 100 tyn in 1993, with the state emblem and value on obverse and reverse respectively [23–24]. Coins of 20 and 50 tenge (cupro-nickel), 100 tenge (silver) and 1000 tenge (gold) have marked anniversaries of independence and honoured historic figures since 1993 [33–34]. Turkmenistan adopted the manat of 100 tennesi in 1993 and coins with the profile of President Saparmyrat Nyyazow have since been released in plated steel [25–29]. Silver 500 manat coins also circulate [35–36] and since 1996 have featured endangered wildlife.

Uzbekistan alone had distinctive coins before 1994, although these were only the tenga and falus struck in the khanates of Bukhara and Khiva during the last years of the tsarist empire. The contemporary steel-clad coins are based on the som of 100 tyin [30–32].

YUGOSLAVIA

The mountainous region of south-east Europe, inhabited by a mixture of ethnic, linguistic, political and religious groups, has been ruled by Greece, Rome, Byzantium, the Ottoman Empire and the Habsburgs. The Balkan mints at Ljubljana, Zagreb, Dubrovnik and Split were significant during the medieval period, producing coinage for local Venetian or Turkish rulers. Serbia was subjugated by the Turks after the decisive battle at Kosovo (1389) and did not regain independence until 1887. Montenegro was alone in precariously preserving its integrity from Turkish domination. As Turkish power waned Russia and Austria carved out spheres of influence, which led to War in 1914, triggered by the assassination of the Austrian Archduke Franz Ferdinand at Sarajevo. Out of the wreckage of World War I emerged the Kingdom of Serbs, Croats and Slovenes, which became Yugoslavia.

Left: Now known as Dubrovnik, in southern Croatia, Ragusa on the Adriatic coast was a major trading centre in the Middle Ages and the origin of the argosy, a large merchant sailing ship. Called the Pearl of the Adriatic, it was noted for the quality of its coinage, especially the silver blasius, named after the patron saint depicted on the obverse. In the 15th and 16th centuries it rivalled Venice in wealth and importance and was an independent republic until 1806, when it was suppressed by Napoleon.

SERBIA AND MONTENEGRO

In the 13th and 14th centuries the rulers of Serbia struck silver dinars as well as imitations of Venetian grossi at Belgrade [1–2]. Coins variously minted in Paris, Birmingham or Vienna were issued sporadically from 1868, based on the dinar of 100 para, with the ruler's profile or the eagle emblem on the obverse and the value on the reverse. After Prince Milan Obrenovich [3–4] assumed the title of king in 1882 coinage was more regularly struck, although under Peter I issues appeared only in 1904 and 1912 [9–10].

The coins of Montenegro, based on the perper of 100 para, began in 1906, with 1, 2, 10 and 20 para with a crowned eagle obverse. Higher values portraying Prince (later King) Nicholas appeared in 1909 with the arms on the reverse[5–6]. Gold and silver coins of 1910 [7–8] celebrated Nicholas's golden jubilee as titular prince-bishop.

YUGOSLAVIA

The Balkan kingdoms were overrun by the Central Powers in World War I, but regained their independence in 1918 and in December that year joined with the southern Slav dominions of the Habsburg Empire, Croatia and Slovenia, to form the Kingdom of Serbs, Croats and Slovenes under Peter I. His son Alexander acted as regent and ascended the throne in 1921. The problems of unifying such a disparate group of territories were immense and were solved only when Alexander assumed dictatorial powers and renamed the country Yugoslavia ("the land of the southern Slavs").

In the face of different languages and scripts (Roman and Cyrillic) the coins introduced in 1920 had an anepigraphic obverse with the royal arms alone, while the reverse had the numerals of value with "Para" in both scripts. Higher denominations, portraying Alexander I, appeared in 1925 [11–12]. When coins were next issued, in 1938, they merely featured a crown on the obverse but were now inscribed with the new country name.

Yugoslavia was overrun by Germany in 1941 and dismembered. Zinc coins with the double-headed eagle were issued in Serbia in 1942, while the puppet fascist state of Croatia issued zinc 1 and 2 kune as well as gold 500 kune in 1941. The half-Croat leader Josip Broz, known as Marshal Tito, eventually drove out the Germans and Italians and restored the country in 1945. Coins now bore the emblem of the Federal People's Republic. They were inscribed in Cyrillic alone [13–14] until the formation of the Socialist Federal Republic in 1963, when the equivalent in the Roman alphabet was added [15–16, 17–18]. From 1965 the denomination was rendered in all four different languages [19–22].

Beginning in 1970 with coins for the FAO "Food for All" programme, Yugoslavia produced commemorative and special issues in denominations from 5 dinara upwards, notably for the Winter Olympics at Sarajevo (1984).

Ancient Warriors

Macedonia, in the heart of the Balkans, has long been the subject of bitter disputes between Serbia, Bulgaria and Greece. It was from here that Philip of Macedon set out to conquer Greece, creating the empire later expanded by Alexander the Great. The Macedonian kingdom of Paeonia was one of the most important sites of ancient coin production and struck silver coins on the Greek model, such as this tetradrachm showing a head of Apollo (obverse) and a Paeonian cavalryman lancing a foot soldier, who is defending himself with shield and spear. Today it forms part of the Republic of Macedonia, which has the epithet "Former Yugoslavia" at the insistence of Greece, whose most northerly province is also called Macedonia.

DISINTEGRATION

After Tito's death in 1980 the six component republics began to drift apart, culminating in the break-up of 1990–1. The secessionist movement began in Croatia and swiftly spread to Slovenia, these republics having formerly been part of Hungary and Austria respectively. Macedonia [23] and Bosnia-Herzegovina also declared their independence, despite strenuous protests from Greece regarding the former and the rivalries of Croatia and Serbia over the latter. In the mid-1990s Serb Orthodox, Croat Catholic and Bosnian Muslim factions fought each other. The Serbs of southern Croatia even formed their own Serbian Republic of Krajina. Serbia and Montenegro alone maintained the fiction of Yugoslavia and coins thus inscribed appeared until 2002, latterly assailed by inflation, which witnessed coins up to 100,000 dinara. The currency was reformed three times in 1992–4 as ten, then a million and latterly a billion old dinara were revalued at one novi dinar [24–25].

Croatia had emerged as a fascist state in 1941 and introduced the kuna (from the word for a marten, reflecting the use of fur as currency in the Middle Ages). On regaining independence Croatia tariffed its kuna of 100 lipa at 1000 old dinara. Coins from 1 lipa to 25 kuna have the numerals of value superimposed on the national emblem on the obverse, with birds, animals and flora on the reverse [26–27]. Commemorative silver or gold coins of 25, 100, 200, 500 or 1000 kuna have appeared since 1994 [28]. Slovenia adopted the tolar (dollar) of 100 stotinov and has aluminium or brass coins with the value (obverse) and fauna (reverse) [29–30]. Many special issues from 5 to 500 tolarjev have appeared since 1991. Macedonia has had coins featuring wildlife since 1993, based on the denar of 100 deni [31–33]. Despite political divisions within the Croat-Muslim Federation of Bosnia and Herzegovina and the Serb Republic, a common currency is used [34–35].

19 20 21 22 23 24 25 26 27 28 29 30 31 32 33 34 35

ALBANIA, BULGARIA AND ROMANIA

These three countries lie in the southern Balkans, but apart from geography they have very little in common. Ethnically, culturally and linguistically, they are each unique. Distinctive coins appeared in the regions as far back as the 5th century BC, reflecting the successive influence of the Greek, Roman, Byzantine and Venetian worlds. Bulgaria was a major power until it fell under Turkish rule in 1395. In modern times, all three countries were kingdoms before World War II and people's republics from the 1940s until the collapse of communism in the 1990s. In the 1890s both Bulgaria and Romania issued gold coins that conformed to the French 20 franc piece, which was the standard in the Latin Monetary Union.

Left: In the 5th and 4th centuries BC the Greek colony of Olbia, a thriving port on the Black Sea, produced large coins cast from copper mined locally. Many of these curious pieces depict leaping dolphins and quasi-religious symbols. Quite unlike the usual Greek coins, they are believed to have originated as votive offerings to the god Apollo.

ALBANIA

The earliest coins in this area were struck at Apollonia (near modern Pojani), a colony founded in 588 BC by Greeks from Corfu. It struck its own coins until 229 BC, when it was annexed to the Roman Republic.

A Turkish province until 1912, Albania was fought over during the Balkan Wars and World War I. It was successively a principality (1914), a republic (1925) and a kingdom (1928). Coinage was not adopted until 1926, based on the lek of 100 qindar. The higher values portrayed President Ahmet Zogu, who later became King Zog I. The bronze or nickel coins were mostly struck in Rome and apart from the double-headed eagle on the 5 qindar and the half lek, motifs drew heavily on those of ancient Rome. The 20 franga of 1922 [1–2] had a reverse showing the Albanian double-headed eagle, but it was superseded in 1926 by a coin portraying medieval hero George Castriota Skanderbeg [3] with the winged lion of St Mark (a Venetian symbol) on the reverse [4]. In 1937–8 gold coins with King Zog facing right [5] had armorial reverses that celebrated the 25th anniversary of independence, the king's marriage and 10th anniversary of his reign [6], shortly before he fled the country. Victor Emmanuel III graced the coins issued in 1939–41.

Enver Hoxha led the partisans during World War II and emerged as head of the People's Socialist Republic, whose aluminium or zinc coins appeared from 1947 [7–9]. Steel or brass coins since 1995 have had various pictorial images on the obverse and a wreathed value on the reverse. Silver and gold coins proliferated from 1968, beginning with a series honouring Castriota Skanderbeg.

BULGARIA

The towns on the Black Sea coast of what is now Bulgaria struck Greek-style coins from the 4th century BC. Chief among them was Apollonia Pontica, which struck drachmae in 450–400 BC showing the Gorgon and maritime motifs such as a crayfish and an anchor [10–13]. Distinctive coins appeared in

Thrace from the 3rd century BC. Handsome drachmae were minted at Odessus (now Varna) in the period of the Mithridatic Wars with Rome (127–70 BC) with the head of Alexander and seated Zeus [14–15], and coins were minted at Serdica as a Roman and then a Byzantine province.

Straddling the northern Aegean and Black Seas, the area was settled by the Bulgars in the 7th century and flourished in the Middle Ages, striking its own coins from the early 13th century [16–17]. It became a principality in 1878, nominally under Turkish control, but joined forces with Eastern Roumelia in 1885 to form Bulgaria. Prince Ferdinand of Saxe-Coburg was appointed ruler in 1887 and proclaimed himself king in 1908.

Coins based on the lev of 100 stotinki were adopted in 1881 [18], with an armorial obverse. The silver (from 1891) and gold (from 1894) portrayed Ferdinand until 1916. Some 1 and 2 leva coins appeared between 1923 and 1941–3, but there were no other coins until 1951 when brass or cupro-nickel pieces from 1 to 25 stotinki were released by the people's republic, which abolished the monarchy in 1946 [19–22]. Further issues appeared in 1962 [23] and 1974 [24].

The return to democracy in 1992 was signalled by new coins from 20 stotinki to 50 leva, with obverses featuring ancient sculpture. In July 1999 the currency was reformed, 10,000 old leva being worth 1 new lev, and brass or cupro-nickel coins from 1 to 50 stotinki had a standard obverse. Numerous gold or silver commemoratives have been minted since the 1960s.

ROMANIA

The Roman province of Dacia bordering the Black Sea has retained the Latin influence in its language as well as its name, although the Christian principalities of Moldavia and Wallachia in the eastern Danube valley were under Turkish rule until 1877. A wide variety of coins was produced in this area from the 3rd century BC, long before the arrival of the Romans. In the Middle Ages the princes of Moldavia and Wallachia struck coins, before and after the area came under Turkish control. Transylvania, now part of Romania, was successively under Hungarian or Habsburg rule, and an independent principality at various times. In each period, it produced distinctive coins.

Reflected Glory

Romania harked back to the time of Michael the Brave (1601) and Ferdinand I in World War I, portrayed alongside King Michael in the gold 20 lei coin of 1944 celebrating the restoration of territories formerly lost to Hungary and Russia. The reverse bore the arms of all 11 provinces, grouped around the crown.

The ruler of the Danubian principalities, Alexander Cuza, was ousted in 1866 and Prince Karl of Hohenzollern-Sigmaringen was appointed in his place. Karl (Carol) proclaimed himself king in 1881. Coins based on the leu of 100 bani, with the arms of the Danubian principalities and inscribed "Romania", were introduced in 1867 [25], followed by a series portraying Carol I (obverse) and the arms (reverse) [26–29]. Few coins below 50 bani were issued for general circulation between 1906 and 1952 [30–31]; in the interim Romania was ravaged by two World Wars, suffered inflation and ceased to be a monarchy in 1947. In the 1950s coins of the people's republic had the communist emblem and the value on the obverse and reverse. A new series in clad steel appeared in 1965–9, marking the change to a socialist republic, and since 1989 coins have reverted to the original title of Romania [32–35] with arms or symbols on the obverse.

GREECE

The cradle of Western civilization and a major contributor to the origin and development of democracy, the arts, architecture and, of course, coinage, Greece fell under the domination of the Roman Empire in the 2nd century BC and was part of the Byzantine Empire until 1453, when it came under Turkish rule. Thereafter coins were struck in various parts of what is now Greece, by the crusader Dukes of Athens [1–2], the Princes of Achaea, and under the auspices of the Knights of St John in Rhodes (until 1522), such as Grand Master Dieudonné de Gozon, who rebuilt the Kingdom of Rhodes in the 14th century [3–4]. Venetian and Genoese trading companies also struck coins in a number of Frankish principalities. Greece retained its distinct language and culture under Turkish rule and a revolt in 1821 triggered off the nationalist movement that led to the creation of a Greek state by 1827. In 1833 the European Powers recognized the sovereignty of Greece, choosing Prince Otto of Bavaria as its king.

Left: Many modern Greek coins use images from coins of ancient Greece: this brass 100 drachma piece of 1990–2000 portrayed Alexander the Great as king of the Macedonians – part of the ongoing propaganda campaign against the independent Republic of Macedonia.

FIRST KINGDOM

The newly independent state revived the ancient coinage system of the drachma of 100 lepta. Copper 1 and 5 lepta appeared in 1828 with a cross above a phoenix, symbolizing the rebirth of the country. Other denominations soon followed, with silver coins portraying King Otto in 1833 [5–6]. Otto was deposed in 1862 and in his place the Powers elected George, second son of King Christian of Denmark [7–10]. He reigned from 1863 to 1913, when he was assassinated during a state visit to Salonika, recently acquired as a result of the Second Balkan War. During his long reign his portrait was extended to the smaller coins. New types appeared in 1912, including holed 5, 10 and 20 lepta with the first essays in pictorialism, reviving the owl [11–12] and Athena motifs from ancient coins.

Relatively few Greek coins portrayed the reigning monarch, so the revolts and factiousness of the ensuing decade are not reflected in the obverses. Constantine I was forced to abdicate in World War I for his pro-German sympathies. Restored to the throne, he was driven out again in 1922 following a disastrous campaign to seize the seaboard of Asia Minor from Turkey. He was briefly succeeded by his son, George II, but he too was ousted, and Greece then became a republic.

FIRST REPUBLIC

The monarchy was overthrown by Eleftherios Venizelos, who had worked closely with the British and French during World War I. The republic lasted until 1935, when George II was restored to the throne. During this period Greece abandoned royal symbolism on its coins; instead the country looked back to the glories of ancient Greece for inspiration, using the helmeted Athena from Corinthian coins for the series of 1926 from 20 lepta to 2 drachmae. In 1930 a nickel 5 drachma coin featured the phoenix derived from the coins of 1828 [13–14], while 10 and 20 drachmae revived ancient types respectively showing Demeter the corn goddess and an ear of wheat or Poseidon the sea god with the prow of a galley. The 5 drachma coin was struck in London and Brussels, distinguished by dots in the berries on the reverse.

MONARCHY RESTORED

Discontent with the republic led to a plebiscite on November 3, 1935, which voted in favour of restoring the monarchy. King George II returned to Athens and was formally restored to his throne on November 25. This was celebrated by gold and silver 20 and 100 drachma coins showing the king and the date of his restoration, although the coins themselves were not actually minted until 1940 [15–16]. The republican coins remained in general circulation and it is remarkable that, apart from these commemoratives, no further coins were issued until 1954 [17–18].

Greece was occupied by Nazi Germany in World War II and suffered inflation for many years, making coinage impractical. George II went into exile in 1941 but was restored for a third time in 1946 and succeeded the following year by his brother Paul, whose profile appears on the middle values of 1954–65 [19–20], though Selene the moon goddess was reserved for the 20 drachmae. Constantine II's reign began auspiciously in 1964 with a 30 drachma silver coin showing the conjoined busts of the young king and his bride, Anne-Marie of Denmark. The permanent series bore his profile and the national arms [21–22].

SECOND REPUBLIC

When a military junta seized power in 1967 Constantine attempted a counter coup. It failed and he fled to Rome. The dictatorial regime of the Greek colonels deposed the king and abolished the monarchy in 1973. Ironically, new coins appeared in 1971 with Constantine's profile (obverse) and the phoenix emblem. Two years later a series appeared with the figure of a soldier superimposed on the phoenix, but the figure was soon removed [24]. The reverse of the series took motifs from ancient coins [23], including the owl and Pegasus, the winged horse [25]. The 1 and 2 drachma coins were inspired by the wars of independence, with portraits of Konstantinos Kanaris and Georgios Karaiskakis [26–7] on the obverse and various motifs symbolic of that period on the reverse [28], but the higher values reverted to classical motifs with Democritus, Pericles, Solon and Homer on the obverse and appropriate pictorial images on the reverse [29–30]. In the 1990s the circulating coinage became a medium for profiling Greek personalities of more recent times [31–32]. Classical motifs, however, have been used for the Greek versions of the euro coinage.

Commemorative coins from 50 to 1000 drachmae (silver) and 2500 to 20,000 drachmae (gold) proliferated from 1975 onward; many had sporting themes, from the Pan-European Games (1981) to the Chess Olympics (1988). For the Athens Olympic Games in 2004 Greece produced a prolific series showing Athenian landmarks and Olympic sports harking back to the Ancient Games. It included a 500 drachma piece portraying Pierre de Coubertin, father of the modern Games, alongside Demetrios Vikelas who organized the first modern Olympics at Athens in 1896 [33–34].

Blend of Ancient and Modern

The best example of the way in which modern Greece identifies with its ancient past is seen in the 10 drachma coins since 1976: the portrait of the philosopher Democritus (*c.* 460–370 BC), who devised the atomic system, is linked to a reverse showing a symbolic representation of an atom.

17 18 19 20 21 22 23 24 25 26 27 28 29 30 31 32 33 34

1 2 3 4 5 6 7 8 9 10 11

ITALY

The history of coinage in Italy goes back to the cumbersome cast copper coins of the 3rd century BC [1–2], but under the influence of the Greek colonies gold staters [3–4] and silver drachmae were struck in various parts of the Italian peninsula from the 4th century BC. As a political entity, Italy dates only from 1861. After the fall of the western Roman Empire in 476, the Italian peninsula was divided into petty kingdoms, city states and papal dominions, each with its own distinctive coins. In the Middle Ages Milan and Florence took a leading role in the revival of realism in coin design, while Venice created a great commercial empire in the Adriatic and eastern Mediterranean, and its coinage was a major influence in that area. Italy was finally unified under Victor Emanuel II of Piedmont, Savoy and Sardinia.

Below: In 1922 Benito Mussolini seized power in Italy and created the world's first Fascist country. While Mussolini wielded dictatorial powers as Il Duce ("the leader"), Victor Emanuel III continued as king. After the annexation of Abyssinia (Ethiopia) in 1936 Victor Emmanuel was styled as King and Emperor and the coins of this period bore dates in the Fascist era as well as the Christian calendar.

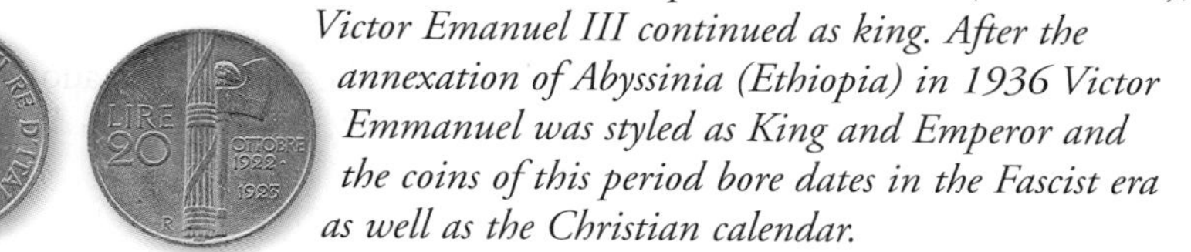

ITALIAN STATES

The Kingdom of Naples and Sicily emerged by 1130, but was under the rule of Spain or Austria from 1502 until 1733, when the Bourbon Prince Carlos became king [5–6]. It was sometimes called the Kingdom of the Two Sicilies, as on coins of Joachim Murat, styling himself Gioacchino Napoleon (1808–15) [12–13]. Sardinia was alternately ruled by Pisa and Genoa before falling to Aragon in 1297. It remained under Spanish rule until 1720, when it became part of the dominions of the House of Savoy and the nucleus of the future Kingdom of Italy.

Powerful families, such as the Sforzas of Milan, the Gonzagas of Mantua and the Medicis of Florence created city-states in the medieval period that came to wield enormous commercial influence and produced attractive gold and silver coins, such as this Florentine half tallero of Cosimo III (1670–1723) [7]. From the 16th century, however, the Italian city-states began to fall under the sway of France, Spain and Austria, and only the Republic of Venice maintained its independence until 1798. A silver ducat of 1676–84 shows the Doge of Venice kneeling before St Mark, the city's patron saint [8–9]. Napoleon Bonaparte briefly redrew the map of Italy in the 1790s, first creating a series of republics and then a kingdom under his personal rule (1804–14). Under Napoleon, coins bore his left-facing profile (obverse) and the crowned and mantled arms of his Italian kingdom (reverse) [10–11].

The Congress of Versailles of 1815 awarded Lombardy and Venetia to Austria; coins with the Lombard crown or the Austrian eagle, based on the scudo of 6 lire, 120 soldi or 600 centesimi, were issued from 1822 until 1866, when the kingdom fell to Italy. Naples and Sicily had a complex coinage based on the ducato or tallero (dollar) [14–15] of 100 grana, but 120 grana were also worth a piastra, 6 tari, 12 carlini or 240 tornese, while 6 cavalli made a tornese. In 1813 the currency was reformed and the franco or lira of 100 centesimi was adopted.

The Duchies of Parma, Modena and Tuscany, as well as the States of the Church, each had distinctive coinage. Piedmont and Sardinia each had their own currency systems, based on the doppia of 2880 denari or the doppietta of 1200 denari respectively, but from

1816 the lira of 100 centesimi was in use and it eventually extended to the whole of Italy.

KINGDOM OF ITALY

The campaign of 1859–60 known as the Risorgimento, led by Giuseppe Garibaldi, resulted in the unification of Italy under the House of Savoy, and coins portraying Victor Emanuel II were introduced in 1861 [16–17]. The Pope, under French protection, held out until 1870, but on the withdrawal of the French garrison Rome finally became the capital of a united Italy.

The reverse of the coins showed the value, but from 1908 onward, a more allegorical treatment was adopted, often using images that harked back to the Roman Empire [18–22]. Exceptionally, between 1894 and 1936, the 20 centesimi had either a crown, a Roman profile or the royal arms on the obverse. The use of imperial imagery increased from 1936 onward, with the rebirth of an empire that Mussolini hoped would encompass the Mediterranean [23]. Italy pioneered stainless steel as a coinage metal (1939) and bimetallic coins (1982).

REPUBLIC

During World War II, Italy was originally allied to Nazi Germany, but it changed sides in 1943 when Mussolini was overthrown, later to be captured and executed by partisans. Umberto II succeeded his father as king in 1946, but by referendum the monarchy was abolished and Italy declared a republic.

After the welter of wartime coins as the currency became depreciated, postwar Italy had a relatively stable coinage, with aluminium 1, 5 and 10 lira coins [24–25], aluminium-bronze 20 lire coins [26–27], stainless steel 50 and 100 lire and silver 500 lire. Allegorical portraits and imagery derived from classical motifs predominated. The size of the coins was reduced in 1951 and cupro-nickel was substituted for stainless steel in the 50 and 100 lira coins in 1993–6. A 200 lire in aluminium-bronze was introduced in 1977 and a bimetallic 500 lire was adopted in 1982 [28–29]. Coins of this denomination continued to be minted in silver as collector's pieces. The 100, 200 and 500 lire were often struck as commemoratives from 1974 onward.

Vacant See

Distinctive coins are issued by the Vatican during the period between the death of a Pope and the election of his successor. These coins, inscribed "Sede Vacante" (Latin for "empty chair"), follow a tradition going back many centuries.

SAN MARINO AND THE VATICAN

The tiny mountain Republic of San Marino, which had been independent since AD 350, began issuing small bronze coins in 1864 and silver in 1898, but Italian coins predominated. Since 1972, San Marino has revived its coinage, producing a different series annually, mainly as tourist souvenirs but also including commemorative gold and silver scudi.

Papal coinage was suppressed in 1870 but revived in 1929, when the Vatican City State was created under the terms of the Lateran Treaty. These coins generally portray the Pope, with religious, allegorical or symbolic motifs on the reverse.

Above: A coin of Pope Pius XI from 1931, showing the papal arms and the Virgin Mary.

FRANCE

The Gaul of Roman times, France became the kingdom of the Franks and, under Charlemagne in the 9th century, the leading power in Europe. Central power weakened in the Middle Ages, with the rise of petty kingdoms such as Brittany and Navarre, and it was not until the early 17th century that France emerged as a highly centralized state. It attained its greatest power under Louis XIV, who came to the throne in 1643 at the age of five [1–2], but the autocratic monarchy was unstable and collapsed in the Revolution of 1789, which led to the First Republic in 1792. This was followed by the Napoleonic Empire (1804–14), the restoration of the monarchy (1814–48), the Second Republic (1848–52), the Second Empire (1852–71), the Third Republic (1871–1940), the fascist Vichy state (1940–4), the Fourth Republic (1944–58) and the Fifth Republic instituted by President Charles de Gaulle, which continues to this day.

Left: Louis Napoleon Bonaparte, nephew of Napoleon I, was elected president of the Second Republic but engineered a coup in 1852, restoring the Bonapartist Empire and taking the title of Napoleon III. On coinage his profile acquired victor's laurels in 1861, following a series of French victories in the campaign for the unification of Italy. France flourished under his rule but the monarchy collapsed as a result of the disastrous war with Germany in 1870–1.

MEDIEVAL COINAGE

Coin production was devolved to the towns and districts of medieval France. Many of the nobility struck their own coins, creating an immense field of study [7–9]. Anglo-Gallic coins were struck in the regions under English rule during the Hundred Years' War.

The regal coinage was reformed by Louis XI (1461–83) after he defeated the English and broke the power of the nobility. Separate coinage continued in Brittany and Navarre until Henry of Navarre took the throne as Henry IV in 1589. The third son of Antoine de Bourbon, Henry established a royal dynasty that was to rule France for the next two centuries.

REVOLUTION AND EMPIRE

In the period prior to the Revolution, French coinage became increasingly complex. The mouton d'or [3–4], a 14th-century gold coin, depicted the lamb of God, and was followed by the ecu d'or [5–6]. Others followed, including the angel, angelot, teston [10–11], pavillon d'or, louis d'or and pistole. Latterly the currency was based on the gold livre of 20 sols or 240 deniers [12–13].

Following the abolition of the monarchy in 1792, some livres and sols were struck in 1793–4 with republican motifs. The transition of power is reflected in the coins portraying Louis XVI but with a reverse showing the

A Record of Longevity

The standing figure of Marianne as a sower of seed was adopted for the silver coinage in 1898 and continued until 1920, but following the currency reform of 1958 she was restored and continued until the advent of the euro.

Above: Marianne, the personification of the French Republic, has been a popular obverse motif. Some of her many guises are shown here on coins of 1872, 1849, 1904 and 1931.

Phrygian cap, fasces and Gallic cock flanking an angel writing a new constitution, with the date expressed as year 5 of Liberty [14–15] in the revolutionary calendar. In this period money rapidly collapsed and coins were replaced by paper currency known as assignats and mandats. In 1794 the currency was reformed and coins based on the franc of 10 decimes or 100 centimes were introduced. These had the head of Marianne, the allegory of Liberty, on the obverse while the reverse bore the value and the date expressed as *L'an* (the year) followed by a number from 4 to 9 (1793–1808).

Although Napoleon had proclaimed himself emperor in 1804, three years elapsed before the first coins bearing the initial N appeared [16–17]. Silver coins portrayed him as first consul and later as emperor.

LATER COINAGE

The Bourbon dynasty was restored in 1814 and silver and gold coins portraying Louis XVIII appeared in 1816 [18–19], followed by those portraying Charles X (1824–30) [20] and Louis Philippe (1830–48) [21–22]. No bronze coins for small change appeared until the overthrow of the monarchy in 1848. After this, Marianne was again portrayed. Silver 1 and 2 francs appeared in 1852, with Louis Napoleon Bonaparte as president, but from 1853 Napoleon III (obverse) and the imperial eagle (reverse) were the norm [23–26]. After the downfall of the empire, the female allegory Liberty, in various guises, was restored.

France was the driving force behind the creation of the Latin Monetary Union in 1865, which created a coinage standard for Belgium, Italy and Switzerland that endured until 1927. The circulating coins of the French Republic rank among the most artistic in the world and from the 1870s reflected a gradual change from Neo-classicism [27–28] to Art Nouveau in the 1890s and Art Deco after World War I. There have also been a wide variety of base-metal alloys, from bronze and nickel before World War I, through the aluminium of the Vichy era and the postwar period before the advent of the "heavy franc" in 1958, to chrome steel, aluminium-bronze and nickel-brass. Many commemoratives have appeared in recent years, often in base metal for general circulation.

MONACO

The tiny principality on the French Riviera has had its own coinage since the late Middle Ages. Modern coinage, based on the French decimal system, dates from 1837, when 5 centime coins were cast in brass or struck in copper along with silver 5 franc pieces. Gold 20 and 100 francs appeared in the 1880s, but lower denominations were not released until the 1940s, conforming to the French specifications [29–30]. Coins were minted sporadically from then until 1974, but since then dates have been changed annually. Some high-denomination commemoratives have appeared in recent years.

Above: Prince Rainier III and the crowned arms of the Grimaldi family.

IBERIAN PENINSULA

The most south-westerly part of Europe was fought over and conquered by Phoenicians, Carthaginians, Greeks and Romans. Silver coins were struck at Gades (now Cadiz) on Greek lines [1–2] and copper denarii appeared before the beginning of the Christian era [3]. The Visigoths and Moors also left their mark on the coinage, but by the 12th century Christian kingdoms were beginning to emerge [4–5]. In the late 15th century the regions of Aragon and Castile were united by the marriage of their rulers, Ferdinand and Isabella [7–8], and the Moors were driven out in 1492 – the very year that Columbus set sail for the New World, whose mineral wealth would make Spain the richest and most powerful nation in Europe. Spain was also one of the major components of the Habsburg Empire in the 16th and 17th centuries and exerted a major influence on its coinage. Portugal was one of the kingdoms to emerge in the 12th century and managed to resist the encroachment of Spain, apart from the period 1581–1640. Both countries won and lost vast colonial empires, followed by political instability, the downfall of monarchy and the rise of fascist dictatorships before the establishment of democracy in the 1970s.

Left: The silver peso a ocho reales, or "piece of eight", featured the Spanish royal arms on one side and a depiction of the Pillars of Hercules (the Straits of Gibraltar) on the other, for which reason it is often known as the Pillar Dollar.

SPAIN

The silver and gold of the Americas flooded Europe from the 16th to the late-18th centuries and transformed the Spanish peso a ocho reales into the world's most popular coin and a role model for the dollar currencies ever since [6]. The gold escudo was worth 16 silver reales, while 34 copper maravedis equalled a silver real. This system was replaced by decimal coinage in 1848 based on the real of 10 decimos or 100 centimos, changed to the escudo of 100 centimos in 1864 and finally to the peseta of 100 centimos in 1868.

In the monarchical periods the obverse portrayed the reigning king or queen, with an armorial device on the reverse. Intermittent coinage during the 1870s [9–10] meant that the first republic (1873–4) came and went without note. Alfonso XIII, born after his father's death, was king from 1886 to 1931, and the early coins of his reign portrayed him successively as a baby and in various phases of childhood.

After the monarchy was overthrown in 1931 a few coins inscribed "Republica Espanola" appeared in 1934–7. In the early years of the nationalist regime, coinage was equally meagre, and it was not until 1947 that something like a regular series was adopted [11–12], with the portrait of General Franco as El Caudillo ("the leader") on the obverse [13] and national arms on the reverse. Although Spain was technically a kingdom from 1949, it was not until the death of Franco in 1975 that its monarchy was restored in the person of King Juan Carlos, grandson of Alfonso XIII.

Spanish coins often have a fixed date, the actual year of production being indicated by tiny numerals within an eight-pointed star, the mark of the Madrid Mint [14]. Conversely, letters after the date are those of mint officials. In recent years some handsome commemoratives have been released, notably for the World Cup football championship (1982) and the Barcelona Olympics (1992) [15].

Explorers Honoured

Many of Portugal's commemorative coins of recent times have focused on the exploits of the Portuguese explorers of the 15th and 16th centuries, not forgetting Prince Henry the Navigator who, though not himself an explorer, established the school of navigation that gave Portugal such a lead in opening up the world.

PORTUGAL

Like that of Spain, the currency of Portugal [16–17] was originally based on the silver real, but higher values were covered by *moeda ouro* (literally "gold money"), hence the term *moidore*. Portugal's commercial power was largely derived from the gold of the Guinea Coast, exemplified by this 4000 reis of João V, 1720 [18–19]. The monarch subsequently received the title "King of Portugal and Guinea".

As Portugal declined in uwealth and importance in the 18th century the value of the real fell to the point at which it vanished altogether. The smallest copper coin was the 3 reis (the Portuguese form of *reales*) but its multiples included the 10 reis [20], vintem (20 reis) [23], pataca (40), tostão (100), cruzado (480), escudo (1600) and the 8 escudo (6400) such as this coin of Carlos IV [21–22]. This cumbersome system continued until the overthrow of the monarchy in 1910, when the escudo of 100 centavos was adopted.

In the closing months of the monarchy, large silver coins celebrated the centenary of the defeat of Napoleon in the Peninsular War or honoured the Marquis de Pombal, the 18th-century statesman who rebuilt Lisbon after the earthquake of 1755. There was a great variety of types in the reis coinage, with the royal effigy or crowned shield (obverse) and value, arms or a cross (reverse). The same approach was adopted in the republican decimal coinage, on which various effigies of Liberty facing left or right [25] replaced the regal portraits. At first the reverses showed either the arms, minus the royal crown, or a wreathed value, but a more pictorial style gradually developed in the 1930s, notably in the silver coins that featured the flagship of the navigator Vasco da Gama [24].

While Portugal's circulating coinage has remained relatively conservative in style and treatment, the commemorative and special issues have escalated in recent years, recording anniversaries of numerous historic events, from the medieval explorations to the revolution of 1974 [26–7].

ANDORRA

The tiny principality of Andorra in the valleys of the Pyrenees is a feudal anachronism: the Counts of Foix (in France) and the Bishops of Urgel (Spain) have ruled it as co-princes since 1278. As a result, French and Spanish currency has circulated freely ever since. Since 1982, however, distinctive coins based on the diner (denier) of 100 centims have been struck, mainly as tourist souvenirs [28–30], along with silver and gold coins aimed at the numismatic market. Some of these coins bear the bust of the Bishop of Urgel (the role of the Comte de Foix has now passed to the President of France), but most feature the arms of the principality. Andorra even produced ecus, but now uses the euro.

Above: Recent motifs on coins of Andorra have ranged from wildlife (such as this Pyrenean goat) to historical figures such as Charlemagne, who granted the valleys their first charter.

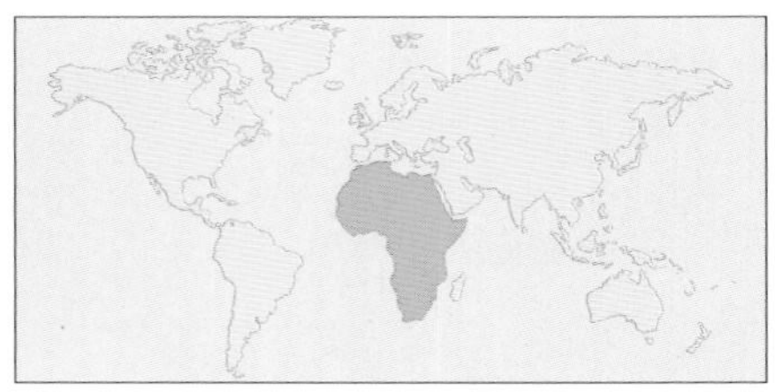

AFRICA

Historically regarded as the Dark Continent, Africa is today home to many of the Third World's poorest countries. Exploited by the rest of the world for centuries and now hampered by colossal debt and unfair trade, it has experienced political turmoil, tyranny and corruption.

NORTH AFRICA

The portion of the continent on the southern shores of the Mediterranean came into contact with the civilizations of Greece and Rome, but long before that period the coastal regions were dominated by Egypt and colonized by the Phoenicians, who created the great power of Carthage, which challenged the might of Rome in the 3rd century BC. Coins struck to Greek standards date from the 6th century BC at Cyrene, such as the horned head of Karneios, counterpart of Apollo [1–2], and from about 410 BC at Carthage, bearing the profile of Tanit, the Carthaginian counterpart of Persephone (obverse) and a horse's head (reverse) [3–4]. Later coins featured entire horses or lions, and both gold and electrum pieces were also struck. The large silver coins, up to 12 drachmae, were heavily influenced by those of Sicily. By 146 BC, Carthage had been conquered and thereafter Roman coins were in use [5–6]. Some coins were also struck by the Berber kingdoms from the third century BC. In the Dark Ages Carthage was overrun by the Vandals but a Byzantine mint flourished briefly, and from the 8th century Islamic coinage was in use. After the death of Haroun al Rashid the power of the Caliphate was divided, and thereafter Ifriquiyah (Africa) became increasingly separate, with its own dynasties issuing Islamic coins in their own names, such as an 8th-century dirham in the name of Haroun's successor [7–8]. By the 14th century the Barbary states (Algeria, Morocco and Tunisia) were emerging; though continuing with the basic Islamic types, they gradually introduced their own distinctive features.

Left: Obverse and reverse of a silver coin of Juba I, king of Numidia in the first century BC. Juba, of Phoenician descent, ruled over Numidia, Mauritania and Libya. In pursuance of his ambitions to create an empire in North Africa he allied himself with the Roman Senate in their struggle against Julius Caesar and struck vast quantities of these coins to finance his campaign.

ALGERIA

The important city and seaport of Algiers was founded in 950 on earlier Phoenician and Roman settlements. Nominally subject to the sultans of Tlemcen, it achieved autonomy in the 15th century and became a commercial centre following the expulsion of the Jews and Moors from Spain in 1492. Although part of the Ottoman Empire from 1518 the Turks gave the Barbary corsairs a free hand, which is reflected in the distinctive coins struck at Timilsan (modern Tlemcen) by Murad III [9–10].

It was to suppress piracy that the French invaded in 1830, annexing Algeria in 1848. Coins modelled on Turkish weights and values were struck at Algiers and Constantine, and also at Mascara and Taqident during the revolt of Abd-el-Kader (1834–47). Latterly

Libya

Nominally part of the Ottoman Empire until 1911, the region of North Africa west of Egypt fell to the Italians in 1934, and they named it "Libia", the Latin name for the territory. Under Turkish rule the pashas, or governors, had struck copper and billon coins for small change, but it was not until 1952 that coins were adopted by this newly created kingdom, with the bust of Idris I on the obverse. The monarchy was overthrown in 1969, and Libya was declared a socialist people's republic, but coins with the republican emblem were not produced until 1975.

the coinage was based on the silver budju of 24 muzuna or 48 kharuba, along with the gold sultani and its subdivisions. French coins were normally circulated, but during World War I token coins were issued by the chambers of commerce. Coins with the head of Marianne, corresponding to the French style but inscribed "Algerie" on the reverse, were introduced in 1949–50. Independence was proclaimed in July 1962 and coins of the Algerian Republic appeared in 1964, based on the dinar of 100 centimes [11–12]. A new series, from the aluminium quarter dinar to the bimetallic 100 dinar coin, was adopted in 1992. A number of commemoratives have been issued since the tenth anniversary of Algerian independence.

MOROCCO

Of immense strategic importance at the western end of the Mediterranean, Morocco was successively ruled by Phoenicians, Romans, Vandals, Visigoths, Byzantines and Arabs. Around 1062 Berber tribes, migrating northwards from Senegal, established themselves at Marrakesh. The Almoravids were so named from the Arabic for "those from the frontier posts". By 1086 they had extended their rule from Algiers to southern Spain. Various dynasties rose and fell, such as the Murabitid [13–14], but the Sharifs of Tafilat gained power in 1660 and have ruled ever since. From this period belongs the dirham struck at Madrid for issue in Marrakesh [15–16]. European rivalries resulted in the partition of Morocco into Spanish and French protectorates in 1912, but sovereignty was regained in 1957.

Coins, struck at Fez, Rabat, Tetuan and Marrakesh, conformed to Islamic styles, although from the early 19th century onward Solomon's seal (a five-pointed star) was a prominent feature [17]. The currency was reformed in the 1890s, based on the rial of 10 dirhams or 500 mazunas, with inscriptions entirely in Arabic except for a date of the Muslim calendar in western numerals. In 1921 the coinage was changed to the dirham of 100 francs, the only decorative feature being a five-pointed star. Following the resumption of independence portraits of Muhammad V appeared on the higher values [19–20]. The currency was changed in 1974 to the dirham of 100 santimat [18].

TUNISIA

The suppression of the Barbary pirates virtually bankrupted Tunis and enabled the French to establish a protectorate in 1881. Previously, successive beys (governors) had issued coins in the name of the Turkish sultan [21–22]. Similar coins, with the Paris mintmark, were struck until 1891, when the franc was adopted. Thereafter, coins were inscribed in Arabic (obverse) or French (reverse). Tunisia became a republic in 1957 and introduced a coinage based on the dinar of 1000 millim [23–26], showing a tree or President Bourguiba on the obverse. A few commemoratives have been issued since 1976.

1 2 3 4 5 6 7 8 9 10 11 12 13 14 15 16

EGYPT AND SUDAN

Pharaonic Egypt had a sophisticated weighed-metal system, which did not require round pieces of metal but relied on standard weights of silver for certain transactions. Athenian tetradrachms were circulating in Egypt by the 5th century BC. Pharaoh Nectanebo II (359–343 BC) struck a gold stater inscribed "Neft Nub" ("good gold") in hieroglyphics and a few silver tetradrachms with indigenous inscriptions are known from around the same period. A distinctive coinage on Greek lines was adopted by Ptolemy I, one of Alexander the Great's generals, who in 304 BC established the Hellenistic kingdom that ended with the suicide of Cleopatra in 30 BC. Greek influence is clearly seen in the tetradrachms of Ptolemy I [1–2] and Ptolemy VI [3–4] of the 4th and 2nd centuries BC. Under Roman rule, Egypt was allowed a subsidiary coinage for local circulation, the output of these coins from the imperial mint at Alexandria being very prolific [5–8].

Left: Ali Bey al Kabir, born in the Caucasus (now Abkhazia), seized power in 1760 and established the Neo-Mamluk Beylicate, repudiating allegiance to the Turkish sultan. Distinctive coins of this period bear Arabic inscriptions on both sides.

BYZANTINE PERIOD

At the division of the Roman Empire Egypt passed under eastern control and Alexandria continued to strike copper nummia until 646 – some years after Egypt fell to the Arabs in 642. These coins were produced in unusual multiples of 3, 6, 12 and 33 nummia. Gold coins were minted sporadically, but later in some abundance towards the end of Byzantine rule, under Heraclius (610–41). The motifs conformed to Byzantine standards, with facing portraits of the emperor and his son Constans on the obverse and the stepped cross or a standing figure on the reverse. Coins portraying Heraclius flanked by the sun and moon were actually struck by Khusru II during the Sasanian occupation of 718–28.

ISLAMIC PERIOD

The Alexandria Mint was one of the casualties of the Arab conquest. When distinctive coins emerged under the Caliphate in the 9th century, coins of the Tulinids [9–10] and Ikshidids [11–12], independent governors in Egypt in the 9th and 10th centuries respectively, were struck at Cairo [13–14], Alexandria and other places. In 969 Egypt fell to the Fatimids, who struck coins in entirely new designs at Cairo until the province was conquered by Saladin in 1171. Thereafter, coins followed the Ayyubid pattern until 1250, when Egypt became the realm of the Mamelukes [15–16]. They were in turn overthrown by the Turks in 1517. Thereafter the coinage followed the Turkish pattern. Ottoman control of Egypt declined in the late 18th century.

KINGDOM OF EGYPT

Though nominally khedive (viceroy) of the sultan, Mehemet (Mahmud) Ali created a dynasty that lasted from 1808 to 1953. The son of an Albanian tobacco merchant, he came to prominence in 1798 when he headed the Albanian–Turkish force despatched by the sultan to counter the French invasion. After the French were ousted by the British he became viceroy. He destroyed the Mamelukes (1811), conquered much of Arabia (1818) and annexed Nubia (1820). He extended his empire to Crete and Morea in Greece (1821–8) and Syria (1831) respectively, but his wish to become sultan of Constantinople was thwarted by the Quadruple Alliance (1840).

The coinage was reformed in 1835 and British coin presses were installed at the Cairo Mint. Nevertheless, the coinage continued to be very similar to the prevailing Turkish types, with the *toughra* on the obverse and elaborate Arabic inscriptions distinguished by the word "Misr" (Egypt) inscribed above the date on the reverse. The currency was based on the guerche or piastre of 40 para, but in 1885 it was extended to the pound of 100 piastres.

Egypt was under British military occupation from 1881 and formally became a British protectorate in 1914, following Turkey's entry into World War I on the side of the Central Powers. It became an independent sovereign state in 1922, when Fuad I was proclaimed king. Illustrated here is a silver 10 piastre coin with dates in both Muslim and Common Era calendars [23–4], struck by the Heaton Mint in Birmingham on behalf of Sultan Ahmed Fuad in 1920, two years before he was elevated to the kingship. Egyptian coins were dated according to the Muslim calendar until 1916, when the currency was reformed and based on the piastre of 10 milliemes; thereafter, dates were given in Arabic according to both calendars [17]. From 1924 onward the obverse bore the bust of the ruler [18–22].

Postman as National Emblem

The image on the Sudanese coins of 1956–71 is that of an Arab postman mounted on a camel, derived from the postage stamps issued from 1898 onward. So familiar was this motif (designed by Colonel E.A. Stanton during the re-conquest of the Sudan) that it became a national icon.

REPUBLIC

King Farouk reigned from 1937 until he was deposed by a military junta in 1952. He was briefly succeeded by his infant son Fuad II, but the monarchy was abolished in July 1953. The Sphinx replaced the bust of Farouk on the obverse of coins, which continued to be inscribed entirely in Arabic, the text reading "Jumhuriyya Misr Al Arabiyya" (Arab Republic of Egypt). Following union with Syria in the form of the United Arab Republic in 1958, the eagle emblem was adopted on the obverse. Syria left this union in 1961 but a decade elapsed before Egypt abandoned the grandiose title and styled itself once more as the Arab Republic of Egypt; the inscriptions on the coinage were suitably amended from 1971 onward [25–26]. The *toughra* was revived as an obverse type in 1984 [31] while higher denominations had a central hole [30], but a more pictorial approach was adopted for the circulating coins in 1992 [27–29]. Many commemorative coins have appeared since the 1960s, often harking back to the Pharaonic period.

SUDAN

This vast country south of Egypt was conquered by Mehemet Ali, seceded in 1881 during the Mahdist revolt, and was re-conquered in 1898. Gold and silver piastres were struck by the Mahdi at Khartoum (1885) and at Omdurman by his successor, the Khalifa (1885–98). From 1898 until 1954 it was an Anglo-Egyptian condominium. Autonomy was followed by the grant of full independence in 1956. Egyptian coins were used until then and the same currency, based on the pound of 100 ghirsh or 1000 millim, was retained. A democratic republic was proclaimed in 1969, signalled on the coins from 1971 by an eagle replacing the original camel motif [32–33]. Most of the special issues since 1972 marked anniversaries of independence or the 1969 revolution. The currency was reformed in 1992 and the dinar of 100 dirhems introduced [34–35].

SOUTH AFRICA

This large country at the southern tip of the continent was for centuries the most European part of Africa in its population and political character. Although the Portuguese first explored it in 1498 it was not colonized until the Dutch arrived there in 1652. The hinterland of the Cape of Good Hope fell to the British during the Napoleonic Wars and was formally annexed in 1814 as the Cape Colony. Discontent with British rule induced many of the Afrikaners (the Dutch settlers) to trek northward and establish independent republics. The subsequent discovery of gold and diamonds in these states led to friction between the Boers (Dutch farmers) and those they defined as Uitlanders (foreign incomers), culminating in the Anglo-Boer War of 1899–1902. Most South African gold was exported and had little effect on the indigenous coinage, and it was not until 1923 that a branch of the Royal Mint was established in Pretoria to produce sovereigns with the SA mint-mark [1–2].

Left: Jan van Riebeeck, portrayed on the obverse of the coins of the South African Republic (1961–9) led the expedition by the Dutch East India Company that founded Cape Town in 1652. His ship, the Dromedaaris, *was depicted on the reverse of the bronze halfpennies and pennies of 1923–60.*

EARLY COINAGE

Ordinary Dutch or British coins were used widely in southern Africa in the 17th and 18th centuries. The first distinctive pieces were issued by the Revd John Campbell, head of the mission station at Griquatown in the territory known as Griqualand, between the Kalahari Desert and the Boer republics. They consisted of copper farthings and halfpennies and silver 5 and 10 pence, depicting a phoenix on the obverse with the name of the mission and numerals of value on the reverse. They were undated but circulated in 1815–16 and are extremely rare. A pattern penny with the profile of Queen Victoria (obverse) and dove (reverse) was produced in Berlin in 1889 [3–4].

Distinctive coinage was first attempted in the South African Republic (Transvaal) in 1874, when gold pounds portraying President Thomas Burgers were struck. Only a few hundred of these Burgersponds were struck. Regular coinage, struck at Pretoria and bearing the bust of President Paul Kruger, was introduced in 1892 [11–12]; it consisted of the bronze penny, silver 3 and 5 pence, 1 shilling [13–14], 2 and 5 shillings [5–6] and gold pound [7–10]. Apart from the smaller silver coins (which showed the value in a wreath), this series bore the arms of the republic on the reverse.

UNION OF SOUTH AFRICA

British coins were in use from 1900 onward, extending from Cape Colony and Natal to cover the former Boer republics, now renamed Transvaal and Orange River Colony. Although the Union of South Africa was proclaimed in 1910 – the former colonies becoming provinces – a distinctive coinage was not introduced until 1923. This series, following British weights and specifications, ranged from the bronze ¼ penny (farthing) to the 2 shillings [15–18]. A curious feature of the 3 and 6 pence from 1925 onward was the depiction of three or six bundles of brushwood on the reverse to denote the value. The obverse portrayed the reigning monarch, with Latin titles, while the reverse was inscribed in English and Afrikaans. A silver 5 shillings was introduced in 1947 to celebrate a royal visit [19]. These coins, with a Springbok reverse, were minted on a regular basis thereafter, as well as appearing in commemorative versions. From 1923 British gold sovereigns and half sovereigns were minted at Pretoria, identifiable by the SA mint-mark, followed by distinctive half pounds and pounds in 1952.

REPUBLIC OF SOUTH AFRICA

The rise of Afrikaner nationalism after World War II, and the implementation of the racially divisive policy of apartheid ("separateness"), led to South Africa becoming a republic in May 1961 and its expulsion from the Commonwealth the following October.

A new currency, based on the rand of 100 cents, was adopted and Jan van Riebeeck replaced the royal effigy [20]. The large brass subsidiary coins [22] were replaced by small bronze 1c [21] and 2c [24] coins in 1965. In 1989, as concerns mounted over costs, three series – red, white and yellow [28–29] – of steel-plated coins were introduced, the colour depending on the usage of copper, nickel and/or tin. Depictions of South African fauna and flora were used on the high denominations [23], while the arms of the republic [25] replaced Van Riebeeck in 1970, interspersed by coins portraying the latest state president [26–27]. The blue crane – the national emblem and a threatened species – appears on the 5c [30].

Above: The rand, named after the reef containing one of the largest gold deposits in the world, started life as a small gold coin in 1961, switched to silver in 1965, then nickel from 1977, to 1990, and finally nickel-plated copper later the same year. For 45 years, however, the reverse design has remained constant, showing a springbok. The protea (right) is the floral emblem of South Africa and has appeared on coins since 1965.

Biblical Allusion

From 1923 the farthing had a reverse motif of two sparrows, an allusion to the rhetorical question posed by Christ (Matthew 10:29): "Are not two sparrows sold for a farthing?" This motif was retained for the reverse of the half cent (1961–83) and extended in 1965 to the cent, where it has continued, in various guises, to this day.

Although South Africa took its doctrine of separateness to the extent of creating four black "homelands" in the 1970s, these territories continued to use South African currency. Bophuthatswana alone produced gold nkwe or platinum lowe bullion pieces in 1987 to mark the tenth anniversary of independence.

The apartheid regime ended in 1994 with the first free elections for all the people of South Africa. In the Afrikaner period, coins had been mainly inscribed bilingually, although some were released in distinctive English or Afrikaans versions. Since 1996, however, coins have been inscribed in Zulu, Venda, Ndebele, Tsonga, Tswana, Sotho, Swati and Xhosa, or other languages indigenous to the country.

The silver rand was a popular medium for commemorative issues from 1967 onward, although a tiny gold rand appeared in 1997 to mark the 30th anniversary of the world's first successful heart transplant, by the South African surgeon Christiaan Barnard. More recently, 2 rand coins have been used as commemoratives. South Africa pioneered modern bullion coins, launching the gold Krugerrand in 1960, followed by the Protea (1986) and Natura (1994) series.

SOUTHERN AFRICA

This term encompasses the countries bordering South Africa (including Lesotho, which is entirely within the boundaries of that country). Three of them were formerly British High Commission territories and the fourth was a German colony, subsequently mandated to South Africa under the name of South West Africa and now called Namibia. They now form a common currency area, with all currencies pegged to the rand.

Left: Although Namibia has a largely pastoral economy, it has considerably developed its offshore fishing industry in recent years. Appropriately, this 5 cent coin, issued as part of the UN Food and Agriculture Organization coin programme in 2000 to celebrate the dawn of the new century, depicts a horse mackerel with the exhortation to "Eat More Fish".

NAMIBIA

Formerly German South West Africa, this vast territory was occupied by South African troops soon after the outbreak of World War I and in 1920 South Africa was granted a mandate by the League of Nations. In 1948 the South African government approached the United Nations with a proposal to annexe South West Africa, but this was turned down. In 1950, when South Africa refused to allow a UN trusteeship, the matter was resolved at the International Court of Justice in the Hague, which ruled against South Africa. The UN terminated the mandate in 1966 but South Africa refused to comply and continued to occupy and govern South West Africa illegally and, moreover, to use it as a base for incursions into Angola. This situation continued until 1988, when South Africa and Cuba withdrew their forces from Angola and steps were finally taken towards independence as Namibia, granted in March 1990.

German currency was used in the colonial period. Namibia continued to use South African currency until 1993, when the Namibian dollar was introduced, on par with the South African rand. Coins from 5 cents to $5, with the republican arms on the obverse and fauna and flora on the reverse, are now in circulation [1–9]. The fifth and tenth anniversaries of independence (1995 and 2000) were celebrated by coins with a multicoloured reverse, and this has been extended to a few other special issues, notably the wildlife series of 1996.

BOTSWANA

Formerly the British Protectorate of Bechuanaland, Botswana became an independent republic in September 1966. Ironically, the first president was Sir Seretse Khama, who had been deposed as Paramount Chief of the Bamangwato and banished following his marriage to an Englishwoman, Ruth Williams, in 1948. He was permitted to return as a private citizen in 1956, entered politics and became the first prime minister (1965) and president a year later. His profile appeared on gold and silver coins celebrating independence and also its tenth anniversary.

Botswana switched from South African currency to the pula of 100 thebe in 1976, remaining on par with the rand. Coins showing the national arms (obverse) and wildlife (reverse) [10–15] consist of the aluminium thebe, bronze 2 and 5 thebe and cupro-nickel higher values. The 25 and 50 thebe coins switched to nickel-clad steel in 1991, while the pula in 1991 and 2 pula in 1994 switched to nickel-brass. A bimetallic 5 pula was added to the series in 2000 and shows a caterpillar devouring a leaf – a message to farmers to be vigilant in pest control [16–17]. A few special issues, including a series devoted to wildlife conservation, have appeared in recent years. Silver and gold coins have also marked the Commonwealth Games (1986), a papal visit (1988) and the International year of Disabled Persons (1991).

LESOTHO

Previously Basutoland, the tiny country of Lesotho is entirely surrounded by the territory of South Africa. A sparsely populated region, it was occupied by refugees from tribal wars, led by Moshoeshoe (1787–1870), who founded a dynasty and established his capital at Thaba Bosiu ("mountain of the night"). Originally named Lepoqo ("disaster", because the region was then famine-stricken), he earned his later name ("shaver") because he dispensed with the beard of an adversary. He withstood the territorial ambitions of Shaka, the mighty Zulu leader, and united the Basotho people through his conciliatory approach to rival tribes. Boer encroachment from the 1830s onward induced Moshoeshoe to seek British protection in 1868 and for a time Basutoland was part of Cape Colony, but from 1884 it was administered by a British high commissioner.

Self-government was granted in 1959, leading to complete sovereignty in 1966. Distinctive coins based on the loti (plural *maloti*) of 100 lisente were introduced in 1979 [18–25]. Moshoeshoe II was twice king (1966–90 and 1995–6), but his meddling in politics infuriated the prime minister, Leabua Jonathan, and resulted in two spells of house arrest, exile (1970) and deposition in favour of his son Letsie III. Moshoeshoe II was restored in 1995 but was killed in a car crash the following year. He was portrayed in military uniform, but during the period when he was deposed the royal arms appeared instead. During the political crises of 1970 and 1990, and also for a few months after Moshoeshoe's death, Ma Mohato (his wife and Letsie's mother) acted as regent. Many of the commemorative coins portrayed Moshoeshoe I on the obverse [22].

SWAZILAND

By contrast with the turbulent politics of Lesotho, Swaziland has been one of the most stable countries in Africa. Sometimes called the Switzerland of Africa because of its mountainous terrain, it lies between the Transvaal, Natal and Mozambique. Though small, it is rich in minerals. Zulu raids induced King Mswati to appeal for British protection and from 1881 independence was guaranteed by Britain and the South African Republic (Transvaal). After the Boer War Britain assumed full responsibility and Swaziland became a High Commission territory. Its independence was granted in 1968.

South African currency was in use until 1974 when a distinctive series, based on the lilangeni (plural *emalangeni*) of 25 luhlanga or 100 cents, was adopted [26–27]. A wide range of circular, polygonal and scalloped shapes made each denomination distinctive, the obverse portraying Sobhuza II [30] and reverses often showing fauna and flora [28–29, 31]. King Makhosetive (Mswati III) has appeared on the coins since 1986 [32–35]. The relatively few special issues include silver and gold coins celebrating the 75th and 80th birthdays of Sobhuza II as well as his diamond jubilee (1981). An unusual feature of some of these coins was a serial number stamped on the reverse.

Africa's Longest-reigning Monarch

King Sobhuza II, born in 1899, ascended the throne in 1921. The year after his diamond jubilee (1982) he stepped down in favour of his grandson Mswati III who was crowned in 1986. In the intervening period, Queen Dzeliwe acted as regent.

AFRICA'S FAUNA

The continent of Africa was relatively stable many millions of years ago, and the fauna that inhabited it then largely survive today. The Sahara Desert and the Great Rift Valley naturally created barriers to the movement of birds and animals, but both were relatively modern (post-glacial) developments. Thus, Africa is home to many species not found elsewhere, while others have their counterparts in India, a relic of the ancient continent Gondwana.

CARNIVORES

The largest and most important of the African carnivores is the lion, which is also found in Asia, indicating its emergence before the continental break-up. Lions were formerly plentiful north of the Sahara but their range has been severely limited by human intervention. As a symbol of strength and courage the lion appears in the heraldry of many countries. As a national icon it has appeared, head alone, on coins of Ethiopia, while an excellent image of a fully grown male lion is featured on the obverse of the coins of the Democratic Republic of the Congo.

By contrast, the leopard has had little recognition, although a very realistic image appears on the reverse of one of the $10 coins issued by Sierra Leone in 2001 with the theme of the Big Five. A full-frontal portrait of a lion appeared on another coin in this series. Distinctive to Africa is the hippopotamus (literally "river horse"), featured on one of the coins issued by Mali in 1960 to celebrate its independence.

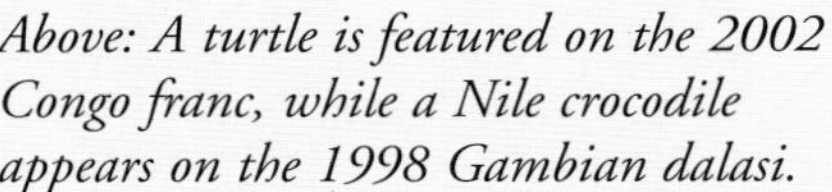

Above: A turtle is featured on the 2002 Congo franc, while a Nile crocodile appears on the 1998 Gambian dalasi.

Above: A coelacanth appears on a coin from the Comoro Islands and the 1998 Ugandan 200 shillings bears a tilapia.

Below: Higher primates are represented in coins by the gorilla from the Congo and the colobus monkey from Eritrea.

Below: Several Botswana coins bear birds, such as the African fish eagle. The 50 cents from the Congo shows a butterfly.

Below: An omnibus issue from several African countries in 1997 showed dinosaurs as part of the Preserve Planet Earth campaign. These coins are from Eritrea (triceratops), Sierra Leone (velociraptor) and Liberia (stegosaurus).

HOOFED ANIMALS

The Cape buffalo, rhinoceros and African elephant were the subject of three coins from Sierra Leone, while another featured the heads of five animals. The elephant of Africa (on many coins from Liberia) is quite distinct in appearance from its Indian counterpart and cannot be domesticated. On the coin from Sierra Leone an adult appears with a baby at its side and a similar motif appears on the 20 shilling coin of Tanzania. The large ears that are a distinguishing feature of the African species are prominent in the 20 cents of Swaziland, and in the coat of arms depicted on the 50 cents the shield has a lion and elephant as supporters.

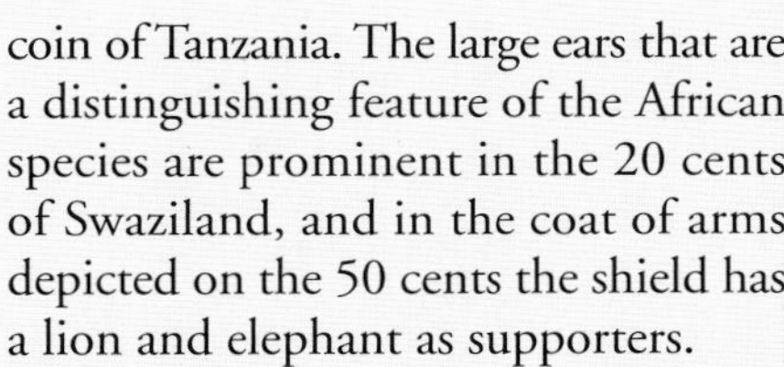

The rhinoceros is mainly found in East Africa although it ranges quite far south, hence its appearance on the 2 pula of Botswana. The single-humped camel was introduced from Arabia as a domesticated animal and is now widely distributed all over North Africa and the Sahara, being featured on coins from Djibouti. Deer are found only in a few parts of former French West Africa. By contrast, the warm grasslands teem with many species of antelope and gazelle, and these graceful animals are a favourite topic on the coins of many countries. Individual species include Loder's gazelle (French

Above: In 2001 Sierra Leone released a set of five large silver coins with the national arms on the obverse and splendid specimens of Africa's Big Five – rhinoceros, lion, leopard, elephant and buffalo – on the reverses.

Equatorial and West Africa), the lyre antelope (French Territory of Afars and Issas, now Djibouti), Buffon's kob (Uganda), the sable antelope (Southern Rhodesia), the Bohor reed buck (Zambia) and, of course, the springbok, which is featured on many coins of South Africa. Africa's only equine species is the zebra, which provides the supporters on the arms of Botswana as well as appearing on the 1 pula coin. Many of the different 2 cent coins of South Africa have featured the white-tailed gnu.

Below and below right: Silver $10 coins were produced in 1996 for "Preserve Planet Earth". Liberia's pair showed a grey parrot and two lovebirds.

OTHER ANIMALS

Africa is home to some of the great anthropoid apes, although few coins have so far been devoted to them. The best example is the gorilla depicted on a coin from the Congo. The aardvark may be found on coins from Zambia and the wildebeest on the 5 kwacha of the same country, while neighbouring Zimbabwe provides an example of a pangolin on the $2 of 1997.

Cattle, sheep and goats are shown on many coins, reflecting their importance to a pastoral economy, while a hare can be found on a Zimbabwean coin. Birds are relatively few, but include the hornbill (Zambia), the crowned crane (Uganda), the heron (Malawi) and the sea eagle (several countries). The national emblem of Zimbabwe is a bird – not a real one but a stylized soapstone carving. Reptiles are represented by the turtle (Congo) and the Nile crocodile (the Gambia). The Congo has even depicted a butterfly on the 50 centimes of 2002 – a subject that has had very short shrift everywhere in the world.

PRESERVE PLANET EARTH

Concern over the endangered fauna of Africa has led to several recent issues of large silver coins giving prominence to species under threat. Many of these have emanated from such countries as Liberia, Eritrea and Sierra Leone and, as a group, they are renowned for their imaginative and realistic portraiture of the animals. From the same countries came a joint issue in 1997 devoted to dinosaurs that roamed Gondwanaland many millions of years ago.

Above: The obverse of Eritrean coins shows a dhow and a camel; the white-tailed sea eagle appears in the arms of Liberia. The reverses show wattled cranes and a Lanner falcon (Eritrea) and a leopard and storks (Liberia).

Below: Coins on an ornithological theme from Eritrea in the "Preserve Planet Earth" programme included this Cape eagle owl.

CENTRAL AFRICA

The area of Central Africa, south of the Equator, consists of the two former Portuguese colonies of Angola and Mozambique, the former Belgian Congo and the territories mandated to Belgium by the League of Nations, and the former colonies and protectorates that made up British Central Africa. These countries were carved out by the various European powers during the "scramble for Africa" in the 19th century.

Left: A brief attempt to weld the colony of Southern Rhodesia and the protectorates of Northern Rhodesia and Nyasaland into a single dominion is recalled by the coins of Rhodesia and Nyasaland, which were issued between 1955 and 1963.

FORMER PORTUGUESE TERRITORIES

Coins for specific use in Portuguese Africa were minted from 1693 onward, while coins struck at Goa in Portuguese India, such as the 1000 reis of José I [1–2], were produced for circulation in Mozambique from 1725. Decimal coins inscribed "Republica Portuguesa" on the obverse, with the name of the territory on the reverse, were introduced in Angola in 1921 [3–4] and in Mozambique in 1936, gradually replacing the coins of the mother country, whose national emblems had given the colonial issues a degree of uniformity.

Both of Portugal's "overseas provinces" were in revolt from 1960 onward, but they gained their independence as people's republics only after the collapse of António de Oliveira Salazar's regime, and the advent of democracy, in Portugal in 1974. Following independence, Mozambique adopted the metical of 100 centimos, and Angola chose the kwanza of 100 lwei (1979). While Angola featured its national emblem on the obverse and numerals on the reverse of its coins [5], Mozambique chose the profile of President Samora Machel and various plants.

Both countries subsequently reformed their currencies. Mozambique switched from centimes to centavos in 1980, while Angola introduced the "re-adjusted" kwanza of 100 centimos, the equivalent of 1000 old kwanzas, in 1995.

FORMER BELGIAN TERRITORIES

Leopold II, King of the Belgians, was granted the Congo in 1885 and governed it as his personal property. This was reflected in the inscription on the coins introduced in 1887, which proclaimed him as Sovereign of the Congo Free State. Revelations of misrule led to it being annexed by Belgium in 1908 and renamed the Belgian Congo [7, 11]. The star emblem of the Free State was replaced by a profile of the king and crowned arms. A palm replaced the latter in 1920 [6], while an elephant replaced the portrait in 1944.

The Democratic Republic of the Congo gained independence in 1960 but was immediately plunged into civil war. Coins issued by the national bank appeared in 1965 [10]. The country's name was changed to Zaire in 1971 and the zaire of 100 makuta was adopted. In the ensuing period, coins portrayed President Mabotu [8–9], but following a civil war in 1997 the country reverted to the previous name and adopted coins featuring a lion (obverse) and various fauna (reverse). Rectangular or triangular coins (2000) publicized the campaign for animal protection.

During the civil war of 1961, bronze coins were struck in the breakaway southern province of Katanga, featuring bananas (obverse) [12] and the bronze crosses [13] used as money before the advent of coinage [14].

Belgium was granted a mandate over Rwanda-Urundi, formerly part of

German East Africa. Congolese coins were used there until 1952, when a series with these names was released. When the Congo gained independence in 1960, coins inscribed "Rwanda Burundi" were adopted. Separate issues in each country appeared in the Kingdom of Burundi (1965) [15–16] and the Republic of Rwanda (1964) [17–18]. Rwanda adopted a new series in 1974–7, with the national arms on the obverse and millet, coffee or bananas on the reverse [19–22]. In 1966, Burundi abolished its monarchy and replaced the portraits of Mwambutsa IV with the republican arms.

FORMER BRITISH TERRITORIES

British and South African coins circulated in the vast territories of the British South Africa Company headed by Cecil Rhodes. Rejecting incorporation in the Union of South Africa (1923) the territory was broken up into the colony of Southern Rhodesia and the protectorates of Northern Rhodesia and Nyasaland.

Above: Pictorial reverses of the 20 ngwee of Zambia, 1985 (left) and 1968-88.

Distinctive silver coins were adopted in 1932 [23–24], followed by holed cupro-nickel halfpennies and pennies in 1934. Coins bore the head of the reigning monarch [25], with pictorial reverses [26–28]. Coins inscribed for use in the Federation of Rhodesia and Nyasaland (1955–64) followed a similar pattern. On the break-up of the federation, Nyasaland became Malawi and Northern Rhodesia became Zambia, both introducing distinctive coins in 1964. Both countries adopted a decimal system based on the kwacha [35–36], comprised either of 100 tambala (Malawi, 1971) [29–30] or 100 ngwee (Zambia, 1968) [31–32].

The former Southern Rhodesia dropped the adjective and then unilaterally declared independence in November 1965. Although the regime, headed by Ian Smith, was declared illegal, its coins continued to portray Elizabeth II until 1970, when a republic was declared and an armorial obverse was adopted. In 1978, Smith signed a pact with moderate African leaders and the country adopted the name Zimbabwe Rhodesia. No coins bearing the double name were ever issued, and in 1980 the country became the Republic of Zimbabwe. Coins thus inscribed, with the emblem of a bird carved from soapstone on the obverse, were issued that year [33–34].

While Malawi and Zimbabwe have produced very few special issues, Zambia has been prolific in releasing large silver coins, often multicoloured and in unusual polygonal or upright oval shapes.

Coins in Two Currencies

The coins issued by Rhodesia from 1964 to 1968 were denominated in both sterling and decimal currencies, on the basis of the pound of 20 shillings or 2 dollars. Thus the shilling of 12 pence was also worth 10 cents. Cupro-nickel coins, which ranged from the 3 pence (2 cents) to the 2 shillings (25 cents), were accompanied by gold coins solely denominated 10 shillings, £1 or £5.

EAST AFRICA

The countries of East Africa were formerly in the British or German spheres of influence and were created as a result of a series of pacts and treaties between these European powers and the various tribal rulers. The area included the offshore islands of Zanzibar and Pemba, governed by the Al-Busaid dynasty, originally from Muscat in Arabia and for centuries the centre of the Arab-dominated slave trade of Africa. The first regular coinage in this region consisted of the bronze pice and silver annas and rupees issued by the British East India Company at Mombasa in 1888–90 [1–6].

Left: Coins of the lower denominations of East Africa had a central hole, with the value and elephant tusks on the reverse and a crown on the obverse. They bore the names and titles of British monarchs, and thus had the distinction of being one of the few issues to be inscribed with the name of King Edward VIII, who ascended the throne in January 1936 and abdicated the following December.

ZANZIBAR

Coins were struck by various seaports along the Swahili Coast from the 11th century, and these remained in use until the arrival of the Portuguese in the 16th century. The sultans of Zanzibar had distinctive coinage in the 19th century. Barghash ibn Sa'id (1879–88) introduced silver ryals and copper pysa in 1882, with Arabic inscriptions on both sides [7–10]. The pysa, however, also featured scales on the reverse, copying the coins of the British East India Company. The rupee of 100 cents was adopted in 1908 and bronze or nickel coins of 1, 10 and 20 cents had a palm tree reverse. Otherwise the sultanate used the coins of the East African Monetary Union. A large silver medal marked the Zanzibar Exhibition in 1905 [11].

FORMER GERMAN EAST AFRICA

Germany obtained trading rights in Dar es Salaam and Witu in 1884 and declared a protectorate in 1891. Six years later the territory was proclaimed a German colony. At first the rupee of 64 pesa was used, and a copper pesa was released in 1890–2 with the name of the German East African Company with the imperial eagle on the obverse and an Arabic reverse. Coins inscribed "Deutsche Ostafrika" were introduced in 1904, based on the rupee of 100 heller, and featured the imperial crown and a wreathed value (heller denominations) or the bust of Kaiser Wilhelm II (rupees). During World War I, German troops fought a skilful guerrilla campaign to the very end, and even produced emergency coins inscribed "D.O.A."

Under the name of Tanganyika, the territory was mandated to Britain in 1920 and became an independent republic in 1961. In 1964 it joined with Zanzibar (where the Arab sultanate had been overthrown) and adopted the name of Tanzania in October that year.

EAST AFRICAN MONETARY UNION

Instituted in 1906, the Union provided a common currency in five territories: British East Africa (the colony and protectorate of Kenya), Uganda, British Somaliland, Zanzibar and latterly Tanganyika. Coins inscribed "East Africa & Uganda Protectorates" were introduced: the low values had a central hole and a crown (obverse) [13], and elephant tusks (reverse) [12, 14], while the silver 25 and 50 cents bore the crowned bust of the monarch (obverse) and a lion and mountains (reverse) [15–16]. Similar coins appeared from 1921 based on the shilling of 100 cents. This pattern continued until 1966, when it was replaced by the coinage of the component states as they gained independence.

INDEPENDENT REPUBLICS

Uganda was granted independence in 1962, followed by Kenya (1963) and Tanganyika (1964). Meanwhile the British Somaliland protectorate had joined with the former Italian colony to form the Republic of Somalia. Initially, the three republics within the Commonwealth continued with the coins of East Africa, but separate issues were adopted when the Union was dissolved in 1966.

The subsidiary coins of the Bank of Uganda retained the Union's ivory tusk motif but the higher values replaced the royal effigy with the arms of the republic [17], while a crested crane superseded the lion on the reverse [18] The composition of the coins was changed in 1976, with copper-plated steel replacing bronze in the lower denominations and cupro-nickel plated steel taking the place of cupro-nickel in the higher values. A new series in stainless or copper-plated steel (1987) had numerals in a floral reverse [19–20]. Inflation in the ensuing decade led to the 1998 series of 50 to 500 shillings, featuring wildlife on the reverse.

Kenya opted for a series with an armorial obverse and a bust of President Jomo Kenyatta on the reverse. In 1968 the reverse inscription was altered but Kenyatta's effigy stayed until 1978. After his death, the portrait of his successor, Daniel Arap Moi, was substituted [21–22], and bimetallic coins from 5 to 20 shillings were added to the series between 1995 and 1998. The very few special issues have commemorated Kenyatta's 75th birthday (1966), the 25th anniversary of independence (1988), the tenth anniversary of Moi as president (1988) and the silver jubilee of the Central Bank (1991).

Julius Nyerere was portrayed on the coins of Tanzania from their inception [23, 25], with mammals, birds and fish on the reverse [24, 26]. As in other parts of East Africa, plated steel has replaced cupro-nickel in recent years [27–28]. The basic circulating series originally ran from the bronze 5 senti to 1 shilingi [29–30]. From 1974, a number of gold or silver high values, up to 2,500 shilingi, marked anniversaries of independence and the Central Bank of Tanzania or publicized wildlife conservation. A polygonal 5 shilingi, released in 1971 to mark the tenth anniversary of independence and contribute to the FAO coin programme, showed agricultural products grouped around the value. This motif was retained for the permanent coins of this denomination. Bimetallic circulating coins of 10 shilingi were introduced in 1987 and 20 shilingi in 1992; both portray Nyerere (obverse) and the national arms (reverse).

Above: Imprisoned by the British during the Mau Mau campaign, Jomo Kenyatta became Kenya's first president.

Wartime Gold

In 1916 gold from the Kironda Mine at Sekengi in German East Africa was coined as 15 rupee pieces, popularly known as Tabora Sovereigns (from the railway workshop where they were struck). The dies were engraved by a Sinhalese prisoner of war, and German regulations decreed that they could be issued only to "residents of the better class."

HORN OF AFRICA

The north-east corner of the continent, bounded by the Red Sea and the north-western part of the Indian Ocean, is described as the Horn of Africa. This region was predominantly in the Italian sphere of influence, since Eritrea and Somalia were Italian colonies or protectorates, while Ethiopia was under Italian occupation from 1936 to 1941. The French controlled the port of Djibouti and its hinterland, while the British established a protectorate over the area on the southern shore of the Gulf of Aden.

Left: Italian coinage was in use in Ethiopia from 1936 to 1941, but coins portraying the Emperor Haile Selassie, dated 1936 in the Ethiopian Era (1944), were issued following the country's liberation. They were struck in Philadelphia, Birmingham or London between 1945 and 1975.

ETHIOPIA

Formerly known as Abyssinia, this large country south of Sudan is the oldest independent nation in Africa, tracing its origins back to the 4th century BC, when it was founded by Menelik I, son of Solomon and the Queen of Sheba. The powerful kingdom of Axum was probably the first country south of the Sahara to issue coins, from the 2nd century AD, including exquisite little gold coins such as the tremissis of about AD 450 [1–2]. Brass or billon coins called mahallak were struck at Harar from 1807 to 1892.

Under Menelik II (1889–1913) Ethiopia emerged from centuries of isolation and rapidly modernized, adopting western-style coinage in 1892 based on the silver talari (derived from the Maria Theresia thaler) of 20 gersh (piastres) or 40 besa. In 1903 the talari was re-tariffed at 16 gersh or 32 besa. A decimal system based on the birr (dollar) of 100 santeems or matonas was adopted in 1931. Coins bore the effigy of the monarch (obverse) and the Lion of Judah (reverse) [3–4].

Haile Selassie was deposed in 1974 and the country became a people's democratic republic in 1976. Coins had a lion's head (obverse) and aspects of agriculture (reverse) [5–6]. A few gold or silver coins of more recent years have marked UN events, such as International Year of the Child (1980) or Decade for Women (1984).

ERITREA

The region on the south-west coast of the Red Sea was annexed by Italy in 1889, and merged with Ethiopia in 1936 to form Italian East Africa. Silver coins from 50 centesimi to 5 lire appeared in 1890, with the crowned profile of Umberto I on the obverse. A silver tallero (dollar) of 1918 showed an allegorical female bust (Italia), with the crowned arms of Savoy (reverse).

The area was under British military administration from 1941 to 1952, when the United Nations declared it an autonomous state federated with Ethiopia, whose coinage it used. This union, unpopular from the start, led to a long-running guerrilla war. By 1991 the Eritrean People's Liberation Front controlled most of the country and the independent republic was recognized in 1993. A series of coins based on the dollar of 100 cents was introduced in 1997, featuring wildlife (obverse) and soldiers with the flag (reverse) [7–16]. Cupro-nickel or silver coins with a camel and dhow on the obverse have proliferated since 1993, celebrating Eritrea's independence or promoting the "Preserve Planet Earth" campaign.

DJIBOUTI

French interest in the Red Sea resulted in trading concessions at the port of Djibouti in 1839. The same year, the British secured the port of Aden on the opposite side of the Bab el Mandeb strait. A protectorate was established in 1884 and the colony of the French Somali Coast proclaimed in 1896.

French coins were generally used, but a series of tokens was issued at Djibouti in 1920–1. Distinctive coins were introduced in 1948 and bore the effigy of Marianne (obverse), with a lyre antelope [17–18] or an Arab dhow and ocean liner (reverse), reflecting the growing importance of Djibouti as a port of call for cruise ships. The name was changed to the French Territory of the Afars and the Issas in 1967, and coins with this inscription but similar motifs (as well as high values depicting camels) were introduced in 1968–9. In June 1977, the country attained its independence as the Republic of Djibouti. Coins retain the reverse motifs of earlier issues but have the national shield and spears emblem on the obverse. [19–22]

SOMALIA

Indigenous coins date from the 14th century and were struck at Mogadishu by Arab traders, conforming to strict Islamic standards. Of particular interest are the undated brass tokens, which were extensively used as small change by Somali Muslims crossing the Red Sea on pilgrimage to Mecca, including types issued by the Italian colonial authorities between 1895 and 1914 [23]. Whereas British Somaliland used Indian rupees and coins of East Africa until 1961, when it was united with the former Italian Somaliland, the latter had distinctive coins from 1909. The rupia of 100 bese bore the effigy of Victor Emmanuel III, with the value in Italian and Arabic on the reverse.

Coins in the Italian currency system were planned, but only the silver 10 lire of 1925, with a crowned bust of the king, was issued. The resumption of Italian rule in 1950 was signalled by coins depicting an elephant or lioness from 1 centesimo to 1 somalo [24–25].

Following the unification with British Somaliland in 1960, to create the Somali Republic, the currency changed to the scellino (shilling) of 100 centesimi [26–27] with an armorial obverse and inscriptions in English and Arabic. Gold coins portraying President Abdulla Osman celebrated the fifth anniversary of independence (1965). After a military coup in 1969, however, Somalia became a democratic republic. Apart from some gold coins of 1970 marking the tenth anniversary of independence and the first anniversary of the revolution, the previous coinage continued until 1976, when the shilling of 100 senti was adopted, with an armorial obverse and various animals on the reverse [28–31]. Although in general circulation, this series was conceived as part of the FAO coin programme. Paradoxically, as true democracy was restored in the 1990s the word "Democratic" was dropped from the inscription. Since 1998 numerous bimetallic coins with multicoloured centres have been produced in sets with such themes, as wildlife and world shipping.

Somalia has been wracked by civil war. The Somali National Movement controlling the former British Somaliland seceded in 1993, and began issuing coins inscribed "Republic of Somaliland" in 1994. The obverse shows a Somali stock dove, both a symbol of peace and the national emblem of the breakaway republic [32–33].

Unique Calendar

Ethiopia has its own Amharic characters to denote numerals, and a calendar that began seven years and eight months after the Common Era (AD). Dates are expressed by separate figures up to ten, then in tens to a hundred, using a combination of multiplication and addition to produce a five-digit date, as shown on the 1969 series.

21 22 23 24 25 26 27 28 29 30 31 32 33

WEST AFRICA

The countries surveyed here are located to the north of the Gulf of Guinea. Four of them were in the British sphere of influence and are now republics within the British Commonwealth, while the fifth, Liberia, was settled by freed slaves returned from the United States and is nominally English-speaking, with close ties to neighbouring Sierra Leone.

Left: Because the low-value coins of British West Africa did not portray the monarch, it was relatively simple to engrave new dies in 1936 bearing the name of Edward VIII as King and Emperor of India. This penny was one of the few coins issued in his name.

BRITISH WEST AFRICA

As in East Africa, a currency board, set up in 1912, provided the coinage in use throughout the British colonies and protectorates of West Africa. Previously, however, coins thus inscribed had been introduced in Nigeria in 1906 and had the distinction of including one of the world's first aluminium coins, the 1/10 penny with a Star of David about a central hole (obverse) and a crown over the value (reverse) [1–2]. From 1908 subsidiary coins were struck in cupro-nickel [3–4]. Coins from 3 pence to 2 shillings were initially minted in silver but switched to brass in 1920. On these denominations a crowned effigy of the reigning monarch (obverse) and an oil palm (reverse) were used for the shilling values [5] and a wreathed value for the 3 and 6 pence denominations [6]. Coins portraying Elizabeth II were in use from 1954 until the four countries achieved independence.

GHANA

The Gold Coast had a silver coinage based on the ackey of 8 tackoe, produced by the Royal African Company between 1796 and 1818. A copper proof tackoe of the first year of issue is shown here [7–8]. It was the first colony to attain independence, together with the mandated territory of Togoland, emerging in February 1957 as the sovereign nation of Ghana, which revived the name of an ancient West African empire. Pence and shillings, introduced in 1958, portrayed Kwame Nkrumah, first the prime minister and later (1960–6) president, of the republic. The currency was reformed in 1965, based on the cedi of 100 pesawas, retaining similar motifs [9–11]. After Nkrumah's overthrow, cocoa beans replaced his image [12], with the national arms dominating the reverses [13–15]. Some coins since 1979 have featured a cowrie, alluding to the currency of earlier generations.

THE GAMBIA

This tiny state along the banks of the River Gambia was purchased by London merchants in 1588 and thus became England's first colony in Africa. Originally a centre for the slave trade, it later became a base for its suppression. It gained independence in 1965, with Elizabeth II as head of state, hence her bust on the coinage [16], whose reverse featured fauna, flora and a sailboat [17]. It became a republic within the Commonwealth in 1970 and new currency, based on the dalasi of 100

Above: The cupro-nickel shilling of the Gambia has an effigy of Elizabeth II (obverse) and an oil palm (reverse).

bututs, appeared the following year, with the effigy of the former prime minister, now president, Sir Dawda Jawara on the obverse, and the republic's arms on the reverse [18].

NIGERIA

The first indigenous coinage of Nigeria (1959) was modelled on that of British West Africa, with the Star of David on the holed coins [19–20] and the crowned bust of the queen on the higher values, with agricultural themes on the reverse [21–22]. Nigeria became a republic in 1963 but the coinage remained unchanged until 1973, when the naira of 100 kobo was introduced. The series featured the republican arms, with pictorial reverses alluding to the country's mineral wealth and diverse agriculture [23–26]. Place of honour on the reverse of the naira was reserved for Herbert Macaulay (1864–1946), regarded as the father of independence.

In 1967, the eastern region broke away and proclaimed the Republic of Biafra. Aluminium coins from 3 pence to 2 shillings, with the palm tree emblem, appeared in 1969. A few silver and gold pieces were struck at the same time to celebrate the second anniversary of independence [27–28], although Biafra ceased to exist in January 1970 following a bloody war.

SIERRA LEONE

An important centre of the slave trade in the 17th and 18th centuries, Sierra Leone was chosen for the first experiment in returning freed slaves to Africa, the aptly named Freetown being established in 1787 [29–30].

Modern coinage, based on the leone of 100 cents, dates from 1964, three years after Sierra Leone achieved independence. Sir Milton Margai, prime minister and, later, the first president, appeared on the obverse with various fauna and flora on the reverse [31–32]. A leone produced for general circulation (1987) used an unusual octagonal format, which was originally applied to bicentennial coins issued to mark the anniversary of Freetown.

Earliest British African Coins

The Sierra Leone Company, set up to settle freed slaves, produced the earliest British colonial coinage issued anywhere in the African continent: the bronze cent (below) and penny; and silver coins from 10 cents to the dollar of 1791. All showed the lion and mountain (from which the country derives its name) on the obverse, and hands clasped in friendship (reverse).

LIBERIA

The country whose name means "the land of the free" was first settled in 1822 by the American Colonization Society, with the aim of repatriating freed slaves. Various settlements combined in 1839 to form the Commonwealth of Liberia, which became a republic in 1847.

A copper cent produced in 1833 showed a man planting a symbolic tree of Liberty, and this was the forerunner to the series of coins of 1896 with the head of Liberty on the obverse and a palm tree on the reverse. Coins were produced very sporadically prior to 1960 and many issues since then [33] exist only in proof sets.

Conversely, Liberia has produced numerous special coins since 1993, often in lengthy thematic series, such as the prolific Pioneers of the West, aimed principally at the American collector market. Other long-running sets since the 1990s have portrayed world statesmen, from Churchill and Roosevelt to Nelson Mandela, Formula One racing drivers, famous baseball players, from Babe Ruth to Reggie Jackson and even the leading characters in the *Star Trek* television series.

SAHARA AND EQUATORIAL AFRICA

Much of this vast region was formerly part of the French colonial empire, and was administered as French West Africa and French Equatorial Africa. To this day the common currency in these regions is issued by the West and Central African States, although some countries have their own distinctive coinage. Although most of the Equatorial region was in the French sphere of influence, both Spain and Portugal managed colonies here, and their successor states likewise now issue their own coins.

Left: Leopold Sedar Senghor, dubbed "the black de Gaulle" was a distinguished teacher, writer and poet who was prominent in the political development of French Africa after 1945, becoming the first president of Senegal (1960–80).

CENTRAL AFRICAN STATES

Ordinary French coins were used in French Equatorial Africa (Middle-Congo, Ubangi-Shari, Chad and Gabon) until 1942, when the region adhered to Charles de Gaulle and the Free French, and coins bearing a Gallic cock (obverse) and the Cross of Lorraine (reverse) were introduced. In 1948 a new type, with the head of Marianne (obverse) and a Loder's gazelle (reverse) was adopted [1–2].

Following the break-up of the French colonial empire in 1958–9, an attempt was made to form a political union comprising Chad, Congo, the Central African Republic and Gabon. Although this failed, an outcome was the monetary union known as the Equatorial Customs Unit, to which Cameroon acceded in 1961. Coins were struck by the authority of the Central Bank of the Equatorial African States, with a standard obverse of three giant eland and a wreathed value reverse [3–8]. The name was changed in 1974 to the Bank of the Central African States. Coins with the new title retained the original motif but from then until 1996 a letter was included to denote the country in which a coin was originally issued: A (Chad), B (Central African Republic), C (Congo), D (Gabon) and E (Cameroon). Equatorial Guinea, a former Spanish colony, issued its own coins in 1969 [9] before joining the Central African States. Conversely the former French Guinea refused to join, and has issued its own coins [10–11] since 1962.

The bank also produces 100 franc coins with the great eland obverse and inscriptions signifying use in the Central African Republic [12–13], Chad, the Congo People's Republic and Gabon. All four have also produced distinctive commemoratives, notably Chad [14] which, in 1970 alone, honoured both Kennedy brothers as well as Martin Luther King, de Gaulle and President Nasser of Egypt.

WEST AFRICAN STATES

French West Africa comprised Dahomey, French Guinea, French Sudan, Ivory Coast, Niger, Senegal and Upper Volta, using French coins until 1944, when a series featuring Marianne and a horn of plenty was introduced. From 1948 to 1958 coins used the Marianne and Loder's gazelle motifs of Equatorial Africa, with the obverse inscription modified. The former mandated territory of Togoland (for which

Odd Man Out

Mauritania only became part of French West Africa in 1920, gaining autonomy in 1958, and becoming the Islamic Republic of Mauritania in 1960. It withdrew from the French Community in 1966 and left the West African monetary union in 1973. It has since issued coins based on the ouguiya of 5 khoums. These have an obverse showing the crescent and star of Islam with palms and the value, while the reverse bears inscriptions in Arabic.

separate coins were issued in 1924–6 and 1948–56) joined the French West African monetary union in 1957, and 5, 10 and 25 franc coins then included Togo in the inscription [15–16].

The coins of the West African States adopted a standard obverse showing an Ashanti gold weight [17], with wreathed values [18–19] or a Loder's gazelle [20] on the reverse.

Since 1980–1, the 10, 25 and 50 franc coins have had reverses showing food production, issued as part of the Food and Agriculture Organization coin programme [21–22]. These coins circulate in Dahomey (now Benin), Senegal, Upper Volta (now Burkina Faso), Ivory Coast, Mali, Togo and Niger [23–24]. Guinea had a currency based on the syli of 100 cauris from 1971 to 1985, when the Guinean franc was adopted [25–26].

In addition to the common currency, several member countries have issued their own coins. Sporadically, coins have been produced by Ivory Coast (1966), Niger (1960), Togo (1977) and Mali (1960–7). Mali's issue of aluminium 5 [28–29], 10 and 25 "francs maliens" underlined the nation's new indepedence from France the previous year, and from the French-backed franc. Dahomey (Benin) and Senegal, meanwhile, have issued quite a number of gold and silver coins [27].

FORMER PORTUGUESE AND SPANISH TERRITORIES

In colonial times, the scattered possessions of Spain and Portugal in the Saharan and Equatorial regions used the coins of their mother countries, but since independence they have produced their own. In the north-west, the former Spanish Sahara was partitioned between Mauritania and Morocco in 1975, but after a long war of independence the Saharawi Arab Republic emerged in 1992. Coins from 1 to 100 pesetas have an armorial obverse and a camel reverse. There is also a prolific output of commemoratives aimed mainly at the Spanish market.

Distinctive coins are issued in the islands of Cape Verde [30–31] and São Tome and Principe, off the west coast of Africa, and in Guinea-Bissau (formerly Portuguese Guinea) on the mainland. São Tome issued coins in 1813, but both territories began issuing decimal coins in 1929–33 with the allegory of the republic and "Republica Portuguesa" (obverse) and arms with the name of the colony (reverse). The word "Colonia" was omitted during the 1960s when they became overseas provinces. In 1975 they became independent republics and have issued their own coins since 1977. All three began with modest series promoting the FAO coin programme but have since moved on to lengthy issues, often of little cultural relevance to their own countries, but aimed primarily at the overseas numismatic trade.

Above: The bronze 20 centavos (1962) of São Tome and Principe, with the Portuguese arms on the obverse.

ASIA

This vast continent, which stretches from the Mediterranean to the Pacific, was the birthplace of coinage. Scholars may argue as to whether it was the inhabitants of Asia Minor (modern Anatolia) or China who first adopted metallic currency, but there is no argument that this is where it all began.

TURKEY

Ancient Lydia, in the territory of modern Turkey, produced the first coins of the western world in the 7th century BC. By the time of King Croesus (561–545 BC) its coins had a lion and bull motif (obverse) and rectangular incuse marks (reverse) [1–2]. After Lydia's conquest by the Persian Cyrus the Great, tiny quarter-sigloi were struck under Darius I [3–4].

Although politically classed as a European country, Turkey lies mostly in western Asia, and from medieval to relatively modern times its coinage owed more to its Asiatic and Islamic background than to European influence. Under Ottoman rule the land of the Turks grew into a mighty empire, which stretched from the Danube to the Persian Gulf and from the Caspian Sea to the Barbary Coast of North Africa. The Ottomans controlled the trade routes between Europe and China and dominated the Mediterranean until their naval power was checked by the Battle of Lepanto in 1571. A century later they even besieged Vienna, but from 1700 their power gradually waned. The Ottoman Empire collapsed in the aftermath of World War I, and the republic that succeeded it was confined to Anatolia and a wedge of territory in eastern Thrace, the last remnant of Turkey in Europe.

Left: Out of an obverse type in which the Arabic letters of the ruler's title were interwoven developed the elaborate calligraphic toughra, *or sign-manual of the sultan, a device that continued to be used on Turkish coins from the 11th to the 20th centuries.*

HELLENISTIC AND ROMAN TURKEY

The Persian Empire declined in the 4th century BC under a succession of weak rulers. Asia Minor was invaded first by Philip of Macedon and then by his son Alexander the Great, who defeated the Persians and annexed the empire, ushering in a period of Greek settlement and rule. After his death, his generals divided his empire among them and struck coins bearing his effigy, such as the tetradrachm struck by Mithridates at Smyrna [5–6]. Under Roman rule (from 63 BC) local issues continued [7–8], latterly in the name of the emperor, such as this early 3rd century bronze coin portraying Severus Alexander [9–10].

MEDIEVAL TURKEY

Anatolia (Asia Minor) formed part of the Byzantine Empire and used its coins [11–12] but from the 10th century onward, it was frequently invaded and overrun by Mongols [13–14] and Turkmens, who established separate dynasties. The Seljuqs of Rum ("land of the Romans") [15], whose capital was the Byzantine city of Nicaea, the Qaramanids, Ilkhanids and others struck coins that were based on Byzantine models but inscribed in Arabic, and sometimes in Greek.

OTTOMAN EMPIRE

In 1453 the Ottoman Turks conquered the city of Constantinople and overthrew the Byzantine Empire. In the ensuing centuries the empire expanded dramatically, from the Caucasus to the whole of North Africa, but by 1914 Turkish dominions in Europe had shrunk to the hinterland of Istanbul (Constantinople), while alliance with Germany and Austria in World War I hastened the end of the empire.

The coins of the Ottoman Empire were struck in copper, silver and gold in a bewildering array of denominations based on multiples of the para, from 3 (*akce* or *asper*) to 240 (*altilik*). In the 17th century, Suleiman II introduced the kurus or piastre, originally a large silver coin worth 40 para. By the 18th century low-grade silver was being used for coins ranging from 1 para upwards, but between 1808 and 1840 the size and fineness of the coins were progressively reduced on eight different occasions as the economy collapsed [18–21]. The gold coinage was infinitely more complex, with numerous coins in different weights and fineness, each distinguished by its own name and issued simultaneously.

The coinage was reformed in 1844 by Abdulmejid, who introduced the gold lira (pound) of 100 silver piastres or kurus; the smaller coins, from 5 para upwards, were struck in bronze [22]. Large bronze piastres bore the Arabic numerals for 40, signifying their value in para. In this series the toughra of the sultan appeared on the obverse, with plain or elaborate surrounds, while the reverse bore the name of the sultan with a regnal year at the top and the date in the Muslim calendar at the foot. Gold coins [16–17] were produced in two types, for trade and mainly for jewellery respectively, the latter being generally thinner and pierced for adornment.

TURKISH REPUBLIC

The Greek invasion of Anatolia in 1921 provoked a resurgence of Turkish nationalism under Mustapha Kemal, who proclaimed a republic at Ankara in 1923 and overthrew the sultanate. The republic adopted the piastre of 100 para, omitting the toughra and

Currency Reform

The Turkish currency was reformed in January 2005, when the yeni (new) lira of 100 yeni kurus replaced a million old lira.

introducing the first pictorial elements: an ear of wheat (obverse) and a spray of oak leaves (reverse), with the crescent and star emblem at the top. These coins continued to be inscribed entirely in Arabic until 1934–5, when the lira of 100 kurus was inscribed in the modified Roman alphabet and the date appeared in the Western calendar [23–24]. In the early versions of the lower denominations the star appeared above the crescent, but from 1949 onward the emblem was rotated so that the star appeared on the left side. Silver coins bore the profile of Kemal Ataturk ("father of the Turks") and a wreathed value [25–26]. Gold coinage was resumed in 1943, with Kemal's effigy (obverse) and an elaborate Arabic inscription (reverse).

INFLATION

Turkey was overtaken by inflation in the 1980s; in the space of 20 years the 50 lira piece was reduced from a large silver coin to a tiny aluminium-bronze piece. In the 1990s base metal coins of 500, 1000, 1500, 2500 and 5000 lira briefly appeared, followed by coins denominated in *bin lira* (thousands of lira). By the end of the 20th century the 100,000 lira was a small aluminium coin [27–34].

In the same period commemorative coins appeared in gold or silver, culminating in the coin issued to celebrate the 700th anniversary of the Ottoman Empire (1999), which was denominated 60,000,000 lira.

PALESTINE, ISRAEL AND JORDAN

The region known as the Middle East forms the land bridge connecting Asia and Africa, and has therefore been an important crossroads of commerce since time immemorial. For the same reason, it has frequently been fought over and, indeed, remains an area of conflict to this day. Palestine (the land of the Philistines) was conquered by the Jews 3000 years ago. Since then it has been successively invaded and occupied by the Assyrians, Persians, Egyptians, Greeks, Romans, Byzantines and Arabs. For four centuries Palestine was part of the Ottoman Empire, before it came under British rule in 1917–18, following the demise of the empire. Britain was granted mandates by the League of Nations to administer the territories of Palestine and Transjordan. These mandates terminated in 1948 and resulted in the emergence of the State of Israel and the Hashemite Kingdom of Jordan.

Left: The Jewish Kingdom of Judaea was under Greek and later Roman rule, but rose in revolt on several occasions. The first Jewish revolt (AD 66–70) was suppressed by the Roman emperor Vespasian, who issued coins to celebrate this victory. He appears on the obverse. The reverse, inscribed "Judaea Capta", shows two Jews under a palm tree, symbolizing their defeat.

JEWISH KINGDOMS

For most of the period before the Common Era, the biblical lands of Judah and Israel used the coinage of foreign invaders and conquerors: the darics and sigloi of Persia, minted locally at Samaria [1–2]; the staters and tetradrachms of Alexander the Great and his successors, such as this coin depicting the goddess Athena but with a Samaritan–Aramaic countermark [3–4]; the Ptolemies of Egypt, exemplified by this tetradrachm of Ptolemy II, struck at Gaza [5–6]; and the Seleucids of Syria.

In 167 BC the Jews under Judas Maccabaeus rose in revolt against the Seleucid emperor Antiochus IV. At one time Jewish coins were attributed to this period, but it has now been proved that they belong to the first rebellion of the Jews against Rome in AD 66–70 [7–8]. In the interim, however, copper pruta circulated as small change and bore a Hebrew inscription on one side and twin cornucopiae on the other [9–10]. During the 1st century BC, Alexander Jannaeus assumed the kingship, and he and his successors struck bronze coins bearing various symbols, such as an anchor, wheel or stars. Although some coins were inscribed in Hebrew, most bore Greek titles. The coins of Herod the Great (37–4 BC) are particularly interesting, as they show increasing Roman stylistic influence. In AD 132–5 the Jews again rose in rebellion, led by Simon Barcochba ("son of the star"), hence the star symbols found on many of the coins of this period. After the revolt was crushed the Romans dispersed the Jews, beginning the Diaspora that continued until the early 20th century.

ISLAMIC RULE

Roman and Byzantine coins were used thereafter, but the encroachments of the Arabs were reflected in coins based on Byzantine models with Arabic inscriptions and motifs [11–12]. Islamic influence began in the 6th century AD, when the Sasanian Khusru II overthrew Byzantine rule. Byzantine gold and copper coins continued to be used in the region until supplies ran out. In the 10th century, Arab mints were established at Iliya Filistina (Jerusalem), Tiberias and Akka (Acre), striking Ikhshidid dinars [13–14]. By the end of that century the concentric designs of the Fatimids were prevalent, as seen in this gold bezant of Acre [15–16], and their coins were copied by much of the Islamic world.

KINGDOM OF JERUSALEM

By the end of the 11th century, the Fatimids had been overthrown by the Christian Crusaders. They established the Kingdom of Jerusalem, which initially extended over much of what is now Egypt and Lebanon. Typical of the Crusader coinage is a denier showing the Tower of David on the reverse [17–18]. The kingdom expired with the fall of Acre to the Mameluks in 1291. While Palestine remained under the rule of the Mameluks and later of the Ottomans, Syrian and Egyptian coins were in use.

BRITISH MANDATE

Under British rule coins inscribed in English, Hebrew and Arabic were issued in Palestine from 1927 to 1948. Those that did not have a central hole bore an olive branch on the reverse [19–25]. Technically the mandate included Transjordan, so Palestinian currency circulated there as well, even though politically it was administered separately. In 1921 the British installed the Emir Abdullah, and in 1923 the lands to the east of the River Jordan became an autonomous state, although they remained under British mandate until 1948.

ISRAEL

The British mandate terminated in May 1948 and the State of Israel was proclaimed on May 14. Coins bearing dates according to the Jewish calendar were introduced, their motifs derived from the coins of the Jewish revolts [26–34]. The currency was originally based on the Palestinian pound of 1000 mils, but in 1949 the lirah israelit (Israeli pound) of 1000 prutah was adopted. Following the monetary reform of 1958 the lirah was divided into 100 agorot. Continuing inflation led to the reform of February 1980 that introduced the sheqel of 100 new agorot (worth 1000 old agorot), but since September 1985 the currency has been stabilized on the basis of the sheqel chadash (new sheqel) worth 1000 sheqalim. In all of these series the biblical themes have continued.

Israel has been a prolific producer of special coins, partly commemorative and partly didactic, upholding the image of the modern state with its roots in ancient Jewish traditions.

JORDAN

The coinage of the Hashemite Kingdom of Jordan, commencing in 1949, is based on the dinar of 10 dirhems or 1000 fils, with inscriptions in Arabic (obverse) and English (reverse) [35–36]. Non-figural motifs were used exclusively until 1968, when a profile of King Hussein appeared on the obverse. In 1996 the currency was reformed and the dinar divided into 100 piastres [37–38]. The few commemoratives since 1969 have mainly marked anniversaries of the kingdom.

Microprocessor Background

Since 1984 a number of definitive and commemorative Israeli coins portraying famous people, such as Theodor Herzl (below right), have had backgrounds formed by the continuous repetition of their names printed by microprocessor.

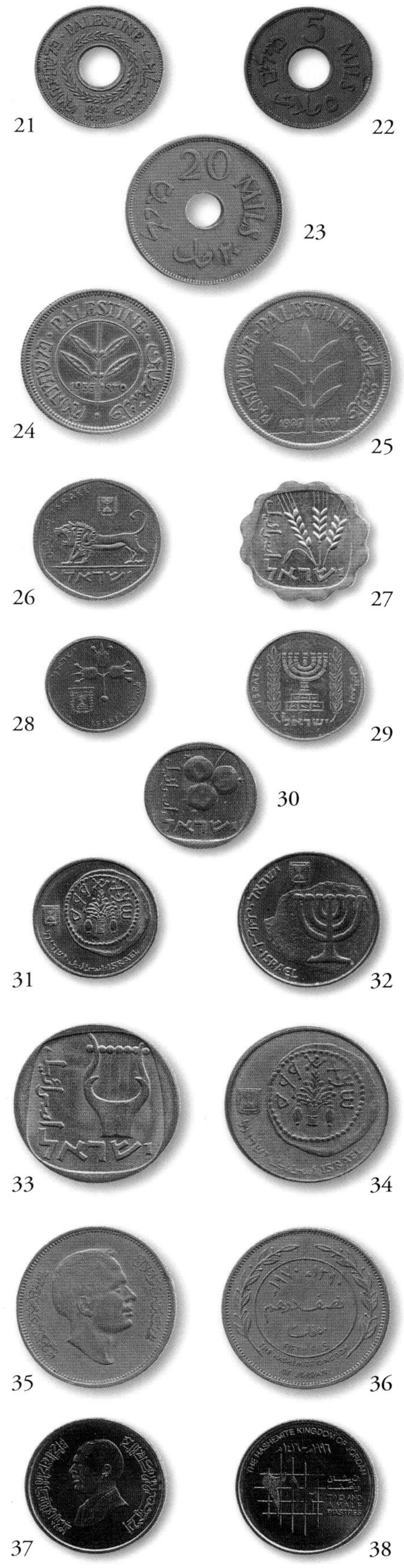

21 22 23 24 25 26 27 28 29 30 31 32 33 34 35 36 37 38

LEBANON, IRAQ AND SYRIA

This group of Middle Eastern countries did not exist until the 1920s, and yet the region has a numismatic history that goes back many centuries. It was successively conquered by the Persians, Alexander the Great, the Romans, Byzantines, Arabs and Crusaders, each of whom left their mark on the coinage of the area. For 400 years the territories remained under Turkish rule, until they were liberated by the Allies during World War I and mandated to the British or French by the League of Nations.

Left: The obverse of the 25 and 100 dinar coins of 2004, the only Iraqi issues since the fall of Saddam Hussein, features a map of Iraq – the historic Mesopotamia, or land between the two rivers, Tigris and Euphrates, which the Arabs styled Al Jazira ("the island") – with dates according to the Western and Muslim calendars.

ANTIOCH

Seleucus I Nicator, who founded the city of Antioch, naming it after his father Antiochus, was one of Alexander the Great's generals. After Alexander's death the generals divided his empire between them and Seleucus gained the territory of Syria and built the Seleucid Empire. Successive Seleucid kings struck coins on Greek models, typified by these tetradrachms of Antiochus II (261–246 BC) [1–4] and Antiochus IV (175–164 BC) [5–6].

No fewer than 12 towns or cities called Antioch struck coins in the classical period [7–8], but of these the most important was Antioch on the Orontes, the capital of the western Seleucid Empire and later of the Roman province of Syria (modern Antakiyah, transferred from Syria to Turkey in 1939). In the Roman and Byzantine periods it ranked third in importance after Alexandria and Constantinople [9–10]. The city was devastated by an earthquake in 526 and rebuilt under the name of Theopolis. It produced a large number of light-weight gold solidi [11–12] in the reigns of Justin II and Maurice Tiberius in the late 6th century.

In the early Islamic period Syria fell under the rule of the Umayyads and Abbasids and struck silver dirhams, notably under Caliph al-Malik, who struck coins at his capital, Damascus, as well as Basra [13–14]. Antioch was liberated in 1098 during the first Crusade and became the capital of a principality that flourished in the 12th century. In this period copper folles [15–16] were struck by Roger of Salerno. Its fall to the Mameluk sultan Baybars in 1268 marked the end of an era that left a rich legacy of copper and billon coins [17–18].

MEDIEVAL DIVERSITY

Antioch was only one of several Crusader kingdoms and principalities that struck gold, silver and base-metal coins in the 12th and 13th centuries, modelled mainly on French deniers, and coins may also be encountered from Acre, Tripoli and Edessa, such as this follis of Baldwin II [19–20]. Meanwhile, Turkic tribes were migrating from Central Asia into the Near East. The Artuqids settled at Hisn Kayfa, while the Zengids occupied Mosul and Aleppo. Their coins are remarkable for their obverses, which bear astrological symbols [21–22] or are derived from classical Greek models [23], while the reverses conform to the Islamic style.

In the 11th century Tughril Beg, leader of the Seljuqs, advanced westward and made himself master of Baghdad. He and his successors extended their empire to the Caucasus and Anatolia. Islamic coinage was struck in many towns in and around Mesopotamia by Seljuqs, Urtuqids,

Royal Portraiture

Unusually for the period, the coins of Iraq portrayed the reigning monarch on the obverse and followed the British custom of profiles facing alternately to the right (Faisal I, 1931–3), then to the left (Ghazi, 1933–9).

Abbasids and Zengids. In the epoch of the Ottoman Empire, from 1516 onwards, coins were struck at Dimishq (Damascus) and Halab (Aleppo), in what is now Syria, and at Mardin, Al-Ruha and Amid in what is now Iraq. The rich variety of coins surviving from this period ranges from the 16th-century gold sultani of Mehmed III, struck at Dimishq [24–25] to the silver dirhams of Haroun al Rashid struck at Basra and the coins of the Zengid Atabegs of Mosul.

IRAQ

Mesopotamia was freed from Turkish rule in 1917 by the British, who were granted a mandate to govern the territory in 1920. It became an independent kingdom in 1921 under Faisal I, whose profile appeared on the coins introduced there in 1931 [26–29]. Similar coins portrayed Ghazi (1933–9) and Faisal II, who was murdered in 1958 when the monarchy was toppled in the first of several military coups. The reverse of the royal coinage, denominated in fils, dirhams, riyals and dinars, bore the value and inscriptions entirely in Arabic. Under the republic, royal effigies were replaced by a motif of palm trees. The relatively few commemoratives issued since 1970 have celebrated such events as peace with the Kurds (1971), oil nationalization (1973) and various anniversaries of the army or the ruling Ba'ath Party.

SYRIA

The League of Nations conferred a mandate on France to rule the Levantine states of Syria and Lebanon. A series of revolts in the 1920s led the French to concede an autonomous republic in Syria (1930), leading to complete independence in 1944. Faisal was briefly king before the French ejected him and the British placed him on the Iraqi throne, and in this period a gold dinar was minted.

Under the French protectorate piastres were inscribed in French and Arabic [30–32]. From 1948 onward, coins bore the eagle emblem of the republic, with Arabic values on the reverse. Subtle changes in inscriptions signified the United Arab Republic (1959–60) and the Syrian Arab Republic (since 1962).

LEBANON

Although the French had a mandate to govern Syria and Lebanon together, they were quick to distinguish between the predominantly Christian Sanjak of Lebanon and Muslim Syria, and as early as September 1920 established the former as the Etat du Grand Liban (State of Greater Lebanon). Coins thus inscribed were adopted in 1924; those without a central hole bore the cedar emblem on the obverse. Some coins from 1929 onward were inscribed "République Libanaise" (Lebanese Republic) although full sovereignty was not granted until 1946 [33, 36]. Few coins were struck during the prolonged civil wars of the 1970s and 80s; those issued since 1968 bear the name of the Banque du Liban (Bank of the Lebanon) [34–35]. A handful of gold and silver coins marked the Lake Placid Winter Olympics of 1980.

Above: Palm trees replaced royal portraits on the coins issued by the Iraqi Republic.

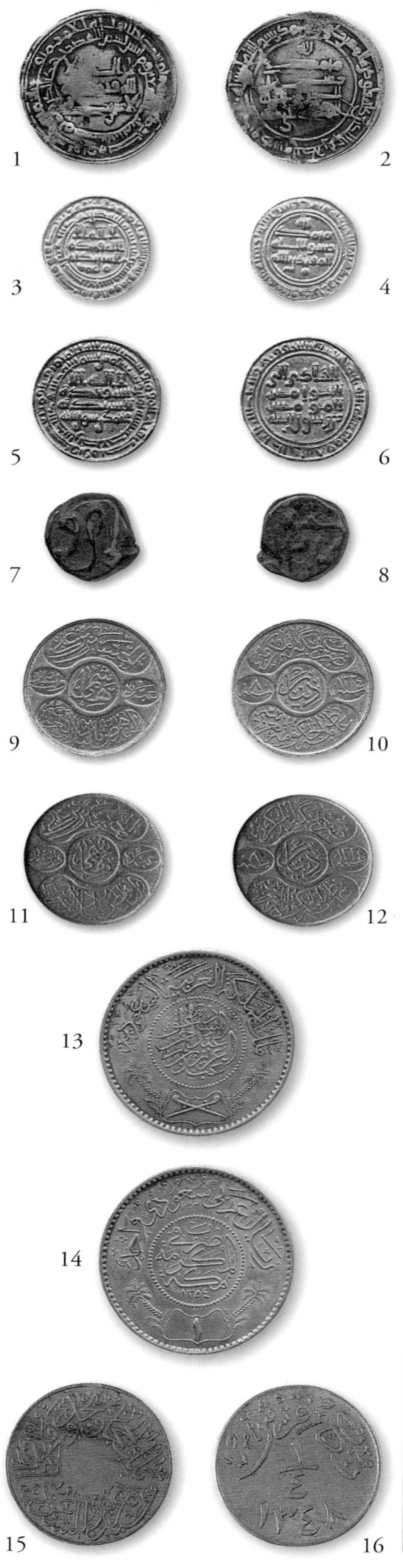
1 2 3 4 5 6 7 8 9 10 11 12 13 14 15 16

ARABIA

A geographical, rather than a political, entity, Arabia is a great peninsula of more than 2.5 million sq km/1 million sq miles between the Red Sea and the Persian Gulf, stretching from the Mediterranean in the north to the Indian Ocean in the south. At its core lies the kingdom of Saudi Arabia; to the south lies the Yemen, while along its eastern and northern borders are a series of smaller countries and petty states whose wealth and importance far exceed their size, as a result of the oil reserves that lie beneath them. Arabia was the cradle of Islam in the 7th century AD, and its language, alphabet, literature, arts and sciences have spread across the world, from Spain and north-west Africa to South-east Asia and the East Indies.

Left: The silver dirham (drachma) evolved in AH 79 (AD 698) and was to become the standard coin of the Islamic world for five centuries. The design of both obverse and reverse was composed entirely of Arabic inscriptions surrounded by circles and annulets. The obverse bears the Muslim declaration of faith while the reverse has a Qur'anic quotation surrounded by the prophetic mission.

CENTRE OF ISLAM

In September 622 Muhammad bin Abdallah fled from Mecca, his birthplace, where he was being persecuted by those who objected to his prophetic mission and teachings on monotheism, to join his followers at Yathrib, later renamed simply Medina ("the city"). This dramatic event was the Hegira or Hijra, from which Muslims date their calendar. Over the ensuing century the followers of Muhammad would create a movement that spread across the known world like wildfire and remains a potent force to this day.

Muhammad led his followers in war on Mecca, in which they were eventually victorious. He consolidated his rule over a unified Arabia, but when he died in 632 he left no son to succeed him. Instead, his powers were divided among two of his fathers-in-law and his two sons-in-law. To the senior father-in-law, Abu Bakr, fell the title of Caliph ("follower"), the spiritual head of Islam.

Arabia was an arid region inhabited by nomadic pastoralists, yet by the 8th century the Arabs had conquered the whole of North Africa and penetrated the Iberian Peninsula. They struck north, south and east, spreading the doctrines of Islam wherever they went. Inevitably as Islam spread, the centre of the religious and temporal power moved away from Mecca and Medina, and by the 9th century Arabia had reverted to the cluster of petty tribal states that had existed before the rise of Muhammad.

RIVAL CALIPHATES

Under the early caliphs, Arabia relied heavily on the gold and silver coins brought to Mecca and Medina by the faithful. By the 9th century, the Abbasids were striking coins at Sana'a and Aden in the Yemen as well as at Makka (Mecca), mostly silver dirhams [1–2]. They were followed by other dynasties such as the Rassids, who minted some beautiful gold dinars at Sana'a [3–4] and even larger coins at Sa'da about 910 [5–6].

Other dynasties that were prolific producers of gold and silver coins included the Ziyadids and Najahids of Zahid, the Sulayhids and the Fatimids. Constantly at war with each other, they fell easy prey to the invading Osmanli Turks who, by 1516, were in firm control. Thereafter Arabia was part of the Ottoman Empire. During this period, however, base-metal coins intended for small change were also struck by local *sharifs* (governors). They were pretty basic pieces, with simple motifs and mint-marks, such as this coin from Mecca [7–8].

SAUDI ARABIA

By the beginning of the 20th century Ottoman power was more nominal than real. From the late 18th century onward Arabia was in the British sphere of influence, the agents of the East India Company having concluded commercial treaties with local rulers from Aden to the Persian Gulf. In the 19th century a power struggle developed between rival factions, and the Turks supported the Rashidis against the Saudis. By 1887 the latter had lost most of their lands and went into exile in Kuwait. But in 1901 Abdul Aziz ibn Saud recaptured Riyadh, capital of the Sultanate of Nejd. He proclaimed himself sultan in 1905 and captured the Turkish province of Al Hasa in 1913.

Ibn Saud struck Hashimi gold dinars of good quality in AH 1334 (1915) [9–10]. Backing the British against the Turks in World War I, he embarked on the conquest of the Hejaz in 1925 and seized most of Asir the following year. To this period belongs the dinar minted in 1923 [11–12]. In 1932, Ibn Saud merged Hejaz and Nejd and founded the Kingdom of Saudi Arabia.

Countermarked coins were used at first, notably the Indian rupee and the Maria Theresia thaler, but a regular coinage based on the dinar of 5 riyals or 100 piastres was adopted in 1916, followed by similar coins, inscribed entirely in Arabic, for Hejaz and Nejd [13–16] and then the series of Saudi Arabia, distinguished by the palm tree and crossed swords emblem, from 1937 onwards [17–19].

A new currency, based on the riyal of 100 halala, was adopted in 1963. The innate conservatism of Saudi Arabia is demonstrated by the strict adherence to Qur'anic teaching and the total absence of any image, human or animal, on the coins [20–23].

United Yemen

In May 1990 the Yemen Arab Republic, also known as North Yemen, joined its southern neighbour to form a single nation state, the Republic of the Yemen. Coins depicting the eagle emblem, modern buildings and the ancient bridge at Shaharah were introduced in 1993.

YEMEN

Coins based on the imadi riyal of 40 buqsha or 80 halala were struck at Sana'a, the capital, from 1902 [24–27], the Mutawakelite Kingdom finally breaking free from the Ottomans in 1916. 1962 the imam was deposed and the socialist Yemen Arab Republic was proclaimed. There was little change in the coinage, other than the Arabic inscriptions, but in 1974 the currency was decimalized, introducing the rial of 100 fils, with an eagle emblem on the obverse [28–29]. A number of gold or silver coins since 1969 have commemorated such disparate subjects as the *Mona Lisa* and the Apollo landing.

The coins of the British East India Company and later of India circulated in British-ruled Aden prior to 1959, when it formed the core of the Federation of South Arabia and adopted the dinar of 100 fils. The reverses of these coins featured crossed *jambiyas* (curved daggers) or a dhow [30–31]. Following a revolution in 1970 the country became the People's Democratic Republic of Yemen, and its coins were subsequently inscribed in Arabic and English [32–33].

GULF STATES

This is the collective term for the small countries on the fringes of Arabia, along the western and southern shores of the Persian Gulf. They were inhabited by Arab tribes, the subjects of Persia or the Ottoman Empire at various times. They were first penetrated by the Portuguese in the 16th century but the British East India Company established trading posts in the early 19th century and in the wake of commerce came treaties of protection with Britain. These relations with the sheikhdoms and emirates of the Gulf terminated in the 1960s, leading to full independence a decade later.

Left: The 100 baisa bimetallic coin of Oman, issued in 1991, celebrated the centenary of coinage in the sultanate. The copper half-anna of 1891, showing a view of the port of Muscat, was reproduced on the reverse. The Arabic numerals signify AH *1411.*

BAHRAIN

This country, ruled by the Al Khalifa family, consists of a cluster of islands that, prior to the discovery of oil in the 1930s, depended on pearl fishing. Revenue from oil has been wisely used to create an ultra-modern state and a major communications and commercial centre. Bahrain attained complete sovereignty in 1971 but introduced its own coins in 1965, with a palm tree obverse and value reverse based on the dinar of 1000 fils [1–2]. A new series, released in 1992, has the values in Western numerals on the reverse [3–10]. A few commemoratives have appeared since the UN Food and Agriculture Organization issue of 1969, including several silver coins portraying the ruler in Arab dress.

KUWAIT

Fearing Turkish encroachment, Sheikh Mubarak of the ruling Al Sabah family, who struck this Kuwaiti baisa in 1887 [11–12], sought British protection in 1899. The agreement was terminated in 1961 and Kuwait became a fully independent country.

Thanks to oil revenue, the Kuwaiti dinar is the world's strongest currency, fully backed by gold. The coins from 1 to 100 fils, introduced in 1961, feature a *sambuke*, or two-masted Arab dhow, with double dates (Christian and Muslim) in Arabic numerals, while the obverse bears the value with the name of the country in Arabic and English [13–16]. A few commemoratives have appeared since 1976, when a silver double dinar celebrated the 15th anniversary of independence with portraits of Abdullah ibn Salim (1950–65) and his successor Sabah ibn Salim (1965–77) side by side. Gold and silver coins of 1981 marked the 1500th anniversary of the Hegira.

OMAN

Although the mint at 'Uman (Oman) operated only occasionally in the 10th century, both gold and silver coins were struck by the Wajihid governors of the province. The dirhams shown here were struck by Ahmad bin Hilal [17–18] and Muhammad bin Yusuf [19–20] between AH 299 and 310, but after about AH 350 coins were supplied from the Yemen.

In 1508 the Portuguese captured Muscat, the capital and chief seaport of the sultanate, in the first European penetration of the Gulf region. In 1650 they were ejected by the Persians, who ruled until 1741, when Ahmed ibn Sa'id seized power and established the dynasty that has reigned ever since. Muscat and Oman was the most powerful state in Arabia until the mid-19th century, when it was weakened by

Prolific Output

Immediately before the Federation of Arab Emirates was formed, many distinctive coins were produced in Ajman, Fujairah, Ras al Khaimah, Sharjah and Umm al Qiwain, a parallel to the unduly prolific stamp issues of the same period and likewise aimed at collectors. Subjects ranged from the World Cup to champions of sport. Sharjah's 5 rupee coin of 1964 was the first in the world to mourn the death of John F. Kennedy.

nomadic attacks. In 1798 it signed a treaty with Britain, which subsequently played a major role in its defence. Sultan Sa'id was overthrown in 1970 by his son Qabus, who dropped "Muscat" from the country's name.

The first coins were quarter and twelfth annas, struck in 1893. They had a pictorial reverse but the following year an all-Arabic non-figural type was adopted. The coinage was reformed in 1945, adopting the Saidi riyal of 200 baisa, with the national emblem, a dagger over crossed swords, on the obverse and Arabic inscriptions on the reverse. Qabus reformed the currency in 1972, adopting the Omani riyal of 1000 baisa. As well as a modified obverse inscription reflecting the change of name, this series has the value in Arabic numerals on the reverse [21–24]. A conservative policy with regard to special issues was followed until 1995, when a lengthy series of 20 silver coins depicting Omani forts was released.

QATAR

This emirate was under Ottoman rule from 1872 until 1916, when the Turkish garrison was withdrawn. Sheikh Abdullah bin Qasim promptly sought British protection, which continued until 1971. The first coins were issued in 1966 and bore the names of Qatar and Dubai, with a gazelle on the reverse [25–26]. A plan to unite with Bahrain and the Trucial States was abandoned and since September 1971 Qatar has been fully independent. Separate coins were introduced in 1973 based on the riyal of 100 dirhem, with Arabic values (obverse) [27] and a dhow and palm tree (reverse).

UNITED ARAB EMIRATES

The sheikhdoms of Abu Dhabi, Ajman, Dubai, Fujairah, Sharjah and Umm al Qiwain [28–29] formed the Federation of Arab Emirates in December 1971, after the withdrawal of British protection over the area formerly known collectively as the Trucial States. In February 1972 Ras al Khaimah joined the federation, which became the United Arab Emirates and began issuing coins thus inscribed in 1973. Its coins are comparatively conservative, with Arabic values (obverse) married to reverses depicting date palms, dhow, gazelle, Mata Hari fish [30–32] and an offshore oil rig.

Above: The diamond-shaped 20 baisa of AH 1359 (1940) was struck by Oman specifically for Dhofar Province.

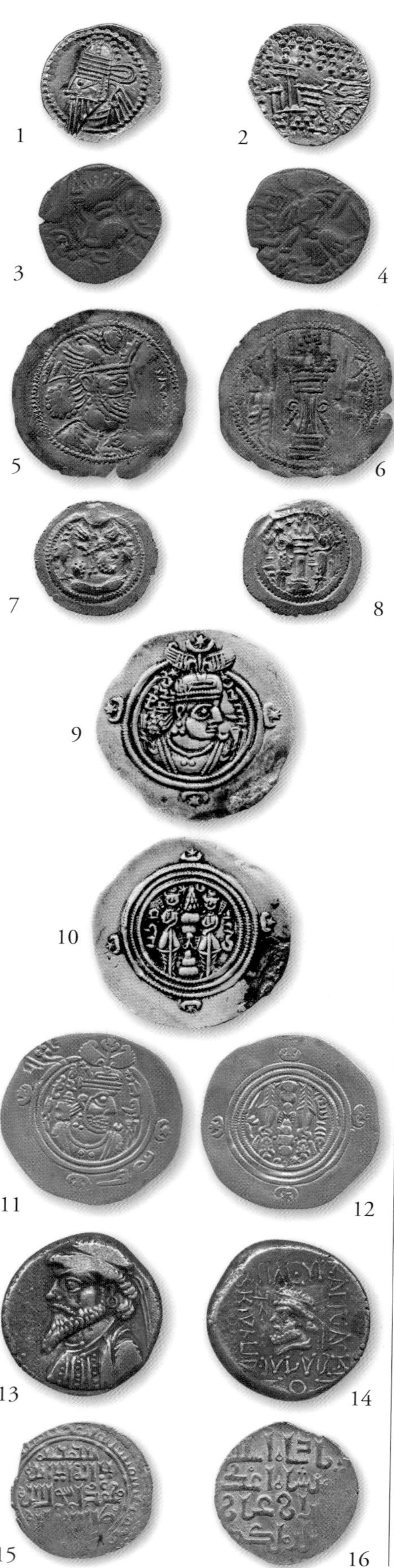

IRAN AND AFGHANISTAN

The Persian Empire embraced the lands now occupied by both modern Iran and Afghanistan, and at its height extended from Asia Minor to the north-west frontier of India, from the Caspian Sea to the Bay of Bengal. In its heyday, more than two millennia ago, it was one of the greatest civilizations and played a major role in the development of early coinage.

Left: Since 1994 Iranian coins of the higher denominations have been struck in bimetallic combinations. Their reverse motifs are derived from ancient art forms featuring stylized flowers.

ANCIENT PERSIA

The art of coinage spread eastward from Lydia, in modern Turkey, in the mid-6th century BC. The Greek historian Herodotus suggested that Darius Hydaspes (521–486) was the first ruler to strike coins, hence the name "daric" applied to the gold piece, equivalent to 20 sigloi (shekels) of silver. Both bore the kneeling figure of an archer – the king himself – on the obverse. These coins were roughly oval in shape and remained unchanged until the fall of the Persian Empire to Alexander the Great in the 4th century BC.

After Alexander, Persia was ruled by various satraps, or governors, who struck silver coins in abundance. In the mid-second century the Parthians overcame their Seleucid (Greek) masters and created a new empire in Persia. Silver coins on the Greek standard portrayed Arsakes, founder of the dynasty, exemplified by this coin of Osroes II dating from AD 190 [1–2]. Latterly, coins had inscriptions of corrupt Greek mingled with Pehlevi, the indigenous language.

The Kushans, a tribe originating in Xinjiang, China, created an empire that flourished from AD 105 to 250 and stretched from Tajikistan to northern India. At its height it produced gold and copper coins [3–4] but virtually no silver. The Kushan Empire declined early in the 3rd century AD, and much of its territory was absorbed by the Sasanians. Ardashir defeated the Bactrians and Parthians and established the Sasanian Empire, which ruled all of Western Asia and originally struck coins with a strong Kushan influence [5–6]. Gold and silver coins were modelled on Roman solidi and Greek drachmae respectively, the latter noted for their very wide, thin flans, later copied by the Arabs. Shown here are a gold solidus of Peroz I (459–84) [7–8] and drachmae of Khusru V (631–3) [9–12]. More orthodox in appearance were the billon tetradrachms of Elymais [13–14], a semi-independent kingdom in what is now south-western Iran, which was conquered by Ardashir.

MEDIEVAL PERSIA

In the 13th century the Mongols, under Genghis Khan, swept across Asia. The Ilkhans of Persia produced spectacular coins in gold [15–16], silver and copper at Tabriz, with the Shia creed of Islam (obverse) and the khan's title in Mongol (reverse). Shah Rukh introduced a new type of dirham, which remained popular from the 15th to the early 18th centuries [17–18] and provided the model for the thin silver coins, which later became smaller and thicker [19–20]. These coins were remarkable for their inscriptions and extensive use of rhyming couplets.

Regal coinage, confined to silver and gold, was struck at numerous provincial mints identified by Arabic abbreviations of their names. Many towns, however, produced their own copper falus, usually featuring animals or birds on the obverse, which serve to identify their origin.

MODERN COINAGE

The bewildering array of weights and values in the Persian coinage was rationalized in 1835 and the currency was based on the toman of 10 krans, 200 shahis or 10,000 dinars. The coins of Persia were consolidated by Shah Nasr al Din in 1876. All the branch mints were shut down and western machinery was installed at Tehran. Coins featured the radiate sun or lion and sunrise emblems [21–22] but from 1897 onward the portrait of the shah was often used.

In 1925 Reza Pahlavi overthrew the Qajar dynasty and proclaimed himself Reza Shah. He reformed the coinage in 1931, creating the toman of 10 rials, 1000 dinars or 5000 shahis. The name of the country was changed to Iran in 1935. In Reza Shah's reign coins reverted to the lion motif with the value in Arabic script [23–24]. His successor, Muhammed Reza Shah, had his profile on coins from 1966 until 1979, when he was overthrown [25–26]. Since then, the coins of the Islamic republic have eschewed portraiture, and mosques, tombs and other landmarks have appeared instead.

AFGHANISTAN

This remote country between Iran and India has been fought over for countless centuries. Distinctive coinage was produced in the area from the 4th century BC onward, notably the issues from the kingdoms of Bactria and Kabul. Lying between the Hindu Kush and the Oxus, Bactria occupied what is now northern Afghanistan and struck coins on the Greek standard, such as this gold stater of 250–230 BC [27–28]. Rectangular copper coins, such as the type by Menander of about 155 BC [29–30], were also produced.

The Kingdom of Kabul, ruled by the White Huns (5th century) and the Turko-Hephthalites (8th century) also minted coins. Afghanistan as a sovereign state developed only from 1747 under the Durrani dynasty, whose coinage aped that of the Mughal Empire, with the same fondness for poetic couplets [31–32]. Copper coins were struck by hand in numerous provincial mints, while gold and silver pieces often appeared in the name of rival contenders for the throne.

A national mint was established at Kabul in 1891 and machine-struck coinage was adopted in a system based on the Kabuli rupee of 2 qiran, 3 abbasi, 6 sanar, 12 shahi, 60 paisa or 600 dinar. These coins bore the state emblem and an Arabic text. In the 1920s coins based on the afghani of 100 pul were struck bearing the *toughra* of Muhammed Nadir Shah. Following the overthrow of Zahir Shah in 1973, coins were issued with a wreathed eagle emblem.

Afghanistan became a democratic republic in 1979, and this regime, under Soviet protection, continued until 1989. In this period, coins with communist-style emblems were struck in Cuba. When Russian forces withdrew, Afghanistan descended into chaos as the Mujahideen fought the Taliban, who established a fundamentalist Islamic state in 1994. The most recent coins of the Islamic Republic of Afghanistan, denominated in afghanis, feature a mosque [33–34]. The date on the reverse is 1383, which approximates to the year 2004.

The Tyranny of the White Huns

The Hephthalites or White Huns were a nomadic people who invaded the Sasanian Empire in the 4th century. They captured Shah Peroz, ransomed him, then used the millions of Sasanian silver coins paid to them as the basis of their own coins, derived from Sasanian, Kushan and Greek types.

17 18 19 20 21 22 23 24 25 26 27 28 29 30 31 32 33 34

BURMA, PAKISTAN AND BANGLADESH

These countries were at one time part of British India, acquired by the Honourable East India Company by conquest in the course of the 18th and 19th centuries. Apart from this, the regions had little in common. Britain fought a long series of wars between 1824 and 1885 to subjugate Burma, which had its own long-established culture and political structure. The territory that is now Pakistan was a major component of the Mughal Empire. It had close ties with Afghanistan, and a coinage with a long and complex history dating back to the pre-Christian era.

Left: The independent Kingdom of Burma was renowned for its distinctive coinage, which had a peacock motif on the obverse and continued until 1885, when it was replaced by Indian coins. Highly prized were the silver kyats, which were subsequently decorated with coloured enamels to make a fashionable form of jewellery at the end of the 19th century.

BURMA

The Kingdom of Arakan struck coins based on Indian designs from the late 7th century, the conch being a popular motif [1–2]. In the Middle Ages, coins of the neighbouring Muslim sultans in Bengal were in use, but Arakanese coins were revived in the 16th century and continued until the 1790s; this 17th-century tanka bears the title "Lord of the White Elephants" used by the Arakan kings [3–6]. In southern Burma, influenced by Malaya, there was a tradition of tin coins from the 17th to 19th centuries [7–8].

Under the last kings, Mindon (1853–78) and Thibaw (1880–5), coins were struck in various denominations (kyat of 5 mat or 10 mu, 20 pe or 80 pyas), the silver kyat corresponding to the Indian rupee and the gold kyat to the mohur. Burma is one of the few countries in relatively modern times to have struck coins in lead for small change; the eighth and quarter pya of 1869 with a hare on the obverse. The quarter pe was struck in different metals: copper (1865), iron (1865), copper again (1878) and latterly brass. Higher denominations featured a lion or peacock on the obverse, with the wreathed value inscribed in words on the reverse [9].

In 1937 Burma was detached from India and granted autonomy, though it continued to use Indian currency. In 1948 it attained independence and left the Commonwealth. Cupro-nickel or pure nickel coins denominated in pyas or pe appeared in 1948–9, followed by the decimal kyat of 100 pyas from 1952. All these coins had the image of a *chinthe* (mythological lion guardian) on the obverse and the value in Burmese script on the reverse. Ironically, in 1966 a new series portrayed national hero Aung San, whose daughter Aung San Suu Kyi, winner of the Nobel Peace Prize, has been under house arrest by the ruling military junta, beginning in 1989. The country changed its name in that year to Myanmar (actually a more accurate phonetic rendering of the indigenous name) and coins with that name in European lettering have been issued since 1999 [10–11].

PAKISTAN

The territory of what is now Pakistan was ruled in turn by Parthians, Kushans and Hephthalites (White Huns), the last-named striking silver coins in the 5th century [12–13]. Later came the Sasanians and the Ghaznavids, who introduced Islam and struck coins at Lahore derived from Afghan types. From Afghanistan the Mughals conquered much of the Indian subcontinent. Multan, where this gold mohur was struck [14–15], was an important mint from the 16th to late 18th centuries. The Punjab was conquered in the mid-18th century by the Sikhs, who produced silver rupees at Lahore [16–17] and Peshawar [18–19] until the mid-19th century, when the region was brought under British rule.

When the British left India in 1947, the subcontinent was divided into the predominantly Hindu Dominion of India and the Muslim Dominion of Pakistan. Coins inscribed "Government of Pakistan" appeared in 1948, with a *toughra* or crescent and star motifs. The rupee of 16 annas gave way to the rupee of 100 paisa in 1961.

The Islamic Republic of Pakistan was proclaimed in 1956, and at first there was no change in the inscription, but English was dropped in 1964 [20–21]. A few 50 paisa or rupee coins have appeared since 1976, mainly to commemorate anniversaries of Jinnah, founder of the state [22–23], or the 1400th anniversary of the Hegira (1981). Gold, silver and cupro-nickel coins of 1977 publicized the Islamic Summit Conference. A set of three large coins in gold or silver appeared in 1976 to promote wildlife conservation.

Family Planning

The population of Bangladesh is increasing at an alarming rate, and even coins are harnessed to the government campaign for family planning. Several coins since 1975 have depicted the ideal nuclear family in an attempt to get this message across.

Pakistan has been under military rule for many years, punctuated by brief periods of parliamentary democracy, but political instability has not been reflected by any changes in the coinage.

BANGLADESH

Situated on the Bay of Bengal, between India and Burma, Bangladesh was formerly the province of East Pakistan. Although sharing the Muslim faith of West Pakistan, it was culturally and historically distinct. In the 2nd and 3rd centuries AD, local Bengal kings issued beautiful Kushan-style coins [24–25]. There were significant developments in the late Gupta period, notably under Sasanka, King of Gauda *c.* 600–30 [26–27], while the silver coins of the Akara dynasty of Bangla Desh in the 10th–11th centuries [28–29] are noteworthy.

In the medieval period, coins reflected Indian, Burmese and Islamic influence. The Ghorids (also dominant in Afghanistan) struck coins, as did the sultans of Bengal. Sultan al-din Iltutmish revived the horseman motif in gold and silver tankas. Chittagong and Dacca (Jahangirnagar) were prolific mints in the Mughal period, while the East India Company struck traditional gold mohurs for circulation in the Bengal Presidency [30–31]

East Pakistan's sense of neglect by the more affluent West Pakistan led to an independence movement. Its people used the techniques of civil disobedience developed by Gandhi in India, provoking massive military retaliation. In support of East Pakistan India went to war with West Pakistan in 1971, and as a result the East declared independence as Bangladesh. Pakistani currency continued until 1973, when the taka of 100 poisha was introduced. Coins feature the *shapla* (lily) national emblem and various symbols of agriculture [32–33]. Significantly, many coins have been issued in connection with the FAO programme and since 1991 a few silver coins have celebrated anniversaries of independence or global concerns such as conservation.

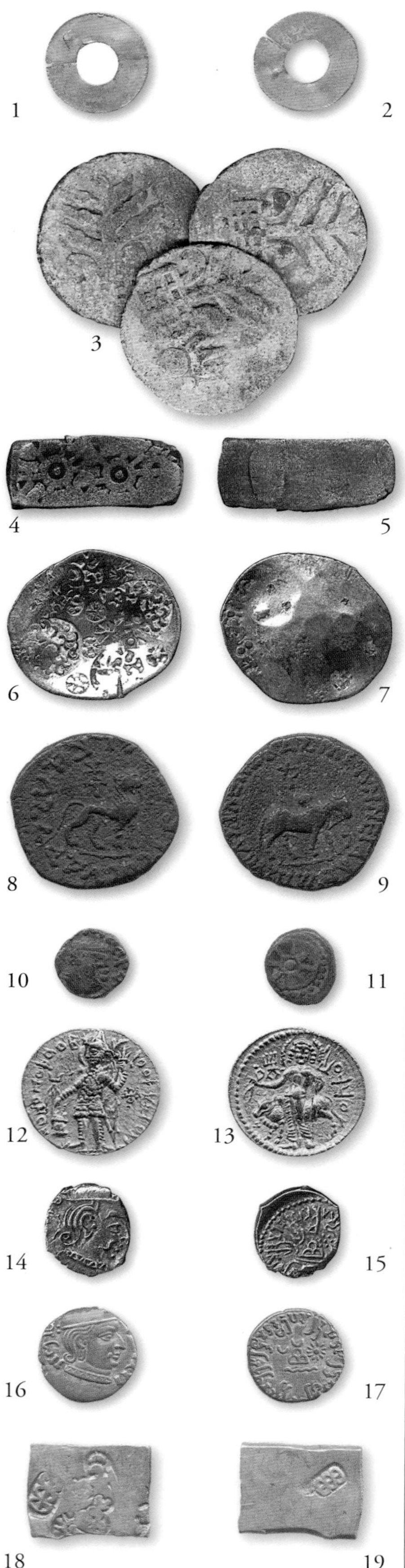

EARLY INDIA

One of the world's largest and most populous countries, India is regarded as a subcontinent, bounded by the Arabian Sea and the Bay of Bengal, and it gives its name to the ocean that lies to the south. It is home to civilizations and religions that date back several millennia and it is probable that coinage originated there quite separately from that of Asia Minor or China, although it very quickly came under Greek influence.

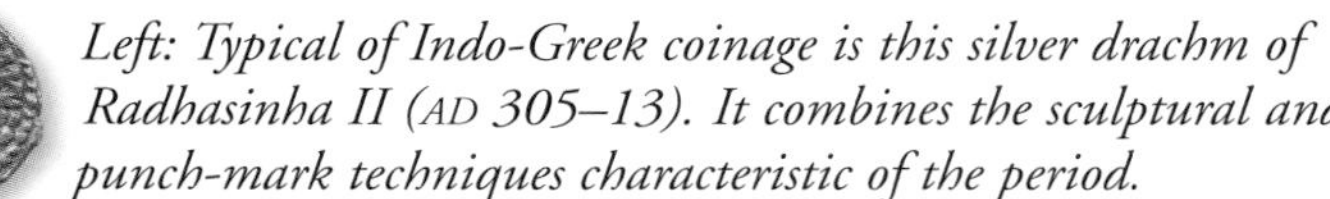

Left: Typical of Indo-Greek coinage is this silver drachm of Radhasinha II (AD 305–13). It combines the sculptural and punch-mark techniques characteristic of the period.

EARLIEST COINAGE

Some of the earliest money in circulation in India consisted of gold discs with a central hole, which doubled as jewellery [1–2], but lead coins were struck by the chiefs of Karnataka in the second century AD [3]. Indian coinage developed along distinctive lines, consisting of pieces of silver or copper, often square or rectangular in shape, with flat surfaces into which various symbols or marks were punched on both sides [4–5].

During the period 600–300 BC, various petty kingdoms and states were producing distinctive coins that drew heavily on the Greek influences of the same period in their weight and style [6–7]. By the 4th century BC, if not earlier, both square and circular coins [8–9] were being cast in copper, with somewhat similar, though less diverse, symbolism. It is clear, from later discoveries of hoards, that these coins circulated all over India.

The empire created by Alexander the Great extended to the Indus and beyond, and the provinces of Parthia and Bactria (lying in what is now Iran) exerted a great influence on the development of Indian coinage, both the copper coins of numerous petty states and the tiny silver hemidrachms, which were rich in mythological symbolism. In the 2nd century BC the Greeks of Bactria encroached on north-west India and struck a wide range of portrait coins. The Greek inscriptions gradually gave way to Prakrit or became very corrupt, and the gods of classical Greece were supplanted by Indian deities, reflecting the rise of the Indo-Scythian kingdoms and the great Kushan Empire, which flourished in the north-west from the 1st century AD and whose coins were apparently influenced by Roman models [10–11]. The Kushans' prolific gold and copper coinage was notable for inscriptions in Persian but written in a corrupt Greek form [12–13]. Portraits of rulers vied with images of the deities pertaining to all the religions of the period, in a style that endured for over 1000 years.

A great number of different types of coinage flourished in the various parts of India. In western India, satraps of Persian origin ruled from the 1st century BC and produced an abundant supply of silver coins featuring a bust of the ruler, down to the time of Swami Rudrasimha III, the last of the satraps of western India [14–15], who ruled in the late 4th century. The western satraps were overthrown by the Guptas, who began to imitate their silver. The Guptas originated in eastern India and spread northward. Their coins were elegant and often adapted Kushan designs [16–20], notably the Lakshmi and lion-slayer types of Chandragupta [21–22]. The White Huns swept aside the Gupta and other Indian civilizations in the 6th century but produced coins modelled on Kushan, Sasanian and Gupta types [23–24].

In central and southern India the Andras struck coins in lead around the beginning of the Common Era; later dynasties in the same area struck

Zodiac Coins

Jahangir authorized a notable series of coins featuring the signs of the zodiac, such as this silver rupee featuring the lion sign of Leo on the obverse. Zodiac coins were also issued by Alexandria, in Egypt, in the 2nd century.

gold coins: these usually depicted the dynastic emblem [25–26], such as the elephant of Malabar or the boar favoured by the Chalukyas of the Deccan, who also produced punch-marked gold pagodas in the 11th and 12th centuries [27–28]. The Chola dynasty struck coins with a standing figure of the ruler on the obverse and the same figure seated on the reverse, a style that was widely copied.

Coinage declined in southern and eastern India in the 6th century, though kingdoms close to Bombay continued to mint coins for some time. A seated figure of Lakshmi was a popular motif for the Kalachuri gold coins of Tripuri [29–30].

MUGHAL EMPIRE

Islam spread to north-west India in the 8th century, but apart from some coins struck in what is now the Indo-Pakistan border area it was not until Mahmud of Ghazna conquered the Punjab in the 11th century that the new culture had much impact on Indian coinage. In 1193 Muhammad bin Sam conquered northern India and established a devoutly Islamic dynasty that lasted until 1399, when Tamerlane sacked Delhi. He created a great Mongol Empire, which stretched from the Mediterranean to the Ganges. As this disintegrated, the Mughals built up an empire that embraced much of modern Afghanistan but gradually spread over the whole of India. The coins of the first Mughal rulers, Baber and Humayun, accorded with the prevailing types of Central Asia [31–32]. However, new designs, sizes and weights were adopted by their successors, notably Jahangir, whose gold coins are among the most splendid in their artistic calligraphy as well as their poetic inscriptions. Square rupees continued under Akbar until the early 17th century [33–34].

Gold was struck only sporadically in the 15th and 16th centuries; there were brief experiments with brass coins but billon was preferred. Under Sher Shah (1539–45) there was a profuse issue of good silver coins, bearing the Kalima (the Islamic confession of faith) and the names of the Four Caliphs, and this set the style for the gold and silver coins that continued until the Mughal Empire was swallowed up by the French and British in the 18th century.

In 1613 Shah Jahangir commissioned the production at Agra of five gold coins with a value of 1000 mohur. These massive coins had a diameter of 203mm/8in and weighed over 12kg/26lb. Their value in modern currency would be £250,000–300,000/$440,000–525,000. Not intended for general circulation, they were presented to various foreign ambassadors. Gold 500 mohurs are mentioned in Jahangir's autobiography, while an electrotype of a 200 mohur is preserved in the British Museum in London. A 100 mohur coin, struck by Jahangir in 1639, had a diameter of 97mm/3.8in and weighed 1094g/2.4lb [35]. Aurungzeb (1658–1707) replaced the Islamic confession of faith with the name of the mint and the date, and this style prevailed until the end of Mughal rule.

Above: A gold coin issued in the reign of Muhammad bin Sam, Sultan of Delhi in the late 12th century.

INDIAN PRINCELY STATES

As the Mughal Empire declined from 1700 onward, many local dynasties sprang up, carving out independent principalities and often warring with each other or seeking alliances with one or other of the European powers gaining control in India. Although the Mughal Empire continued in name until 1857, by 1800 its powers had largely passed to the British East India Company, which exercised control to a greater or lesser extent over the princely states. After the suppression of the Sepoy Mutiny most of India came directly under British rule, but the rest was ruled indirectly through the medium of more than 1000 autonomous states. Even as late as 1947, when India gained independence, no fewer than 675 principalities remained. By 1950 the last of them had been abolished. At least 125 states produced their own coinage, mainly in the period from 1800 to 1900, though a number continued to issue coins until the 1940s.

Left: This gold mohur bearing the crowned bust of Victoria as Empress of India was struck at the Calcutta Mint in 1885. Copper and silver coins of this type were also issued from 1877 onward and were issued by the states of Alwar, Bikanir, Dhar and Dewas. Before she was proclaimed Empress of India in 1877, coins in the name of Queen Victoria had been struck in India from 1862.

MONETARY CONFUSION

Virtually every state had its own currency system, a situation complicated by the fact that there was very seldom a fixed ratio between copper, silver or gold. Values tended to vary according to the decrees of the local potentate, which could not have facilitated trade between the states. Certain denominations were widespread, such as the gold mohur, the silver rupee and the copper paisa, based on the coins of the Mughal Empire. Indeed, many coins included the name of the Mughal emperor in their inscriptions, presenting a nominal semblance of unity and adherence to the imperial principle. This silver rupee of Jaipur names the Mughal emperor Ahmed Shah Bahadur [1–2]. By the late 19th century, however, many coins bore inscriptions referring to Queen Victoria of "Inglistan" (England). As late as 1948 Jodhpur was still producing coins in the names of George VI and Hanwant Singh [3–4].

Some of the states in north-west India, such as Awadh and Hyderabad, produced copper falus [5–6] or gold ashrafi [7–8], reflecting their commercial and political ties to Persia or Afghanistan. States in the Kutch region, such as Bhavnagar, Porbandar and Junagadh [11–12], had silver kori and half kori and copper dhinglo, dokdo [13–14], dhabu [15–16] and trambiyo. Also shown is a gold coronation kori from Kutch [9–10]. The inhabitants of Cochin used chuckrams, puttuns and fanams, while neighbouring Travancore also had anantarayas. The silver tamasha circulated in Kashmir, while copper cash and the gold pagoda paralleled the silver rupee and its subdivisions (right down to the tiny 1/32 rupee) in Mysore. The pagoda was the chief gold coin of the southern Indian states, and the issues of Mysore were very prolific [17–20].

INSCRIPTIONS

Most of the state coinage had legends in Persian (Farsi) or Nagari script, but it was often crude and blundered and therefore difficult to read. Fortunately, various symbols, approximating to mint-marks, were also included, and it is on these that collectors generally rely in order to assign their coins to the correct state. In general, coins often present an appearance of Arabic, with one or more horizontal lines dividing the text. English inscriptions were confined to the coins issued in Bikanir, Travancore and Jaora.

IMAGES

The exceptional use of Queen Victoria's crowned bust has already been mentioned, but she also appeared bare-headed on the rupee and mohur of Bhartpur in 1858. In the Muslim states, the use of effigies was usually frowned upon, but the Hindu states made occasional attempts at portraiture. Sayaji Rao III, Gaekwar of Baroda, was profiled on gold and silver coins [21–22], while the last mohurs and rupees of Bikanir bore a full-face bust of Ganga Singh.

An exception to the exclusion of portraits is to be found on the coins of Bahawalpur (now part of Pakistan) whose ruler, Sadiq Muhammad Khan, appeared bare-headed or wearing a fez on copper coins and silver rupees minted in 1940, although most of his coins featured his *toughra*, or sign-manual [23–4]. Travancore stuck gold sovereigns and half-sovereigns with the bust of Maharajah Rama Varma V. His successor, Bala Rama Varma II, appeared in profile on the copper chuckrams of 1938–45.

The Hindu kingdom of Tripura in Bengal had a long tradition of pictorial coins. These were mostly silver tankas or ramatankas with a horse and trident reverse, but other motifs included an allegorical scene alluding to the conquest of Chittagong [25–26], and the ritual bath in the River Lakhmia [27–28]. The nazarana mohur of Dhar (1943) had an armorial obverse and a Farsi inscription on the reverse [29–30]. A coat of arms, along European lines, also appears on the mohurs (1912–14) and silver half rupee (1923) of Assam, the rupees of Tripura and the mohurs of Rewah.

Both a portrait obverse and armorial reverse occur on coins of Datia, Indore and Gwalior. Scenery and landmarks are conspicuously absent, with the solitary exception of Hyderabad, which featured its Char Minar monument on the obverse of most coins from 1903 to 1948 [31–32], although a toughra was used in the series of 1911–30. The silver coins of Mewar (1931–2), struck in the name of "a friend of London" (Bhupal Singh), are unique in having a panoramic scene on the obverse [33–34].

Most of the coins were non-figural, although occasionally a pictorial element crept in, as in the paisas of Baroda, which showed a dagger or sword, or the paisas of Derajat, Lunavada and Elichpur, with their crude figures of lions. The coins of Indore featured a sacred cow and also used the motif of a radiate sun, while Tonk showed a horse and Mysore favoured the elephant.

The Mughal emperor Jahangir (1605–28) produced a handsome series depicting the signs of the zodiac [35–36]. The only coin known to have been issued by Rajkot appeared in 1945 and had the state arms (obverse) and the rising sun (reverse). A sun face obverse, sometimes with a kneeling cow reverse, appears on many of the coins of Indore [37–38].

Royal Portrait

Machine-struck cash and chuckrams of Travancore not only bore the denomination in English but also had the monogram RV on the obverse, denoting Maharajah Rama Varma VI (1885–1924). However, his successor, Bala Rama Varma II (1924–49), exceptionally placed his own portrait on the chuckram.

23 24 25 26 27 28 29 30 31 32 33 34 35 36 37 38

COLONIAL AND MODERN INDIA

In 1498 Vasco da Gama rounded the Cape of Good Hope and reached India by sea. Within a few years the Portuguese had established trading posts on the west coast, but they were soon overtaken by the Dutch, Danish, French and British, all of whom formed settlements on the east and west coasts. All the foreign settlements produced distinctive coinage.

Left: Coins with the crowned profile of George VI circulated until 1950, when the series inscribed "Government of India" was introduced. Among the patterns of 1947–9 were square 2 anna pieces, one with a peacock in side view and one face on, displaying its tail.

PORTUGUESE INDIA

Although Bombay passed from the Portuguese to the British as part of the dowry of Catherine of Braganza in 1660, Portugal continued to have a major interest in the subcontinent. Its settlements gradually declined but it retained Goa, Damao and Diu until 1962, when they were seized by the Republic of India.

Crude copper tanga [1–2] were produced at each settlement, each with its own currency system. Thus the rupia of 2 pardao or xerafim [3–4] in Goa was worth 480 reis, while in Diu the rupia was worth 10 tanga or 40 atias or 150 bazarucos or 600 reis. In 1871 the currency was reformed on the basis of the rupia [5–6] of 16 tanga or 960 reis, and coins inscribed "India Portugueza", with the profile of Luiz I (obverse) [7–8] and the royal arms (reverse) were introduced. After Portugal became a republic coins mainly featured the arms and cross emblems [9–12]; the escudo of 100 centavos was adopted in 1958.

DANISH INDIA

The Danes established trading posts at Pondicherry and Tranquebar, on the south-east coast of India, in 1620, but sold their remaining interests to the British East India Company in 1845. Crude copper or silver dumps denominated in cash and fano (fanams) respectively, with the crowned royal monogram (obverse) and the date and value (reverse), were produced until 1845, but they are now very rare.

DUTCH INDIA

The United East India Company of the Netherlands had a number of settlements that issued their own coins in the 18th and early 19th centuries. These included Negapatam, ceded to the British in 1784; Tuticorin, ceded in 1795; and Cochin, ceded in 1814. The last of the Dutch trading posts, at Pulicat, was transferred to British rule in 1824. Illustrated here is a tiny silver rupee of Jagannathpur [13–14] and a lead bazaruk of the Dutch East India Company [15–16].

FRENCH INDIA

The French did not take an interest in India until 1664, when the Compagnie des Indes Orientales was formed. Trading posts were established between 1666 and 1721, from Surat on the west coast to Balasore on the Bay of Bengal. There were inland settlements at Arcot in south India and at Chandernagore and Murshidabad in the north-east. Following the defeat of the French by Clive at Plassey (1759), France lost all its settlements apart from Pondicherry, which, in 1954, voted to join the Republic of India. Copper and silver coins based on the rupee of 64 biches (paisa) were augmented by fanons (fanams) and caches (cash). Apart from an issue of 1836–7 most coins were undated and very crude. The basic type of the silver fanon (2 royalins) showed a European crown on the obverse and the fleur de lys of France [17–18] but in deference to local custom a Hindu crown was later substituted, often reduced in the smaller coins to little more than a jumble of dots [19–22]. The copper cash showed a single fleur de lys, or a mere fragment in the smaller denominations. Coins of British India were used from 1848.

Architects of Modern India
Following the death of Jawaharlal Nehru in 1964 rupee coins with his dates of birth and death were struck for general circulation until 1967. This set the precedent for coins marking the birth centenaries of Mahatma Gandhi (1969–70) and Nehru himself (1969).

BRITISH INDIA

The territories of the British East India Company, developed from 1660, were divided into the Presidencies of Bengal, Madras, Malabar and Bombay (now Mumbai). Each produced coins that conformed to either the Hindu or Muslim coinage systems [23–24], based respectively on the pagoda of 42 fanams or 3360 cash, and the gold mohur (such as this coin of the Bengal Presidency in the name of the Mughal Shah 'Alam II [25–26]) of 16 rupees or 256 annas. The vast majority of coins were inscribed in Farsi, but Madras used Nagari script, as shown on this silver half pagoda of 1808 [27–28]. The Bombay coinage featured the bale-mark emblem (obverse) and scales (reverse) from 1791 onward, and an armorial obverse was gradually adopted from 1804.

Standard coins for the whole of British India were introduced in 1835. The copper denominations [29–30] featured the arms of the East India Company while the silver coins portrayed the reigning British monarch; all coins had a wreathed value reverse. Shown here is a gold restrike of the copper half anna of 1892, with Victoria as Empress [31–32]. A new reverse, featuring a tiger, was adopted in 1946 when nickel replaced silver in coins from 2 annas upwards. As a wartime economy measure the pice (quarter anna) was redesigned in 1943, retaining the original diameter but reducing the metal content by means of a large central hole [33–34]. These coins continued until 1947 and are of immense interest as they were struck at Lahore, Bombay and Pretoria (South Africa) as well as Calcutta. As well as three different types of crown, there are variations in lettering and the presence or absence of mint-marks.

REPUBLIC OF INDIA

In August 1947 the British handed over power to the Muslims of Pakistan and the mainly Hindu government of India. The Dominion of India became a republic in 1950. In the first decade of independence the old coinage system, based on the rupee of 16 annas or 64 pice, was retained. The obverses of 1950–7 were inscribed "Government of India" around the Ashokan column, while the reverses bore the denomination in English and Hindi surrounding a pictorial motif.

In 1957 the rupee of 100 naye (new) paise was adopted. The column of Ashoka continued but now with the country name in Hindi and English, while the reverse motifs prominently featured the numerals of value [35–36]. The use of various shapes, begun under the British, was considerably extended, each value having a distinctive shape. The designs were subtly modified in the 1970s and 1980s, but in 1988 a new series of pictorial reverses was released [37–38].

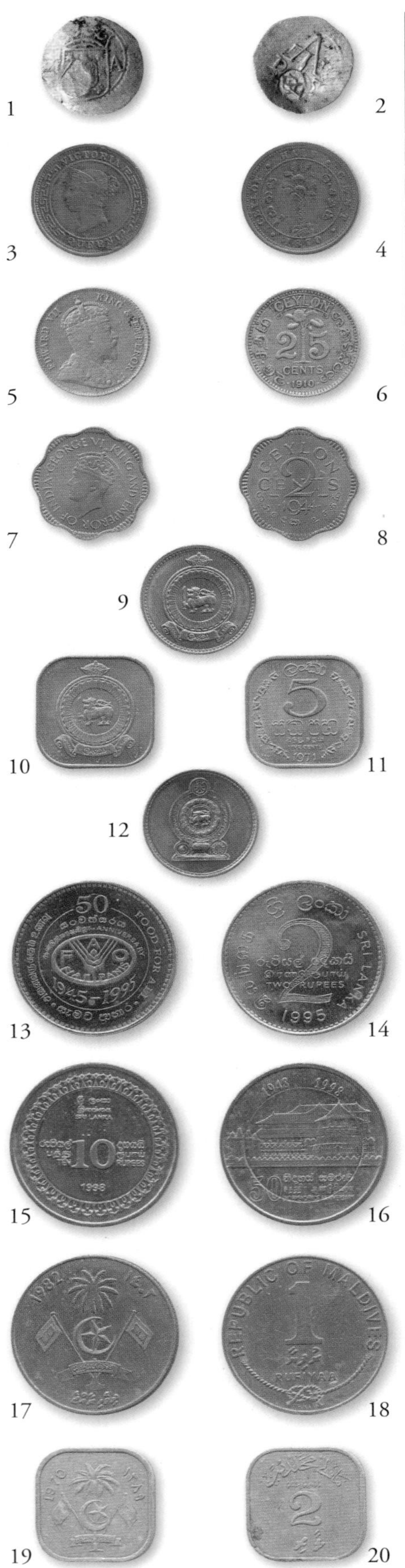

INDIAN OCEAN

A number of islands in the Indian Ocean, which were formerly part of the British or French colonial empires, issue their own coins. They range from Sri Lanka (formerly Ceylon), which has a coinage dating back to the 1st century BC, to the territories that have adopted distinctive coins only in quite recent times.

Left: Following the capture of the island of Ceylon from the Dutch in 1796, and its proclamation as a British crown colony six years later, copper coins were issued by the British in 1802. They bore an Indian elephant on one side and the value or the effigy of George III on the other.

SRI LANKA

The ancient coins of this island followed the pattern of the Chola dynasty of northern India, who subjugated the indigenous Veddahs and ruled until 1408. Ceylon then came under Chinese control until the arrival of the Portuguese in 1505. They, in turn, were supplanted by the Dutch in 1658. Local coinage was produced in each of these eras, mainly silver tangas such as this specimen from 1642 [1–2].

During the last year of the 18th century the British conquered the Dutch territories and made the island into a crown colony in 1802. The British retained the Indo-Dutch currency system, based on the rixdollar, on par with the rupee and divided into 48 stivers, each of 12 fanams. From 1839 to 1868 British third and quarter farthings [3–4] and silver threehalfpence also circulated in Ceylon, in addition to the local coinage. In 1872 the currency was decimalized, and the rupee of 100 cents was adopted. Bronze coins of this series bore the profile of the reigning monarch (obverse) and a palm tree (reverse) while the silver, or later nickel, coins had the value in numerals in an ornamental reverse [5–8].

Ceylon became a dominion in 1948 but continued to issue coins with the monarch's effigy until 1957. Thereafter the national emblem was substituted in a series introduced in 1963, with inscriptions in Sinhala and Tamil instead of English [9–11]. In 1972 the island became a republic under the name of Sri Lanka ("resplendent island"). A modified version of the coinage was adopted in 1975 [12]. A few commemoratives have been produced since 1957, when the 2500th anniversary of Buddhism was celebrated [13–16].

MALDIVE ISLANDS

This archipelago west of Sri Lanka was an independent sultanate from 1153 and had its own coins inscribed in Arabic from the 17th century. It became a British protectorate by agreement with the Governor of Ceylon in 1887. The rupee of 100 lariat (singular *larin*) became the rufiyaa of 100 laari in 1954, when the Maldives reverted to a sultanate after a brief period as a republic. Until 1968, when the second republic was proclaimed, coins bore the arms of the sultanate [17–20]. Since then coins have had pictorial motifs and numerals of value. Gold and silver coins in recent years have highlighted events or anniversaries of international importance.

MAURITIUS

Named after Prince Maurice of the Netherlands, this island was under Dutch control from 1598 to 1710, when it was acquired by the French,

Living Fossil

The coelacanth, a species of fish that existed 400 million years ago and pre-dated the dinosaurs, was believed to be long extinct when a live specimen was caught off the Comoros in 1938. Since then others have been found. This "living fossil" appears on a coin of the Comoros issued in 1984 to mark the World Fisheries Conference.

from whom it was captured by the British in 1810. At first the British retained the French currency of the livre of 20 sous; they then briefly issued coins in fractions of dollars [21–22] with a crowned anchor obverse, before adopting the rupee of 100 cents in 1877. Thereafter, coins portrayed the reigning monarch with the value on the reverse. From 1934, the silver coins had a pictorial reverse.

Mauritius became an independent state within the Commonwealth in 1968. Its coins continued to portray Elizabeth II until 1987, when the bust of Sir Seewoosagur Ramgoolam, the first prime minister, was substituted.

SEYCHELLES

Like Mauritius, this island group passed to Britain from France in 1810. It used the coinage of Mauritius until 1939, when distinctive coins, portraying the reigning sovereign, were introduced. These had the value on the reverse, but 5 and 10 rupee coins were added in 1974–9, with images of a beach scene and a turtle respectively. The Seychelles became an independent republic in 1976 and adopted a series of coins portraying the president, Sir James Mancham, with fauna and flora on the reverse, but an armorial obverse was adopted the following year while retaining the same reverses [23–26]. Since 1983 there has been a prolific output of special issues marking all manner of events worldwide.

MADAGASCAR

A French protectorate from 1886 and a colony from 1896, Madagascar used French currency until 1943, when coins bearing the Free French emblem were introduced, followed in 1948–53 by a series showing the head of Marianne. The island became the Malagasy Republic in 1958 but did not issue coins thus inscribed until 1963, with poinsettia (obverse) and a zebu (reverse). It became a democratic republic in 1975 and reverted to the name of Madagascar in 1996, when the five-pointed star of the democratic republic reverted to the poinsettia emblem [27, 29]. Many coins are denominated in both French and local currencies, at 5 francs to the ariary [28, 30–32].

COMOROS

This archipelago came under French protection in 1886, and coins denominated in francs and centimes, but inscribed entirely in Arabic, were produced in 1890. Formerly a dependency of Madagascar, the Comoros attained self-government in 1961 and had coins with the effigy of Marianne and palm trees from 1964. It became a federal Islamic republic in 1975 and introduced coins inscribed in Arabic and French with the four stars and crescent emblem, with pictorial reverses [33–38]. Coins portraying Said Mohamed Cheikh celebrated independence.

Above: Gold crescent obverse, and silver pictorial reverse, issued as part of the Comoros 'independence series'.

INDOCHINA

The name Indochina was given collectively to the French colonies and protectorates in South-east Asia, on the eastern side of the peninsula shared with Thailand. The area was originally occupied by peoples from the Yellow River valley of northern China, who migrated as a result of ethnic cleansing during the Han dynasty. In the 2nd century BC, the Chinese conquered Indochina and controlled it until AD 938, leaving the indelible mark of Chinese culture. In more recent times the kingdoms and states of Annam, Tonkin, Cambodia, Cochin-China and Laos emerged. The French penetrated this area in the early 19th century and gradually gained control, creating the states of Cambodia, Laos and Vietnam.

Left: That the French regarded Indochina as the jewel in the crown of their colonial empire is reflected in the style of the coinage from 1879 to 1954, which is rich in the symbolism and allegory of the French Republic, with very little concession to local character.

FRENCH INDOCHINA

The extraordinarily diverse coinage of the region was gradually superseded from 1879, when the French introduced a uniform currency throughout the areas under their control. These coins had the inscription "République Française" on the obverse and "Indochine Française" on the reverse, the former usually accompanied by an allegorical subject and the latter with the value in European and Chinese characters. The coins were denominated in piastres of 100 sapeque, on par with the franc of 100 centimes.

Since it came under the control of the Vichy French government, Indochina was nominally an ally of the Japanese, who occupied it in World War II. French rule was restored in 1946 and new coins were then introduced. They were inscribed "Union Française" and "Federation Indochinoise", and bore the head of Marianne and ears of corn [1–4].

VIETNAM

This country occupying the eastern coast of the peninsula was formerly divided into Tonkin (north) and Annam (south). It gained complete independence from China in 1428 and developed into a mighty empire. Its prosperity was reflected in the wealth and diversity of its gold and silver coinage, which ranged from cast bent rings or "banana bars" and copper dongs to the beautiful tien and lang series of circular coins [5].

After the country came under French control, the emperors continued to rule. The last of them, Bao Dai (1926–55), was deposed in 1945 by the communist Viet Minh under the leadership of Ho Chi Minh. Ho established a provisional government in the north and struck dong, xu and hao coins with a five-pointed star [6–7] until 1954, when the Democratic Republic of Vietnam was established and aluminium coins with the communist emblem around a central hole were introduced [8–9].

Bao Dai fled from Hanoi to Saigon, where the French created the state of Vietnam in 1949. Aluminium coins of 1953 featured profiles or portraits of three women side by side [10–11]. In 1955, Bao Dai was deposed and (South) Vietnam became a republic. Coins inscribed "Viet-Nam Cong-Hoa" were issued, with rice plants or bamboo on the obverse and the value on the reverse [12–16].

CAMBODIA

The Khmer people have inhabited the region to the west of Vietnam for at least 2000 years. The Khmer Empire controlled much of South-east Asia at its zenith in the 12th century, but under attack from its neighbours it declined considerably. It sought French protection in 1863 and was incorporated in French Indochina in 1877.

Cambodia issued coinage based on the silver tical up to 1885, with tiny uniface pe depicting animals, birds or flowers. King Ang Doung imported British presses to mint coins such as the silver tical of 1847 with a view of Angkor Wat [17–18]. A series portraying Norodom I and dated 1860 (but not released until 1875) was produced in Belgium [19–20]. Independence was restored in 1949 under Norodom Sihanouk; coins inscribed "Royaume du Cambodge" appeared in 1953 [21–22]. The riel of 100 sen was adopted in 1959, but the previous motifs were retained.

In 1970, Sihanouk was deposed and the Khmer Republic was proclaimed by Lon Nol. No circulating coins appeared under this regime, although some gold and silver pieces were struck at the Royal Mint in 1974, shortly before the regime was toppled by Pol Pot. The People's Republic of Kampuchea abolished money. Apart from an aluminium 5 sen of 1979 [23–24], there were no coins until 1988 when some commemoratives began to appear. Pol Pot was ousted in 1989 and the State of Cambodia emerged the following year with coins thus inscribed. In 1993 Prince Sihanouk returned as head of state and the Kingdom of Cambodia was restored [25–26].

LAOS

Fa Ngum created the first kingdom known as Lan Xang ("land of a million elephants") in the 14th century and established his capital at Luang Prabang. The kingdom originally included parts of Thailand and Yunnan province in southern China, but it gradually declined and by the early 19th century it had come under Thai control, whose coinage was widely used. The French established a protectorate in 1893. Autonomy was granted in 1949 but by 1953 the government was at war with the communist Pathet Lao. Laos gained independence in 1954, but civil war erupted in 1960 and continued until the creation of the Lao People's Republic in 1975.

Aluminium holed coins were introduced in 1952, based on the kip of 100 centimes [27–30]. Coins featuring the star and the hammer and sickle emblem were released in 1980 [31–32]. Large gold and silver coins were issued in 1971, and have reappeared since 1985.

United Country

After a long-running war between north and south, Vietnam was unified in 1976 as the Vietnam Socialist Republic (Cong Hoa Xa Hoi Chu Nghia Viet Nam) and coins thus inscribed have been used ever since. These have a star and cogwheel emblem on the obverse and a reverse bearing the value in currency based on the dong of 10 hao. Coins from 5 to 10,000 dong have been struck in brass, cupro-nickel or silver in recent years to mark the Olympic Games or to promote nature conservation.

Above: A silver bullion piece struck by the Chinese in 1943–4, denominated in kip, for trade in Laos.

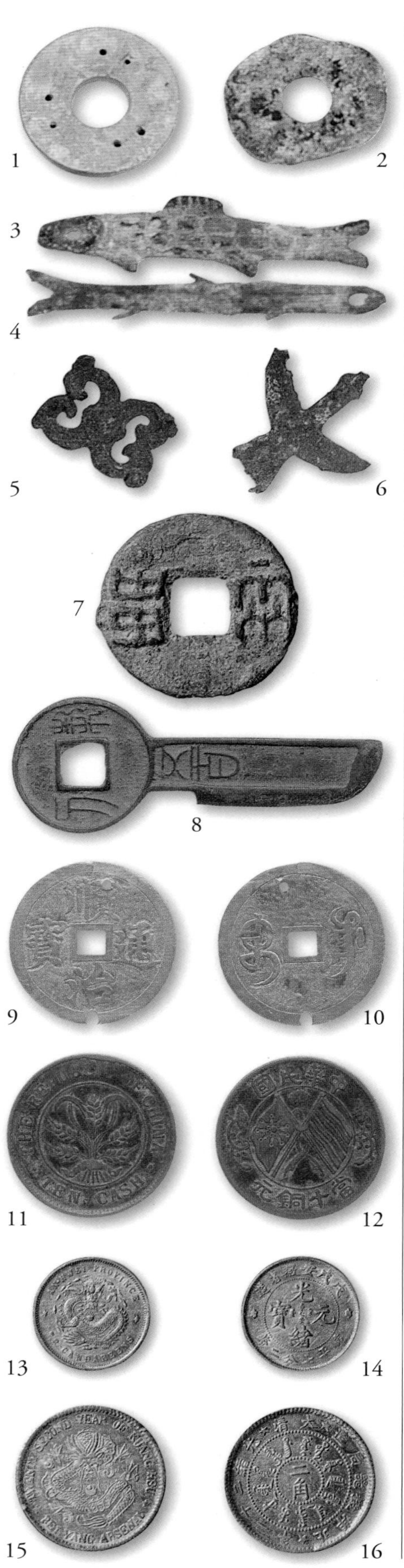

CHINA

China is one of the world's largest countries, covering an area of almost 10 million sq km/3.7 million sq miles. It extends from Central Asia to the Pacific, and from the Gobi Desert to the Gulf of Tonkin. It is also the most populous nation on earth, with around 1.3 billion inhabitants. The Chinese were among the chief originators and developers of coinage. Their cash – distinctive copper coins with a square hole punched out of the centre – continued in use for nearly two millennia.

Left: The Dragon silver dollars, which were first struck at the Guangdong Mint in 1889, became the standard throughout the Chinese Empire. The weight of these coins was fixed at 7 mace and 2 candareens, the mace being a tenth of a tael.

ANCIENT CHINA

The bronze implements pioneered as currency by the Zhou dynasty were roughly contemporary with the very first coins of Asia Minor, but in China the former were actually predated by stone rings fashioned from limestone [1–2]. In addition to the well-documented "knife" and "spade" currencies, a variety of other implements circulated in the periods of the Zhou and Warring dynasties, including "bell money", "fish money" [3–4], imitation cowries and various other bronze artefacts used in barter [5–6].

The flattened, round copper discs known as cash [7], which more closely resemble today's circular coins, probably made their first appearance in the 4th century BC, although a handsome knife currency [8] reappeared at the beginning of the first millennium, thanks to the ruler Wang Mang. Cash often circulated alongside other items, such as the jewellery money of amulets and charms [9–10] exchanged under the Qing dynasty (1644–1911).

CHINESE EMPIRE

Although copper cash continued to circulate well into the 20th century, with many provincial variations, a standard unified coinage on western lines developed after the establishment of the central mint at Tianjin in 1905 [11–12]. Coins were struck rather than cast in the traditional manner. Subsidiary coins of values up to 20 cash were struck in brass, copper or bronze with a dragon motif, while silver coins were denominated from 10 cents to one dollar.

Tianjin manufactured the dies used at many of the provincial mints. In addition to the general issues for circulation throughout the empire, numerous provincial series were struck at regional mints in Anhui [13–14], Chihli [15–16], Fengtian, Fujian, Heilongjiang, Henan, Hubei, Hunan, Gansu, Guangxi, Guangdong, Guizhou, Jiangnan, Jiangxi, Jiangsu, Jilin, the Manchurian Provinces, Shaanxi, Shanxi, Shandong, Sichuan Xinjiang, Yunnan and Zhejiang. In some of these vast provinces there were several mints, each producing distinctive coins. In Xinjiang, for example, local coinage was produced at Aksu, Kashgar, Kucha, Urümqi and Wuxi in the latter period of the empire.

CHINESE REPUBLIC

The system of provincial and local mints continued after the republic was proclaimed in 1912. Indeed, it expanded in the 1920s and 1930s, as central government weakened and China disintegrated into regions controlled by warlords [17] followed by the long struggle between the Kuomintang ("national people's party") [18–22] and

Birds of Ill Omen

Silver dollars were issued in 1932, the reverse showing a junk with the rising sun in the background and three birds at the top. This seemed innocuous at the time, but the rising sun was the emblem of Japan and the birds were deemed to symbolize the Japanese air raids on Manchuria. The junk dollars were re-issued in 1933–4 with the sun and birds removed and in this form they were restruck during World War II in the USA, with an inscription added to celebrate victory over the Japanese.

the communists led by Mao Zedong. The situation was also exacerbated by wide variations in the value of currency in different parts of China, and latterly by inflation.

The bronze coins struck by the central government under the National Revenue Board had crossed flags on one side and the value in Chinese and English on the other, often incorporating a floral motif. Gold and silver coins portrayed Sun Yat-sen [23], Yuan Shi-gai [24] and other prominent figures. Interestingly, coins appeared in 1926 to commemorate the wedding of Pu Yi, the last emperor of China, who had abdicated in 1912. A new series portraying Sun Yat-sen was introduced in 1936 with a reverse reproducing an ancient bu coin.

Both the central government and the provinces produced numerous silver dollars portraying political and military leaders. Among the provincial issues, those coins issued under Japanese auspices in Manchukuo (Manchuria) in the name of the Emperor Kang De (formerly Pu Yi) in 1932–45 are particularly noteworthy.

PEOPLE'S REPUBLIC

A soviet republic was proclaimed by Mao Zedong in 1931 and coins with a five-pointed star or the hammer and sickle superimposed on a map of China were issued in those areas under communist control. Extremely rare coins were also struck under communist auspices in various regions under local soviets [27–30], including some with very crude portraits of Lenin.

Although the People's Republic of China was proclaimed at Beijing in October 1949 it was not until 1955 that a regular coinage was introduced, based on the Renminbi yuan of 10 jiao or 100 fen, with a uniform obverse showing the state emblem and a wreathed value reverse. These motifs have been in use in the fen denominations for half a century without change. The jiao, first struck in copper-zinc in 1980, switched to aluminium in 1991 [25–26], when the 5 jiao, originally in the same alloy, switched to brass. In both values a new reverse incorporated a peony blossom. The yuan first appeared as a circulating coin in 1980, struck in cupro-nickel with mountains on the reverse, but changed to clad steel in 1991 with the peony reverse.

Silver and gold commemoratives have proliferated since 1980, mainly in yuan denominations, although they include the silver 5 jiao of 1983, which celebrated the seventh centenary of the sojourn of Marco Polo. Latterly, these commemorative and special issues have appeared in long series with specific themes, from the Olympic Games to the autonomous regions, founders of Chinese culture, poets and Chinese inventions. China has also produced tiny gold 3 and 5 yuan with a giant panda on one side and the Temple of Heaven in Beijing on the other. The Panda series has become immensely popular worldwide, even leading to issues in platinum since 1993 and large silver versions since 1997.

FLORAL COINS OF ASIA

More than in any other part of the world, the coins of Asia display a penchant for floral themes. The universal appreciation of flowers for their beautiful forms, colours and scents, combined with the fact that some species are associated with particular countries because they grow only in those regions, is reflected in the prevalence of flowers as national emblems. Thus, they provide a ready means of identification on coins.

FLORAL ORNAMENT

Because of the traditional Islamic objection to figural motifs based on living creatures (both animal and human), the preferred ornament on much of the coinage of Islamic states is floral. Plants and flowers, often stylized, may be found on the reverse of the contemporary coins of Pakistan. Whereas European and American coins might use laurel or oak leaves for wreaths, Asian countries often favour leaves of *padi* or rice plants, and these may be found on coins of many countries in South-east Asia. Rice plants at the flowering stage are featured on the coins of South Vietnam, Thailand and Burma (Myanmar), while rice plants and a pineapple can be found on a coin from Thailand marking World Food Day.

Below: Coins from Burma (top, and large central coin), East Timor (top-right and bottom-left), and Vietnam, showing rice blossom and panicles.

The lower denominations of the coins issued by the People's Republic of China since 1991 feature sprays of peonies and other blossoms on the reverse. Flowers have also featured on the reverse of the large multiple tugrik coins of Mongolia since 1996, celebrating the Lunar New Year, as well as the series issued by South Korea to mark the Olympic Games of 1988. Since 1983, China has produced annual issues of bullion coins in silver or gold with the theme of the giant panda. As its diet consists solely of bamboo shoots, these plants invariably appear in the designs, showing the various stages of bamboo growth.

FLOWERS AS NATIONAL SYMBOLS

The chrysanthemum is the chief means of identifying the coins of Japan, and its similarity to the rising sun (a popular obverse motif) explains its appearance. For the Japanese the flower is a traditional symbol of the sun, and the symmetrical arrangement of its numerous petals represents perfection. It features in the Japanese imperial crest and the emperor's throne.

In the majority of coins issued in Japan since the arrival of Western-style coinage in 1873, a chrysanthemum blossom appears at the top of the reverse, but in the bronze sen of 1898–1915 it formed the central motif on the obverse. In many coins a wreath of chrysanthemum leaves surrounds the value. Other flowers have sometimes been featured, notably the *kiri-mon* (*Pawlonia imperialis*) on the sen of 1916–38 and the 500 yen since 1981, and the mass of cherry blossom on the 100 yen since 1967.

Above (clockwise from top-left): A chrysanthemum on a Chinese 1 jiao, the Rose of Sharon from Korea, plum blossom on a 5 jiao, the Bauhinia motif on a Hong Kong dollar obverse.

Below: Kiri-mon blossom on the Japanese 100 yen (top). Phalaenopsis and cattleya orchids on coins of Taiwan (below).

Many of the petty kingdoms of ancient India struck small copper coins with crude flowers. The reverse of the silver rupees under British rule had floral motifs, and in the George V and VI series the thistle, rose and shamrock of

Above (clockwise from top-left): Water lily (Iran), Hibiscus rosasinensis *(Malaysia), Jasmine (Indonesia) and Shapla (Bangladesh).*

the United Kingdom were surmounted by the lotus blossom of India. Among the coins of the modern republic, however, the lotus is the dominant motif in the Food and Agriculture Organization pair of 1970–1.

In Korea the five-petalled hibiscus known as the Rose of Sharon appeared at the top of the reverse in the issues of the empire (1898–1909) and has also featured as the chief motif in the high-value gold and silver coins of South Korea. The five-petalled plum blossom is the national flower of Taiwan and has appeared on the obverse of several coins, while the reverse of the yuan of 1960 also showed a dendrobium orchid. This theme was expanded in the 1 jiao coins of 1967–74, which featured a phalaenopsis orchid, while the 5 jiao depicted a cattleya.

The *shapla* or water lily is the emblem of Bangladesh and thus provides the principal motif for the obverse of the coinage, while a water lily may also be found on the reverse of the bimetallic 250 rials of Iran. The lotus is the emblem of Sri Lanka and thus appears above the value on the rupees since 1963. Gold-plated lotus flowers appear on the reverse of Nepal's silver 500 rupee coin of 1996.

The coins of Israel, derived from the ancient coins of the Jewish revolts, abound with plant life, from grapes to pomegranates, but the only true flower used on the coinage graces the obverse of the sheqel: this is the tri-lobed lily *yehud*, a pun on the word *yehudi* (Jew). Jasmine has appeared on several coins of Indonesia, usually in a subordinate position, but it takes centre stage on the reverse of the 500 rupiah coins issued since 1991.

Both Hong Kong and Macao, the former British and Portuguese colonies, adopted flowers as their national emblems, featured in the flags introduced when they became special administrative zones of China. The bauhinia orchid appears on the obverse of the entire series of Hong Kong, whereas the lotus of Macao has yet to be featured on its coins. The *Hibiscus rosasinensis* has appeared on the reverse of Malaysian coins as a wreath around the value, but in the 1989 series it is more prominent, appearing above the values on the obverse. The orchid *Vanda* 'Miss Joaquim' is the national flower of Singapore and two blossoms have flanked the numeral on the reverse of the cent since 1986. Continuing this theme in the higher denominations are the fruit salad flower (5c), jasmine (10c), powder-puff plant (20c), yellow allamanda (50c) and periwinkle ($1). When a $2 coin was added to the series in 1992 the reverse featured *Vanda* 'Miss Joaquim' in all her glory.

Above (clockwise from top-left): full-colour Camellia (China), Pomegranate (Israel), Periwinkle (Singapore), a floral wreath (China) and the fruit salad flower on a Singapore 5 cents.

Above: Turkish coins of the 1990s had a wealth of floral designs, including (clockwise from top-left) the Carnation, Rose, Cedar and Tulip blossom.

Turkey has a long tradition of incorporating leaves into its coin designs, from the intricate leaf patterns drawing from Saracenic art in the Middle Ages to the olive, laurel and oak wreaths of many modern coins. In the 1990s, however, as inflation rose astronomically, a new series denominated in bin lira (thousands of lira) had a floral theme, with cedar blossom (2.5), tulip (5), carnation (10) and rose (25) motifs on the reverse.

PRETTY AS A PICTURE

Special or commemorative coins that have a flower as their principal motif are surprisingly few in number. When Thailand hosted the ninth World Orchid Conference in 1978 a silver 100 baht coin had a spray of orchids across the reverse. In 1999 China issued two large 10 yuan silver coins. One was gold-plated and depicted a Chinese rose on the reverse, while the other showed auspicious camellia blossoms in full colour.

CHINESE TERRITORIES

On the fringes of China are several countries that were once part of its territory and are now independent, or conversely are now part of China, having had an independent existence with distinctive coinage. They include the former British and Portuguese colonies of Hong Kong and Macao.

Left: The ruined façade of St Paul's Cathedral, depicted on several coins, is one of the most impressive sights in Macao. The edifice is a reminder of the heyday of this former Portuguese colony, and was a bastion of Christianity in the Far East in the 17th and 18th centuries.

HONG KONG

China ceded the island of Hong Kong ("fragrant harbour") to Britain in 1841 at the end of the First Opium War, and a 99-year lease on adjacent territory on the mainland was granted in 1898. On the expiry of the lease Britain ceded the colony to the People's Republic in 1997. It has since been a special administrative zone, retaining its currency based on the dollar of 100 cents.

Locally struck coins were introduced in 1863, all but the tiny mil (one-tenth of a cent) bearing the crowned bust of Queen Victoria [1–2]. This established a precedent for all the coins down to 1997, with a reverse showing the name and value in English round the circumference and the corresponding Chinese characters in the centre. The sole exception was the 50 cents with the bust of Edward VII [3–4] on the obverse: its value in English appeared in the centre, with the name and date around the top and the Chinese equivalent around the foot.

The traditional formula continued with the coinage of Elizabeth II, three different effigies being used between 1955 and 1992. A silver 20 cents with the bust of Edward VII appeared in 1902–5, and this denomination was revived in 1975 as a nickel-brass coin with a scalloped edge [5–6]. Cupro-nickel $1 (1960), $2 (1975) and $5 (1976) had a reverse type showing the crowned lion emblem of the colony surrounded by the name and value in English and Chinese [7–8].

In preparation for the retrocession, a new series, with a bauhinia flower (obverse) and numeral (reverse) was introduced in 1993 and this included a bimetallic $10 piece [9–12]. A coin of this type with a pictorial reverse was released in 1997 for the opening of the Harbour Bridge. Gold $1000 coins began in 1975 with the Queen's visit, and since 1976 similar coins have greeted the Lunar New Year [13–14].

MACAO

The Portuguese acquired the peninsula of Macao with the islands of Taipa and Coloane as a trading post in 1557, although it did not acquire full colonial status until 1887. Portuguese coins were used until 1952, when a distinctive series based on the pataca of 100 avos was adopted. The obverse showed the crowned globe and shield emblem of Portugal, while the reverse bore the value in European and Chinese scripts [15–16]. A new series, with a shield (obverse) and Chinese characters (reverse) came into use in 1982 [17–18], and a pictorial issue appeared from 1992–3 [19–24] in anticipation of Macao returning to China in 1999 as a special administrative zone.

Commemorative silver and gold coins since 1974 have marked the opening of the Macao-Taipa Bridge and the Macao Grand Prix as well as the Lunar New Year [25–26]. An unusual feature of many modern coins has been the depiction of the ruins of St Paul's instead of the customary arms.

TAIWAN

The island of Taiwan, formerly known as Formosa, was occupied by Japan in 1895 but returned to China in 1945. Thither came the remnants of the Chinese nationalist forces when the communists drove them from the mainland. Since 1949, Taiwan has been the seat of the Republic of China (ROC), led by Chiang Kai-shek and his successors. Most coins since 1949 have featured Sun Yat-sen (obverse) and a map of the island (reverse) [27–28], with inscriptions entirely in Chinese and dates in years since the foundation of the republic in 1911. The 5 and 10 yuan, introduced in 1965, depict Sun's mausoleum at Nanking on the reverse. Many of the yuan coins since 1966 have portrayed Chiang Kai-shek.

Relatively few commemorative coins (from 10 yuan upwards) have appeared, honouring leaders of Chinese nationalism [29–30] or marking anniversaries of the republic. A silver 1000 yuan of 1996 marked the first popular elections, with side-by-side portraits of President Lee Teng-hui and Vice President Lien Chan on the obverse.

MONGOLIA

Once a mighty empire that conquered China and extended as far as Hungary, Mongolia came under the rule of the Manchus in 1691. In 1921, with Russian support, it asserted its independence and became a people's republic. Coins based on the tugrik of 100 mongo were issued from 1925, with the national emblem, followed by communist symbols in 1945 when Mongolia severed its last links with China. The collapse of communism led to the creation of the democratic state of Mongolia in 1990. Since 1994 coins have reverted to the emblem of the 1920s [31–32]. Mongolia has also produced a vast number of special coins, ranging from the Chinese New Year to the Japanese Royal Wedding of 1993. While coins in general circulation are inscribed in Mongol, in both the indigenous script and a modified form of Cyrillic, special issues are invariably inscribed in English.

Above: Flowers and candles depicted on sample coins from the Central Mint of Taiwan in the 1960s and 1970s.

Commercial Advertising

Gold and silver coins were issued by Macao in 1978 to mark the 25th anniversary of the Grand Prix. They depicted racing cars blazoned with advertising for Seiko, Luso Banking and even Rothman Pall Mall cigarettes, which appeared in the photograph supplied to the coin designer. The colonial authorities took exception to this so the coins were hurriedly withdrawn and replaced by designs without advertisements. The "advert" versions are now extremely rare.

HIMALAYAN STATES

Two of the countries that lie in the Himalayas, between China and India, have managed to preserve their independence, despite having been under the protection of their more powerful neighbours at various times. On the other hand, although it is now classified as an autonomous region of the People's Republic of China, Tibet has been under Chinese control since 1950, when its distinctive coinage was suppressed.

Left: In 1966 Bhutan celebrated the 40th anniversary of the accession of Maharajah Jigme Wangchuk with the issue of a set of seven coins. The four lower values were denominated in Indian currency, but the top values were 1, 2 and 5 sertums and were struck in gold or platinum.

TIBET

Nominally a tributary of China for many centuries, Tibet embraced Buddhism in the 8th century and thereafter became increasingly isolated from the outside world. A British military mission from India, led by Sir Francis Younghusband, invaded it in 1903. Influenced by the British, Tibet formally declared its independence in 1913, but this was suppressed by China in 1950. Following a revolt in 1965 it was made an autonomous region.

The coins of neighbouring Nepal were used from 1570, but in the 1720s Nepal began striking coins with a lower silver content for use in Tibet, based on the tangka of 15 skar or the srang of 10 sho or 100 skar. This was unsatisfactory and around 1763 the Tibetans began producing coins for themselves. From this early period dates the Suchakra Vijana tangka [1–2], but such coins were produced by hand in small quantities. A mint opened at Lhasa in 1791 under local auspices and struck Kong-Par tangkas, but was quickly suppressed by the Chinese, who opened their own mint in Lhasa in 1792 and struck silver sho in the name of Emperor Qianlong [3–4]. Sino-Tibetan coins continued intermittently until 1909–10, when the copper skar [5–6] was struck in the name of the Chinese emperor Xuantong (Pu Yi).

In the independent period, the Tibetan authorities struck a wide range of coins, from the copper skar to the gold srang [7–8] with a lion obverse and various motifs, notably the prayer-wheel, on the reverse. Even after the Chinese invasion of 1950 a few coins with the lion on a background of mountains continued as late as 1953.

BHUTAN

This landlocked Himalayan kingdom was conquered by Tibet in the 9th century and had a similar theocratic form of government. The southern part was annexed by Britain to India, but the northern part became a hereditary kingdom in 1907 and attained full independence in 1971.

For countless centuries, Bhutan had a wholly agricultural economy: self-sufficient in foodstuffs it relied on barter in all transactions, and barter is still widely practised. It had no coinage of its own and, when the need began to arise in the 18th century, it made use of the silver debs or half rupees of the Indian state of Cooch-Behar. About 1790 it began striking its own coins, originally in the same weight and fineness as the Cooch-Behar coins, but from 1820 onward debased by an admixture of lead or other metals, so that latterly debs were mostly copper or brass, with a silver wash to give them the appearance of precious metal. The design was very simple, with three lines of characters separated by horizontal lines, but including a symbol that helps to place them in chronological sequence, rather like the mint-marks

Nepalese Symbolism

The coins of Nepal are rich in the aniconic symbolism of Buddhism and Hinduism. While the obverse of the 50 paise coin since 1994 has featured the plumed crown of the Shah Dev dynasty, the reverse incorporates some of the items that compose the *ashtamangala* (the eight auspicious symbols). The date, in Hindi and Devanagari script, is 2051 in the Vikrama Samvat Era, 57 years ahead of the Common Era (that is, 1994).

on medieval English coins. They consisted mainly of the deb [9–10] and rupee [11–12] of debased silver.

This primitive coinage was replaced in 1928 by a series based on the Indian rupee of 64 pice. The obverse bore the bust of the ruler, Jigme Wangchuk, but the reverse was divided by horizontal and vertical lines to form nine compartments, with an inscription in the centre and ornate symbols in the others. They were undated but bore the symbol of the earth dragon in the Chinese zodiacal cycle. When re-issued they bore the iron tiger, dating them to 1950, though this symbol was retained when the half rupee was re-issued in a reduced weight to conform with the Indian coins current in 1967–8. In the interim a series based on the Indian rupee of 100 naye paise celebrated the ruler's 40th anniversary, followed in 1974 by a series portraying Jigme Singye Wangchuk, based on the sertum of 100 ngultrums or 10,000 chetrums [13–14]. Various Buddhist symbols appeared on the reverse.

Since 1974 Bhutan has produced numerous gold and silver coins for occasions ranging from royal anniversaries to international sporting events.

NEPAL

Distinctive coins, mainly square copper dams [15–16] were struck by several of the Himalayan mountain states from the late 15th century. Silver coins of good quality were produced at Patan [17–18] and Bhatgoan [19–20], while both circular and square mohars with their subdivisions were minted at Kathmandu [21–28].

In the late 18th century Prithvi Narayan Shah, ruler of Gurkha, welded these states into a single kingdom and struck silver mohars [29–30]. After his death Nepal suffered a long period of instability, reflected in the clay token inscribed in Newari, which was used as small change [31–32]. Order was restored in the 1840s when the Rana family established a hereditary premiership that took real power away from the king. This continued until 1950, when a popular uprising deposed the Rana prime minister and restored the power of the monarchy.

Prior to 1932 Nepal had a very complex currency system, based on the rupee of 2 mohar or 4 suka, 8 ani, 16 dak, 32 paisa or 128 dam [33–34]. Gold, silver and copper coins were struck on circular flans with geometric motifs contained in a square format (obverse) and a segmented device resembling flower petals (reverse). The currency was simplified in 1932 when the rupee of 100 paisa was adopted. Pictorial elements, such as crossed kukris, a hoe or a stylized lotus gradually crept in from that time. Symbols of the monarchy, such as the crown or sceptre, were depicted on the obverses [35–36]. Very few coins portrayed the ruler, King Tribhuvan, though he appeared on rupees of 1953–4.

A 2 rupee denomination was introduced in 1982 and thereafter became the preferred medium for commemoratives and special issues [37–38]. Previously, a few silver coins from 10 to 50 rupees had served this purpose. In more recent years both gold and silver coins of very high face values have appeared, including a gold bullion series denominated in asarfi.

KOREA

The "land of the morning calm" occupies a peninsula in north-eastern Asia, bordering China. The country allegedly had its own distinctive civilization over 4000 years ago, but recorded details date only from the 1st century BC, while the name Korea (Koryo) appeared in 935, when three kingdoms were merged into one. It came under Japanese influence in the late 19th century, became a protectorate in 1905 and was annexed in 1910. Liberated in 1945, it split along the 38th parallel: the north, under communist influence, became the People's Democratic Republic of Korea, and the remainder the Republic of Korea. Despite the collapse of communism everywhere else, North Korea remains a totalitarian state and Korea is still divided.

Left: The bronze 1 chon, the basic currency unit, was introduced in 1902. Japan's growing confidence is reflected by the imperial eagle, crowned and armed with sceptre and orb, and the fact that the inscriptions were mostly in Japanese.

KOREAN EMPIRE

Korea had a copper cash currency, on Chinese lines, for many centuries from AD 996 [1–2]. In the 17th century a new series, known as *shang ping* (stabilization money), was introduced [3–4]. A second series followed around 1742. The coins were cast at numerous mints all over the country, while each of the government ministries in the capital, Seoul, also produced them. They are identifiable by marks in the form of Chinese ideograms derived from a book entitled *Thousand Character Classic* (because the text consisted of exactly 1000 characters, none of which was repeated). These coins continued until 1888 when small silver and bronze coins, from 1 to 3 chon, were introduced [5–8].

Coins struck from modern presses were adopted in 1888, based on the warn of 1000 mun. The currency was reformed in 1892, when the silver yang of 100 fun was struck [11–12]; in 1893, the hwan of 5 yang or 500 fun was introduced [9–10], but this system was superseded a decade later by the won of 100 chon. Apart from the denomination, which was in English, all inscriptions were rendered in Chinese characters, and a phoenix or dragon was depicted on the obverse. During the brief reign of the last emperor, Kuang Mu, a few gold 10 and 20 won coins were struck. Following annexation by Japan in 1910, only Japanese coins circulated until liberation in 1945.

NORTH KOREA

The Cairo Conference of 1943 had decreed that Korea should be "free and independent" and presumably a unified sovereign state, but towards the end of World War II the Soviet Union declared war on Japan and invaded Manchuria and Korea from the north in 1945. At the same time, American forces landed in the south, and later that year the Potsdam Conference decided that Korea should be partitioned at the 38th parallel.

When the Soviet authorities barred the entry of UN personnel to supervise free elections in 1948, leading to reunification, the elections went ahead in the south and as a result the Republic of Korea was formally proclaimed on August 15. Unsupervised elections took place in the north ten days later and the Democratic People's Republic, with its capital at Pyongyang, was inaugurated.

In 1950 North Korean forces rapidly overran the south. US forces held on to Pusan and this became the bridgehead for the UN counterattack. The communists were on the point of defeat when China intervened, and the conflict see-sawed back and forth until 1953, when an armistice was arranged. The two Koreas have been in a state of warlike confrontation ever since, and all attempts by the UN to revive plans for reunification have foundered.

No coins were issued in North Korea until 1959, when three aluminium pieces, denominated 1, 5 and 10 chon, were released, with the communist emblem on the obverse and value on the reverse [13–14]. The chon was reissued in 1970 and the 5 chon in 1974. These coins may be found with or without one or two stars flanking the numeral on the reverse [15–16]. A 50 chon appeared in 1987 with an emblem obverse, but the reverse depicted a Chulima rider; this coin also had a fixed date, with or without stars on the reverse. Higher values, from 1 to 10 won, in cupro-nickel, appeared from 1987, invariably commemorating Kim Il Sung, the "Comrade Great Leader". A vast number of gold and silver coins have been issued in more recent years [17–20].

Ironclad Battleship

The 50 hwan coins of 1959–61 and the bronze or brass 5 won coins of South Korea since 1966 have featured the so-called turtle boat invented by Admiral Yi Sunsin. With a fleet of these ironclad vessels he defeated the Japanese in Chinhai Bay in 1592, an action as decisive as the English defeat of the Spanish armada by Sir Francis Drake four years earlier.

A singular feature of the circulating coinage in the Democratic People's Republic from 1959 onward was the three-tier system, indicated by the presence or absence of five-pointed stars alongside the numeral of value on the reverse. Coins without stars were for general circulation among the people of the country; those with one star at the side of the numeral were issued to visitors from China and the former countries of the Soviet bloc; while those with two stars flanking the numeral were restricted to visitors from all other countries, who were compelled to exchange dollars, pounds and other "hard" currencies. As no new circulating coins have been produced since 1978 it is assumed that this system is still in force. The star system did not apply to the commemorative and special issues, which were anyway aimed very largely at the overseas market, as reflected in their thematic character.

SOUTH KOREA

The hwan of 100 chon was adopted in the south, but no coins appeared until 1959 when a series of three, from 10 to 100 hwan, had a numeral obverse and pictorial reverses showing, respectively, a rose of Sharon, a turtle warship and a bust of the first president, Syngman Rhee [21–22].

The currency was reformed in 1966 and the won (worth 10 hwan) was introduced. In this series the pictorial images occupied the obverse and the numerals the reverse [23–26], with a mixture of subjects, including the Pul Guk pagoda and the turtle warship, while the ship's inventor, Admiral Yi Sunsin, was portrayed on the silver 100 won. The permanent series has remained relatively stable since then, the only major change being the adoption of cupro-nickel in 1970 for the 100 won [27–28].

Since 1975, when the 30th anniversary of liberation was celebrated, South Korea has issued a number of silver and gold coins, though the range of subjects commemorated is much wider and less politically inspired [29–32].

JAPAN

The Empire of Japan consists of an archipelago off the north-east coast of Asia. According to legend it was founded in 660 BC by Jimmu Tenno, a descendant of the sun goddess Amaterasu. It is still believed that Japanese emperors are directly descended from him; they accede to the throne by divine right and are, effectively, living deities. For this reason, the image of the emperor remains sacred, and royal portraits never appear on coins. The sun symbol, which adorns the national flag, has appeared on some Japanese coins.

Left: The gold koban, introduced in 1601, resembled a large upright oval flat plate with a ribbed surface, on which various circular stamps were impressed . Sometimes an inscription was applied in black ink. Oban were similar pieces worth ten times as much.

ANCIENT JAPAN

The Japanese adapted Chinese coinage to their own purposes and introduced bronze cash in AD 708. From then until the middle of the 10th century coins of this type were issued with distinctive marks for each reign, but from then onward no regal issues were made at all, and the gap was filled by imitations of Chinese cash produced under the authority of the various *daimyos* (provincial nobility). During the Shogunate (1603–1867), there were many interesting and unusual coins. In 1624 the copper kwan-ei was introduced, and numerous variations appeared over the ensuing two centuries, augmented in the 19th century by the copper ei-raku and bun-kyu sen.

Unlike China, Japan made extensive use of gold and silver coinage from the 16th century onward, in the form of the large, flat oval oban and koban, oval silver chogin [1–2] or the small rectangular bu [3]. A notable oblong issue of 1765 was struck from confiscated silver ornaments.

MODERN JAPAN

When Emperor Meiji ascended the throne in 1867 he immediately dismissed Yoshinobu, the last of the shoguns, who had been the real rulers of Japan since the 17th century. Having restored imperial government he embarked on a comprehensive policy of westernization. In a single generation, this transformed Japan from a feudal backwater to an industrialized world power. One of Meiji's first reforms was the currency. Hitherto there had been no fixed ratio between gold, silver and copper, but he installed a Western-style mint at Osaka in 1869 and the following year coins based on the yen of 100 sen or 1000 rin were released. Illustrated here are the obverse and reverse of a copper pattern for the tiny 1 rin coin of 1870 [4–5].

The yen, derived from the Chinese word yuan (dollar), was originally a gold coin [6–7], but its size was reduced in 1874 and it was discontinued in 1880, as the public preferred the silver yen. Coins of this type [8–9] were minted regularly until 1914. Gold coins of 10 yen [10–11] and 20 yen [12–13] were introduced in 1871 and 1870 respectively. The former was struck until 1910, while the latter survived to 1920. The 20 yen was briefly revived in 1930–2, but coins of that period are very rare. When the 10 yen was revived in 1951 it was a small bronze coin. The tiny bronze rin was not minted after 1884, but the 5 rin or half sen continued until 1919.

Since their inception, modern Japanese coins have been dated by the regnal year of the emperor, and this has been inscribed entirely in Japanese since 1916, year 5 of the Taisho era.

Early types depicted a dragon or phoenix [16–17] as well as the chrysanthemum in a wreath [14–15] or as a central motif [18–19], but a greater degree of pictorialism crept in during World War II, with Fujiyama (1 sen), a peregrine falcon (5s) and a stylized flower (10s). The character for *dai* (great) was dropped from the country name following the defeat of Japan. New designs adopted late in 1945 were the peace dove (5s), rice (10s) [20–21], the phoenix and corn sheaf (50s) [22–23] and flowers (yen). Prior to 1948 the characters making up the country name were read from right to left, but this was reversed thereafter. A blend of symbolism and pictorialism developed in the postwar period; sometimes images that had previously been treated symbolically were rendered more realistically, as in the 50 yen of 1955–8, in which the chrysanthemum appeared as an actual flower, with leaves and stalk. Since 1955 the yen has been the smallest coin [24–25].

Postwar inflation led to higher denominations for everyday circulation. The first 100 yen piece appeared in 1957 as a silver coin but switched to cupro-nickel in 1967 [26–27]. When a 500 yen was required in 1982 it was struck in cupro-nickel from the outset. Similarly the metal used for the lower denominations was downgraded. The 10 yen, which had been a gold coin when it was last minted in 1910, was revived in 1951 as a bronze coin. The obverse featured the ancient temple of Hoo-do in an arabesque frame, and this continues to the present day. Similarly, the gold 5 yen was struck until 1912 and next emerged in 1948 as a brass coin with the parliament buildings on the reverse.

COMMEMORATIVE AND SPECIAL ISSUES

Japan did not produce commemorative coins until 1964, when silver 100 and 1000 yen publicized the Tokyo Olympic Games [28–29]; both coins had symbolic motifs, although the obverse of the 1000 yen also featured Fujiyama wreathed in cherry blossom. Coins of 100 yen marked the Osaka Expo of 1970 [30–31] and the Sapporo Winter Games of 1972 [32–33].

Thereafter the pace of special issues quickened. Since 1985 coins of 500 yen have been the preferred medium for special issues, with occasional silver (5000 yen) or gold (10,000–100,000 yen). The 500 yen coins are struck in cupro-nickel and circulate generally. They cover all kinds of current events, from the opening of Narita Airport, the Selkan Tunnel and the Seito Bridge to the Asian Games and other sporting events. Royal events have also been celebrated, from the diamond jubilee of the Emperor Hirohito (1986) to the enthronement of Akihito (1990). No portraits were used, of course, the first occasion being marked by a view of the imperial palace and the second by a picture of the state coach. The centenaries of the cabinet system (1985), parliament (1990) and the judicial system (1990) are celebrated by coins.

High Value

Japan was one of the first countries to introduce a base-metal high-value coin for general circulation. The 500 yen coin, launched in 1981, was worth about $2.50 or £1.30 at the then-current rate of exchange. The obverse depicts the paulownia flowers of the imperial *kiri-mon.*

Below: Of the current series, the brass 5 yen and cupro-nickel 50 yen have the distinction of being holed coins.

INDONESIA AND THE PHILIPPINES

Two great archipelagos extend the continent of Asia across the western Pacific. Indonesia, the world's largest island group, stretches along the Equator for more than 5000km/3000 miles, from the southernmost tip of Asia to northern Australia. The Philippines, much smaller and more compact, lie off the east coast of China. Both groups came in contact with Europeans in the 16th century, becoming colonies of Holland and Spain respectively; both were overrun by the Japanese in World War II.

Left: The silver coins of the Philippines, 1903–21, show Liberty with Mayon volcano in the background (obverse) and the emblem of the USA (reverse), symbolizing American control of the islands after the Spanish–American War of 1898.

NETHERLANDS EAST INDIES

Numerous kingdoms and sultanates spread across the East Indies and issued Islamic coins inscribed in Arabic and local languages. Shown here is a range of tiny gold coins of the 13th–17th centuries from Sallendra in Java [1]. These continued during the early period of Dutch rule, interrupted during the Napoleonic wars by the British occupation of Java and Madura (1811–16), when coins with the emblem of the British East India Company were briefly in use. The company also held Sumatra from 1685 until it was ceded to the Dutch in 1824; in that period copper kepings had the company emblem on one side and Arabic inscriptions on the other.

Coins equating the Dutch gulden with the Java rupee were supplied from Holland. They bore the crowned arms (obverse) and the VOC monogram of the Dutch East India Company or the name and date (reverse) [2–3], and supplemented a wide range of local pitis, kepings and rupees produced on various islands. During delays and shortages, makeshifts known as "bonks" were roughly cut from copper or tin rods. In 1856 the gulden of 100 cents was adopted and a new series with arms (obverse) and Arabic inscriptions (reverse) was released [4–5]. A new type of bronze cent was introduced in 1936 with Dutch, Malayan and Javanese inscriptions round a central hole and rice panicles or flowers on obverse and reverse [6–7]. After Holland was overrun by Germany, some coins were struck in 1941–5 at the US mints in Philadelphia, Denver [8–9] or San Francisco, identifiable by their mint-marks after the date.

INDONESIA

The Netherlands Indies were occupied by the Japanese in 1942–5 and used the occupiers' currency. The Japanese fostered the nationalist movement, which had begun in the 1920s. The United States of Indonesia was proclaimed in August 1945 but a four-year campaign ensued before the Dutch finally bowed out. Coins inscribed "Indonesia" were introduced in 1951–2 [10–15]. Most featured the mythical *garuda* (the national bird) although the 50 sen [16–17] portrayed Dipanegara, who led the struggle for independence against the Dutch in the 18th century.

In the 1960s inflation drove coins out of circulation. Although the currency was reformed in 1965 (100 old rupiah to one new rupiah) no coins appeared until 1970–1, by which time the rupiah was the smallest denomination. This series had different pictorial motifs (fauna [18–19], flora and landmarks [22–25]). In later years, 5 rupiah coins appeared sporadically, promoting family planning [20–21] and serving as small change, but it was not until 1991 that a general issue of coins was resumed. In this series, from 25 to 1000 rupiah, the garuda obverse was combined with pictorial reverses [26–27]. Relatively few gold and silver commemoratives, mostly celebrating anniversaries of independence, have appeared since 1970. Separate issues of coins with the bust of Achmed Sukarno on the obverse, were produced for the Riau archipelago (1963–4) and West Irian, formerly Netherlands New Guinea (1964–71). Both sets had fixed dates of 1962.

TIMOR

This island in the Lesser Sunda group was partitioned between the Netherlands (west) and Portugal (east) in 1859. West Timor was incorporated with Indonesia from 1950, but East Timor remained under Portuguese rule and had coins in the Portuguese colonial style. In 1976 it was occupied by Indonesia, triggering off a long-running war that culminated in the attainment of independence in December 1999. The Democratic Republic of East Timor was later proclaimed, and distinctive coins with pictorial motifs, based on the escudo of 100 centavos, were introduced in 2004 [28–32].

Cowboys

The reverse of the 100 rupiah of Indonesia since 1991 shows the national sport of cow-racing.

PHILIPPINES

An extensive copper and silver coinage was produced in the Philippines in the Spanish colonial period, based on the peso of 8 reales, with subdivisions of quarto and octavo real. The obverse showed a lion resting on twin hemispheres, while the crowned arms of Spain occupied the reverse. A wide range of foreign coins, with appropriate countermarks, circulated in the 19th century before the currency was reformed in 1861, and the peso of 100 centimos was adopted, with the head of the monarch (obverse) and crowned arms (reverse) [33–34].

Under American rule from 1898 the currency changed to the peso of 100 centavos, and this continued until 1967, when the names changed to piso and sentimo. The seated or standing figure of Liberty appeared on the obverse, while the reverse featured the American eagle and shield until 1935 [35–36], when the Commonwealth of the Philippines was proclaimed with a measure of autonomy. Although the shield on the reverse changed, the coins continued to bear the name of the United States of America.

Occupied by the Japanese in 1941 and liberated in 1944–5, the Philippines became an independent republic in July 1946, but coins reflecting this change did not appear until 1947 and most denominations did not appear with the republican arms until 1958. An entirely new series portraying national heroes was released in 1967 [37–38] and since then has undergone changes in metal, size and shape, with pictorial reverses replacing the original arms or seal devices in 1983. The current coins, introduced in 1995, have the value on the obverse and arms on the reverse.

In 1903 the Commission of Public Health established a leper colony on the remote island of Culion. Special coins, from half centavo to 1 peso, were struck by Frank & Company with the caduceus emblem on the reverse. In 1927 a new series portrayed José Rizal with the national arms on the reverse.

MALAYSIA AND SINGAPORE

The countries in this group were all formerly under British rule and have maintained close ties through membership of the Commonwealth since they attained independence in the 1960s. They formed part of the great Javanese empire of Majapahit and converted to Islam in the 14th century. From the 15th century onward the coins of the numerous petty states generally conformed to Islamic standards. Johor struck octagonal gold kupangs with Islamic inscriptions [1–2], but for small change Chinese-style cash, such as the tin jokoh of Perak [3], or the silver tanga, such as this example from Melaka of 1631 [4–5], were preferred. The Portuguese and Dutch penetrated the region in the 16th and 17th centuries, followed by the British East India Company, which acquired the strategically important island of Penang off the coast of Kedah in 1786.

Left: The tenth anniversary of the Republic of Singapore was celebrated by the silver $10 of 1975, with a pictorial reverse emphasizing its importance as one of the world's largest commercial ports.

STRAITS SETTLEMENTS

This British crown colony was formed in 1825 by combining the trading posts at Penang – shown here are copper pattern cents of 1788–1810 [6–9] and a quarter-dollar of 1788 [10–11] – and Melaka with Singapore, the settlement founded by Stamford Raffles in 1819. Coins bearing the name of the East India Company but denominated in the local currency, based on the dollar of 100 cents, appeared in 1845 with the profile of Victoria (obverse) and wreathed value (reverse) [12–13]. The name was changed in 1862 to "India Straits", then to "Straits Settlements" in coins from 1872 to 1935 [14–15].

BRITISH NORTH BORNEO

This territory was administered by a chartered company until it was overrun by the Japanese in 1942 and declared a crown colony in 1946. It changed its name to Sabah on joining the Federation of Malaysia in 1964. Coins bearing the company arms were struck by the Heaton mint from 1882 until 1941 [16–17].

SARAWAK

The land of the white rajahs came into being in 1840, when the Sultan of Brunei granted territory on the island of Borneo to James Brooke, a British adventurer who had quelled a rebellion on the sultan's behalf, and whose initials appear on this copper keping [18–19]. In 1888 the state of Sarawak was placed under British protection. It was occupied by the Japanese in 1942 and ceded to the British Crown in 1946 by Sir Charles Vyner Brooke, who is portrayed on the silver 20 cents of 1910 [20–21]. It joined Malaysia in 1963. Sarawak issued its own coins from 1841 to 1941, with the profile of the rajah (obverse) and a wreathed or encircled value (reverse).

MALAYA

The Currency Board of Malaya was established shortly before World War II and uniform coinage for use in the Straits Settlements and the Malay States was introduced in 1939, with the crowned profile of George VI (obverse) and the value (reverse) [22–23].

Although it was interrupted by the war, this coinage was resumed in 1945 and continued until 1956, though no coins were dated after 1950. A new series, with the crowned bust of Elizabeth II, circulated from 1954 to 1961 and was inscribed "Malaya and British Borneo" on the reverse [24–25].

MALAYSIA

The Malayan Federation was formed in February 1948 by Melaka and Penang with the nine Malay states. It became an independent member of the Commonwealth in 1957 and used coins of Malaya and British Borneo.

In September 1963 the Malayan Federation joined with North Borneo (Sabah), Sarawak and Singapore to form the Federation of Malaysia. Coins inscribed "Malaysia", in currency based on the ringgit of 100 sen, were introduced in 1967, when the Currency Board was dissolved. The standard obverse featured the parliament building in Kuala Lumpur and the crescent and star emblem, while the reverse bore the value [26–29]. A new series, with a floral obverse and indigenous artefacts on the reverse, was introduced in 1989 [30–31]. Commemorative coins have appeared since 1969.

SINGAPORE

This island at the tip of the Malay Peninsula became a separate crown colony in 1946. It joined Malaysia in 1963 but seceded in August 1965 to become an independent republic.

Singapore continued to use the coins of Malaya until 1967, when a distinctive series based on the dollar of 100 cents was adopted. This followed the same pattern as the coinage of Malaysia, with the value on the reverse, but from the outset had different pictorial motifs on each obverse: birds and fishes on the middle values, with a fountain and high-rise apartment block (1 cent) [32] and Singapore's trademark mythical beast, the Merlion ($1). Armorial types with flora and fauna on the reverse have been used since 1985 [33–34]. Commemoratives have appeared since 1973, and there have been annual issues for the Chinese Lunar New Year since 1991.

South-east Asia's Own Olympics

Coins with seven interlocking rings have marked the four-yearly South-east Asia and Pacific Games, involving Malaysia, Singapore, Indonesia and the Philippines.

BRUNEI

This sultanate arose in the 16th century and eventually ruled most of Borneo and even parts of the Philippines but declined in the early 19th century. It was eventually confined to a small area near the mouth of the Brunei River. Its fortunes recovered after World War II thanks to the discovery of oil in the region; it is now one of the world's wealthiest countries.

Cash or pitis of lead or tin appeared briefly about 1700, but it was not until 1868 that tin coins were re-introduced, with the state umbrella (obverse) and text in Jawi script (reverse). Western-style bronze coins, struck by Heaton of Birmingham, appeared in 1887, before Brunei adopted the currency of the Straits Settlements and later of Malaya. On the dissolution of the Currency Board distinctive coins were resumed, portraying Sultan Hassanal Bolkiah (obverse) [35] with ornamental motifs (reverse) [36–38]. New portraits were adopted in 1977 and 1993.

Gold and silver commemoratives have appeared since 1977, with various portraits of Sultan Hassanal on the obverse, mainly celebrating royal events or national anniversaries.

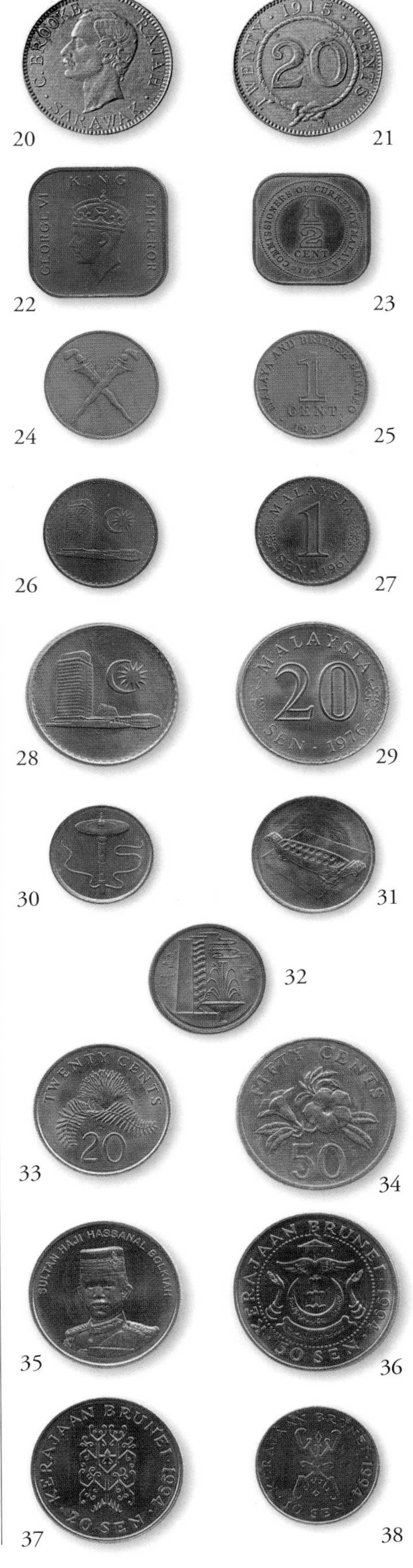

THAILAND

The ancient kingdom, known to its inhabitants as Muang Thai ("land of the free"), was the only country in South-east Asia never to fall under the control of a European power. Malay, Mon and Khmer kingdoms prospered in the region before the arrival of the Thai people, who began their migration from southern China and Laos during the 6th century. The emergence of a Thai-dominated nation began with the rise of the Sukhothai kingdom in the mid-13th century, under which distinctive bullet-shaped coins first emerged. In 1782 Rama I moved the capital to Bangkok and founded the dynasty that endures to this day. The Dutch, French and latterly the British played a part in the westernization of the country.

Left: The 10 baht coin of 1987, celebrating the anniversary of the Asian Institute of Technology, shows King Rama IX himself lecturing to students. It is one of many recent coins to show the hands-on approach of the royal family in everyday life.

SIAM

Silver and tin units were circulated in antiquity by the Indochinese kingdom of Funan [1–2], and later by the Mon people of Dvaravati [3–4]. In the north-east, the Kingdom of Langchang used bar-shaped coins of varying lengths, known as "leech money" [5] or "tiger tongue money", throughout the 16th and 17th centuries. More widely, gold and silver bullet-shaped coins developed from the original "bent rings" and endured as currency until the end of the 19th century [6–7]. The pieces had a standard weight based on the baht (15.4g/½oz), which was used as a unit of weight until the 1930s.

Bullet money was gradually superseded by western-style coinage from 1859 [8–9], the year in which Queen Victoria sent Rama IV a coining press as a gift. From then until 1937, coins were minted in a range of denominations, based on the baht on par with the tical and tamlung and worth 4 salung, 8 fuang, 16 sik, 32 pai, 64 att [12–13] or 1280 solot, while 20 baht equalled a chang.

From the outset these coins combined symbolism with images of Buddhist shrines and temples. In 1887 a series with the bust of Rama V (Chulalongkorn) was adopted [10–11], while the reverse of the lower values depicted a heavenly nymph, seated with a shield and spear, looking suspiciously like Britannia on British coins [14]. Buddhist symbolism continued on the higher values. The currency was reformed in 1908 and reduced to the baht of 4 salung or 100 satang, but similar types continued. Coins of this period were struck in many different metals, including tin, bronze, brass and cupro-nickel as well as silver and gold.

THAILAND

The new name was officially adopted in place of Siam by royal decree of June 1939. To this period belongs the bronze holed satang [15–16] followed by tiny tin or aluminium coins [17]. In September 1945 the country reverted to the older name but since May 1949 has been known as Thailand. Coinage continued to be inscribed solely in Thai characters until 1945, when western numerals were briefly used to denote value and date (in the Thai calendar). Most coins, however, have continued to be inscribed solely in the indigenous script. Definitive coins bear the effigy of the reigning sovereign. Rama IX (Bhumifhol Adulyadej) ascended the throne in 1946 as a teenager and many different portraits of him have been used. Sometimes the differences are very subtle, such as the effigies with one or three medals on the king's chest, or the portraits of the 1980s with or without a space between the collar and the lower hairline. The present series, from the tiny aluminium satang [17] to the bimetallic 10 baht, was introduced in 1987. It has the king's portrait on one side and symbolism, royal insignia or temples on the reverse [18–22].

COMMEMORATIVE AND SPECIAL ISSUES

An extraordinary feature of modern Thai coinage is the wide range of commemorative and special issues, the vast majority of which are produced in base metal for general circulation and add considerable interest to the everyday currency. They have been produced in denominations of 1, 2, 5, 10 and 20 baht in cupro-nickel. Although many have the portrait of Rama IX on the obverse this is by no means standard. In many cases, conjoined busts of the king and Queen Sirikit have been used, facing left or right [27–28]. Other coins have devoted the obverse to the Princess Mother [30] and the various princes and princesses of the blood royal. In effect, Thai coins are the nearest thing today to the portrait gallery of the Roman emperors. The coins that portray the junior members of the royal family are invariably intended to celebrate events in their lives, from the investiture of Prince Vajiralongkorn as crown prince (1972) [29] to royal birthdays and weddings. These are as assiduously chronicled in coins as the anniversaries of the king's reign. In some cases the formal portrait gives way to a more pictorial treatment. Thus the Food and Agriculture Organization coin of 1977 showed the king instructing a farmer, while coins of 1991, celebrating the award of a Magsaysay (Philippines) scholarship to Princess Sirindhorn showed her working with children (obverse) and the decorative scroll of the award (reverse).

When it comes to the centenaries of national institutions, an appropriate pictorial motif appears on the reverse, but conjoined busts or facing portraits side by side of Rama IX and one of his ancestors are commonly featured on the obverse. Triple portraits have been used in coins marking the centenary of the Thai Red Cross (1993) and the 72nd anniversary of Chulalongkorn University (1989). The reverses of these coins tend to be symbolic in character [23–26] – again the parallel with the allegories of the Roman Empire is close. A more pictorial approach has been used in coins publicizing wildlife conservation [31].

Graduation Coins

When Princess Sirindhorn and her sister Chulabhorn graduated from university, their success was celebrated by sets of three coins in 1977 and 1979, with their portraits on the obverse, and appropriate symbolism on the reverse.

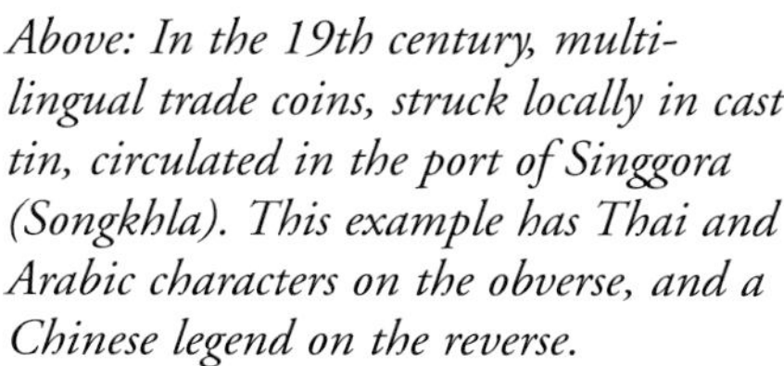

Above: In the 19th century, multilingual trade coins, struck locally in cast tin, circulated in the port of Singgora (Songkhla). This example has Thai and Arabic characters on the obverse, and a Chinese legend on the reverse.

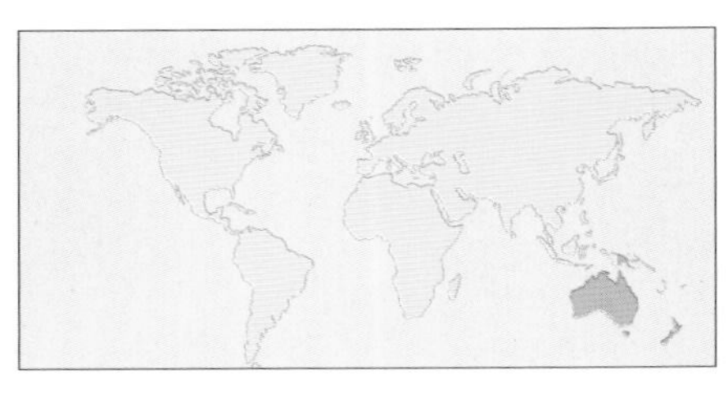

AUSTRALASIA AND OCEANIA

This vast area in the Pacific Ocean includes Australia, the world's smallest continent, together with New Zealand and a number of archipelagos scattered over the eastern and southern Pacific. The area was first traversed by Europeans in 1521 but was not properly surveyed until the 18th century, largely as a result of the three voyages of the British explorer and navigator Captain James Cook. All the territories have been subject to European colonization, primarily of British and French origin.

AUSTRALIA

Although Chinese, Spanish and Portuguese navigators sighted the great southern land it was not until 1770 that its east coast was properly surveyed by James Cook, who named it New South Wales because of an imagined similarity to that part of Britain. The first permanent settlement took place in 1788 when the penal colony at Port Jackson was founded. The six Australian states of New South Wales, Van Diemen's Land or Tasmania, Western Australia, South Australia, Victoria and Queensland were settled as colonies during the period 1823–59. They joined together in 1901 to form the Commonwealth of Australia. The country is a member of the Commonwealth, with Elizabeth II as head of state.

Left: A polygonal 50 cent coin was issued in 1970 to celebrate the bicentenary of Captain Cook's first voyage to the Pacific, during which he charted the east coast of Australia.

PRE-DECIMAL COINAGE

With a few exceptions, the Australian colonies used the coins of the mother country, and this continued for several years after the Commonwealth of Australia was formed. The silver threepence, sixpence, shilling and florin (2 shillings) were introduced in 1910 and bore the right-facing crowned bust of Edward VII, who died that year, with the Commonwealth arms on the reverse. The left-facing bust of George V was substituted the following year, when the bronze halfpenny and penny were added to the series [1–4]. These coins had a prosaic reverse with the value in words across the middle.

A new series appeared in 1938 with the bare-headed profile of George VI and pictorial images on the reverse. A kangaroo appeared on the bronze coins [5–6], while the silver featured ears of wheat (threepence) [7] or a merino ram (shilling), but the sixpence retained a modified version of the arms and the florin [8] had a more elaborate crowned version of the arms. These reverse motifs were retained for the series of 1953–64, with the profile of Elizabeth II on the obverse [9]. A crown (5 shillings) with a Tudor crown on the reverse was restricted to 1937–8. The florin was the medium for coins celebrating the jubilee of federation (1951) and the Queen's visit (1954) [10].

GOLD COINS

The only regular coinage produced in the 19th century consisted of gold sovereigns and half sovereigns [11–14]. Following the discovery of gold in South Australia, pound coins with a crown (obverse) and value with the weight and fineness around the circumference (reverse) were minted at the Government Assay Office in Adelaide in 1852 [15–16]. Three years later a branch of the Royal Mint opened at Sydney and began coining sovereigns and half sovereigns with the profile of Queen Victoria (obverse) and a crown over "Australia" within a wreath (reverse) – the first coins to bear the name of the continent.

Australian coins continued until 1870 [17–18] but thereafter Sydney struck gold coins conforming to the prevailing British designs [19–20], distinguishable by the S mint-mark alongside the date. Branch mints were later opened at Melbourne (1872) [21–22] and Perth (1899). Production of gold sovereigns ceased in 1931.

DECIMAL COINAGE

Australia switched to the dollar of 100 cents in 1966. The bust of Elizabeth II by Arnold Machin appeared on the obverse [23], while reverses up to 20 cents featured examples of Australia's unique wildlife [24]. The circular silver 50 cents bore an elaborate version of the arms; when it next appeared, in 1969, the coin was struck in cupro-nickel with a polygonal shape. The series was re-issued in 1985 bearing the Maklouf profile [25] and in 1999 with the Rank-Broadley obverse [26]. The 1 and 2 cent coins were discontinued in 1991 and aluminium-bronze coins denominated $1 (1984) [27] and $2 (1988) [28] replaced banknotes.

Bimetallic $5 coins also appeared in 1988 but this denomination has since been largely employed as a commemorative. Australia has produced a vast range of commemoratives and special issues [29–31] in recent years, many in thematic series, in silver, gold and platinum and including, recently, coins with coloured surfaces.

KEELING COCOS ISLANDS

Ordinary Australian coins circulate in the overseas dependencies of Christmas Island and Norfolk Island. In the Keeling Cocos Islands, however, a distinctive series was issued in 1977, based on the rupee of 100 cents. It bears the bust of John Clunies-Ross (obverse), the self-proclaimed king of the islands in the 19th century, and a palm tree (reverse). Previously, various plastic and ivory tokens for use by workers in the coconut plantations were produced in 1910–13 and 1968 [32].

Holey Dollar and Dump

The first distinctive coinage in Australia, authorized in 1813 by Governor Lachlan Macquarie, consisted of Spanish silver dollars with their centres cut out and tariffed at 15 pence, while the outer rings were circulated at 4s 9d. The work of cutting the coins and stamping them to denote their new value was entrusted to William Henshall, a convicted forger. In 1988, Australia issued a pair of legal tender silver coins, consisting of a 25g/1oz holey dollar and a 25 cent dump, as part of the celebrations marking the bicentenary of the first colony.

17 18 19 20 21 22 23 24 25 26 27 28 29 30 31 32

AUSTRALIA'S COMMERCE AND INDUSTRY

Australia is not much smaller than the United States of America, yet the ratio of population is 14.3 to 1. Most Australians live within a few miles of the coast and vast regions of the interior are either sparsely populated or uninhabitable. When the first British settlement was established at Botany Bay in 1788 the indigenous population of the continent has been estimated at about 60,000 Aborigines, nomadic tribes which had lived there for thousands of years. Although Australia had been discovered by the Chinese in the 15th century and sighted by the Portuguese a century later, colonization was hampered by its remoteness from the civilized world.

WOOL

Captain Cook explored and charted the east coast of Australia in the course of three voyages between 1770 and 1777, but it was only in 1788, after the loss of the American colonies, that Britain took serious notice of the great southern land – and then only as a dumping ground for convicts. Its very isolation was originally regarded as its chief asset.

Below: 200 escudo coin from Portugal, 1995 highlighting the Portuguese exploration of Australia in 1522–5.

Above: 50 cents portraying explorers George Bass and Matthew Flinders and the shilling showing a Merino ram.

Attempts to penetrate the hinterland were baulked by the Blue Mountains and it was not till 1813 that Wentworth, Blaxland and Lawson (on a $5 of 1993) found a way through. They were rewarded by the sight of vast grasslands. As a result, pastoralism became Australia's first major industry, favoured by the flatness of the terrain. Vast areas of desert or semi-arid land, however, meant that the population density might be reduced to one or two sheep per square mile. Nevertheless, the number of sheep exceeded 100 million by the end of the 19th century. By 1940 there were 123 million – the largest sheep population anywhere in the world. By that time Australia possessed a quarter of the world's sheep resources (meat and wool). About 80 per cent of the wool exported is Merino, a fine wool highly favoured in the textile industry. A Merino ram appeared on the shillings of 1938-63 symbolizing an industry that generated a revenue of £55,000,000 a year in the 1930s, compared with about £20,000,000 for cattle and dairy products. Elizabeth MacArthur who introduced the breed, is portrayed on a $5 coin of 1995 with a flock of sheep in the background. Although these animals were bred primarily for their wool, the export of meat rose sharply after the introduction of refrigeration in the mid-19th century. Today, the lean meat of sheep bred in the Outback is particularly favoured in Islamic countries from Indonesia to Arabia. The great

Above: $10 of 2002 marking the 150th anniversary of the Adelaide pound.

Below: The original Adelaide pound of 1852, minted from locally mined gold.

importance of wool to the Australian economy is reflected in the 50c of 1991 issued to mark the 25th anniversary of decimal currency; the Merino ram was the motif on the reverse.

GOLD

The population of the Australian colonies remained small till the 1850s. In 1851 gold was discovered in Victoria more or less simultaneously at Bathurst and Anderson's Creek near Melbourne, shortly followed by the vast deposits at Ballarat. This triggered off a gold rush and by early 1852 prospectors from Europe, America and China were pouring through Melbourne at the rate of 2,000 a week. Though gold was the

Above (clockwise from top-left): George V sovereigns of 1921–6 with mintmarks above the dates: the Melbourne 'M', the Sydney 'S' and the Perth 'P' with obverse.

Below: Dollar celebrating the 130th anniversary of the Melbourne Mint, its gateway flanked by the two sovereigns.

most important metal in terms of value, copper, silver, lead, tin and later tungsten were also discovered, creating the core of Australia's wealth and greatly stimulating its population growth. The gold rush era is featured on a $5 coin of 1995.

This had a direct bearing on the money in circulation. Australia relied on British coins but it seemed logical to refine and coin gold in Australia itself rather than ship the raw metal back to England. In 1852, a mint which struck gold pounds was established in Adelaide. The obverse featured a crown while the reverse bore the value surrounded by the weight and fineness of the metal. A mint opened at Sydney in 1853 and struck gold sovereigns from 1855 onwards, with a profile of Queen Victoria on the obverse and a crown over AUSTRALIA on the reverse. These distinctive coins continued till 1870 when the Sydney Mint was redesignated as a branch of the Royal Mint in London. Thereafter, it struck British gold sovereigns, distinguishable solely by the initial letter S alongside the date on the reverse.

Another branch mint was opened at Melbourne in 1872 and struck sovereigns with the letter M. Finally a mint at Perth in Western Australia began striking sovereigns in 1899. The Sydney mint closed in 1926 and is now a museum. Although the production of gold sovereigns ceased in 1931 the Melbourne and Perth mints continue to this day, the former striking circulating and commemorative coins, while the latter concentrates mainly on bullion pieces such as the Kookaburra (silver), Nugget (gold) and Koala (platinum) series. In recent years, the use of mint marks has been revived, the letters C (Canberra), M (Melbourne) and S (Sydney) being found on some coins from 1993 onwards. And gold even accelerated the path of democracy; the miners' rebellion at the Eureka Stockade in 1854 (on a coin of 2004) marked the advent of workers' rights.

Above: The reverses of coins marking the 150th anniversary of the Eureka stockade (left) and Cobb & Co mail-coach.

Below: Reverses of centennial coins marking the Darwin-Adelaide Railway.

COMMUNICATIONS

Up to the 1850s, communication between the six colonies of Australia was by coastal shipping, but the gold rush of 1851-2 stimulated attempts to provide overland communications. In 1853, Freeman Cobb and three fellow Americans established the American Telegraph Coach Line, soon changed to Cobb & Co, and secured a Royal Mail contract to carry mail and passengers between Bathurst and Bourke. The network of mail-coaches spread rapidly across the continent, and the company enjoyed a high reputation for reliability. To this day Australians use the word 'cobber' to mean a good friend. A silver $5 coin was belatedly issued in 1995 to celebrate the 150th anniversary of the company and features a mail-coach on the reverse. The first railway opened in 1854, but today the major routes include the Indian-Pacific, from Perth to Sydney, and the 'Ghan', from Adelaide to Darwin, so-called because Afghan camel-drivers ran the supply route while the line was under construction. Coins of 2004 celebrated the 150th anniversary of the railway system, while subsequent commemoratives have marked the opening of air routes, including the Queensland and Northern Territory Air Service – better known today by its acronym QANTAS – and internal air services, including the Royal Flying Doctors (on coins of 1998).

NEW ZEALAND

The Dominion of New Zealand is a member of the Commonwealth and has Elizabeth II as its head of state. It consists of two large islands and has an area rather larger than that of the United Kingdom but with only a twentieth of the population. Its economy is based on agriculture, with wool, meat and dairy products accounting for the bulk of its exports.

Left: In 1977, New Zealand celebrated the Queen's Silver Jubilee with a silver dollar showing the house at Waitangi where the treaty of cession was signed in 1840, echoing the Silver Jubilee crown of 1935, whose reverse had depicted the signing ceremony.

The Maori who migrated from Hawaii between the 10th and 14th centuries called the islands Aotearoa, "the land of the long white cloud". Abel Jan Tasman was the first European to sight the land and named it after the Dutch province of Zealand. Its coast was surveyed in detail in 1769 by James Cook, who annexed it to Britain. This rash act was ignored by the home government and for more than half a century New Zealand was visited only by whalers and sealers. By 1814, missionaries were establishing posts around the Bay of Islands and adventurers came in search of gold. In 1840, Captain William Hobson signed the Treaty of Waitangi with Maori chiefs and New Zealand was annexed as a dependency of New South Wales. A silver crown issued in 1935 for the silver jubilee of George V pictured the meeting of Hobson and the Maori chief, Waka Nene.

New Zealand was detached from New South Wales in 1852 and granted self-government. In the 1860s the population rose sharply following the discovery of gold, but continuing wrangles over land resulted in the Maori Wars of 1861–71. In the 1890s, New Zealand declined to join the Australian colonies in federation and became a separate dominion.

EARLY COINAGE

Remarkably, New Zealand used British coinage well into the 20th century. Periodic shortages of coins were met by the traditional expedient of tradesmen's tokens, which began in 1857 and amounted to about 150 different types by 1881 when they were discontinued, although they continued to circulate until 1897. Later, Australian coins circulated alongside British ones.

New Zealand introduced distinctive silver coins in 1933, with the crowned bust of George V [1] on the obverse and various pictorial motifs on the reverse: Maori clubs (threepence) [3], the extinct *huia* bird (sixpence) [4], a Maori warrior (shilling) [2], a kiwi (florin) [5] and arms (half crown). Bronze coins did not appear until 1940, when the halfpenny featured a *tiki* or Maori idol [7] and the penny a *tui* bird [8]. These reverse types continued in later issues, with the profiles of George VI (1937–51) [6] and Elizabeth II (1953–64). Beside the centennial florin of 1940, silver crowns were issued on three occasions, for the silver jubilee (1935), the royal visit (1949) and the coronation (1953) [9]. To mark the centennial (1940) a half crown was issued [12], and half crowns were also issued in 1962 [10–11].

DECIMAL COINAGE

New Zealand adopted the dollar of 100 cents in 1967, with coins in bronze (1 and 2 cents) or cupro-nickel (5 cents to $1). The Machin bust of the Queen appeared on the obverse, while the reverse motifs were a stylized fern leaf (1 cent) [13], kowhai blossom (2 cents)

Non-Event

In 1949 a crown featuring a silver fern leaf and the Southern Cross was struck at the Royal Mint and shipped to New Zealand to celebrate the visit of George VI. The trip was cancelled on account of the king's illness, but the coins were issued anyway. When Queen Elizabeth and the Duke of Edinburgh visited New Zealand five years later no coins were issued to mark the occasion.

[14], tuatara (5 cents) [16], Maori *koruru* or carved head (10 cents) [15], kiwi (20 cents) [17], Captain Cook's brig *Endeavour* with Mount Egmont (Taranaki) (50 cents) [18] and the national arms crowned and flanked by fern leaves [19]. The 50 cent coin was re-issued in 1969 with an edge inscription to celebrate Cook's bicentenary.

Apart from the 1 and 2 cents (discontinued in 1988), the basic series has continued to this day, with the more mature effigies of the Queen by Maklouf (1986) [20] and Rank-Broadley (since 1999). In 1990 the large cupro-nickel dollar was replaced by a smaller aluminium-bronze coin featuring a kiwi [24]; at the same time a circulating $2 in the same alloy depicted a great egret [21] while the 20 cents now showed a tiki flanked by Maori curvilinear panels [23].

COMMEMORATIVE COINS

To mark the 150th anniversary of annexation in 1990 the circulating coins were temporarily replaced by issues showing a stylized bird (5 cents), a Maori sailing canoe (10 cents), Cook's ship (20 cents) and tree-planting (50 cents); the dollar showed the signing of the Treaty of Waitangi.

Large dollars in cupro-nickel or silver were produced extensively from 1969 to commemorate historic anniversaries and events, including royal visits in 1970, 1983 and 1986, while royal birthdays, jubilees and wedding anniversaries [22] have also been assiduously celebrated. New Zealand hosted the Commonwealth Games in 1974 and 1989, issuing a single coin the first time and a set of four the second time. In more recent years coins have marked the Rugby World Cup and the Olympic Games. A series of 1992, ostensibly honouring Columbus, included coins in tribute to Kupe, the mythological leader of the Maori migration to New Zealand, as well as Tasman and Cook. A $5 coin of 1990 paid tribute to the Anzac forces of World War I, while a $20 of 1995 saluted the bravery of Charles Upham, the New Zealand double winner of the Victoria Cross.

New Zealand does not possess its own mint and has therefore relied mainly on the British Royal Mint for its coins, but this has given rise to some curious errors. In 1967 a consignment of bronze 2 cents was struck with the obverse of the Bahamas 5 cents instead. In 1985 a supply of cupro-nickel 50 cent coins was found to have the Canadian dollar reverse showing a Voyageur canoe. While examples of the Bahamas error are quite common, only nine of the Canadian hybrid coins have so far been recorded.

Above: A dollar depicting Mount Cook, known to the Maori as Aorangi, was issued to celebrate the 1970 royal visit.

NEW ZEALAND DEPENDENCIES

Several countries in the South Pacific are dependencies of New Zealand. Coins of the latter originally circulated in these territories – and still do, in the case of Niue – but in more recent years, indigenous coinages have developed, and these are inscribed with the names of the islands and relevant pictorial reverses.

Left: The British oarsmen and gold medallists Sir Matthew Pinsent and Sir Steve Redgrave are portrayed on the reverse of the $50 coin issued by Niue to mark the 1992 Olympic Games. Steve Redgrave holds the record as Britain's greatest Olympian, winning gold medals at five consecutive Olympic Games from 1984 to 2000.

COOK ISLANDS

This archipelago of 15 islands some 3000km/2000 miles north-east of New Zealand is named in honour of James Cook, although the Spaniard Alvaro de Mendaña was probably the first European to sight it, in 1595, while the Portuguese Fernandes de Quieros landed there in 1606. Cook visited the islands in 1773, 1774 and 1777 and named them the Hervey Islands, after one of the lords of the Admiralty.

The Cook Islands had their own monarchical system, but in 1888 Queen Makea Takau sought British protection. They were annexed by New Zealand in 1901 but were granted internal autonomy in 1965, though New Zealand continues to be responsible for defence and external affairs. The islands used New Zealand coins exclusively until 1972, when a series bearing the Machin bust of Elizabeth II [1, 3, 5] was introduced. These coins followed the weights, alloys and specifications of their New Zealand counterparts, with pictorial reverses featuring a taro leaf (1 cent), pineapple (2 cents), hibiscus (5 cents) [2], orange (10 cents) [4], fairy tern (20 cents) [7], bonito fish (50 cents) [6] and Tangaroa, the Polynesian god of creation ($1) [8]. The reverse of the 20 cents changed in 1972 to depict a Pacific triton shell. The series was re-issued in 1978 with an edge inscription marking the 250th anniversary of the birth of Captain Cook, and the same device was repeated in 1981 to celebrate the wedding of Prince Charles and Lady Diana Spencer. In 1987 the Maklouf profile was substituted, the size of the dollar reduced and a scalloped shape adopted on the dollar, while a $2 coin depicting an island table and a $5 showing a conch shell [9] were introduced.

Numerous commemorative or special issues have appeared since 1986 [10–11], notably the series of 16 (1996) featuring world wildlife and the multicoloured coins depicting the cartoon character Garfield (1999).

Above: Dollar issued by New Zealand in 1970 to mark the bicentenary of the discovery of the Cook Islands.

NIUE

Discovered by Cook in 1774 and originally named Savage Island, Niue was originally administered as part of the

Cook Islands but has been a separate dependency of New Zealand since 1922. New Zealand coins are still in general circulation and Niue must be unique among the nations of the world in not having introduced a base-metal circulating coinage of its own. This defect, however, has been more than remedied since 1987 by the release of a considerable number of commemorative or special coins in denominations from $1 to $250, in cupro-nickel, silver or gold. The overwhelming majority are from $5 upwards and in fact it was not until 1996 that Niue got around to issuing a $1 coin, with a reverse depicting HMS *Bounty*, scene of one of the most famous mutinies in the history of the Royal Navy.

While some coins have the Maklouf profile of Elizabeth II on the obverse, the majority bear the crowned arms of New Zealand instead [12]. The first coins were of $5 denomination and portrayed the tennis stars Boris Becker [13] and Steffi Graf. This set the tone for subsequent issues; tennis is a sport that has been rather neglected on the coins of other countries, but from Niue have come coins honouring Martina Navratilova and Chris Evert as well as Steffi Graf (1988), the final between Germany and Sweden in the Davis Cup (1989) and a further issue devoted to Steffi Graf (including silver $50 and $100 as well as $250 gold coins) in the same year. After that, Niue looked elsewhere and, discovering that soccer was a lucrative theme, issued coins portraying such football stars as Franz Beckenbauer and even the entire Italian squad (1990). Themes of other series range from endangered wildlife to war heroes such as Douglas MacArthur and Admiral William Halsey, and Cook's voyages of discovery vie with the Soviet Union's Luna 9 moon landing.

First Rounded Triangle

To the Cook Islands goes the credit for producing the world's first triangular coin with rounded edges, the $2 of 1987–94: both circulating and proof versions were minted in each year.

TOKELAU ISLANDS

About 3000km/2000 miles north of New Zealand lie the Union or Tokelau Islands – Atafu, Nukunono and Fakaofo – whose inhabitants are Polynesian by race and Samoan in language and culture. These remote atolls were acquired by Britain in 1889 and bandied about for many years, at times administered as part of the Gilbert and Ellice Islands Protectorate and then, from 1926 to 1948, attached to Western Samoa. Since then they have been a New Zealand dependency.

In 1978 a cupro-nickel dollar was issued, merely inscribed "Tokelau" with the date round the top, over the Machin bust of Elizabeth II (with neither her name nor titles) [14]. What appeared to be Morse code running round the rim were patterns of three dots representing the three atolls. The reverse depicted a breadfruit with the value in Samoan ("Tahi Tala") [15]. An edge inscription proclaimed "Tokelau's First Coin". This established the pattern for subsequent coins, from $1 [16–17] to $100, and though the Maklouf profile was adopted in 1989 the Queen's name remains conspicuously absent. The reverses depict aspects of island life, although a series of 1991 featured salient events in the Pacific War, from the attack on Pearl Harbor to the raising of the Stars and Stripes on Iwo Jima.

10

11

12

13

14 15

16 17

PNG, NAURU AND VANUATU

Apart from Nauru (formerly Ocean Island), these countries lie to the north of Australia. They include Vanuatu, formerly the New Hebrides, which was administered by France and Britain as a condominium, and the eastern part of New Guinea (the world's largest island after Greenland), which was formerly partitioned between Germany and Britain. The western portion of New Guinea was once part of the Dutch East Indies and is now Irian Barat, part of Indonesia.

Left: The toea, *or Emperor of Germany bird of paradise, is not only featured on coins of Papua New Guinea but has lent its name to the unit of currency.*

GERMAN NEW GUINEA

The southern portion of east New Guinea was annexed by Queensland in 1883. A year later Germany annexed the northern part, which became Kaiser Wilhelmsland. British and German coinage circulated in the respective territories, but in 1894–5 a distinctive series for use in Kaiser Wilhelmsland was produced by the New Guinea Company, whose German name appeared on the obverse of the bronze 1 and 2 pfennig coins, with the value on the reverse. The higher values, comprising the bronze 10 pfennig, silver half, 1, 2 and 5 marks and the gold 10 and 20 marks, had an obverse showing the *toea* (the national bird), with a wreathed value on the reverse [1–5]. Shortly after the outbreak of war in August 1914 German New Guinea was invaded and occupied by Australian forces. In 1920 Australia was granted a mandate by the League of Nations and ordinary Australian coins were adopted.

BRITISH NEW GUINEA

The administration of the southern portion, known as British New Guinea or Papua, passed from Queensland to the British Crown in 1888, but was transferred to the Commonwealth of Australia in 1901. It became a self-governing territory in 1906. British or Australian coins were used until 1929, when cupro-nickel halfpennies and pennies were introduced as small change, followed by the cupro-nickel threepence and sixpence, and the silver shilling, in 1935. A singular feature of the coinage was that all five denominations had a central hole [6–7]. The obverse bore a Tudor crown flanked by two maces on the two lowest values and the shilling, while the others featured the crown and royal monogram flanked by the date. The reverses had the name of the territory, value and date, with cruciform or geometric patterns in the middle.

A bronze penny was adopted in 1936 with the monogram of Edward VIII, and was one of the few distinctive colonial coins of his short reign [8–9]. New pennies with the "GRI" monogram appeared in 1938 and 1944, with sporadic issues of higher values up to 1945 [10–11].

PAPUA NEW GUINEA

The Japanese invaded New Guinea in 1942 and a ferocious campaign ensued before Commonwealth forces regained control. A mandate from the United Nations was granted in 1946 and in 1949 Papua and New Guinea were united. In 1973 the territory was granted self-government, and full independence as a member of the Commonwealth was achieved in 1975.

Coinage was introduced that year, based on the kina of 100 toeas, the eponymous bird of paradise appearing on the standard obverse, with other examples of fauna on the reverse [12–13]. Simultaneously a gold 100 kina portrayed the prime minister, Michael Somare. Coins from 1 to 20 toeas have been issued in the same designs ever since [14–19].

A few heptagonal 50 toeas appeared in the 1980s, solely as commemoratives, but the crown-sized 5 and 10 kina are the preferred medium, together with gold 100 kina. The relatively few special issues have included coins for the visit of Pope John Paul II (1984) and the Commonwealth Games (1991). An enormous 25 kina in enamelled silver appeared in 1994 to mark the centenary of the first coinage.

Heptagonal Coins

In 1980 Papua New Guinea introduced a 50 toea denomination and adopted the seven-sided format pioneered by Britain. It has so far been confined to coins commemorating the South Pacific Festival of Arts (1980) and the Ninth South Pacific Games (1991).

NAURU

One of the world's smallest and most isolated countries, the Republic of Nauru has an area of just 21sq km/8sq miles and a population of 13,000. It has the curious distinction of being the only country in the world without a capital. Composed largely of phosphate deposits, now exhausted, Nauru could eventually disappear as the island succumbs to rising ocean levels resulting from global warming. Some of the phosphate revenue was invested in Australian real estate, notably Nauru House, one of the highest buildings in Melbourne, but having enjoyed the highest per capita income of any Third World country, Nauru is now on the brink of bankruptcy. In the 1990s the islanders attempted to create a tax haven, but this ended in 2004. Recently the island's main revenue has come from Australia, which uses it as a detention centre for asylum seekers.

Discovered in 1798 by a whaler, John Fearn, who named it Pleasant Island, Nauru continued as a tribal kingdom with mixed Melanesian and Polynesian inhabitants until 1888, when it was annexed by Germany as a dependency of New Guinea. The exploitation of the phosphate deposits began in 1905. Nauru was occupied and administered by Australia from 1914 and invaded by Japan in 1942. In 1947 the United Nations placed it under joint British, Australian and New Zealand government until it became an independent republic in 1968 under the presidency of Hammer de Roburt. Australian coins are in everyday use but silver $10 and gold $50 pieces have been issued by the Bank of Nauru since 1993 to commemorate the Olympic Games, the World Cup, the Queen Mother [20] and other subjects of global interest.

VANUATU

Named the New Hebrides by Captain Cook in 1774, these islands east of Papua New Guinea were declared a neutral zone in 1878, administered jointly by British and French naval officers. A condominium was proclaimed in 1906, but the only distinctive coins were those provided by the French after 1966 (see "French Pacific Islands").

In 1980 the country became an independent republic within the Commonwealth and adopted the name of Vanuatu. Coins thus inscribed, with the national emblem (obverse) [21, 23] and flora or seashells (reverse) [22, 24], were struck in denominations from 1 to 100 vatu. Several FAO coins have appeared [25–26], along with coins from 10 to 100 vatu celebrating the end of the Victorian era (1995), the Olympic Games, Captain Cook and the 25th anniversary of the Voyager 1 spacecraft – an eclectic mixture.

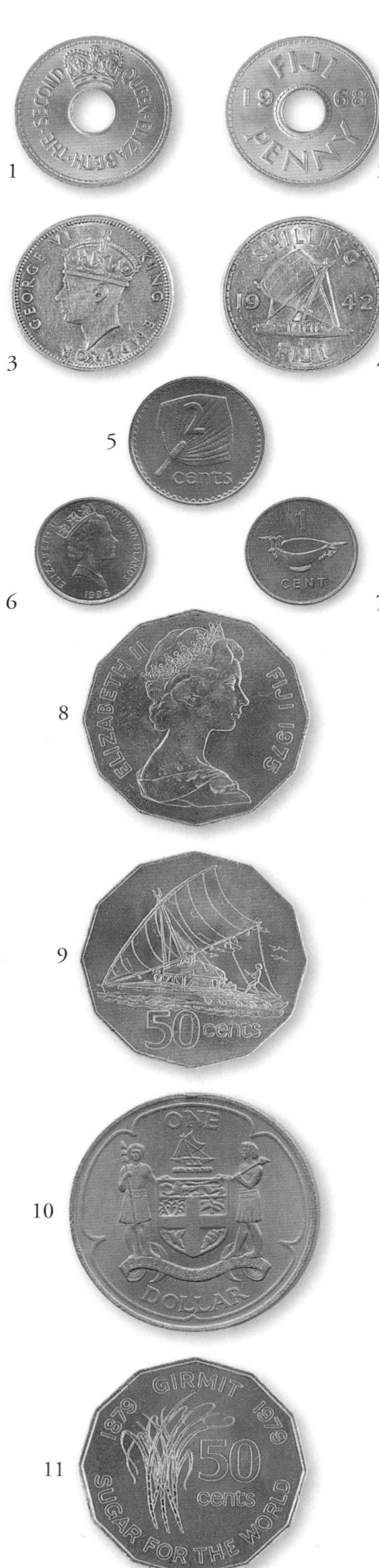

FIJI, SOLOMONS, KIRIBATI AND TUVALU

These countries are archipelagos scattered over the south-western Pacific. Though all three were sighted by European navigators in the 16th and 17th centuries they were surveyed by Captain Cook in the 18th century and thereafter fell within the British sphere of influence.

Tuvalu, formerly the Ellice or Lagoon Islands, was claimed for the British Crown in 1892 by the captain of HMS Royalist, *depicted on the $20 of 1993.*

FIJI

In 1643, Abel Jan Tasman was the first European to sight Fiji, and the islands were visited by James Cook in 1774. William Bligh and the loyal members of the crew of HMS *Bounty*, set adrift in an open boat by the mutineers, sailed through the Fiji group on their epic voyage to Timor (1789), but it was not until 1840 that the islands were comprehensively surveyed.

Traders and adventurers arrived in 1801 in search of sandalwood, and by 1850 there was a sizable and cosmopolitan population in Suva, the capital. By that time the islands were united under King Cakobau, but in 1874 incessant tribal warfare induced him to seek British protection in order to restore law and order. In the colonial period the British developed the sugar industry, bringing in indentured coolies from India. When Fiji attained independence in 1970 the Indian majority were held back by the indigenous Fijians, a dangerous situation that resulted in two military coups in 1987, the declaration of a republic and Fiji's expulsion from the Commonwealth. It was re-admitted in 1997.

British (from 1881) and Australian currency (from 1910) was in circulation until 1934, when distinctive coins were introduced. The holed halfpenny and penny were originally struck in cupro-nickel, then brass (1942) and bronze (1949), with a crown and the name of the monarch on the obverse and the country name, value and date on the reverse [1–2]. Thus Fiji was one of the few colonies to issue coins in 1936 in the name of Edward VIII. The silver sixpence, shilling and florin appeared in 1934, with a crowned bust of George V on the obverse and reverse motifs of a turtle, outrigger canoe [3–4] and colonial arms respectively. A 12-sided nickel-brass threepence was added in 1947, featuring a thatched hut between palm trees on the reverse. These coins, with the crowned effigy of the monarch, continued until Fiji adopted the dollar in 1969. A new series bore the Machin bust of the Queen and artefacts representing indigenous culture: kava bowl (1 cent) [6–7], palm-leaf fan (2 cents) [5], ceremonial drum (5 cents), throwing club (10 cents), *tabua* (whale's tooth) on a braided cord (20 cents), sailing canoe (50c) [8–9] and arms ($1) [10], the specifications following the Australian standard. The Maklouf effigy of the Queen has been used since 1986.

Numerous commemorative coins have appeared since independence in 1970. In addition to conventional circular coins Fiji has experimented with pentagons, polygons [11–13] and even segments which, when fitted to similar coins from Western Samoa and the Cook Islands, form a complete circle.

Pacific Conflict

The Solomon Islands were the scene of some of the fiercest fighting between Japanese and US forces in 1942–3, especially on Guadalcanal. From 1991 onward, several coins were issued to mark the 50th anniversaries of the battles of the Coral Sea and Guadalcanal, beginning with a dollar commemorating the Japanese attack on Pearl Harbor.

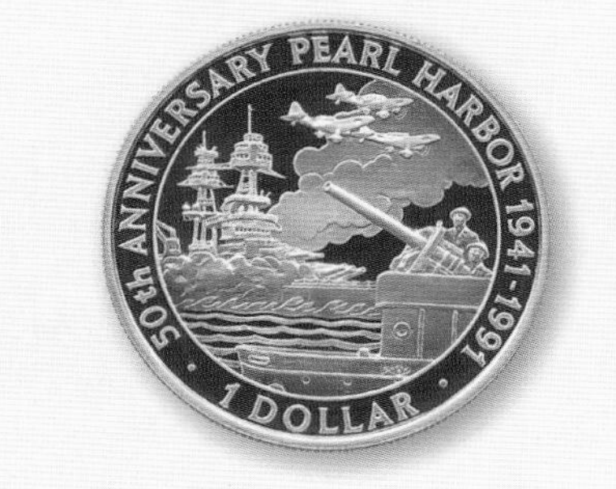

SOLOMON ISLANDS

Discovered in 1567 by the Spanish, these islands were partitioned between Germany and Britain and were declared protectorates in 1885 and 1893 respectively. The German islands were occupied by Australia in 1914 and in 1976 the protectorate was abolished. Since becoming an independent member of the Commonwealth the islands have issued coins portraying Elizabeth II with indigenous artefacts on the reverse, as well as numerous commemoratives [14–19].

KIRIBATI

Pronounced "Kiribas", the islands' name is the Polynesian rendering of "Gilbert", as they were previously thus named after Captain Thomas Gilbert, who first visited them in 1778. With the Ellice Islands, the Gilberts were administered from Fiji as a British protectorate, becoming a crown colony in 1915. The Phoenix group was added in 1937 and the Central and Southern Line Islands in 1972. These sparsely populated islands are spread over more than 2.5 million sq km/1 million sq miles of ocean, but their total land area is relatively small. The Gilbert Islands became a separate colony in 1976 and a republic within the Commonwealth in 1979, adopting the present name. Until then Australian currency was in use, but Kiribati has since issued its own coins, with arms (obverse) and indigenous fauna (reverse) on the low values and a sailing canoe and thatched hut on the dollar coins [20–21].

TUVALU

Formerly the Ellice Islands, this group has an area of 25sq km/10sq miles, and constitutes one of the world's smallest independent republics. In 1974 the inhabitants voted to separate from the Gilbert Islands and in 1976 became a "constitutional dependency" of the British Crown, under the name of Tuvalu. Complete independence for the population of 9000 was achieved in October 1978. Distinctive coins were adopted in 1976, bearing the Machin effigy of Elizabeth II with marine fauna on the reverse [22–23]. Since 1994 the Maklouf profile has been substituted. A few silver ($5, $10 or $20) and gold ($50 or $100) coins have appeared since 1976, marking anniversaries of independence or royal events, from the wedding of Prince Charles and Diana Spencer (1981) to the Duke of Edinburgh Award and birthdays of the Queen Mother.

Fitting the Pieces Together

Kiribati has produced relatively few special issues, although they include segmented Millennial coins resembling pieces of a jigsaw puzzle (1997), inscribed with the Latin for "times are changing".

FRENCH PACIFIC ISLANDS

Second only to Britain, France was the major colonial power in the South Pacific, and it still maintains a strong presence in that region. The Bank of Indochina established branches at Nouméa, New Caledonia, in 1888 and at Papeete, Tahiti, in 1905 and was responsible for paper money. French coins were in use until 1949, when separate issues for the French territories were introduced. The Bank of Indochina was succeeded in 1965 by the Institut d'Emission d'Outre-Mer (Overseas Issuing Institute), whose initials appear on the obverse of the nickel coins issued since 1975 [6, 14]. Separate issues are made for French Polynesia and New Caledonia, the CFP ("Change franc Pacifique" or "Pacific franc exchange") franc being tariffed at 1000 to 8.38 euros.

Left: An image of Moorea, one of the most spectacularly beautiful islands anywhere in the world, is featured on the 50 franc coins of French Polynesia.

FRENCH POLYNESIA

Porinetia Farani, as it is known in the local language, is a French overseas collectivity, comprising several island groups scattered over 2.5 million sq km/1 million sq miles of the South Pacific, with a total land area of 4,200 sq km/1,600sq miles and a population of 270,000. The largest island is Tahiti, which is also the location of the capital, Papeete. Captain Cook visited Tahiti in 1769, naming the archipelago the Society Islands, and Captain Bligh of the *Bounty* spent some time there in 1788–9 gathering breadfruit plants, which were to be established in the West Indies as food for the plantation slaves. Pomare II converted to Christianity in 1797 and British missionaries were in a favoured position until 1843, when France established a protectorate that became a colony in 1880 when Pomare V abdicated. The Society Islands joined the Marquesas and the Tuamotu archipelago in 1903 to form the colony known collectively as the French Settlements in Oceania.

French coins were used until 1949 when French Oceania attained self-government within the French Union. Aluminium coins from 50 centimes to 5 francs had the allegorical figure of Marianne on the obverse and a palm-girt scene on the reverse [1].

In 1957 the territory was renamed French Polynesia and chose to remain within the French Community. Coins in the same designs as those of 1949, but inscribed "Polynésie Française" on the reverse, were adopted in 1965 [2]. Higher denominations (10, 20 and 50 francs), struck in nickel, were added in 1967, with the head of Marianne (obverse) [5–7] and reverse motifs of a carved pole [3], frangipani blossom [4] and the jagged peaks of Moorea respectively. A 100 franc coin with the Moorea reverse, struck in nickel-bronze [8], was added to the series in 1976.

French coins also circulate widely, reflecting the continuing military presence associated with the testing of nuclear devices at Mururoa Atoll. Since January 1996, however, nuclear testing has been discontinued and the military garrison greatly reduced. Today the main sources of revenue come from tourism and the cultivation of *noni* fruit for the pharmaceutical industry.

NEW CALEDONIA

This archipelago 1800km/1100 miles east of Australia was discovered in 1774 by Captain Cook, who bestowed on it the name then used by poets to denote Scotland. As in Tahiti, British missionaries brought Christianity and a measure of Western civilization, but it was the French who established a protectorate there in 1853. They used it as a penal settlement, deporting many thousands of Communards in the aftermath of the abortive revolution of 1870–1. Normal colonial development began only in 1894.

New Caledonia used French coins exclusively until 1949 but, following its establishment as an overseas territory within the French Community in 1946, aluminium coins for small change were introduced. These had the same obverse as the coins of French Oceania [9] but the reverse featured the *kagu*, the national bird [10–11]. Nickel coins appeared in 1967 with the head of Marianne on the obverse [14] and on the reverse a Melanesian sailing pirogue, or flat-hulled canoe (10 francs) [12], zebu cattle (20 francs) [13] and a hut surrounded by Norfolk Island pines (50 francs) [15]. Nickel-bronze 100 francs with the pines reverse were added to the series in 1976.

Associated with New Caledonia are the three tiny volcanic islands of Uvea (Wallis), Alofi and Futuna, known as the Wallis and Futuna Islands, lying between Fiji and Samoa. The group was discovered by the Cornishman Samuel Wallis in the 18th century, but Christianized by French missionaries who arrived in 1837, and French protectorates were established over the islands in 1887–8. Each island has its own king to this day. In 1959 the inhabitants voted to become a separate overseas territory, thus severing political dependency on New Caledonia. A French overseas collectivity since 2003, the territory continues to use the coinage of New Caledonia.

NEW HEBRIDES

Named the New Hebrides by Captain Cook in 1774, because of a fancied resemblance to the islands off the west coast of Scotland, these islands east of Papua New Guinea had previously been visited by the Portuguese Pedro de Queiros (1606) and the Frenchman Louis de Bougainville (1768). Rival missionaries and sandalwood traders established themselves in the islands throughout the 19th century and urged their respective countries to annex them. Even British settlers favoured French protection when their own government seemed indifferent. An ad hoc dual system developed, but was unsatisfactory in regard to the settlement of civil disputes. The situation was aggravated by periodic uprisings by the indigenous inhabitants. In 1878 France and Britain negotiated a deal whereby the islands were declared a neutral zone, administered jointly by British and French naval officers, but this was impractical and led eventually to joint rule. A condominium was proclaimed in 1906, with two separate police forces and a judicial system headed by two judges (British and French) and a president, who could be neither British nor French, appointed by the king of Spain.

British, French and Australian currency was used but the only distinctive coins were those provided by the French authorities from 1966 onward, with the head of Marianne on the obverse and indigenous carvings on the reverse [16–20]. In 1980 the New Hebrides achieved complete independence, becoming the Republic of Vanuatu, a member of the British Commonwealth (see "PNG, Nauru and Vanuatu").

Reference to Earlier Currency

The squiggles flanking the carved mask on the reverse of the 10 and 20 franc coins of the New Hebrides are pieces of *tridacna* or clam shell, used as money before the advent of coinage.

POLYNESIAN KINGDOMS

Polynesia (from the Greek for "many islands") is the generic name for the vast number of islands scattered across the central Pacific from Hawaii in the north, whence the hardy seafaring Polynesians set out to colonize the other island groups in the 10th and subsequent centuries. The tribal communities eventually developed into kingdoms with their own coinage.

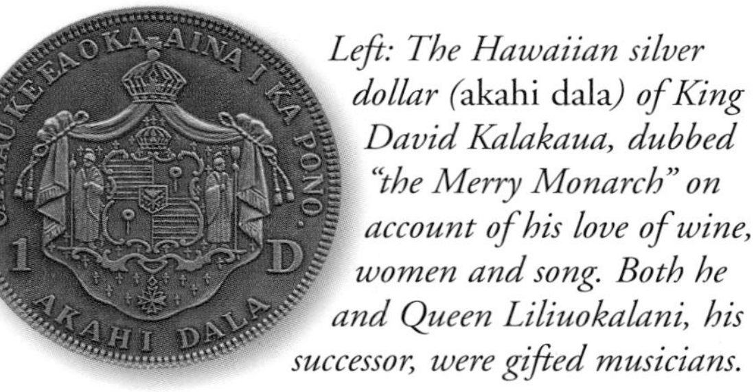

*Left: The Hawaiian silver dollar (*akahi dala*) of King David Kalakaua, dubbed "the Merry Monarch" on account of his love of wine, women and song. Both he and Queen Liliuokalani, his successor, were gifted musicians.*

HAWAII

This archipelago was visited by Captain James Cook in 1778. At that time the eight main islands were under the rule of petty kings and tribal chiefs, but by 1795 Kamehameha I had welded them into a single nation. American missionaries and traders gradually transformed Hawaii, creating the sugar and pineapple industries and bringing in indentured labourers from Japan and the Azores. American businessmen engineered the downfall of the monarchy in 1893, and for a brief period in 1894 Hawaii was a republic before it was admitted to the USA in 1898, becoming a territory in 1900 and a state in 1959.

Copper cents with a facing bust of Kamehameha III on the obverse and the value in the Hawaiian language on the reverse appeared in 1847. A regular coinage was introduced in 1881–3, with the profile of David Kalakaua on the obverse [1–2]. The reverses featured a crowned value (5 cents), wreathed values (10 cents and ⅛ dollar) and the crowned arms (quarter, half and dollar). Coins with the bust of Queen Liliuokalani dated 1891 or 1895 (the latter bearing a striking resemblance to the Syracusan decadrachms of the 5th century BC, complete with dolphins surrounding the portrait) were commissioned by Reginald Huth, a wealthy British collector, and are regarded as patterns. Restrikes or imitations of Hawaiian coins have been produced in recent years as tourist souvenirs.

TONGA

Named the Friendly Islands by Captain Cook in 1773, Tonga is an archipelago in the South Pacific, south of Samoa and east of Fiji. Intertribal warfare was brought to an end by Taufa'ahau, who adopted the name of King George Tupou I when he converted to Christianity in 1845. Aided and abetted by the British missionary Shirley Baker, who became prime minister, he united the islands into a single kingdom by 1862. Tonga became a self-governing British protectorate in 1900 and a fully independent kingdom within the Commonwealth in 1970.

The coinage of Britain, and latterly of New Zealand, circulated in Tonga, and the first indigenous coins were the gold pieces of 1962 called the koula (from the Tongan word for "gold") with its half and quarter. A standing figure of Queen Salote appeared on the koula and half koula and a profile on the quarter koula, with the royal arms on the reverse. Circulating coinage, based on the pa'anga of 100 seniti, was adopted in 1967, with Salote's effigy on the obverse [3] and various reverse motifs of a giant tortoise (1 and 2 seniti), wreathed value (5 and 10 seniti) and the coat of arms (20 and 50 seniti and 1 pa'anga) [4]. These coins were posthumous, as Salote had died in 1965. A series of seven coins, including the platinum hau (100 pa'anga) and its subdivisions, also appeared in 1967 to celebrate the coronation of her son and successor Taufa'ahau Tupou IV, with his portrait (obverse) and arms (reverse), followed by a permanent series with his profile replacing his mother's [5–7]. A series introduced in 1975 bore a facing bust of the king in military uniform, with motifs promoting the Food and Agriculture Organization programme [10–11]. Since then Tonga has produced numerous coins in all shapes and sizes [8–9] for a wide range of topics, often issued in thematic sets. These have ranged from veteran and vintage cars to celebrate the automobile centenary [12–13] to sporting events such as the Olympic and Commonwealth Games and the America's Cup yacht races, as well as tributes to members of the British royal family [14].

Christmas Coins

From 1982 to 1988 Tonga released heptagonal coins to celebrate Christmas, with appropriate reverse motifs ranging from Dürer's *Praying Hands* to the Three Wise Men. Struck in cupro-nickel for general circulation, they were also minted in silver, gold or platinum in very limited editions.

Despite its comparative remoteness, Tonga has made a big splash in the coin world with a number of startling innovations. As well as the first gold coins from Oceania, Tonga experimented with high-denomination coins (the hau worth 100 pa'anga) struck in palladium, a rare metal of the platinum group. In the 1980s, when the bullion value of silver rose sharply, a number of special issues were struck in silver-plated cupro-nickel. Some coins of 1967–8 were countermarked to commemorate the king's 50th birthday or the anniversary of Salote's death, in much the same way that stamps are overprinted for this purpose.

WESTERN SAMOA

The islands of Samoa were discovered by the Dutch Jacob Roggeveen in 1772 but were later the subject of a three-cornered tussle between Germany, Britain and the USA. Although the group had an indigenous monarchy, it was partitioned between Germany and the USA in March 1900, and the eastern portion remains under US rule. In 1914 German Samoa fell to forces from New Zealand, which was granted a mandate by the League of Nations. Western Samoa remained under this mandate until it attained independence in 1962.

Distinctive coins were introduced in 1967, based on the tala (dollar) of 100 sene (cents) [15–16]. The obverse bore the profile of Malietoa Tanumafili II, a direct descendent of the kings of Samoa, who holds his position for life, although it is intended that his successors should be elected for five-year terms. The reverses focus on various fruits [19–20], with the state arms on the tala. Since 1969 Western Samoa has issued a large number of special coins, commemorating the Queen's silver jubilee [17–18] and featuring sporting events such as the Commonwealth and Olympic Games [21–22] and the Americas Cup yacht races, while local heroes such as Robert Louis Stevenson (known as Tusitala – "the teller of tales") [23–24] and German governor Dr Wilhelm Solff are not forgotten.

10 11 12 13 14 15 16 17 18 19 20 21 22 23 24

GLOSSARY

Some of the more commonly used terms are given below.

Accolated *see* **conjoined**.
Adjustment The filing down of a blank to reduce it to the correct weight before striking, revealed by file marks on the surface.
Ae Abbreviation of *aes* (Latin, "bronze"), used to denote copper, brass or bronze.
Aes grave (Latin, "heavy bronze") Heavy coinage of the Roman Republic from 269 BC.
Aes rude (Latin, "rough bronze") Irregular lumps of bronze used as money before the adoption of regular coinage, *c.* 400 BC.
Aes signatum (Latin, "signed bronze") Regular bars or ingots cast to a standard weight, stamped to guarantee their weight, 289–269 BC.
Alliance coinage Coins struck by two or more states in conjunction.
Alloy Mixture of metals, such as bronze (copper and tin).
Altered Deliberately changed, usually to increase the value of a coin (such as changing a common date to a rare one by filing one of the digits).
Aluminium Lightweight silver-coloured metal used for coins of low denominations.
Aluminium-bronze Durable, gold-coloured alloy of aluminium and copper.
Amulet Coin whose design confers talismanic properties, often pierced and worn to ward off evil spirits. *See also* **touchpiece**.
Anepigraphic coin Coin with no inscription.
Angel Gold coin named for its image of Archangel Michael, first used in France in 1340 and introduced to England in 1465, with a value of 6 shillings and 8 pence.
Annealing Process of heating and cooling metal to relieve stresses before it is processed.
Annulet Small circle used as an ornament or spacing device in inscriptions.
Antoniniani Roman imperial coins named after the emperor Caracalla (Marcus Aurelius Antoninus) in whose reign they were first minted.

Ar Abbreviation of *argentum* (Latin, "silver").
Assay Test to determine the fineness of precious metal.
Attribution Identification of a coin by such data as the issuer, date, reign, mint or denomination.
Au Abbreviation of *aurum* (Latin, "gold").
Barbarous Descriptive of coins struck by Celtic and Germanic tribes in imitation of Greek or Roman coins.
Base metal Non-precious metal or an alloy containing neither gold nor silver.
Bath metal Inferior bronze alloy used at Bath, England, for casting cannon, but also employed by William Wood of Bristol to produce tokens for Ireland and colonial America.
Beading Border of raised dots round the rim of a coin.
Billon Alloy of copper with less than 50 per cent silver.
Bimetallic Made of two different metals or alloys; such coins usually have a centre in one metal and outer ring in another.
Bimetallism Descriptive of coinage consisting of coins in two different metals with a fixed ratio between them, such as gold and silver or silver and bronze.
Bit (1) Segment of a coin that has been cut up in order to circulate at half or one quarter the value of the entire coin. (2) Nickname of the 1 real piece that circulated in North America in the 17th and 18th centuries, worth one eighth of a dollar, or 12½ cents.
Blank Disc of metal cut or punched out of a strip or sheet, on which a coin is struck. Also known as a flan or planchet.
Blundered inscription (1) Jumbled lettering in inscriptions on barbarous coins, reflecting the illiteracy of the makers copying Greek or Roman coins. (2) Unreadable inscription as a result of a mis-strike.
Bon pour (French, "good for") Inscription on 1920s French tokens used during a shortage of legal tender coins.
Bourse Area in a coin exhibition where dealers sell their wares.
Bracteate (from Latin *bractea*, a thin piece of metal) Coin struck on such a thin blank that the image impressed on one side shows through on the other.
Brass Alloy of copper and zinc.
Brockage Mis-struck coin with only one design, normal on one side and incuse on the other, caused when a struck coin clings to the die and strikes the next blank to pass through the press.
Bronze Alloy of copper and tin.
Bullet money Globular pieces of silver with impressed marks, used as currency in Thailand from the 14th century until 1904.
Bullion Precious metal whose value is reckoned solely by its weight and fineness.
Bullion coin Coin struck in precious metal, now usually with an inscription giving its weight and fineness, whose value fluctuates according to the market price of the metal.
Buyer's premium Percentage of the purchase price at auction paid by the winning bidder to the auction house.
Carat (US karat) Term used to denote the fineness of gold, being 1/24 of the whole. Thus 22 carat gold is .916 fine.
Cartwheel Nickname of the British penny and 2 pence copper coins of 1797, weighing respectively 1oz/28.35g and 2oz/56.7g, with raised rims resembling cartwheels.
Cased set Set of coins in mint condition, packaged by the mint.
Cash (from Portuguese *caixa* and Tamil *kacu*, a small coin) Cast circular coins in copper or bronze with a square central hole, used as subsidiary coinage in China.
Cast coins Coins made by pouring molten metal into moulds, rather than by striking discs of metal with dies.
Clad Descriptive of a coin with a core of one metal covered with a layer or coating of another.
Clash marks Mirror-image traces found on a coin struck with dies that have been damaged by having been previously struck together without a blank between them.
Clipping Removing slivers of silver or gold from the edge of coins, an illegal but widespread practice until the 1660s, when milled coins began to be struck with grained edges.
Cob Irregularly shaped silver piece sliced from a bar of silver and crudely stamped for use in Spanish America in the 16th to 18th centuries.
Coin Piece of metal marked with a device and issued by a government for use as money.
Coin weight Piece of metal of exactly the weight of a known coin, used to check weight and fineness of matching coins.
Collar Ring within which the obverse and reverse dies operate to restrict the spread of the blank between them; it is often engraved with an inscription or pattern that is impressed on the edge of the coin.
Commemorative Coin struck to celebrate a historic anniversary or personality or publicize an event.
Conjoined portrait Obverse portrait with two heads or busts in profile, facing the same direction and overlapping. Also known as accolated or jugate.
Convention money Coins struck by neighbouring states and mutually acceptable; specifically the issues of Austria and Bavaria, which spread to other German states in the early 19th century.
Copper (1) Metal widely used for subsidiary coinage for more than 2500 years, usually alloyed with tin to make bronze, but also alloyed with nickel or silver. (2) Nickname for small denomination coins.
Coppernose Nickname derived from the debased English silver shillings of Henry VIII because the silver tended to wear off the king's nose, the highest point of the obverse.
Counter Piece resembling a coin but actually intended for use on a medieval accountancy board or in gambling.
Counterfeit Imitation of a coin for circulation, intended to deceive the public and defraud the state.
Countermark Punch mark applied to a coin to change its value or authorize its circulation in a different state.
Crockards Debased imitations of English silver pennies, produced in the Low Countries and imported into England in the late 13th century.

Crown gold Gold of 22 carat (.916) fineness, so called because it was first used in England in 1526 for the gold crown; it remains the British standard.
Cupellation (Latin *cupella*, little cup) Refining process used to separate gold and silver from lead and other impurities in a bone ash pot called a cupel; used in assaying to determine the fineness of precious metals.
Cupro-nickel (US copper-nickel) Alloy of copper and nickel.
Currency Money of all kinds, including coins, paper notes, tokens and other articles, passing current in general circulation.
Current Descriptive of coins and paper money in circulation.
Cut money Coins cut into smaller pieces to provide proportionately smaller values for general circulation.
Debasement Reduction of a coin's precious metal content.
Decimal currency Currency system in which the basic unit is divided into 10, 100 or 1000 subsidiary units.
Demonetization Withdrawal of coins from circulation, declaring them to be worthless.
Denomination Value given to a coin or note of paper money.
Device Term derived from heraldry for the pattern or emblem on a coin.
Die Hardened piece of metal bearing the mirror or wrong-reading image of a device, used to strike one side of a blank.
Die break Raised line or bump in a relief image caused by a crack in the die.
Dodecagonal Twelve-sided.
Dump Coin struck on a very thick blank.
Eagle US gold coin with an American eagle obverse and a face value of $10, circulating until 1933.
Ecclesiastical coins Coins struck under the authority of an archbishop or other prelate, prevalent in the Middle Ages and surviving in coins of the Papacy.
Edge The side of a coin, perpendicular to the obverse and reverse surfaces, which may be plain, inscribed or grained.
Edge inscription Lettering on the edge of coins designed to prevent clipping.
Edge ornament Elaboration of the graining on milled coins designed as a security device.

Effigy Portrait or bust on the obverse of a coin.
Electrum Naturally occurring alloy of gold and silver prevalent in the ancient coins of the Mediterranean region; it was also known as white gold.
Encased money Stamps enclosed in small metal discs and used in lieu of coins during the American Civil War and in Europe during and after World War I.
Engraving Technique of cutting designs and inscriptions in dies used for striking coins.
Epigraphy Study of inscriptions engraved in stone or metal, usually to determine the date and provenance of an artefact so inscribed.
Erasure Removal of the title or effigy of a ruler from coinage issued posthumously, notably in Roman coins of Caligula and Nero.
Error Mistake in the design or production of a coin.
Exergue Bottom segment of the face of a coin, usually divided from the rest of the field by a horizontal line and often containing the date or value.
Face Obverse or reverse surface of a coin.
Face value Value of the denomination applied to a coin, distinct from its intrinsic value.
Facing Descriptive of a portrait facing to the front instead of in profile.
Fantasy Piece purporting to be a coin but either emanating from a non-existent country or never authorized by the country whose name is inscribed on it.
Field Flat part of a coin between the legend and effigy or other raised parts of the design.
Flan *see* **blank**.
Forgery Unauthorized copy or imitation, produced primarily to deceive collectors.
Frosting Matt finish used for the high relief areas of proof coins to contrast with the polished surface of the field.
Globular Descriptive of a coin struck on a very thick dump with convex sides.
Gold Precious metal used for coins since the 7th century BC.
Grade Description of the condition of a collectable coin for the purposes of valuation and trade.
Graining Pattern of close vertical ridges around the edge of milled coins, originally devised to eliminate the fraudulent practice of clipping. Also known as reeding or milling.
Gun money Emergency Irish coinage of 1689–91 struck from gunmetal by the deposed James II in order to pay and supply his troops during the Williamite or Jacobean War.
Hammered Descriptive of coins struck by hand, using a hammer to impress the dies.
Hoard Group of coins buried or hidden in the past.
Holed coin (1) Coin minted with a central hole. (2) Coin pierced after striking, to wear as jewellery or a talisman.
Hub Right-reading metal punch used to strike working dies.
Incuse Descriptive of an impression that cuts into the surface of a coin.
Ingot Piece of precious metal, cast in a mould and stamped with its weight and fineness.
Intrinsic value Net value based on the metal content of a coin, as opposed to its nominal or face value.
Iron Metal used in primitive currency such as the spits of ancient Greece, and for emergency coinage in both World Wars.
Jeton (from French *jeter*, to throw) Alternative term for **counter**.
Jugate (from Latin *jugum*, yoke) Alternative term for **conjoined**.
Key date The rarest date in a long-running series.
Klippe Coin struck on a square or rectangular blank hand-cut from sheet metal, originally in a time of emergency.
Laureate Descriptive of a design incorporating a laurel wreath, either adorning the brows of a ruler or enclosing the value.
Legal tender Coin declared by law to be current money.
Legend Inscription on a coin.
Long cross coinage English pennies first issued by Henry III, on which the arms of the cross on the reverse reached to the rim.
Lustre Sheen or bloom on the surface of an uncirculated coin.
Maundy money Set of small silver pennies distributed by the British sovereign to the poor on Maundy Thursday (preceding Good Friday), a medieval custom still enacted. Ordinary coins were originally used but special 1, 2, 3 and 4 pence coins were first minted in 1822.
Milling Mechanical process for the production of coins, in use from the 16th century.
Mint Establishment in which coins are produced. Also used as a grading term.
Mint set Coins still enclosed in the package or case issued by the mint.
Mint-mark Mark on a coin identifying the mint at which it was struck.
Mirror surface Highly polished, flawless surface of the field of a proof coin.
Mis-strike Coin on which the impression of the die has been struck off-centre.
Moneyer Mint official in pre-industrial era responsible for striking coinage of legal weight and quality.
Mule Coin whose obverse and reverse designs are wrongly matched. Can be comprised of different denominations or even separate foreign currencies.
Nickel Base metal used extensively in coinage as a substitute for silver, frequently alloyed with copper to make cupro-nickel.
Non-circulating legal tender Coins that, though technically valid for use, do not circulate in practice (such as silver and gold commemoratives). Abbreviated to NCLT.
Numismatics (from Latin *numisma*, coin) The study and collection of paper money, coins and medals.
Obverse "Heads" side of a coin.
Off-metal Descriptive of a coin struck in a metal other than that officially authorized.
Overdating Method of changing a date without the expense of engraving an entirely new die. One or more digits are altered by superimposing other numerals using a punch.
Overstrike Coin produced when a previously struck coin is substituted for a blank, on which traces of the original design remain.
Patina Surface quality acquired as a result of environmental interaction over time, such as the oxidation of metal.

Pattern Design piece prepared by a mint for approval by the issuing authority, not actually put into production. Patterns may differ from issued coins in metal or minor details, but many bear designs quite different from those eventually adopted.
Pellet Raised circular ornament, sometimes used as a spacing device in the inscription.
Pieces of eight Nickname for Spanish silver 8 real coins.
Piedfort (US piefort) Coin struck on a blank of two or three times the normal weight and thickness.
Pile Lower die bearing the obverse motif, the opposite of the trussel.
Planchet *see* **blank**.
Platinum Precious metal first used for coins in Russia in 1819 and occasionally in recent years for proof coins.
Plate money Large, cumbersome copper plates used as money in Sweden, 1643–1768.
Privy mark Secret mark incorporated in a coin design as a security device or to identify the particular die used.
Profile Side portrait often used on the obverse of coins.
Proof Originally a trial strike but in recent years a coin struck to a very high standard, often in precious metals.
Punch Piece of hardened metal bearing a design or lettering used to impress a die or a coin.
Recoinage Process of recalling and demonetizing old coins, which are then melted down and made into new coins.
Reeding *see* **graining**.
Relief Raised parts of the design.
Restrike Coin produced from the original dies, but long after the period in which they were current.
Reverse "Tails" side of a coin, usually featuring arms, the value or a pictorial design.
Rim Raised border around the outside of a coin's face.
Scissel Clippings of metal left after a blank has been cut; sometimes a clipping accidentally adheres to the blank during striking, producing a crescent-shaped flaw.
Scyphate (from Greek *scypha*, skiff or small boat) Cup-shaped, used to describe Byzantine concave coins.
Sede vacante (Latin, "vacant see") Inscription used on issues of ecclesiastical mints between the death of a prelate and the election of his successor.
Series All the issues of a coin of one denomination, design and type, including modifications and variations.
Short-cross coinage English pennies on which the arms of the reverse cross fell far short of the rim.
Siege money Emergency currency issued under siege.
Silver Precious metal widely used for coinage from the 6th century BC onward.
Slabbing Method of encapsulating a coin permanently, particularly in a rectangular plastic case, to prevent deterioration.
Specie (Latin, "in kind") Money in the form of coins, especially of precious metals.
Steel Metal refined and tempered from iron and used in a stainless or chromed version for coinage since 1939. Copper-clad steel is now extensively used in place of bronze.
Tin Metal used for small coins in Malaysia, Thailand and the East Indies, and in British halfpence and farthings (1672–92). It is more usually alloyed with copper to form bronze.
Token Coin-like piece of metal, plastic or card issued by merchants, local authorities or other organizations, often during periods when government coinage is in short supply, but also produced extensively as a substitute for money.
Touchpiece Coin kept as a lucky charm and often pierced to wear as jewellery, notably the English gold angel, which was believed to cure or ward off scrofula, a skin disease known as the King's Evil.
Trade coin Coin produced for use outside the country of origin as part of international trade, such as British and American trade dollars.
Truncation Stylized cut at the base of the neck of a portrait, sometimes the site of a mint-mark, the engraver's initials or a die number.
Trussel Upper die used in hammered coinage bearing the reverse design, the opposite of the pile.
Type A major variety of a series of coins.
Type set Set comprising one coin of each type in a series.
Uniface Coin with a device on one side only.
Vis-à-vis (French, "face-to-face") Descriptive of a double portrait in which the two heads face each other.
White gold Ancient term for **electrum**, which differs from the modern definition.
Year set Set of coins produced annually by a mint, usually containing a specimen of each coin issued by the mint during the year.
Zinc Metal alloyed with copper to produce brass; zinc-coated steel was also widely used in Europe during both World Wars.

GRADING TERMINOLOGY

You will find below the various terms given in catalogues and dealers' lists to denote the perceived state, or 'grade', of a coin, with the higher grades given first.

Fleur de Coin (FDC) or **Brilliant Uncirculated (BU** or **B. Unc.)** Denotes coins in the very finest possible condition with full original lustre, no surface marks or edge knocks. Usually reserved for descriptions of proof and de luxe coins.
Uncirculated (Unc.) The highest grade applicable to coins struck by high-speed presses for general circulation. These coins should have full original lustre, which may have darkened with age to produce an attractive patina. Otherwise the surface should be flawless.
Extremely Fine (EF) Indicates a coin in virtually pristine condition but showing slight signs of handling. It should have every detail of the engraving clearly delineated but will have lost some of its original lustre.
Very Fine (VF) Coins show slight evidence of wear on the highest points of the design, notably the hair on portraits and the ridge at the truncation of the bust. In modern coins this is the lowest grade for practicable purposes and to purchase a coin in any lesser condition would be a waste of money. Dealers do not normally offer modern coins in lower grades unless they are very scarce. Older material, however, may be acceptable.
Fine (F) To the uninitiated such a coin may seem perfectly acceptable, but look closely and you will see that the higher points of the design are worn smooth and the lettering is noticeably thicker and less clearly defined, especially in the serifs (the little spurs on capitals) which may have all but disappeared.
Very Good (VG) A misuse of language as a coin with this description would be in pretty poor condition. In such coins little of the fine detail will be present and the overall impression would be blurred and worn.
Good (G) Now means the complete opposite. A coin in this state would be worn smooth all over and the date would be just readable. For that reason alone collectors will keep such a coin if a particular year is so scarce that the chances of finding a better specimen might be remote.

Lower grades, such as **Fair**, **Mediocre** and **Poor** have almost vanished from the scene and would only be considered if the coin was seldom available in a better condition. These terms are usually reserved for medieval coins which have been clipped or have irregular shapes with chunks missing – which is, in fact, a not uncommon situation for many coins from the 10th to 16th centuries. Also included in these categories are coins which have been pierced for wear as pendants, the only exception in this case being the gold angels of medieval Europe, which were believed to guard the bearer against disease, and which are still highly valued by auctioneers and collectors.

INDEX

A
admission tokens 82
advertising 221
Afghanistan 203
Africa 12, 69, 172
  Equatorial Africa 190–1
  fauna 180–1
aircraft motifs 79, 145
Albania 162
albums 65
Algeria 172–3
allegory 18–19
alloys 38–9
aluminium coins 39, 121, 149, 151
  Nigeria 188, 189
  Vietnam 214
America 96
American Numismatic Association (ANS) 61, 90
American tokens 35
Andorra 171
anepigraphic coins 139, 160
angel 130, 168
Anglo-Saxon coinage 10, 22, 23, 71, 130
Angola 182
animal motifs 79
  Africa 180–1
  Argentina 120
  Ascension 123
  Caribbean 108, 109
  Latvia 155
  Queen's Beasts 123
  Svalbard 127
anna 184, 201, 205
  square 210
annual coins 81
Antigua and Barbuda 108
Antilles 105
Antioch 196–7
Arabia 12, 25, 54, 198–9
Argentina 120, 121
Armenia 158
Ascension Island 123
ashrafi 208
Asia 192
Aspects of Medicine on Ancient Greek and Roman Coins 78
Australia 234–5, 236–7
Austria 148–9
Azerbaijan 158

B
Bahamas 104

Bahrain 200
baisa 200, 201
balboa 113
bamboo tokens 13
Bangladesh 205
bank tokens 96
Barbados 104
barter 10–11
  Tatarstan 159
base metals 39
basic currency units 77
battleship coins 225
beer tokens 83
Belarus 159
Belgium 71, 138
Belize 113
Benin (Dahomey) 190, 191
Bermuda 104–5
bezant 195
Bhutan 222–3
Biafra 189
bimetallic coins 39, 84
  Italy 167
  Oman 200
Birmingham Mint 72
births 80
blasius 160
bogus coins 84
Bohemia 150
Bolivia 118
boliviano 114, 118
Borneo 230
Botswana 178–9
bourses 10, 91
boxes 64–5
bracteates 25, 43
brass coins 39, 85, 119, 121, 151, 186
brass tokens 187
Brazil 12, 13, 116–17
British Somaliland 184, 185
British tokens 34, 35
British Virgin Islands 109
bronze coins 16, 17, 18
brothel tokens 82
Brunei 231
bu 226
Buddhist motifs 80, 212, 223
building motifs 78
Bulgaria 162–3
bullet coins 232
bullion coins 33, 39
  Canada 97
  China 79
  Laos 215
  Perth Mint 73, 81
  South Africa 177
Burkina Faso (Upper Volta) 190, 191
Burma 204
Burundi 182–3
Byzantium 19, 20–1, 26, 71, 156, 174, 192

C
cabinets 65
Cambodia 215
Cameroon 190
Canada 13, 96–7
Cape Verde 191
Caribbean 87, 104–5, 106–7,108–9
Carthage 172
Cartwheel coins 49, 132
cases 64–5
cash 14–15, 42, 210, 211, 216, 224
cast coins 42
catalogues 66–7
Cayman Islands 106, 107
Celtic coinage 22, 40
cent 7, 34, 98, 99, 105, 184–5, 189, 230
centavo 113, 114, 117, 118, 119, 171, 191
centime 41, 182
Central African Republic 190
Central America 112–13
Chad 190
Chile 118–19
China 12, 13, 14–15, 40, 216–17
chogin 226
chon 224, 225
Christian motifs 20, 56, 71, 177
Christmas coins 249
Christmas Island 235
chronograms 55
chuckram 208, 209
circulating coins 47
clad coins 39
Classical images 56, 78–9
clipping coins 50
coelacanth coins 213
coin clubs 90
coinage 6
  cast coinage 42
  denominations 36–7
  hammered coinage 42–3
  industrial developments 46–7
  milled 44–5
  money of necessity 34–5
  special production techniques 48–9
  specifications 40–1
Coincraft catalogues 66
coins 6–7, 9, 95
  buying and selling 90–1, 92–3
  cleaning 62–3
  condition 60–1
  great collections 59
  housing collections 7, 64–5
  preserving condition 62
CoinTalk 92
Colombia 115
colon 112, 113
coloured coins 107
commemorative coins 80–1
  Afghanistan 203
  Arab Emirates 201
  Canada 97
  Cook Islands 240

  Gibraltar 137
  Greece 165
  India 211
  Isle of Man 52
  Israel 195
  Japan 227
  Macao 220, 221
  New Zealand 239
  Niue 241
  Olympic Games 109, 128–9, 155, 165, 170, 197
  Queen's Beasts 123
  Rome 18, 19
  Solomon Islands 245
  Switzerland 141
  Switzerland 141
  Taiwan 221
  Thailand 233
  United States 100–1, 102–3
  Virgin Islands 109
Comoros 213
Congo 182–3, 190
Cook Islands 240, 241
copper 16, 34–5, 39, 126, 157, 136
  Siberia 157
Costa Rica 112
counterfeiting 50–1
  penalties 51
countermarks 87
cow-racing coins 229
Croatia 10, 49
crosses 182
crown 81, 122
Crusader coins 25, 75, 195, 196
cruzeiro 117
Cuba 106
currencies 32–3
  early 12–13
  German states 143
  Rhodesia 183
Cyprus 136
Czech Republic 151
Czechoslovakia 150–1

D
dam 223
Danzig (Gdansk) 153
dates 7, 21
  Ethiopian calendar 187
dealers 90–1, 92
deaths 80
debasement 50
decimal coinage 124–5
  Australia 235
  New Zealand 238–9
  United Kingdom 133
definitives
  Canada 97
  United States 98–9
Democritus 165
denarius 18–19, 23, 24, 25
  Jerusalem 79, 194
denier 18, 23, 24, 25, 136, 195
Denmark 70, 124–5
denominations 21, 36–7, 76–7
dhabu 208
dies 43
  die production 46–7
  die variations 86
dime 7, 98
dinar 18, 24, 26, 173, 175, 195, 196, 197, 198, 199
  Kuwait 200
dirham 26, 27, 172, 173, 196, 197
  Oman 200
Djibouti 186–7
dokdo 208
dollar 32–3, 76, 96, 117, 230, 231, 248
  Bermuda 105
  Canada 96, 97
  China 217
  countermarked 87
  Guyana 1177
  holey dollar 235
  Jamaica 107
  New Zealand 238–9
  quarter dollar 6–7, 102–3
  silver half dollar 100–1
  silver trade dollars 14, 33, 76
  United States 98, 99, 100–1
Dominica 108
Dominican Republic 106, 107
dong 215
doubloon 33
drachma 10, 17, 26, 77
  Bulgaria 162–3
  Carthage 172
  Greece 164–5
  India 206
ducat 25, 33, 148, 150
dump 235
Dutch East Indies 13, 228
dynastic coins 26

E
eagle 49, 100
East African Monetary Union 184–5
eBay 93
economic upheaval 75
ecu 81, 137
Ecuador 114–15
Egypt 13, 27, 36, 174–5
El Salvador 113

electrum 16, 17, 38
elongates 85
England 31, 32, 37, 130–1
  pictorial coins 56
engraving 43
ephemera 89
Eritrea 186
errors 86–7
escudo 110, 115, 118, 119, 170, 171, 229
Estonia 155
Ethiopia 186, 187
euro 81, 146, 147, 168
Europe 69, 124
  medieval European coinage 24–5, 31, 56

F
fairs 7, 90, 91
Falklands 123
falu 208
family planning motifs 205
fano 210, 211
fantasy coins 85
FAO (Food and Agricultural Organization) coins 74, 79, 161, 178, 185, 187, 191, 200, 205, 233, 249
farthing 35, 40, 57, 77, 130
  South Africa 176, 177
fifty pence 41, 133
Fiji 244
Finland 24, 70, 127
floral motif coins 218–19
florin 25, 33, 117, 244
forums 91
franc 41, 138, 139, 140–1, 162
  Africa 190, 191
  Indochina 214
  Madagascar 213
  Polynesia 246
France 24, 31, 37, 168–9
  Africa 190–1
  pictorial coins 56, 57
Franklin Mint 48, 73
French Indochina 214
French Polynesia 246

G
Gabon 190
Gambia 188–9
gaming tokens 83
Gandhi, Mahatma 211
George Cross 137
Georgia 158–9
Germany 13, 24–5, 31, 37, 142–3, 144–5, 146–7
  mints 31, 46
  pictorial coins 57
Ghana 188
Gibraltar 137
gold 10, 16, 38–9, 236–7
gold coins 16, 18, 24, 25, 29
  Australia 234–5, 236–7
  England 37
  France 168
  gold trade coins 33
  lei 163
  peso 119
  United Kingdom 132, 133

  United States 98–9
gourde 11, 106–7
grading coins 60–1
graduation motifs 233
graining 51
Greece 16–17, 31, 32, 36, 164–5
  pictorial coins 56–7
Greek Coin Types and Their Identification 78–9
Greenland 125
Grenada 109
groat 24, 117, 130, 131
gros 24, 25, 136
guarani 120–1
Guernsey 134
Guidebook of United States Coins 66
guides 66–7
guilder 117
Guinea 190, 191
guinea 36, 37, 84
gulden 7, 25, 57
guldengroschen 148
gun money 69, 131
Gupta Empire 29
Guyana 116, 117

H
Habsburg Empire 148
Haiti 11, 106–7
half crown 133
halfpenny 57, 130, 133
hammered coins 42–3
Handbook of United States Coins 66
hau 249
Hawaii 69, 248
Heaton Mint 230
Hellenistic coins 28–9
heptagonal coins, Papua New Guinea 243
heptagonal coins, Tonga 249
high-speed production 46
Hindu motifs 223
Hispaniola 106
Hogge Money 104–5
Honduras 112–13
Hong Kong 220
hubbing 47
Hudson's Bay Company 10, 97
Hungary 148, 149
hwan 224, 225

I
Iceland 125
imperial coins 71
incuse coins 49, 51
India 12, 13, 28–9, 40, 68, 69, 206–7, 208–9, 210–11
Indian Head Penny 99
Indochina 214
Indonesia 228–9
industrial developments 46–7
inflation 117, 144, 145, 149
intaglio coins 49
Ionian Islands 137
Iran 202–3
Iraq 197
Ireland 68, 69, 131, 135
  Barnyard series 57, 69
Islamic coins 26, 27, 29, 174, 194–5
  Arabia 80, 198–9
  non-figural motifs 54–5
island coinage 69
Isle of Man 38, 39, 134–5
Israel 68, 194–5
Italy 24–5, 166–7
Ivory Coast 190, 191

J
Jamaica 106, 107
Japan 12, 13, 40, 226–7
Jersey 134
jeton 89
jewel-studded coins 48
jiao 217
jokoh 230
Jordan 194, 195

K
Kazakhstan 159
Keeling Cocos Islands 13, 235
Kennedy, John F. 201
Kenya 184, 185
kina 242–3
Kiribati 245
klippe 41
koban 13, 226
kopek 40, 127, 155, 156–7
Korea 224–5
kori 208
koula 248
krone 124–5, 126, 127
Krugerrand 33, 39
kuna 10, 49, 161
kupang 230
Kushans 28–9, 202
Kuwait 200
kwacha 183
kwanza 182
kyat 204
Kyrgyzstan 159

L
Laos 215
Latin Monetary Union 169
Latvia 154–5
leather tokens 13, 35
Lebanon 197
lei 163
lempira 113
leper coins 115, 229
lepta 164
Lesotho 179
Liberia 189
Libya 173
Liechtenstein 141
lilangeni 179
lira 18, 27, 167, 187, 193
  Turkey 193
literature 66–7, 78–9, 85
Lithuania 154
Livonia 155
livre 18, 213
loti 179
Low Countries 71
Luxembourg 71, 139
Lydia 16–17, 38, 192, 202

M
Macao 220, 221
Macedonia 17, 32, 161
Madagascar 213
Madrid Mint 170
Malawi 183
Malaya 230–1
Malaysia 231
Maldives 212
Mali 191
Malta 136–7
manilla 13
Marianne 168, 169, 173, 187, 191, 213, 214, 246, 247
mark 10, 76–7
  German New Guinea 242
marks 16
  countermarks 87
  marks of value 37
  secret markings 50
marriages 80
Mauritania 191
Mauritius 212–13
medals 73, 137
medical motifs 78
Mesopotamia 13
metal 13, 38–9
Mexico 110–11
microprocessor motifs 195
Middle East 13, 26–7
miliaresion 21
military anniversaries 81
milk tokens 82–3
milled coinage 44–5
  security edges 50–1
mints 6, 30–1, 72–3
  Egypt 174, 175
  Mexico 110, 111
  mint-marks 7, 50, 72
  private mints 72–3
  Russia 156
  South Africa 176
mission coins 176
model coins 84
mohar 223
mohur 205, 207, 208, 209
Moldova 159

Monaco 169
money of account 37
money of necessity 34–5
Mongolia 221
Mongols 26–7
Monumental Coins: Buildings & Structures on Ancient Coinage 78
Morocco 27, 173
Mozambique 13, 182
Mughals 29, 207
mules 87, 123
multiple denominations 37

N
naira 189
Namibia 178
Nauru 243
Nehru, Jawaharlal 211
Nepal 223
Netherlands 40, 71, 138–9
New Caledonia 246–7
New Guinea 69, 242
New Hebrides 247, 243
New Zealand 238–9, 240
ngwee 183
Nicaragua 113
nickel 7, 57
  metal 39, 99
Niger 190, 191
Nigeria 188, 189
Niue 240–1
noble 130, 131
nomenclature 61
Norfolk Island 235
North Korea 224–5
Norway 70, 127
notgeld 145
numismatics 6–7, 9
  assessing coins 60–1
  buying and selling coins 90–1
  catalogues 66–7
  coin lookalikes 84–5
  collecting by country 68–9
  collecting by denomination 76–7
  collecting by group 70–1
  collecting by mint 72–3
  collecting by period 74–5
  commemorative collections 80–1
  errors and varieties 86–7
  housing coins 7, 64–5
  looking after coins 62–3
  online trading 7, 92–3
  origins 58–9
  patterns, proofs and ephemera 88–9
  pictorial collections 78–9
  tokens 82–3
Nyasaland 183

O
obol 10, 17, 136
obsidional (siege) currency 31, 35, 131
Oceania 12, 234
Olympic Games 80, 109, 128–9, 155, 165, 170, 197

Oman 200–1
Ottoman Empire 27
ouguiya 191

P
pa'anga 248, 249
packaging 89
pagoda 208, 211
paisa 205, 208, 209, 210, 211, 223
Pakistan 204–5
Palestine 194
Panama 113
paper money 15
Papua New Guinea 242–3
Paraguay 120–1
Paris Mint 46, 47
patagon 138
patterns 48–9, 88
peca 116
penny 7, 18, 34, 57, 133
  Indian Head Penny 99
  silver penny 23, 24, 32, 36, 50, 130, 131
periodicals 67
Persia 27, 32, 194, 202–3
Perth Mint 72
Peru 118, 119
peseta 170
peso 14, 33, 96, 112, 113
  Argentina 120
  Chile 118–19
  Colombia 115
  Cuba 106
  Mexico 110, 111
  Philippines 229
  Spain 170
pfennig 24, 43, 75, 144, 146, 147, 242
Philippines 228, 229
piastre 41, 136, 175, 193
pice 184
pictorialism 56–7, 78–9
pieces of eight (*peso a ocho reales*) 170
piedforts 48–9
pile and trussel 43
Pistrucci, Benedetto 99, 133
plastic tokens 13
platinum coins 249
play money 85
PNGs (philanumismatic covers) 89
Pobjoy Mint 38, 48, 49, 73
Poland 24, 152–3
polish 63
polygonal coins 41
Polynesia 248–9
portraiture 6, 18–19, 52–3
  Anglo-Saxon 22
  Hellenistic 17, 52
  India 208, 209
  India 209
  Iraq 197
  Roman 52, 53
  Thailand 233
Portugal 171
postman emblem 175
pottery tokens 13
pound 18, 45, 51, 77
  Burgerspond 176
  Israeli 195
price guides 67
proofs 47, 48, 88
pruta 194, 195
pula 178
punches 28, 42, 43
PVC 65
pysa 184

Q
Qatar 201
quarter 6–7, 102–3

R
rand 177, 178
reale 107, 110, 115, 170
regal coins 74
reis 116–17, 171, 210
religious symbolism 71
Renaissance 6
Rhodesia 183
rial (riyal, ryal) 41, 79, 184, 201
roller presses 44–5
Romania 159, 162, 163
Rome 6, 18–19, 20, 22–3, 30, 32, 36, 37, 52, 53
  mints 18, 30, 31
  pictorial coins 56
rouble 126, 156–7, 158, 159
Royal Canadian Mint 49, 73
Royal Mint 41, 46, 48, 49, 73
rupee 29, 86, 184, 199, 201
  India 208, 209, 210, 211
  Pakistan 205
  square 207
  Sri Lanka 212
  Tabora Sovereign 185
rupiah 229
Russia 40, 156–7, 158–9
Russian Federation 158
Rwanda 182–3

S
Saharawi Arab Republic 191
saiga 23
salvaged coins 63
San Marino 167
São Tome and Principe 191
Sarawak 230
satang 232, 233
Saudi Arabia 27, 199
scalloped edges 41
Scandinavian Monetary Union 124, 126
sceat 10, 23, 130
schilling 148–9
Scotland 131
segmented coins 245
Seljuqs of Rum 27
Senegal 190, 191
sequin 25
Serbia and Montenegro 24, 160
serrated edges 41
Seychelles 213
shape 40
shekel (sheqel) 36, 195, 202
shells 12–13
shilingi 185
shilling 10, 57, 77, 130, 131, 187, 244
shooting festival coins 141, 148
Siam 232
Siberia 157
siege coins 31, 35, 131
Sierra Leone 189
Sierra Leone Company 189
silver 39, 118, 150
silver coins 16, 18
  silver cordoba 113
  silver half dollar 100–1
  silver nickel 99
  silver penny 23, 24, 32, 36, 50, 130, 131
  silver thaler 149, 150
  silver threepence 6
  silver trade dollars 14, 33, 76
  silver yuan 14, 33
Singapore 231
Singapore Mint 49
sixpence 57, 176, 244
skar 222
skatiku 10
Sloakia 151
slot machine tokens 83
Sobhuza II of Swaziland 179
solidus 19, 21, 23, 25, 26, 196, 202
Solomon Islands 245
Somalia 185, 187
sou 34
South Africa 176–7
South America 114–15, 116–17, 118–19, 120–1
South Georgia and South Sandwich 123
South Korea 225
South-east Asia and Pacific Games 231
sovereign 33, 38, 75, 84, 86, 130, 209
Soviet Union 156–7
Spain 24, 170
Spence, Thomas 34
Spink & Son catalogues 66
spoof coins 84
sporting events 80
srang 222
Sri Lanka 212
St George and the Dragon 99, 133
St Helena 122
St Kitts and Nevis 108–9
St Lucia 109
St Vincent 109
Stalin, Joseph 151
Standard Catalog of World Coins 66
stater 18, 22, 28, 130
steam-powered machinery 46
steel coins 149, 159
  Italy 167
Straits Settlements 230
stuiver 105, 117
sucre 114
Sudan 175
sultani 197
sun motif 55
Svalbard 127
Swaziland 179
Sweden 70, 126
Switzerland 140–1
sycee 40
Sylloge of Coins of the British Isles 67
Syria 197

T
Tabora Sovereign 185
Tahiti 246
Taiwan 221
talent 16, 36
tanga 210, 212, 230
Tanganyika 184
tangka 222
tanka 205, 209
Tanzania 184, 185
Tatarstan 159
testoon 52–3, 77, 130
tetradrachm 7, 22, 28, 174, 192, 194, 196, 202
Thailand 13, 40, 232–3
thaler 33, 41, 53, 57, 199
  Austria 148, 149
  German states 142–3
thickness 40
Third Reich 145
threepence 41, 57, 176
thrymsa 23, 130
Tibet 222
Tibetan Fake Coins and Fantasy Countermarks 85
tical 215
Timor 229
Timor-Leste 57
tin coins 204, 230, 232
titles 54–5
tobacco tokens 83
toea 242, 243
Togoland 190–1
Tokelau Islands 241
tokens 13
  collecting 82–3
  money of necessity 34–5
Tonga 248–9
toughra 27, 55, 175, 193, 209
trade coins 32–3
tram 158
transport tokens 83
treasuries 6
tremissis 19, 23, 186
triangular coins, Bermuda 105
triangular coins, Cook Islands 241
Trinidad and Tobago 104, 105
Tristan da Cunha 11, 123
Tsarist Russia 156
Tunisia 173
Turkey 27, 192–3
Turkmenistan 159
Turks and Caicos Islands 106, 107
Tuvalu 245
twenty pence 49

U
Uganda 184, 185
Ukraine 159
United Arab Emirates 201
United Kingdom 37, 132–3
  pictorial coins 57
United States 37, 98–101
  colonial coins 70
  mints 7, 31, 46, 48
  pictorial coins 57
  Presidents 74
  state quarters 1999-2008 102–3
Uruguay 120, 121
Uzbekistan 159

V
value of collections 7, 91
Vanuatu 243, 247
Vatican City State 68, 167
Venezuela 114
Victor Emanuel III of Italy 59
victoriate 18
Vietnam 13, 214, 215
Viking coinage 23, 126, 131

W
wallets 65
wartime shortages 34, 35
wax models 47
Weimar Republic 144–5
Western Samoa 249
White Huns 29, 203
won 224, 225

Y
Yemen 27, 199
yen 226, 227
yuan 217
  silver yuan 14, 33
Yugoslavia 160–1

Z
Zaire 182
Zambia 183
Zanzibar 184
Zimbabwe 183
zinc coins 149, 153, 160–1
zloty 152–3
Zodiac coins 207, 209

PICTURE ACKNOWLEDGEMENTS

The publishers would like to thank A H Baldwin and Sons Ltd, London for their kind assistance in supplying a substantial number of images from their photographic archive for use in this book.

All images in the book were supplied by Dr James Mackay and A H Baldwin and Sons Ltd, London unless otherwise indicated below.

(Note: t= top; b = bottom; l = left; r= right)

2: The Mary Evans Picture Library; 6bl: The Art Archive/Museo della Civilta Romana Rome/Dagli Orti; 6br: The Art Archive/Musée du Louvre Paris/Dagli Orti (A); 10tr (in panel): The Mary Evans Picture Library; 10bl: The Mary Evans Picture Library; 11t: The Mary Evans Picture Library; 11m: The Mary Evans Picture Library; 11b: Mary Evans/Meledin Collection; 12t: The Art Archive/Dagli Orti; 12bl: The Mary Evans Picture Library; 15tl: The Mary Evans Picture Library; 15tr: The Art Archive/Victoria and Albert Museum London/Eileen Tweedy; 17br The Art Archive/Archaeological Museum Naples/Dagli Orti (A); 18b: The Art Archive/Rheinische Landesmuseum Trier/Dagli Orti; 20t: The Art Archive/Bodleian Library Oxford; 21bl: The Mary Evans Picture Library; 23tr; The Mary Evans Picture Library; 24t: The Art Archive/Sienese State Archives/Dagli Orti (A); 26br: The Art Archive/Bodleian Library Oxford; 30tr: The Mary Evans Picture Library; 32bl: The Art Archive/American Museum Madrid; 34br: The Art Archive/Musée Carnavalet Paris/Dagli Ortii; 36bl: The Art Archive/Musée du Louvre Paris/Harper Collins Publishers; 37tr: The Art Archive/Ministry of Education Tokyo/Laurie Platt Winfrey; 38bl: The Art Archive/Templo Mayor Library Mexico/Dagli Orti; 42br: The Art Archive/Museo Correr Venice/Dagli Orti; 43t: The Art Archive/Dagli Orti (A); 46tr: Mary Evans Picture Library; 46bl: The Mary Evans Picture Library; 47: All images on this page appear courtesy of the Perth Mint, Western Australia; 48bl: Courtesy of the Perth Mint, Western Australia; 49tl: Courtesy of the Perth Mint, Western Australia; 50tr: The Mary Evans Picture Library; 51bl: Courtesy of the Perth Mint, Western Australia; 51br: The Mary Evans Picture Library; 56tr: The Art Archive/Archaeological Museum Ferrara/Dagli Orti (A); 58t (coin of Holy Roman Emperor Charles V): The Art Archive/Dagli Orti (A); 59bl: The Mary Evans Picture Library; 59br: The Mary Evans Picture Library; 63br: Courtesy of the Perth Mint, Western Australia; 64m (Discover Australia collector's folder) courtesy of the Perth Mint, Western Australia; 65bl: Courtesy of the Perth Mint, Western Australia; 67tr: Web page reproduced by permission of the American Numismatic Association; 68tr: Web page reproduced by permission of the American Numismatic Association; 69br (Discover Australia coins): Courtesy of the Perth Mint, Western Australia; 71tr: The Mary Evans Picture Library; 72br (in panel): Courtesy of the Perth Mint, Western Australia; 75t: The Art Archive/Culver Pictures; 78br: Courtesy of the Perth Mint, Western Australia; 81tr (in panel): Courtesy of the Perth Mint, Western Australia; 82bl: The Mary Evans Picture Library; 83tr: The Mary Evans Picture Library; 91tr: Web page reproduced by permission of the American Numismatic Association; 90bl (in panel): Image reproduced by permission of the American Numismatic Association; 90tr: Web page reproduced by permission of the American Numismatic Association; 100 (coin 1–6): supplied by Heritage Galleries and Auctioneers (HeritageAuctions.com), Dallas, TX, USA; 115 (coins 18–19): supplied by New World Treasures, Iron Mountain, MI, USA; 136 (coin inset, top): supplied by Said International Ltd, Valletta, Malta; 149 (coins in pane): supplied by Guenter Roeck, www.theresia.name/en; 243 (coin 20) supplied by Chard (1964) Ltd, www.24carat.co.uk.
Paul Baker supplied the following images of coins: 79mr (Iranian rial showing mosque); 84bl (Hong Kong 'play money'; 85tr (Euro plastic token); 85mr (elongate coin); 87tl (curved clip on Sudanese coin); 108 (coins 11, 14 and 15); 115 (coins top-left, in panel; coins 21–22); 120 (coins 12–13); 122 (coins 3–4; 6–11); 123 (coins 12–15); 133 (coins 24–26); 141 (coins 12–13; 16–17; 20–23); 144 (coins 3–6); 145 (coins 15–20); 146 (coins 6–7; 10–11); 147 (coins 21–32); 151 (coins 12–15); 152 (coins 12–13); 153 (16–19; 24–25); 154 (coins 8–9; 12–17); 155 (coins 22–27 and 29–30); 159 (coins 33–36); 160 (coins 9–14; 17–18); 175 (coins 32–33); 178 (2–7; 9; 14–17); 179 (coins 24–25; 34–35); 186 (coins 7–18); 187 (coins 26–27; 30–33); 188 (coins inset, bottom-right; 16–17); 189 (coins 27–28); 190 (coins 1–2; 15–16); 191 (28–29); 198 (coins 15–16); 199 (coins 22–27; 32–33); 201 (coin bottom-right, inset); 202 (coin top, inset); 203 (coins 33–34); 208 (coins 13–16); 209 (coins bottom-left, in panel; coins 33–34); 213 (coins 27–38); 214 (coins 1–4; 8–9) 215 (coins 23–26; 31–32); 218 (top-right Korean coin depicting Rose of Sharon); bottom-right group of three Japanese and Taiwanese coins); 222 (coins 13–14); 224 (coins inset, top-left; 13–14); 225 (coins 15–16; 29–32); 227 (coins 20–23; 28–33); 228 (coins 10–13); 229 (coins 35–36); 238 (coins 1–2; 10–11); 240 (coins 1–6); 241 (coins 10–11; 14–17); 242 (coins 6–11); 243 (coins 21–22); 244 (coins 1–4; 8–9; 11); 245 (coins 12–19; 22–23); 246 (coin inset, top-right; 2; 6); 247 (coin in panel; coins 14–19); 248 (coins 1–4; 6–9); 249 (coins 17–20; 23–24).

Photography: Mark Wood took the photographs appearing on 8; 45bl; 60tr; 61bl; 62tr; 62bl; 63t (in panel); 63bl; 64bl; 65br (in panel); 66tr and br; 90br; 93tr and 94.

USEFUL WEBSITES

Auctions and shopping
Amazon www.amazon.com
Ebay www.ebay.com
Heritage Auctions Galleries www.ha.com
Paypal www.paypal.com

Dealer directories
Most reputable dealers now run their own websites. Although there are far too many to list here, Coin Resource is a useful portal site offering links to American and worldwide dealers on the web, in addition to links to the websites of auctioneers, magazines, mints and suppliers:
www.coinresource.com/directory
Many national numismatic associations also offer country-specific directories of dealers.

Discussion forums
Coin Talk www.cointalk.org
Coin Site www.coinsite.com

Grading, standards and advice
Independent Coin Grading Company
www.icgcoin.com
Professional Coin Grading Service
www.pcgs.com
Professional Numismatists' Guild
www.pngdealers.com

National numismatic associations
For a global directory of national associations and shows, go to NumismaLink:
www.numismalink.com/societies.html

1867
CONFEDERATION
CONSTITUTION
1982
CANADA
1834 TORONTO 1984
DOLLAR
UNITED STATES OF AMERICA
HALF DOLLAR
EIN KRONA
ISLAND 1999
IN GOD WE TRUST
1926
50 CENTIMES
2002
TURKS & CAICOS ISLANDS
1969
ONE CROWN
ESTADO DA INDIA
ESTADOS UNIDOS MEXICANOS
REPUBLIC OF KENYA
10
TEN SHILLINGS 1994
BANKY FOIBEN'I MADAGASIKARA
2003
MEDIO BALBOA
1689
1989
BRITISH WEST AFRICA
1936
YUN-NAN-PROVINCE
SIMON BOLIVAR 1783-1830
1973
REPUBLIC OF THE GA
1998
HONG KONG
1000
5
CENTAVOS
CROWN 1935
2 F
AFRIQUE EQUATORIALE FRANÇAISE
100
PATACAS
BOLIVAR LIBERTADOR
REPUBLICA DE COLOMBIA
WINTER OLYMPICS LAKE PLACID USA
ONE CROWN
BANQUE CENTRALE DE MAURITANIE
1997
20
OUGUIYA
UNION MONETAIRE OUEST
100
FRANCS
1977
25
CENTAVOS
20
MILS
WAITANGI DAY
ONE DOLLAR
1
PESO
1861
BANCO CENTRAL DE RESERVA DEL PERU
1994